Educated for Change?

Muslim Refugee Women in the West

A volume in
Education Policy in Practice: Critical Cultural Studies

Series Editors
Edmund (Ted) Hamann, *University of Nebraska-Lincoln*
Rodney K. Hopson, *Duquesne University*

Education Policy in Practice:
Critical Cultural Studies

Edmund (Ted) Hamann and Rodney K. Hopson, Series Editors

Educated for Change?

Muslim Refugee Women in the West

by

Patricia Buck
Bates College and Matawi, Inc.

and

Rachel Silver
Matawi, Inc.

Information Age Publishing, Inc.
Charlotte, North Carolina • www.infoagepub.com

Library of Congress Cataloging-in-Publication Data

Buck, Patricia.
Educated for Change? : Muslim Refugee Women in the West / by Patricia Buck
and Rachel Silver.
p. cm.
Includes bibliographical references.
ISBN 978-1-61735-620-9 (paperback) -- ISBN 978-1-61735-621-6 (hardcover) --
ISBN 978-1-61735-622-3 (e-book)
1. Muslim women--Education--Western countries. 2.
Women--Education--Western countries. 3. Muslim women--Social conditions.
I. Silver, Rachel. II. Title.
LC2410.5.B84 2011
371.828'297--dc23

                    2011035163

Printed in the United States of America

[Never] has it ever been argued, whether in Mary Wollstonecraft's day, when European women had no rights, or in our day and even by the most radical feminists, that because male domination and injustice to women have existed throughout the West's recorded history, the only recourse for Western women is to abandon Western culture and find themselves some other culture. The idea seems absurd, and yet this is routinely how the matter of improving the status of women is posed with respect to women in Arab and other non-Western societies.

Women and Gender in Islam
Leila Ahmed
(p. 244)

In memory of Safia Ahmed

CONTENTS

FOREWORD

Bradley A. U. Levinson and Margaret Sutton

It is a delight for us to introduce you to this stunning ethnography of refugee women's education by Patti Buck and Rachel Silver. This is a work not only of acute intellect but also of strong heart. Buck and Silver have experienced both the joys and the sufferings of their subjects first hand. They identify with the plight of Somali refugee women, and this identification allows them to engage in a practice of empathetic reflexivity, or what Faye Harrison (2008) and Virginia Dominguez (2000) would call a politics and ethnography of love. The result is an amazingly rich, insightful, and emotive account of these women's lives, and of the educational processes that accompany them on their journeys from Somalia to the United States. It is also a cutting-edge scholarly work. Bringing this rich ethnographic body of evidence to bear, the authors speak insightfully to central intellectual questions of the twenty-first century.

Buck and Silver started their work with Somali refugee women at an adult education center in the Northeastern city they call Milltown, where they taught and volunteered. Eventually, they decided to document and study the ways these women negotiated life in the educational settings of their new home. In this way, Buck and Silver contribute to the insightful body of literature concerning Muslim women and their education in the west. Like Raissiguier's (1997) work among young Algerian women in France and Sarroub's (2005) in the upper Midwestern United States, Buck and Silver demonstrate "that these women of the global South wield the power to observe, deliberate, and act as agents in the creative endeavor of living."

Educated for Change?: Muslim Refugee Women in the West, pp. xi–xiii
Copyright © 2012 by Information Age Publishing
All rights of reproduction in any form reserved.

Yet they were not content only to study the "context of reception," as sociologists would refer to the new places where immigrants settle. Rather, they decided to study and understand the context from which the women came. To that end, they spent several months over the course of a few years studying life for Somali women in both the refugee camp of Dadaab and the Somali immigrant neighborhoods of Kenya, all of which served as weigh stations between Somalia and settlement in the United States. As a result, Buck and Silver have gifted us a multilayered, multisited ethnographic account of the full refugee-immigrant experience. In this regard, the authors squarely enter debates concerning the power, efficacy, and values of international institutions that assume mandates for transnational migrants. As they observe,

> the political tension and outright conflict between the West and the Islamic East results in human displacement and the need for an international humanitarian aid apparatus to come into play, [therefore] it makes sense to look at refugee policy as part of an examination of Islamic East/West relations.

Herein they neatly synthesize a critical perspective on international development and humanitarian assistance organizations, in which (1) both forms of international transfer are of a piece; (2) and geopolitics creates the need for the "aid" institutions themselves (see de Haan 2009). As the authors observe repeatedly, one manifestation of the nexus of geopolitics and humanitarian assistance is the creation of "quasi states" such as Dadaab, under the auspices of the UNHCR (United Nations High Commissioner for Refugees).

In another sense, too, Buck and Silver bridge local, national, and global scales. Throughout their account, they draw attention to the salience of two clusters of discourse that structure expectations and possibilities for these women's lives in Milltown. These discourses they represent, alternately, as "traditional nativist" and "Enlightenment liberal." One of the signal triumphs of their book is their ability to demonstrate how such broad historical discourses, formed at the national and even international level as approaches to diversity and national identity, become contextualized locally in ways that really matter for refugee women. In this regard, the authors speak to contemporary debates about cosmopolitanism and transnational identities. Their nuanced representations of the choices made by the women that they studied and the meanings of these choices in their lives vividly illustrate Martha Nussbaum's (1997) claims that "real cultures are plural." In their own words:

> During the course of our study, we met women who self identified as traditionalist, others who aspired to Westernize, and many who explored the

myriad possibilities in between. Diversity among Somali women indicates that an essential Islamic East/West oppositionality is spurious.

This book contributes an important angle to understand how education policy is appropriated in practice. In this case, the most relevant policies are those of the UNHCR and USCIS (United States Citizenship and Immigration Services) governing the settlement of new immigrants and refugees, as well as the adult education center where the Somali women live and study many hours each day. Buck and Silver are able to show how a "liberal Enlightenment" discourse generally informs policy at each of these levels. This discourse invites, even requires the refugee women to become the "good immigrant of liberal imagination." While liberal enlightenment discourse provides a seemingly palatable alternative to the depredations of nativism, Buck and Silver also show us how such discourse, assimilationist to the core, still ultimately contradicts some of its own principles, and thereby compromises the possibility of fuller democratic recognition and participation.

Finally, as discussed in the conclusion, the authors' endeavor goes beyond the fine scholarship presented here to action informed by the work as a whole. Both in their consultation with the agencies studied in this monograph and through the creation of the NGO *Matawi*, Buck and Silver provide an inspiring model of engaged public scholarship.

PREFACE

Somalia, a predominantly Muslim country on the Horn of Africa, fell to civil war in 1991. Thousands were killed in the ensuing chaos. Thousands more were displaced. Unfortunately, conditions in Somalia have only worsened in the intervening decades. Over the course of time, it is estimated that up to a million Somalis have died due to the conflict (Global Security, 2010), while Somalia's neighboring countries have seen an influx of well over 600,000 refugees from the war torn land. Qafis, Bartan, and Mooro,[1] three camps that make up the Dadaab camp system in northeast Kenya, now comprise the largest single refugee population in the world at a staggering and ever increasing 370,000 plus inhabitants (United Nations High Commissioner for Refugees [UNHCR], 2010). All Somalis who successfully cross the border into Kenya are eligible to apply for refugee status and its concomitant rights and protections.

For most, asylum translates into years spent languishing in the circumscribed existence of camp life where movement, economic activity, citizenship rights, and participation in farming or herding are all severely restricted. A lucky few among the camp population finds their way onto UNHCR resettlement lists. One day—after years of waiting—an even smaller number steps off planes onto the territory of one Western nation or another. Once in the United States, Canada, Denmark, or another of the handful of nations worldwide that accepts asylees from Somalia, they restart lives. One of the unexpected results of the war and widespread migration has been to increase female refugees' educational opportunities.

Whether in Kenya or a Western nation, in strikingly new surroundings, as refugees, many Somali girls and women have gained newfound access to schooling. The unexpected result of war literacy levels among Somali girls and women have historically been among the lowest in the world (United Nations Development Programme [UNDP], 1998). Given nearly

Educated for Change?: Muslim Refugee Women in the West, pp. xv–xvii
Copyright © 2012 by Information Age Publishing

two decades of bloody struggle, one might reasonably expect that such trends would continue or even worsen. Yet, while enrollment within Somalia has likely fallen, those who safely flee across the border into Kenya can claim asylum with the UNHCR and thereby become candidates for a host of social services including public primary and secondary schooling. Ironically, for Somali girls and women, one of the worst humanitarian crises of our time entails a significant advantage.

International law posits that access to primary education is a universal human right (International Covenant on Economic, Social and Cultural Rights, 1966). While far from realizing the letter of the law, the UNHCR does provide basic education to a significant portion of its camp population. In 2008, UNHCR reports spending $1,734,338 of its $6,304,840 Kenyan operational budget on educational programming, thereby enrolling roughly 50% of Dadaab camps' primary school aged population in school (UNHCR Global Report, 2008). Since the formation of the Dadaab camps in 1991, the percentage of female primary school students has reportedly risen from the single digits to a current 45%. For those few who receive resettlement to Western nations, basic, secondary, adult, higher and continuing educational opportunities have become widely available and on an even more gender-equal, even compulsory, basis.

In what follows we offer an anthropological examination of what newfound access to schooling means in the everyday lives of Somali refugee girls and women. We focus especially on the strategies refugee women employ in their utilization of schooling as a space and process through which to affect and respond to the sociocultural changes associated with the forced migration of the Somali community. Our study took place in two locations touched by the displacement of Somali citizens: the Dadaab refugee camps and Milltown, a small city in northern New England that has served as a Somali resettlement site since 2001.

NOTE

1. While Dadaab is the actual name of a town in Northeastern Kenya, in order to protect participants' anonymity, we use pseudonyms for each of the three camps located in Dadaab, as well as for Milltown, a small city in the United States to which a significant population of Somalis has resettled. All participants have been given pseudonyms.

ABBREVIATIONS

BPRM   Bureau on Populations, Refugees, and Migration

CEDAW   Center for Elimination of All Form of Discrimination
        Against Women
CEE   Critical Educational Ethnography
CO   Cultural Orientation
FAIR   Fairness and Accuracy in Reporting
FGC   Female Genital Cutting/Circumcision
FGM   Female Genital Mutilation
GAD   Gender and Development
GBV   Gender Based Violence
GSL   Greater Somali League
GTZ   German International Cooperative Enterprise
HI   Handicap International
ICU   Islamic Courts Union
IOM   International Organization on Migration
JVA   Joint Voluntary Agency
KCPE   Kenyan Comprehensive Primary Examination
KCSE   Kenyan Comprehensive Secondary Examination
NCCK   National Council of Churches of Kenya
NGO   Non-governmental Organization
NRC   Norwegian Refugee Council
OIOS   Office of International Oversight Services
SCK   Save the Children United Kingdom
SNL   Somali National League
SNM   Somali National Movement
SPM   Somali Patriotic Movement
SRC   Supreme Revolutionary Council
SYL   Somali Youth League
TANIF   Temporary Aid For Needy Families
TBA   Traditional Birth Attendants
TFGT   Transitional Federal Government
USC   United Somali Congress
USCIS   United States Citizenship and Immigration Services
VCT   Volunteer Counseling and Testing
WFP   World Food Programme
WUSC   World University Services of Canada

ACKNOWLEDGMENTS

Our research methods are intricately entwined with our activism. A component of our work with the Somali community has been to found a nonprofit organization entitled Matawi (meaning "branches" in Swahili), with a mission to support education, civic engagement, and leadership development in the global refugee community. Matawi's work features an initiative to raise funds to support Dadaab women who wish to attend university (The Dadaab Young Women's Scholarship Initiative) as well as a platform for the collection of research conducted with the Somali community. We see ourselves as advocates for Somali girls and women and, as such, strategically use the research process to gather the voices and perspectives of our participants and to actively involve them in the process of constructing knowledge about themselves and their communities. Accordingly, among other research activities, study participants conducted interviews, documented their stories first hand, and served as our translators. We are deeply grateful for their insights and dedication.

The Somali women and girls and their families, neighbors, and friends with whom we worked in both locations demonstrated a generous willingness to share their lives and experiences with us and, perhaps most notably, revealed time and again tremendous bravery and grace in the face of the most unimaginable of circumstances. There is no greater inspiration than the women's consistent desire to create better lives for themselves, their families, and indeed, our world, in spite *and* because of what they have endured. Nevertheless, the process of constructing a narrative about peoples' lives by definition reflects and is limited by the authorial perspective. As such, we accept full responsibility for everything written in this text.

We would also like to thank our editors Bradley Levinson and Margaret Sutton for their perceptive commentary throughout our process of craft-

Educated for Change?: Muslim Refugee Women in the West, pp. xix–xxi
Copyright © 2012 by Information Age Publishing
All rights of reproduction in any form reserved.

ing and, eventually, expanding the scope of *Educated for Change?* to encompass two distinct locations. They guided us carefully as we experimented with different theoretical frameworks and remained patient throughout. To readers of a particular chapter or chapters—Bill Corlett, Fatuma Hussein, Ismail Ahmed, Leslie Hill, Kathy Schultz, Trish Niesz, Molly Blackburn, Sarah Jewett, Rebecca Herzig, and Thea Abu El Haj—as well as readers of our entire manuscript—Abdi Samatar, Lisa Smulyan, Peggy Gilman, Helen Regan, Emily Kane, Margaret LeCompte, Jill Reich and Jen Sandler—we are deeply grateful for your generosity of time and wisdom. Each of you indelibly shaped our project for the better. Patti also wishes to thank Kathy Schultz, Kathy Hall, Fred Erickson, and Marvin Lazerson for shepherding her in the field of ethnographic research.

In Kenya, we have more people to thank than we can possible name. To our friends at the aid agencies in Nairobi and Dadaab, specifically: Mohammed Qazilbash, Chege Ngugi, Bud Crandall, Musa Dagane, Boniface Kanyi, Theresiah Nthiana, and Fanuel Onyuka Randiki at CARE; Dr. Marangu Njogu, Norah Gaiti Kariba, Winfred Kiunga, Jeremiah Orina, and Patrick Boro at Windle Trust Kenya; Francesca Bonnelli, Alexandra Kaun, and James Karanja at the UNHCR—thank you for the endless ways in which you facilitated our stays, imparted your knowledge about life in Dadaab, and made our time in Kenya an all around pleasure. Thank you to Cindy Horst for many thought-provoking conversations and your willingness to help orient us to the landscape of Dadaab. To the student researchers in participating Windle Trust Advanced English and Form Four Classes, we learned as much or more from you as we could possibly impart in our workshops. Thank you for offering us such unique vantage points from which to view camp life.

In Maine, we would like to gratefully acknowledge the teachers at the Milltown Adult Education Center (MAEC) for generously granting us access to your classrooms. Thank you Ann Kemper for facilitating our research at the Center and for presenting research findings with us at different conferences as the project progressed. To Ellen Alcorn and Bill Blaine Wallace, thank you for your hard work and perseverance in helping to execute a truly memorable memoir project, which resulted in publication of the anthology *They Were Very Beautiful. Such Things Are*, all proceeds of which benefit the Dadaab Young Women's Scholarship Initiative. We would like to recognize the Bates students from Patti's classes who together clocked thousands of hours volunteering at MAEC, as well as Sarina Rosenthal who generously helped us prepare the manuscript for completion. We would also like to acknowledge the Board of Directors of Matawi for committing their time and energies to the cause of refugee education.

We are grateful for the financial support from Bates College, the Kathleen Curry Akers '41 Fund, the Roger C. Schmutz Research Grants, Yale University's Pre-Dissertation Fellowship, Yale Council on African Studies' Lindsay Fellowship as well as a grant from the John Anson Kittredge Educational Fund.

We cannot complete this project without thanking the owners and staff at two lovely Portland area institutions—the North Star and Café 158—whose delicious food, comfortable chairs, beverages, and kind check-ins kept us fueled to write this book. (Little did you know when we first made our entrances the sheer number of hours that we would clock at your establishments). Last but not least, a warm-hearted thank you to our family and friends—and in particular Bonnie, Bill, Chris, Bill, Tom, Ricky, Laurie, Louis, and Nathan.

SERIES EDITORS' INTRODUCTION

Recentering the Critical in Sociocultural Ethnographic Studies

Rodney Hopson and Edmund T. Hamann

For people who have been dispossessed and forced to leave for an uncertain destiny, rejected time and again, returned to the sea or to the no man's land of border zones; for these unwanted expatriated, it seems that all attempts at exalting the achievements of exile are but desperate efforts to quell the crippling sorrow of homelessness and estrangement. The process of rehabilitation which involves the search for a new home appears to be above all a process by which people stunned, traumatized and mutilated by the shifts of event that have expelled them from their homelands learn to adjust to their sudden state of isolation and uprootedness. (Minh-ha, 2011, p. 29)

With great hopes for contributing to a similar process of rehabilitation and adjustment as captured in Trinh Minh-ha's lines above, this book, *Educated for Change? Muslim Woman in the West* by Patti Buck and Rachel Silver, is the first book in the series of Educational Policy in Practice: Critical Cultural Studies under our new editorial team. (The founding editors, Bradley Levinson and Margaret Sutton, contribute the foreword to this volume.)

Like many of the volumes in the series, this one follows in the traditions of comparative education and educational anthropology and consid-

Educated for Change?: Muslim Refugee Women in the West, pp. xxiii–xxv ers how the study of educational policy and practice, in a critical sense, may affect the exiled, refugee, estranged, and *othered* woman in the contemporary United States and Africa. In this case, Buck and Silver, display what this means through incredible shifts of events across borders, cultures, nation-states, and formal educational experiences.

Like Minh-ha's (2011) account of refugees, who are unwanted, homeless, stateless, and "dispossessed not only of their material belongings but also of their social heritage" (p. 30), *Educated for Change?*, is more than the story of access on two continents to schooling in the lives of Somali girls and women. In the chapters that follow, the book depicts, in a multisited ethnographic account, the complexities, contestations, and triumphs of schooling, globalization, race, and gender in the African diaspora, weaving together narratives and counternarratives about women in Dadaab, Somali and Milltown, United States. While it is uncommon to end a book title with a question mark, *Education for Change?* resounds with both moral and logistic questions—How well do educational institutions serve these girls and women? What would serving them well entail—and from that we return to the book series' concern with education policy and practice, as both policy and practice are intended as the vehicles through which society endeavors to express and realize "what should be."

Educated for Change? follows in the footsteps of other books in the book series, with one stated emphasis. That is, the Buck and Silver book is grounded in sociocultural ethnographic analysis of political, religious, and cultural dynamics that take place among the lives of Somali refugee women and the encounters they face with access to schooling and citizenship in northeastern United States. By examining the complicated social lives of Fatima, Asha, Haali, Roda, Nimo, Amina, Fathia, and others between refugee camp and ESL classrooms, as well as the embedded policies and practices of the United Nations High Commissioner for Refugees (UNHCR) and the No Child Left Behind (NCLB) Act, the book is "a locally informed, comparatively astute, ethnographically rich account of how people make, interpret, and otherwise engage with the policy process" (Levinson & Sutton, 2001, p. 4).

Even more, the book elaborates an explicit critical turn in anthropological, ethnographic, and cultural studies (cf. Collins, 2011; McCarty & Warhol, 2011, in press; McCarty, Collins, & Hopson, 2011) regarding recent discussions of the critical sociocultural turn in language policy and planning, challenging the global intersections and interventions that perceive schooling as a natural, apolitical, "good," and nonideological institution. Their book is not only rich in ethnographic detail, portraying the range of discourses and meanings, the stories of the Somali women in Dadaab and Milltown are fundamentally critical of the immigration and schooling institutional contexts in which the women and girls face, giving voice to a set of realities faced by refugee women of color and attempting to plant seeds that unsettle and transform those realities to a realize greater equity and social justice.

Ultimately, it is a delight to start our editorship of this series with such a strong and insistent manuscript. Consider this an invitation to contribute to the series in similar ways as Buck and Silver have done, both in explicating policy as complex social practice and interrogating meaning of policy in and as practice, while offering ideas for rehabilitation and to counteract the shifts and displacements of peoples and communities that take place in schooling and educational settings among diverse nation-states and institutional contexts.

CHAPTER 1

IN THE CONFLUENCE OF ISLAMIC EAST AND WEST

Muslim Girls and Women in School

Somali refugee girls and women encounter increasing educational opportunities at a tenuous moment in time. In the post-9/11 world, the perceived
dichotomy between the Islamic East and the West has seized the collective
imagination. For nearly a decade now, the citizenry, media, and government of postindustrial European and North American countries have sustained a heightened level of interest in Muslim history, culture, economics,
and politics. Some of the discourse could be characterized as responsible
and even geared toward the development of greater mutual understanding
and tolerance. In such cases, the range of beliefs and practices within Islam
is highlighted. Attention to the dangers of fundamentalism might be balanced with stories about moderate Muslims' efforts to define Islam as a
responsive, compassionate and just belief system. As if offering a nod to
one's own accountability in the creation of the problem of Islamic East/West
antagonism, it has also been noted that Western colonial, Cold War, and
military interventions have often worked to the detriment of peaceful
development within Islamic societies. With regard to Muslims living in the
West, constructive approaches tend to point to those aspects of constitutional government that embrace religious and cultural pluralism.

Of course, much of the discussion and decision making with regard to
relations between the West and the Islamic East has been, at best, ill or

Educated for Change?: Muslim Refugee Women in the West, pp. 1–33
Copyright © 2012 by Information Age Publishing
All rights of reproduction in any form reserved.

underinformed and, at worst, highly reactionary and intentionally incendiary in nature. Unfortunately, badly informed and politically motivated chauvinism makes for good ratings. Like a roadside accident, it draws attention even as it inevitably slows progress. Similarly, fear mongering and the resultant populist impulse to go on the offensive in the name of national self-defense make effective, if opportunistic, political strategy. As a result, representations of Islamic extremism figure prominently in Western news media and politics, heightening antagonism within the West toward Islam and Muslims. Postcolonial scholar Said refers to "subtle and persistent Eurocentric prejudice against Arabo-Islamic peoples and their culture" as Orientalism (Windschuttle, 1999). The unfortunate effects of the Orientalist focus on extremist elements of Islam have been to polarize Western citizenry while discounting calls for restraint; propagate an image of Muslims as violent, underhanded, and oppressive; signal the desirability for modernization of Muslim culture; and provide a ready-made justification for further Western imposition into sovereign nations.

When Islam is discussed from Western points of view, analysis of the ways in which gender is used as an implicit principle of social organization frequently serves as a key thematic. Again, strands of the conversation about gender in Islam have been nuanced and convey a genuine appreciation of diversities of perspective and practice. Other depictions are less sanguine. At its heart, Orientalist renderings of gender in Islam focus on women's oppression. Here a virtual (dirty) laundry list of cultural practices has become familiar: women are obligated to cover in public; women are largely confined to the private, domestic sphere; young girls are sold into early marriages; female circumcision puts young girls at risk of infection and death and denies women sexual pleasure; sex segregation symbolizes the constraint, control, and diminishment of women's roles in society; girls and women are prohibited from attending school; and, marriage, divorce, and inheritance laws favor men. Nor, is the former list an exhaustive one as these and still more gender salient elements of Islamic culture and society are run through the courts of public opinion all over the Western world. A seeming affront to Western liberal sensibilities, purported gender based oppression has been skillfully exploited as a rationale for war. In the United States, the Bush-Cheney administration cultivated an international gender politics in which the West positioned itself as the heroic savior of Muslim women. In coordination with the release of a state department report on the condition of Afghan women, in a November 2001 speech, Laura Bush suggested improvement in Afghan women's lives as a rationale for the recent declaration of war against Afghanistan. Stabile and Kumar (2005) argue that in such political discourses about Afghan women:

two narrative traditions and practices converge: that of the protection scenario and that of Orientalism. Both traditions draw much of their rhetorical force from discourses of imperialism. The argument about protecting women, used as justification for the bombing of Afghanistan, combines elements of both traditions. (p. 6)

In virtual lockstep with political rhetoric, media often portrayed Afghan men as violent oppressors while U.S. and allied forces free women from the literal and figurative binding of Islam bearing hitherto shrouded heads to the light of day and opening school doors to eager young female minds (Stabile & Kumar, 2005).

A related gender politics has emerged with regard to domestic Muslim populations in the West. The governments of France and Belgium have placed increasing legal restriction on the use of Muslim identified female dress in public. In both cases, a ban on such garb in schools preceded the more far reaching prohibition, and thus, schools served as an experimental space from which subsequent social change was leveraged. In their rationale, French officials argue that covering represents a threat to secularism or *laicism*, the very defining feature of what it means to be French (Killian, 2003). Further, proponents of the ban argue that Muslim culture forces women to wear clothes that are hot and impractical and in doing so oppresses. Accordingly, by outlawing such garb, Westerners protect Muslim women. President Sarkosy explained the ban saying, "France is 'united around a certain idea of personal dignity, particularly women's dignity" (2010). Simultaneously, officials argue that such clothing can hide bombs or other weaponry used for terrorist activity. The oxymoronic coupling of the latter two justifications simultaneously situate Muslim women as passive victims of Muslim males' authoritarianism and virulent perpetrators of violence against the West.

Orientalist preoccupations with the act of veiling and the provision of schooling justify war, regulate women's bodies, evoke a chauvinistic fear that Islam threatens the Western way of life, and position Western men as heroes and women as models of an enlightened feminine. However, while the Orientalist approach utilizes the provision of schooling as one mechanism through which to affect sociocultural, gender specific change in Muslim communities, unlike efforts to justify military intervention or criminalize veiling, it would be overly simplistic to regard all Western based efforts to increase Muslim women's access to schooling as a totalizing inscription of Western knowledge/power paradigms on members of the Muslim community. In fact, the education of Muslim women by Western stakeholders often occurs as a part of international development and refugee aid policy in which the religious and ethnic identification of those served varies widely. Further, in countless development and refugee aid contexts with significant Muslim populations, activists, development workers, missionaries, humanitarian aid staff members, and educators work to improve Muslim girls' and women's access to schooling. They undoubtedly do so with myriad motivations including personal career development, evangelical zeal, and a commitment to the realization of greater equity and social justice.

Beyond stakeholders' varied individual inclinations, public policy shaping Muslim girls' and women's access to schooling in war torn, poverty stricken, and/or refugee situations—in short in areas where circumstances have afforded the West significant degrees of power over Muslim communities—also evolves from compound, often contradictory motives. Military strategizing (as in Afghanistan and Iraq), protection of oil interests (as in Iraq, Nigeria, and the Sudan), negotiation of tenuous regional ethno-religious politics (such as in Palestine), inhibition of terrorist activity (such as in Afghanistan, Somalia, and Kenya), development aspirations (such as across the African continent and the East), and humanitarian aid concerns (such as across the African continent and the East) all propel policy in unique, regionally definite ways.

Outside of multifaceted intents and methods underlying the provision of education to Muslim girls and women, the emphasis on attainment of gender equity in educational access within refugee policy and practice in particular is subject to numerous and contentious critiques. Some argue that in providing education and taking on a gender equity agenda as well as other programs of social improvement, the UNHCR has overextended itself and thus fails to realize its original mandate to provide adequate security and protection against refoulement (Loescher, 2001). In this vein it is noted that the UNHCR falls short of enforcing human rights laws particularly in regard to gender based violence and thus exhibits ill-conceived policy priorities (Fox & Hasci, 1999).

Others contend that while the UNHCR acts as a quasi-state, there are no democratic means through which it is held accountable by its refugee citizenry. Whether the focus on girls' and women's school is the appropriate priority misses the point, which is that in doing so the UNHCR exercises an improper use of power (Verdirame & Harrell-Bond, 2005).

Another potent critique asserts that the language of charity employed by the UNHCR and its contracted nongovernmental organizations (NGOs) elides the extent to which donor states are responsible for problems that give rise to the political violence to which girls and women often fall victim. Such criticism can also be applied to the vernacular employed by charitable, often faith based organizations that assist in refugee resettlement in the West. According to critics with an historical eye, the West's responsibility for contemporary disorder in Islamic states including Somalia, Iraq, and Afghanistan is rooted in exploitative colonial histories, Cold

War era interference, predatory lending practices, structural adjustment policies that starved the public sector of resources, and outright military force (Herpa, 2009).

Still others see the provision of schooling, whether in camps or within Western states, as an ethnocentric intervention that strips indigenous cultural knowledge, values, and skills (Aikman, 1999). Relatedly, some argue that through access to formal education, sponsorship of community education campaigns (around HIV/Aids, domestic abuse, and family planning), and resettlement in the West, the West foists an alien vision of gender equality upon its dependents (Pratt, 1986; Salmon, 1997).

In the years spent working with Somali men and women, we were frequently confronted with conservative Somalis who rejected all attempts to pursue gender equity as an imperialistic enterprise. Conversely, we also came to know Somali men and women who complained that not enough was done to achieve gender equity within international refugee aid policy. In the latter case, Somalis echoed feminist proponents who argue that the focus on access in policy obscures substantive issues of educational inequality within schools that serve refugee populations (Unterhalter, 2005).

In sum, while it may be possible to roughly parse Western-based discourse on Islam, the Islamic East, and Muslim people as either responsible or incendiary, it would be unwarranted to characterize efforts to provide Muslim girls and women with access to schooling as similarly binary. Somali refugee girls' and women's improved access to schooling post-displacement is neither a straightforward realization of cynical maneuverings of neoconservatives and cultural imperialists nor purely beneficial and well executed. The provision of educational opportunity for Muslim girls and women by Western parties is a complex, controversial, and precarious undertaking.

Making schooling available to Muslim girls and women is contentious in part because education is by definition an act of change. Across place and time and regardless of method, education entails cognitive, cultural, social, economic, and political transformation. The education of Muslim girls and women within Western institutional contexts in an era defined by tension between the Islamic East and West necessarily brings heightened sensitivity to any and all forms of change among the various stakeholders. When one speaks about the education provided by Western (quasi) governmental bodies to female forced migrants from a failed, postcolonial state in which girls' and woman's literacy rates are extremely low, one logically engages lines of inquiry about, *What sort of change is brought about by the incorporation of displaced Muslim girls and women into the Western educational paradigm? Whose interests are served by the changes wrought when Muslim girls and women gain newfound access to Western-style schooling? How does participation in schooling shape*

Muslim girls' and women's relationship to the new communities into which they have entered? What impact does Muslim girls' and women's access to schooling have upon their relationship to their own families and the larger Muslim community in the diaspora? Finally, how do the answers to the preceding questions speak to the ways in which Muslim female students' perspectives, actions, and experiences contribute to a gender salient conversation about relations between the Islamic East and the West that transcends simple dualism.

We live in a time at which the provision of education for Muslim girls and women serves as a focal point in the West's struggle over the relative influence of the West versus that of the Islamic East in matters of war, governance, and culture. Yet, there is a stunning absence of Muslim refugee girls' and women's voices on the matter. To date, there has been a near complete failure among Western stakeholders to gather, disseminate, or respond to Muslim girls' and women's perspectives with regard to schooling. While ostensibly executed in the name of democracy building, the realization of human/civil rights, and movement toward greater gender equality; attempts to increase Muslim girls' and women's access often position recipients as inanimate objects. It goes without saying that Muslim women do not share equal representation at Western decision making tables whether on local school boards or as leaders within the international governance bodies. Nor, do they have a say in the creation or daily operation of the institutions through which such decision-making happens. It is well understood that the provision of schooling serves as a tool of sociocultural transformation at spaces of cultural encounter, yet, the beneficiaries have little influence over the West's project to educate Muslim girls and women. It is our hope that an in depth ethnographic study of Somali women's schooling in the diaspora will begin to address the exclusion of Somali girls and women from the larger conversation. In our multiyear investigation of women's schooling (in the Dadaab refugee camps of northeastern Kenya and at an adult learning center in Milltown, New England) we find that female refugee students use schooling as a means to engage in sophisticated negotiation of the varied formulations of gender implicit in Western and Islamic Eastern sensibilities. In the process they open up new possibilities for creative gender work within a point of juncture. Accordingly, the voices of female Somali refugee scholars have the potential to reconfigure the reductionist dualism that dominates relations (and talk about relations) between the Islamic East and the West.

The Study

We have worked continuously with the Somali diasporic community since the fall of 2002 and anticipate doing so well into the future. Between

2001 and 2003, approximately 1,200 Somali refugees came to Milltown, a small, postindustrial city in northern New England (Nadeau, 2003). For the majority of these refugees, Milltown is a site of secondary resettlement to which they have relocated after initial stays of at least a year in large urban centers. For the first phase of our research, we tutored, taught, and conducted a 3-year ethnographic investigation at the Milltown Adult Education Center (MAEC). Throughout this time, we had the opportunity to work closely with roughly 20 Somali refugee women as they negotiated their new lives in Milltown and at MAEC.

We joined a liberal arts college community located within Milltown at the same time as Somali refugees arrived in significant numbers to the area, Rachel as an undergraduate student in the fall of 2001 and Patti as faculty the following fall. Individually, we followed local events and reactions to the cultural and demographic changes brought about by the influx of refugees. We each attended relevant community gatherings, demonstrations, and meetings organized by both Somali and longtime Milltown residents.

In the fall of 2002, Rachel enrolled in one of Patti's classes. Aware of MAEC's unique presence as a gathering place of many new Somali community members, Rachel requested to complete the service-learning component of the course at MAEC. That semester, Rachel tutored and completed journal entries that depicted vivid scenes from MAEC. She described adult learners who used their time at MAEC to practice reading and writing, exchange valuable information about local employment and housing opportunities, and share their experiences and frustrations as Muslims and Africans in the post-9/11 United States. Taken by these images, Patti began to make regular visits to MAEC. Soon the two of us began to envision an ethnographic study that would capture the rich texture of this newly diverse institution set within one of the most racially homogenous states in the country. In the fall of 2003, we met with Sue Davis, MAEC's counselor coordinator, to propose an ethnographic investigation of student meaning making around gender, schooling, and social change.

Sitting together around the large, rectangular table in the central ELL tutoring room, the three of us also imagined how Patti and Rachel could participate at MAEC in ways that were relevant and responsive to MAEC's needs. Sue asked Rachel to develop and implement MAEC's first organized citizenship course while Patti described how Rebecca, MAEC's level four English Language Learners teacher, expressed interest in having her observe and guest teach in her class.

Our resulting ethnographic study spanned 3 years of extensive participant observation, throughout which we maintained a steady presence as volunteers at MAEC and occupied various roles. After first tutoring for a year and a half, Rachel taught the citizenship class while Patti observed Rebecca's ELL 4. Together, we attended MAEC's informal weekly women's group in which a diverse gathering of immigrant and refugee women voluntarily met to discuss a range of issues of concern in their daily lives. During the summer of 2004, Patti began teaching MAEC's entry-level ELL class every morning. Rachel joined to co-teach the daily course in the fall of 2004 and continued to do so until she moved from Milltown a year later. For several years, Patti maintained a steady presence at MAEC and arranged for hundreds of education students to complete thousands of service learning hours in MAEC's ELL program.

The second phase of our research includes four trips of varying lengths to Kenya. Interested in seeing for ourselves the context from which Somalis lived before their arrival in Milltown, we planned an initial visit to Nairobi in 2005-2006. During our time in Nairobi, we met with representatives from governmental and non-governmental organizations that work with Somali refugees in Kenya, including: the UN High Commission on Refugees (UNHCR), CARE Kenya,[1] as well as the International Organization on Migration (IOM). We also observed two 3-day Cultural Orientation sessions for U.S.-bound Somali refugees. Such fieldwork provided an initial glimpse at the challenges facing Somali refugees in Kenya and allowed us to begin planning our time in the Dadaab refugee camps.

The majority of our fieldwork in Kenya has taken place in Dadaab. Approximately 60 km from Kenya's Somali border, the three encampments that comprise Dadaab (Qafis, Bartan, and Mooro) are home to over 370,000 refugees, approximately 98% of who are Somali. In the spring of 2007 CARE Kenya contracted Patti to conduct an ethnographic investigation of factors that hinder female achievement in camps schools. At the time Dadaab featured a school system enrolling approximately 39,550 students (CARE, 2007).[2] Participation, performance, and retention levels within camp schools, however, are deeply gendered in ways that favored males.[3]

Our initial visit to Dadaab, from February to May 2007, combined participant observation in and outside of CARE schools with interviews and focus group discussions.[4] Focus groups were comprised of female Form Four[5] students in each of the three camps as well as female primary school teachers in Qafis. We also conducted individual interviews with: CARE educational supervisors, CARE and Windle Trust[6] teachers, female secondary school students, female Form Four leavers, female World University Services of Canada (WUSC) scholarship recipients, a former CARE education coordinator, minority students and their parents, as well as school headmasters and administrators. Finally, we conducted four week-long workshops on community-based ethnographic research methods with groups of English-proficient adult and Form Four refugee students.[7] As a component of the workshops, participants carried out a series of interviews with community members and wrote final analytic essays or reports. Research topics chosen by workshop participants included women and girls' participation in schooling as well as a range of other local, context-relevant queries around refugee perceptions of life in Kenya and the camps.

In 2008 we returned to Dadaab, where Patti had been hired as a consultant to CARE's Education Sector. Rachel visited as a graduate student in African Studies at Yale University. In addition to spearheading a project geared toward increasing tertiary educational opportunities for Form Four leavers,[8] we conducted two memoir groups. The groups were held in Qafis and Bartan and followed the memoir-gathering format developed by Chaplain Bill Blaine-Wallace in his work with HIV/Aids patients. In the Blaine-Wallace format,[9] participants meet regularly for as many sessions as there are group members to share life stories in an open-ended fashion. While in Dadaab, we ran two groups with 9 participants in Qafis and 11 in Bartan. Group members included female Form Four leavers, family members of educated women, secondary teachers, primary teachers, and mentors chosen by female students in Dadaab. Finally, Rachel co-facilitated a book group and discussion circle of female Form Four leavers in Qafis.[10]

It is worth noting that, due to logistical limitations, we were not able to spend nearly as much time in Dadaab as we did in Milltown. As a result, data drawn from the former site features interview data while that gathered in Milltown is much more observational in nature. We strongly prefer rich observational data and believe that, unfortunately, our portrait of Dadaab is less textured than that offered for Milltown. In what follows we seek the point of view of the study participants. In asking how the women made sense of school, we take a particular authorial subject position in which, as participant ethnographers, we seek the emic, or insiders' perspective. In asking how they "do" school" we assume a particular position with regard to a long standing question in the study of culture concerning the relative determinism of structural forces versus the ability of individuals to exert agency. By attending to the forms of active engagement employed by participants in the school sphere, we purposefully focus on their proactive efforts to apply their will within an admittedly highly delimited set of possibilities.

The attempt to capture women's agency in action is a deliberate move on our part, which reflects not only the abstract notion that individuals can exercise their will in the world but, more significantly, that these women of the global South wield the power to observe, deliberate, and act as agents in the creative endeavor of living. We purposely focus on their everyday actions and interactions in order to contest more common representations of Somali girls and women in the diaspora as vulnerable (refugees), oppressed (Muslim women), discriminated against (Blacks), backward and underdeveloped (members of the global South), and shameless opportunity seekers (refugees and/or welfare recipients). We have discovered that Somali refugee women work hard for the sake of personal achievement, in order to assist their families, and with the aim to secure citizenship in a world defined by diversity, competition, and dynamism. We find that, for the young scholars, schooling serves as a space in and process through which to negotiate gender salient sociocultural change at the turbulent confluence of myriad collapsed, reconfiguring, and emergent cultural and historical influences and structuring forces.

Why Explore Islamic East-West Relations Through a Multisite Study of Muslim Refugee Women's Schooling?

Talk about Islamic East-West relations at points of cultural juncture is often framed with regard to whether the Islamic belief structure is compatible with secular, democratic ways of life and governance (Fattah, 2006). To state the obvious, there is also deep concern about terrorist proclivities among followers of radicalized Islam. Thus, in working with Somali refugees, we have selected a population that, given Somalia's lack of state structure, prolonged civil chaos, and the increasingly strength of the al-Qa'ida-linked al Shabaab movement, agitates the West's worst fears. In the process, we provide a countervailing image. We are provided an invaluable opportunity to portray the rich variance within Muslim people and communities. In demonstrating the struggles, achievements, and desires extant within a population of Muslims from whom the West believes it has much to fear, we hope to lessen fear, increase knowledge, and modestly improve relations between the Islamic East and the West.

Conversely, there is concern from within the Western left and among citizens of predominantly Muslim occupied states, such as Somalia, that the so-called expansion of democracy is really an imperialistic mission in disguise. Certainly, democracy as a way of life and a formal governance structure has gone global. Recently, the West, and the United States in particular, has loudly espoused the virtues of democracy in its foreign policy and even foisted democratic political processes and structures upon Muslim countries through military invasion and occupation. It is also true that we live in an era in which democratically governed nations of the West have come together to form supranational agencies, organizations, and corporations that enjoy profound reach across the globe through peaceful, if well leveraged, means. Some maintain that the individual and/or conjoined hegemony of democracy, neoliberalism, and postwest-phalian regimes of global governance "are every bit as arrogant and free-dom-threatening as communism was" (Fraser, 2005, p. 138; Hardt & Negri, 2000).

On both ends of the spectrum lie fear of totalitarianism, a nebulous anxiety that, if allowed to flourish, either the West or Islam will, in politi-cal theorists Nancy Fraser's (2005) words, "subjugate human spontaneity to the false necessity of social determinism" (p. 139). And, thus, out of an anxiety held in common, we are "locked together in a self-propelling destructive cycle" in which "the mutually reinforcing projects of 'jihadism' and the 'war on terror'... generate new forms of menace to humanity" (p. 134).

We posit that the sensible antidote to alarm about possible absolutism is plurality in voice and decision making. If we accept the twofold premise that there is a rift between the Islamic East and West—often manifested via interrogation of gender norms within Islam—and that the split lends complexity to efforts to enroll Muslim refugee girls and women in school-ing, then we must also understand that an examination of Muslim, refu-gee girls' and women's school lives provides an opportunity to examine Islamic East/West relations in a poly-vocal manner. While extremes of per-spective are highlighted in much public discourse, in reality the middle ground between the West and Islamic East takes up much more metaphys-ical space than the polarities themselves. Accordingly, the vast interior should be afforded greater attention than is currently the case. Listening to the voices of Muslim female students offers a point of possibility that we seek to locate and depict in rich detail.

Girls and Women as Active Producers of Culture

Muslim female students are at a juncture of the Islamic East and the West. In some cases they are used as mere props in divisive politics. However, they hold much more promise. By looking at girls' and women's perspectives, actions, and experiences, we appreciate their part in drafting the ever-evolving narrative of Islamic East-West relations. Muslim girls and women are active meaning makers and producers of culture, which is not to say that they are producing one culture or speaking with one voice. Somali women in the diaspora do not speak for all Muslim women, nor do all Somali women speak with one voice. Individual women have their own voices, per-spectives and experiences. During the course of our study, we met women who self identified as traditionalist, others who aspired to Westernize, and many who explored the myriad possibilities in between. Diversity among Somali women indicates that an essential Islamic East/West oppositionality is spurious. There is so much internal difference within the West and within the Islamic East that to propose a master narrative of discord is simply inaccurate. We attempt to move beyond Orientalist discourse in which Muslim women are either made passive to the Western gaze or the oppression of Muslim men or they are imagined as covertly violent radicals. By looking at women in Dadaab and in Milltown, we examine two sites of cultural encounter between the West and Islamic East in which Muslim girls' and women's active production of meaning is made visible. Girls and women must choose between different ways of being: maintaining certain cultural traditions and beliefs, adopting Western ones, and/or actively creating something new and unique through hybridization. When such decision-making capacity is made evident, the women's self-identification and efficacy as active subjects becomes apparent.

The women in our study have been victims of political violence in a Muslim country. Recent stories from Somalia feature terrorism, piracy, prolonged civil disorder marked by extreme violence, and the stoning of women for adultery and other causes. All strike Westerners as barbaric and inexcusable. The narrative construction of events in Somalia by the Western media heightens the already active proclivity to view Muslim women as passive victims to be pitied and saved by the West. Accordingly, by demonstrating that Somali refugee women are, in fact, active agents who think and act in complex and assertive ways, not passive pawns of either the West or the Islamic East, we offer a powerful counternarrative to what has become a normalized portraiture of Muslim women and relations between the Islam East and the West.

Multiple Sites Highlight the Particular

The multisite nature of the current study is also a fitting way to reflect upon Islamic East/West relations as the Somali community in each location develops distinct strategies for grappling with unique sets of social, political, cultural, and economic realities. Accordingly, highlighting the regional nature of Islamic East/West relations further deconstructs a master binary narrative. For, when we are able to diversify our image of Somalis, we effectively refute the notion that there is a universal way of being Muslim and reveal the minority status of members of the Islamic radical right.

Finally, while our main objective is to show some of the variety within Muslim communities and people, because so much of the political tension and outright conflict between the West and the Islamic East results in human displacement and the need for international humanitarian aid apparatus to come into play, it makes sense to look at refugee policy as part of an examination of Islamic East/West relations. The use of two study locations allows for consideration of the transnational nature of refugee policy, and thus, breeds an appreciation for the delicacy of relations. For example, it is widely accepted that Somalis, and refugees in general, fantasize about being relocated to the West, particularly the United States (Horst, 2006). For Somali refugees, *buffism*, a Somali word used to describe the longing for resettlement in the United States, is weighed against the knowledge that the United States currently plays an unpopular interventionist role in their home country. If resettlement prospects did not exist, the balance between the desire to belong and resentment for intervention would likely be lost and Somalis could very well become increasingly anti-American as they languish in camps that are effectively human warehouses. The vital function resettlement plays in maintaining Somalis' hope for a better future underscores the significant role international and transnational refugee policy plays as a whole in ever-evolving Islamic East-West relations.

Theorizing Somali Women's Schooling: Power, Knowledge, and Flexible Citizenship

Whether in Dadaab or Milltown, Somali women live at a point of cultural, political, and economic confluence. They live in spaces defined by the coming together of opposition from the Islamic East and West. In Dadaab, the tension is expressed in various ways, which we will describe in greater detail in forthcoming chapters. One of these is worth describing at this early point in order to give an inkling of the polarity between what stakeholders commonly refer to as "traditional Somali culture" and the Enlightenment agenda of the UNHCR. The UNHCR subcontracts its services to various NGOs. The NGOs that the UNHCR works with are largely based in Western countries or, if local, receive the bulk of donations from Western states. Many have a faith based (Christian) component. One of these includes the National Christian Churches of Kenya (NCCK). The role of NCCK in Dadaab is to provide health and reproductive education. They run an anti(female) circumcision campaign for which they employ young Somali male incentive workers as community educators. Working on the campaigns puts the young men in a difficult position. They have to confront conservative members of the Somali community, which places them in great physical danger, in order to earn a small stipend that supplements the meager food rations provided by the UNHCR. They also stand to gain favor among NGO staff. That the UNHCR deliberately contracts a Christian organization to promulgate an anticircumcision message suggests the perception on the part of the UNHCR that Somalis hold very different world views on issues related to women's roles in the family, community, and society at large and could not be entrusted with the responsibility of upholding the desired platform. The fact that the young male incentive workers report facing a threat of violence and social marginalization within their community as a result of their work confirms the assessment of divergence is at least accurate in relation to a portion of the Somali community.

A fissure between the Islamic East and West is also apparent in Milltown. In fact the divide is in some ways more readily apparent in Milltown, where letters to the editor in the local paper frequently and publicly vocalize anti Somali sentiment in a way that does not occur in Dadaab. Milltown has also experienced multiple hate crimes targeted at Somali newcomers and episodes of violence between White and Somali youth.

While division exists in both locations, the parties in question do not exercise tensions on equal terms. Power differentials are obvious. In Dadaab, they are evident in material and political realities. Refugees rely on the UNHCR for food rations and all social services. They must compete for a limited number of school seats. Refugees are prohibited by Kenyan law from paid labor. The UNHCR is allowed to provide a very small stipend to refugees for what is termed "incentive work." If they want an exception to laws that prohibit movement out of their camp, they must depend on the UNHCR to provide waivers to suitable to Kenyan government officials. Without a functioning state government refugees have no right to vote. The UNHCR alone determines who gets what benefits and for what reason.

In Milltown material and political inequities are also quite evident. Milltown is a postindustrial city with high unemployment rates. Somalis rarely have marketable skills or necessary credentials and so rely on social welfare benefits that, although generous in comparison to others states, maintain a basic level of subsistence. As refugees, Somalis are not eligible to apply for US citizenship for five years and thus, again, have no right to vote.[12]

In both locations power differentials are not only visible in material realities or in the lack of refugee political rights but also in relation to cultural or knowledge forms. Western ways of reasoning and being have been thoroughly institutionalized in schools, government, health care, prisons, and various social services that serve the displaced Somali population. Foucault theorizes the intimate interconnection between forms of knowledge and the exercise of power arguing that particular ways of knowing are given heightened value through institutionalization. Contemplating the Modern era, Foucault argues that faith in the progressive potential of humanity to create an ordered and just society underlied the creation of a variety of social institutions; i.e., prisons, schools, and hospitals. Drawing on Foucault (for heuristic purposes as opposed an act of positivist historicism) as applied to ethnographic study, or the study of ethnically or otherwise culturally identified groups, we can imagine that two distinct ways of knowing and acting in the world can emerge within two different communities. The resultant knowledge forms might be quite distinct, even opposing. Through institutionalization within the apparatai of a society that encompasses both ethno-cultural groups, one group's way of knowing—say, progressive humanism in the case of Foucault's favored Modern era—is elevated above the other.

In the process, the primary ethno-cultural group itself gains status as bearers of prestigious knowledge. Those familiar with the secondary informal (noninstitutionalized) knowledge can hope to lift their own status either through institutional change or co-optation of the primary group's knowledge via access to status quo institutional structures. Thus, power relations are mediated through institutionalization of particular forms of knowledge and over time competing knowledge forms often fade, become crystallized as a subversive alternative, and/or become subtly woven into the fabric of the primary knowledge form. Interestingly, the knowledge-power connection is maintained through self-regulation as change agents rarely successfully overturn institutionalized forms of knowledge wholesale, thereby leaving individuals to seek forms of personal success and belonging through deliberate appropriation and subscription to established norms.

As a disciplinary technology, international refugee law exemplifies Foucault's proposed dynamic of self-regulation and universalization in action. Refugee law was created by Westerners in response to widespread displacement caused during World War II. Accordingly, through a presumption of universal individual rights, already well established in the constitutional democracies of the nations that crafted and signed the declaration into law, a particular worldview became inscribed in a piece of legislation that would go on to impact millions of people across the globe. While today's refugees, who often come from communitarian and/or theocratic societies, may share little ideologically with the individualistic and secularism underlying international refugee law, they actively seek asylum via means of the law, thereby claiming rights based on a notion of equality between individuals. Their life thereafter is irreparably shaped by the contours of Westernized refugee policy and practice.

While refugee law may serve as a fitting example of the disciplining and normalizing effect of the institutionalization of particular forms of knowledge, Foucault is clear that the ability to regulate in this manner is not limited to governments. Power is a relational matter for Foucault and thus is not a fixed quantity to be uncomplicatedly held in the hands of politicians. Rather, government is itself an institutional apparatus inscribed with certain knowledge forms at the expense of others. However qualified, governing bodies—local, national and supranational—do enjoy considerable latitude in the shaping of ancillary institutions aimed at the production of universal, normalized knowledge and a citizenry versatile in select knowledge forms.

For example, in providing public schooling to their citizenry, governments offer individuals an opportunity to engage in self-improvement and develop skills needed to thrive in society. The curriculum, pedagogy, and rewards and punishment systems within schooling are synonymous with the knowledge valued by the government. One could envision a democratic government placing an emphasis on the development of critical thinking skills among its citizenry. Regardless of the form of government, the purposes of schooling commonly include: familiarizing the citizenry with national history and language in order to foster a sense of national unity, teaching skills needed within the national or regional economy, and conveying particular moral codes, that is, religious orthodoxy or humanism, according to which a nation/society can operate effectively.

Schooling's function as a disciplinary apparatus holds true in regard to the schooling provided refugees. Promises of jobs and resettlement, as well as respect as evolved modern Somalis, are held out to those who perform well academically. The autonomous subject position also remains relevant. Dadaab students fight for evermore limited seats as they move from primary through secondary school. Eventually hundreds will compete for the roughly 40 scholarships that provide a means for them to leave the camps for further study. Because they are individually accountable for achievement of school success, the disciplining function of schooling—where they learn English, read the canon, and study diligently for hours a day—is realized on their backs, through their own labor.

As institutions with their origins in the Modern era, it should not be surprising that Foucault's vision remains applicable to schooling. Even his understanding of the panopticon holds true. Dadaab and Milltown students are forever under the surveillance of peers, teachers, and family members. In Dadaab, all are well aware that the end game is a scholarship that will take them out of the camps and that the means through which scholarships are awarded is performance on a single exam, the Kenyan Comprehensive Secondary Education examinations (KCSE), one final zero sum game test. Fittingly, they are also surveying themselves through constant comparison to others, ritualistic efforts to increase performance, denial of sleep in order to study, and internal chastisement for underperformance. A similar dynamic holds true in the United States, where students are often learning English for the first time. Under the shadow of No Child Left Behind policy, newcomers' test scores resulted in several local Milltown schools being labeled "failing." Accordingly, community members carefully attend to the educational progress of the refugee English language learners. And, study participants are only too conscious of their place under the microscope. The women we worked with monitored their own progress toward being able to respond to their neighbors' angry accusations, threats and demands that they "learn English or go back to Africa." Further, in the United States, scarce jobs go to those who speak English, learn to read and write, maintain timeliness, and dress in ways suitable to employers. In short, the hope for employment demands that women appropriate Western skills, dress, and habits. Accordingly, through schooling, women learn to discipline themselves in order to one day gain employment and social acceptance.

Whether poststructuralist or otherwise theoretically identified, educational scholars have long understood schooling's role as a normalizing and organizing social institution. Consider Bowles and Gintis' (1976) sociological examination of schooling's function to reproduce social class stratification, Bourdieu and Passerons' (1990) analysis of schooling as a mechanism through which cultural capital is transmitted, and Willis' (1977) ironic discovery that working class boys' class based resistances to schooling perpetuate class hierarchies. More recently, world culture theorists point to an increasing homogeneity in schooling across the globe. World culture theorists believe that individual nation states seek legitimacy by taking on Western education "scripts" (Dale, 2000). Accordingly, wide-scale adoption of Western governance structures, curricula, and pedagogical practices lead to greater isomorphism in education across the globe. Schools become secularized, similarly organized into particular disciplines, the curriculum within disciplines is standardized, and reward systems are geared toward individual accomplishment.

The image Dale (2000) paints is certainly reflected in the Kenyan camps, where the UNHCR has adopted the Kenyan national curriculum, itself modeled after the British system reflecting a colonial past. Teachers are certified through a national system that mirrors Britain's and many in the West. Classrooms and institutional layout also resemble those in the West though are much more modest. All details echo classrooms that first appeared in the modern era and largely remain intact to the present day. In the United States, again the same applies. Students learn a standardized curriculum in "egg carton" classrooms. At the most advanced levels of adult English language learning, students learn the material for the U.S. citizenship test. The test is of American history and government and successful performance is dependent upon one's ability to hear, speak, read, and write English.

However accurate Foucault is at depicting schooling as a disciplinary apparatus, it is also true that he wrote about the institutionalization of particular forms of knowledge before many of the transformations that characterize the current global era had occurred. Political philosopher Fraser (2010) writes:

> Foucault mapped the contours of the disciplinary society just as the ground was being cut out from under it.... The irony is plain: whether we call it postindustrial society or neoliberal globalization, a new regime oriented to "deregulation" and "flexibilization" was about to take shape just as Foucault was conceptualizing disciplinary normalization. (p. 117)

For Fraser, the problem with reading contemporary society through a Foucauldian lens is that the rapid globalization of the past two decades has undermined the universalizing potential of disciplining apparatus. The nation no longer enjoys the same irrefutable authority it once did. While Foucault had a decentered understanding of the mechanisms of power, he did assume that the society within which processes of normalization occurred were coterminous with national borders. In the current global era, however, ideas, people, and money cross borders at unprecedented rates of speed and quantity and in the meantime, reorder economies across the globe. Diversity in ideas and people coupled with dramatic reconfiguration of national and regional economies bring contestation over what comprises the norms for which disciplinary power might be attuned as well as the form(s) and content(s) of the discipline(s) and the arbiter(s) of the power themselves.

Several educational ethnographies offer empirical grounding for this sea change in the ontology of contemporary society. Critical educational ethnographers (CEE) often examine sites of cultural encounter and in doing so, emphasize localized acts of resistance and/or appropriation of what might otherwise be understood as homogenizing, Western derived reform processes. CEE scholars interpret the seeming global isomorphism of curricula and bureaucratic structures as obscuring more deeply resonant differences. For example, more often than not disagreement over even the most entrenched education policy and practice exists within nations and between supranational bodies, suggesting the salience of conflicting models of education. Further, the gap between policy and practice may be wider than between policies as individuals, communities, nations, and regions appropriate educational models to suit local needs, habits and desires. Finally, homogeneity in educational nomenclature conceals that "a model diffused in name only does not have the same significance as a model that actually affects behavior all over the world" (Anderson-Levitt, 2003, p. 17).

The work of those skeptical of the notion that Westernization acts as a totalizing force falls into three subgroups[12]: Research that traces policy reform implementation from the top (Western derived national education policies) down (through state/district/province to the school level)

(Anderson-Levitt & Diallo, 2003; Brook Napier, 2003; Jungck, 2003; Vavrus, 2006); research that interrogates the point of contact between universal education policy and local knowledge, tradition, and practices. Such scholarship often centers on the experiences and meaning making of those at the very local level in regard to education policy reform (Randle, K. & Brady, N. 1997; Hatch & Honig, 2003; Luykx, 1996; Ouyang, 2003; Rival, 1996; Rosen, 2003; Stambach, 2003). And, finally, research that examines far reaching educational policy that originates outside of Western derived models (Aikman, 1997; Barlett, 2003; Reed-Danahay, 2003; Segal-Levit, 2003; Toh & Floresca-Cawagas, 1997). In each case, as CEE scholar Vavrus (2005) contends in her investigation of structural adjustment policies in Tanzania, ethnographic studies of policy share "an emphasis on relations of power, on cultural practices that affect policy interpretations, and on sustained engagement with residents in a local setting" (p. 176).

Fraser (2010) offers a useful way to think about the layered, multi-vectorial denormalization that occurs at sites of cultural encounter. She argues that the new global regime calls for study of *flexibilization*. Due to decades of deregulation and the decentering of the nation in favor of transnational processes and bodies, she argues that flexibility has emerged as a new method of self-regulation. In addition to its use as an economic concept referencing multinational production streams that require low inventories and the ability to rapidly move sites of manufacture in response to the availability of low cost labor, Fraser defines a corresponding human process of flexibilization. Flexibilization of the self entails being held accountable to navigate contested ideological terrains and material realities that transcend national boundaries. Here Fraser echoes Ong's (1999) examination of Hong Kong business elite, who in seeking multiple national citizenships, have

> adopted a kind of "flexible citizenship" in the wake of Tiananmen Square and with a view to Hong Kong's patriation.... Caught between British disciplinary racism and China's opportunistic claims of racial loyalty, between declining economic power in Britain and surging capitalism in Asia, they sought a flexible position among the myriad possibilities (and problems) found in the global economy. (p. 123)

For Ong (1999), flexibility is both a product and a condition of late capitalism. The process of flexibilization is a product of an undermining of state sovereignty manifest in globe trotters' leveraging of national belonging. In this postnational world, residents of global cities belong to a plane of citizenry which rises above individual nation-states. Perhaps, for example, the primary identities of jet setting Londoners share more in common with their counterparts in New York City, Bangkok, and Hong Kong than in the countryside of Yorkshire.

While Somali refugee women may cross many national borders, they could hardly be considered flexible citizens with the same connotation of choice, influence, and status as cosmopolitan Londoners or Ong's business elite. However, their flexibility does involve sociopolitical change that requires a negotiation of (quasi) national environments dominated by contrasting ideologies in which the sovereignty of the nation state has been called into question. In Dadaab, refugees, aid workers, and observers alike reference Somali traditionalism and UNHCR espoused enlightenment as opposing ends of an ideological polarity. In Milltown, a triad between liberalism, nativism, and Somali traditionism presides.[13] While enlightenment, traditionalism, liberalism, and nativism are not fixed concepts but rather contested and localized, each bears very real discursive and materially consequences in the lives of Somali women. Study participants were often treated as pawns in the tug of war played out between the most vocal (or institutionally powerful) proponents of these ideologies. However, the women's work in school demonstrates that, while they felt and acknowledged the polarity (in Dadaab) or the threefold discursive currents (in Milltown), they did not see themselves as pawns but rather as active agents *flexibly* negotiating between and making sense of these different worldviews *as well as* their areas of overlap.

In her ethnography of Sikhs in London, Hall (2002, p. 150) notes that "contradictions within and between classificatory systems ... allow spaces for the negotiation, contestation, and reinterpretation of difference" (p. 150). Indeed, we found that Somali refugee women worked to break down the ideological architecture in which they found themselves, discovered (or created) spaces for negotiation, contestation, and reinterpretation of difference, while at the same time they carefully constructed new lives and ways of being in often dire circumstances.

And so, we take several valuable lessons from Foucault, Fraser, and Ong as we look upon Somali women's schooling. First, the schism between the Islamic East and the West occurs at an historical moment in time in which ways of knowing and being long inscribed in institutional forms dating to the Modern era; that is, schooling, is increasingly vulnerable to changes wrought by globalization. Further, due to deregulation, resultant economic shifts, and the underresourcing of public spaces/institutions, individuals are increasingly asked to flexibly negotiate highly charged cultural, social, and economic arenas making decisions of great consequence. And finally, that they do so illustrates agency, if not the realization of social justice.

A Story From Dadaab

In May and June of 2008, we ran a memoir-gathering group in two of the three subcamps that comprise Dadaab. Each group's composition included four or five young women who had recently completed secondary school in the refugee camp. As a group, the young women selected a female mentor, a primary school teacher, and a secondary school teacher whom they approached to join. Each graduate had also invited a family member to participate. Groups met daily for as many meetings as there were members. With the exception of a secondary teacher who was an ethnic Somali, Kenyan national and one who was from mainland Kenya, all were refugees who had fled Somalia's civil war. During each session, one group member shared a story that reflected his or her unique life experiences. At the beginning of each session, we offered a simple introductory prompt that invited participants to tell us what they would like the group to know about them. Participants told their stories in the language of their choice. One of the young women translated, either from English to Somali for the benefit of family members who did not speak English or from Somali to English for our benefit. All conversations were recorded and later transcribed.[14]

Leyla,[15] a gregarious and warm 19-year-old, translated most frequently. After coming to Kenya as a child with her mother in 1992, Leyla enrolled in school and would become one of the first generation of girls to complete school in Dadaab. The following excerpt is from her story:

> My name's Leyla Abdi Mohammed and I live in the Bartan refugee camp and I'm also a Form Four graduate of 2007. During these days when I was in school, I had faced some challenges, and this has not been a problem [only] to me only but it also happens to most of the Somali girls.
>
> In my secondary school I can remember … an incident … in the afternoon when schools—usually lessons end at 4 in the afternoon. We used to remain in school and revise our books. There were also other eleven talented girls who used to be in my class. We used to urge one another in our challenges that we are facing as refugee girls and a way out. We used to ask each other in the morning session, "How many hours had you been awake last night?" If one says, "I had been revising for two hours," we used to shout at that one. We used to tell her, "sleeping doesn't help [you], but do [as] much [as] you can—just add two other extra hours, even if you are feeling sleepy! For example, if you feel like you are feeling sleepy, just get a bowl of water and put it under your legs there and as you shiver, then you won't feel sleepy." And we used to use also coffee.
>
> The other thing is that in the afternoon sessions we used to go from school at late hours. I can recall every evening we used to meet a certain man on the way. He used to look at his watch and glance at us with a gloomy face. And when we were on the way we used to also shout [to each other],

"What are the things you have learned today?" and "What can you recall?"
We used to ask each other such questions. Accidentally one of my friends
the other day reminded me, "Do you see this man?" is what she said. She
says, "when he approaches us every evening, maybe he's a business man
who comes from the market, and he keeps on watching us every evening
and he glances us with gloomy eyes, I don't know what's up with him." I told
her, "Leave him alone. A day will come while we are walking majestically on
this way and we shall also enjoy the fruits of our education of today."

For young women in Dadaab, seeking an education represents a break
from tradition and they are well aware that many disapprove of the venture. The censure is especially bitter toward those rare few, like Leyla and
her friends, who continue past the primary level and hope to complete
secondary school. As Leyla's narrative suggests, together and for one
another's benefit, these pioneers co-construct arguments in defense of
their decision to pursue education beyond puberty, the traditional age of
marriage eligibility. In fact in response to the resistance they feel from
community members, they develop both discursive and material strategies for making it through the four grueling years of high school. They
tutored each other so that no one fell behind in a particular subject; they
carried friends to the camp hospital when one fainted from painful menstrual complications due to the type of female circumcision commonly
practiced among Somalis[16]; they pooled money from their extremely limited resources to purchase schoolbooks and solar lamps which they then
rotated among their homes in order to allow for nighttime study. Meanwhile, their male classmates, who were permitted out of their homes after
dark, gathered at the well-lit school campuses every evening. Before the
(KCSE) examinations, the cumulative end-of-high-school exams that
solely determine one's eligibility for university, one group of women
rented a small home in which they could study and sleep without the distraction of otherwise routine domestic chores. As Leyla conveys, the
young women supported each other in the face of stigmatization by traditionalists within the community and even advocated for one another
when threats of arranged marriage emerged. Yet, even as they rejected
the imagined and explicit commentary of disapproving community members and worked collectively to support one another's progress, they were
not in the position to simply exert their own will. Rather they reasoned,
cajoled, and compromised with various members of Dadaab community
in order to stay enrolled. Such maneuvering often took place within their
families. Leyla shared:

When I was in Standard Eight another incident happened to me. Before the
preparation of the exam a certain man came to my mom while he proposed
that, "I want to marry your daughter." My mom came to me the other night

and she explained to me, "This man is going to America and he has some dollars. So kindly, we are in such a critical condition; he may help us out to be out of this condition. Kindly, I need you to marry this man."

I had to object the idea. I told her, "Have you ever seen me discuss with a man or any proposal I have been made towards a man?" She said, "No." I told her, "I want you to accept my request and kindly apologize and kindly forgive me and let me continue my studies." She didn't give me a clear result at that time. Later on after three nights I had to think of all sorts of solutions so that I can convince my mother and she can chase away this man. During the third night when it was midnight I had to wake her up from sleep. I told her, "I have a discussion with you tonight. Be patient with me for the hours that I'll be sharing my views with you." Then she said, "Accepted."

Later on, I explained to her all the hardships she was undergoing at that time and all the possible efforts she was making for me. I convinced her that "I am the first born of the family, yet you don't have any son of yours who will be assisting you. So I'm in the position of both the first-born of the family and acting like a baby boy for you and it will happen if you leave me like this one day it will happen that you will not receive support from any other person except through my hand and I will make sure that before you live all prosperous life that I won't even look or glance at the sight of men."

I tell her, "What you require from this man is only wealth and wealth gets ended easily like that." I promised her that by any means I'll be assisting her except if she's saved from death, both of us. I also make one promise with her—If she allows me to continue with my studies today, then next time when I finish high school or any other possible solutions of my education, any status it will be, any proposal that she makes towards me concerning about marriage, I will accept from her that day, but not today. And I won't make any proposal towards men without her consent.

And that's how it happened. And my mom had to accept my request. She said, "Starting from this moment there will be no point of argument of marriage and you will be continuing with your studies unless or otherwise you bring for me a man and you say, 'This man is what I want' … You [will] finish your studies. I won't disturb you anymore." I also made that promise and I'm still in that process and I never intended even to have a discussion with anyone.

In the described exchange with her mother, Leyla framed education as an economic investment through which she would be better able to provide support in the future. She also etched out a careful concession with regard to marriage, promising to resist distraction and, if allowed to complete school, accept any arrangement later proposed by her mother. Leyla was careful not to break gendered expectations held of youth, but rather in absence of a male heir, she cast herself as the son of the family. In doing so, she successfully negotiated a highly charged terrain and was allowed to complete her secondary education. She and her peers faced multiple, at times conflicting, conventions of community members who would have her marry and remain in the domestic sphere; Kenyan teachers who praised her work ethic, assertiveness, and ability; humanitarian aid staff who assured her that she was a leader of a new generation of sophisticated Somali women, and family members who tried to ascertain the best approach to protecting their daughters' and all other family members' best interest.

At the time of writing, both Leyla and her mother had fulfilled their ends of the bargain. Selected from among a highly competitive pool of applicants, Leyla worked for Save the Children and, with her salary, sustained her mother and brother. She remained unmarried and eagerly awaited any opportunity for tertiary education. Imagining the opportunity for further schooling, Leyla described a better life of broad social change:

> I know education is the key to being successful in life. It's the only thing—for one, when you're literate person, one thing which is good is that you'll be able to know of your rights and the rights of others. Secondly, you will become an independent person who doesn't need any help from any person and that uses his book and pen to do so. With the aid of education I am also sure if it becomes possible I'll be able, in a position, to help the future generation, the upcoming generation.
>
> Through my education I will also be sure that I'll break the inequality that exists in the Somali community, that is the segregation of women and the low empowerment of women in the Somali community and I'll guarantee if I'm told I'll continue my studies that such status will no longer exist and we shall also break them and some of the barriers that women are facing—they will no longer exist during our generation time.

In adroitly casting herself in the role of the son in order to continue schooling, Leyla pulled a piece of Somali tradition—the educational privilege afforded to boys—into the present in order to envision a different future altogether, a future in which the very gender norms she used to justify her continued enrollment no longer exist. It is a future at once bold and new, yet linked without disruption through narrative device to a cultural history. It is a future in which Leyla remains at once unmistakably Somali and in which what it means to be a Somali woman has undergone considerable transformation.

A Story From Milltown

Across the diaspora in Milltown, during winter months of 2008, Patti held another memoir-gathering group that included undergraduate students from the college where she teaches and adult Somali refugees who had resettled locally. Some of the major topics that arose in Milltown discussions included: childhood memories, educational experiences, family life, details of resettlement to the United States, aspects of refugee life, religion, marriage and divorce, encounters with violence, language barriers and challenges faced within the United States. While many themes reflect challenges and opportunities unique to life as Somali Muslim refugees resettled in the post-9/11 United States, others resonate with those relevant in Dadaab. The following story was shared by Asha who, like most Somalis in Milltown, relocated to Maine after an initial period in a larger American city.

My name is Asha Ahmed. I have been in the United States since January 2004. When I arrived I had two sons, my younger sister and my husband. I had my third son Abdikadir who was born here. After the third child, I got divorced from my husband. I have only been living in Milltown for five months. I go to adult education for English language four days a week. I am attending job training develop[ment] three times a week. I have never worked in Maine but I am taking literacy and skill classes to go to work and get a position. I like Milltown because there are a lot of resources for my development.

My son, who is seven, is now better off than me with English reading and writing. Omar, my son, is the one who helps me with my spelling and explains things to me that I don't understand. So Omar is tutoring me at home so that I can catch up with my English. Noor, my other son, has very limited Somali language so Omar interprets between Noor and me. I have to give Noor instructions [but] I can't speak English, so I have to use Omar who is the second person in the house giving instructions. Noor went to daycare when he was 2½, then preschool, kindergarten, so he was away from me as I worked and tried to go to school. So I lost him language-wise then and he communicates in English and spending more time speaking it.

So Noor has better English than me. I think it is a good thing because I feel Noor is in the system and picked up the language in a much better way and I am proud of him. Omar is telling me 'Mom, Noor can't understand you. You better start learning English quickly and you better learn it good.' So he was not spending a lot of time with me, more at the daycare and I am proud of him. So, again, even the childcare itself there is limited Somali interaction. So I look at it from the positive side its good for me, its better for me I will have kids that are educated and can help me as I struggle.

At the beginning, in the resettlement system I had an interpreter that told me everything and gave me the numbers to call and people to contact.... At the beginning, it was like I was somebody who could not speak or hear anything because I didn't know what people were saying. Everything was communicated through the interpreters. I feel like I'm being squeezed, in Somali we say, "ciriri." I'm in a situation where I have no way to do anything and I felt overwhelmed by not being able to ... [I] felt as if I was being left out on what people were saying because I could not interpret it....

The first thing I do now is look at where I was three years and I feel that I have come a very long way. I'm ok now, I feel even comfortable talking to and interacting with people and I think I will be very comfortable if I go to work with people who speak English and just say, "What's up?" I don't feel tied down now [and] if I don't understand I will not be shy. I feel that now I am able to approach people and say, "I don't know this. Can you show me this?" and if I want to contribute I can just express myself.... I feel like at this point that I am almost getting to self-sufficiency and that I will be able to help care of myself language wise, skills wise and knowing where the resources are and I am very grateful that I am getting more support and I am able to comprehend what is available for me.

Thousands of miles from the harsh desert environment of Dadaab, Asha no longer faced a situation as dire as Leyla's. Indeed, life in Milltown represents an expansion of opportunity for Somali women, most of whom have never attended school prior to resettlement. Relative to Dadaab, in the United States, sufficient educational offerings exist to match the demand of entry-level learners and the mainstream cultural environment has normalized, even compelled, Somali women's participation in schooling. While Asha confronted challenges that might have interfered with her ability to attend classes, such as caring for her three children in an unfamiliar environment and the frustratingly slow pace of learning to read and write for the first time as an adult in a foreign language, she poignantly framed education as the ticket to self-sufficiency, mobility, and adaptation in a globalized world. Assurance in education's promise led Asha to decide that the United States presented the best option for herself and her family, just at it sustained her through initial days of hardship upon arrival in New England. She recalled:

The first thing I felt was the cold. We even felt that it was cold before we got there. And during the flight, the first things I saw was white, everything covered with snow. That was terrifying.... The kids did not sleep that [first] night. They were coughing and wheezing and we just knew they were cold. In Somali we say, "the cold that entered you," were exposed. In the morning, the kids [were] taken to hospital and given syrup and meds and felt fine. We then came back home. With all that snow, I said to myself, "Oh my God, I better go die in [Kenya]. I cannot die here. I can deal with the heat and no food in [Kenya], but what am I going to eat out here with all this snow on the ground?"

At least I knew that there was some hope there, out of all this cold and what I am going through. But if I think of where to go, I know if I went to back to [Kenya], my hope was finished.... There was nothing to hope for, nothing to do. But here at least I know my kids will learn and go to school. That is where I found the strength to hold on. My niece came here and went to middle school, almost out of high school and going to college. That kind of success I hope for my kids and myself. That's what got me through the snow and cold.

Asha unequivocally expressed gratitude for her newfound access to schooling and the doors of communication and economic opportunity it allegedly opened. Nonetheless, Asha took the space to reflect upon different ways of being she observed in the U.S. and proudly defended the cultural mores and gendered norms prominent in Somalia and later, Kenyan refugee camps.

> The children in America and Africa are totally different. Culture and tradition it very important in my country and not so much in America. In Africa, there is gender gap from early age. It is totally different here as long as they are the same age they can hang out, work together, and be together. We were brought up in a life that a young girl prepares to get married. Things are totally different here. You have to wait until you are 18 to be legal to get married. So we have to know the difference and distinctions.
>
> I was 15 in my first marriage. I had my first child at 16 and I'm 24 now. I am happy I had children very early. But my older son looks like my younger brother. People always ask me about it. But I am comfortable with it.
>
> American 24-year-old woman have wasted a lot of years. I am 24 now with three kids and you don't have kids? You have wasted a lot of time. You better hurry up and get married! We never thought about children as a burden. We had to raise the child, feed and take care of the child. But here you guys think about it as being hard because people are busy with school.

Asha prides herself on the ability to at once take advantage of the opportunities afforded by schooling and fulfill her role as a mother of three children at age 24. Asha's lifeway represents the best of both worlds for her—as a young woman she can become educated and parent at an early age—despite the fact that her situation does not entirely resemble the norm in either Somalia, where she likely would not have accessed formal education, or in the United States, where, as she noted, increasingly few women have multiple children by age 24. Indeed, even Leyla was not afforded the ability to do both in Dadaab. For, if Leyla had been married or impregnated as early as 16, she would have been forced by all parties involved to drop out of camp schools.

Beyond their radically distinct locations, Leyla and Asha share much in common. Both are Somali migrants forced from their homeland by violence and material deprivation. Each has lived a significant portion of her life in the Dadaab refugee camp. Asha had also arrived in Dadaab in the early 1990s and stayed for 15 years before being awarded resettlement to the United States. While Dadaab is situated within Kenya's isolated and majority Muslim Northeastern province, the camp is managed by the UNHCR and, as such, forms a unique island of Western influence amidst an otherwise barren and isolated desert landscape. As such, each lives within a region strongly imbued with a Western zeitgeist, a worldview readily apparent in the organization and daily practices of schooling.

The women from Dadaab and Milltown use schooling as a space and process to flexibly negotiate belonging in new (quasi) national contexts in ways that reflect and actively incorporate elements of a shared Somali history. In *Mistrusting Refugees*, Daniel and Knudsen (1995) write that to be fully human "is to be able to partake of a culture, where culture is seen as yet another domain of sign activity but a domain that is public, shared, and quasi-conventional" (p. 11). By definition, the refugee experience is about the disruption of culture, place, and nation. Refugees enter host countries at a break point in a sequence of cultural meaning. Daniel and Knudsen describe the shock of existence in such a space of absolute syntagmatism "where information cannot be related to something preexisting (i.e., made into at least a partially redundant form) meaning cannot exist" (p. 3). The refugee women involved in our study use their engagement in the schooling process as an opportunity to bridge the chasm that separates personal pasts and the new domain of sign activity into which they enter upon arrival in Dadaab and the United States. In drawing upon an understanding of Somali culture rooted in the past—in a homeland from which they have fled and may never safely return—in order to shape a present in such a way as to direct themselves toward an equally imagined, yet qualitatively different future as Somali women in the diaspora, the scholars engage in a "weaving" (Berns McGown, 1999) effort. Through such indexing and entwining of experience, refugees reengage in the very human pursuit of claiming belonging through evocations of heritage. Anthropologists Ashworth and Graham (2005) describe such weaving or heritage work as the:

> ways in which very selective material artifacts, mythologies, memories and traditions become resources for the present. The contents, interpretations and representations of the resources are selected according to the demands of the present; an imagined past provides resources for a heritage that is to be bequeathed to an imagined future. (p. 4)

As an instrumental process, the women's weaving or heritage work involves pasts "reinvented to reflect new presents" (Ashworth & Graham, 2005, p. 4). Selective acts of remembrance serve as mechanisms in the crafting of collective sense of self within a larger and new (in this case supranational and United States) community. They selectively use the old to both make sense of a changed environment and circumstances as well as to create change in and for themselves.

While Somali women's efforts are not as blatantly about the acquisition of multiple national citizenships as is the case for Ong's Hong Kongers, as a whole, Somali refugee women's efforts to apprehend induction into new (quasi) national contexts is manifold and synonymous with what Ong (1999) refers to as *flexible citizenship*. In Ong's (2003) ethnographic depiction of Cambodian immigrant lives in the United States, she identifies citizenship work as "the interconnected everyday issues involved in shaping poor immigrants' ideas about what being American might mean" (p. xvii). Like McGown and Ashworth and Graham, Ong highlights newcomers' ideas and actions. Ong's conceptualization, however, imagines remembrance as one among many ways in which newcomers may be "active participants within institutional constraints and possibilities" (p. xvii). She conveys an improvisational performance out of which some form of belonging is the end goal.

Ong's broad based depiction mirrors our own findings. In both Dadaab and Milltown, schools physically bring together diverse community members with widely varied experiences, beliefs, and practices. It is through ensuing extemporized negotiation that Somali newcomers etch out ways of belonging in the Somali diasporic community as well as the larger national or quasi-national community they have entered. Through everyday flexible negotiation in and around school, Somali women intellectually break down the discursively constructed dyad or triad that characterize their ideological environs. They do so through a number of practices. First, they carve out particular ways of being Somali women that are unique to the context in which they find themselves. Second, they negotiate power relations at a number of levels (e.g., intrafamilial, intracommunal, and intercommunal) and in doing so draw upon their own agency within a landscape of structurally dominating forces. Finally, they craft new ways of belonging in two highly charged sociopolitical contexts.

Map of the Book

We present our study in two geographically bound sections. Part 1 features Kenya's Dadaab refugee camps and Part 2 is set in Milltown. In Chapter 2 we interrogate the concept of *traditionalism* within Somalia through a outline Somali political and educational history. In Chapter 3 we offer a portrait of Dadaab in which Western derived enlightenment ideology shapes the institutional organization of camp life. In Chapter 4 we explore refugees' various responses to the highly symbolic polarities of Somali traditionalism and Western enlightenment. Topics we discuss in Chapters 3 and 4 have parallel articulations in Milltown (see Chapter 9). In both Part 1 and 2, we focus on how Somali girls and women utilize schooling to negotiate the complex and particularized cultural ecologies of Dadaab and Milltown (Chapters 5 through 7 and 10 through 12). A middle "bridging" chapter between Parts 1 and 2 details the trajectory through which refugees from Dadaab come to live in Milltown. Finally, in Chapter 13 we review our findings and consider how Muslim refugee women's increasing access to schooling speaks to relations between the Islamic East and the West. We end with an afterword that describes the ways in which our own identities and the *politics of love* (Dominguez, 2000) have shaped our project and ongoing relations with the Somali diasporic community.

NOTES

1.   At the time of our study, CARE Kenya served as the UNHCR's primary implementing partner for services in Dadaab. Since completion of the manuscript, the UNCHR has transformed management structure in the camp, increasing the number of implementing partners contracted to work in Dadaab and dividing responsibilities once held exclusively by CARE among new and older stakeholders.

2.   Given a number of factors, Somali refugees face protracted stays in Dadaab. While thousands of Somalis have left Kenya to resettle in what now constitutes a worldwide Somali diaspora, most who remain in the camps have been there for over a decade. Repatriation is precluded by deteriorating conditions in Somalia. Kenyan refugee policy prohibits integration and resettlement options in countries of the global North are competitive and limited. Accordingly, development of a comprehensive school system in Dadaab has been of priority among camp residents and nongovernmental service providers.

3.   Enrollment in primary schools is 61% male to 39% female, while secondary schools are 84% male to 16% female. After class three, only one girl per six boys enrolls in school. Of the 40% of Somali children currently out of school, 70% are girls (UNHCR, 2005). In addition to gender-based discrepancy in participation levels, girls' performance on the Kenyan Certificate of Primary Education (KCPE) and Kenyan Certificate of Secondary Education (KCSE) examinations consistently lags behind that of their male counterparts.

  Prior to our study, CARE Kenya had already implemented a range of initiatives geared toward bolstering girls' enrollment and retention, including: the dispensation of incentives to families who enroll their daughters, provision of culturally appropriate uniforms with hijabs for girls, installation of separate restroom facilities on school grounds, distribution of sanitary supplies, as well as implementation of affirmative action policies to ensure equitable distribution of scholarships.

4.   Interview protocol was crafted specifically for each interviewee. Because aforementioned interviewees were primarily fluent English speakers, interviews were conducted in English with a Somali-speaking translator present

in case translation became necessary. The project translator was a young Somali woman who had completed schooling in Dadaab.

5.   The Dadaab school system follows the Kenyan curriculum as developed by the Kenyan Institute of Education and the Kenyan National Examinations Council. Heavily influenced by the British, education in Kenya follows the educational infrastructure and policies in place at the time of independence, which features an 8-4-4 system, with Standards One through Eight in Primary School and Forms One through Four in Secondary.

6.   Another implementing NGO in Dadaab, Windle Trust Kenya offers English language courses to adult students, supplements the CARE school system with resources such as solar lamps, and facilitates the distribution of WUSC scholarships. The latter places high-achieving Dadaab graduates in 4-year Canadian universities on scholarship and grants them Canadian permanent residency. WUSC scholarships are highly competitive.

7.   We conducted 4 week-long workshops on ethnographic research methods with the following groups: female Form Four students in Qafis Secondary School, advanced Windle Trust English students in Qafis and Mooro, as well as upper-intermediate Windle Trust students in Mooro. In total we had approximately 60 participants. Workshop content highlighted triangulation of research topics through the gathering of multiple perspectives and was participatory and student-centered.

    Workshops with Windle Trust advanced classes formed a component of the English course curriculum students were required to complete for graduation. Students in each of the two advanced classes chose either to craft their own research topic or to explore girls and women's participation in camp schooling. Individualized topics included: influence of the media in Dadaab refugee camps, violence against women, activities of CARE's Water and Environmental Sanitation Sector, perceptions of food distribution process, relations between Somalis and ethnic minorities, drug use in Qafis camp, refugee perspectives on life in Kenya, refugees and health, and the impact of restricted movement on refugees, among others, and provided extensive contextual and supporting data on life in the camps. The Form Four girls and upper-intermediate Windle Trust women's class focused research on girls and women's schooling, each choosing three interviewees from the following list of choices: secondary school girls, primary school girls, PTA members, teachers, parents (both of school-going girls and girls who had never enrolled in school), girls who had dropped out of school, girls who never attended schools, school-boys, camp chairwomen, CARE education sector staff, and minority students. Interviews by student field researchers were primarily conducted in Somali and translated by the students into English, although some occurred in English or other languages spoken in the camps by minority populations. While each of the Windle Trust groups completed the workshops and subsequent research as part of their class requirements, Qafis Form Four girls were individually paid a small monetary token for participation. Each girl's family supplemented stipends to purchase rechargeable lamps for study purposes.

8. The goal of Patricia Buck's consultancy was to build relationships between the Dadaab community, U.S. institutions of higher education, and the Somali diaspora (through NGOs/CBOs) in order to foster additional scholarship, livelihood, and cultural opportunities for the Dadaab refugee community, particularly females. The 2008 partnership between CARE Kenya and Patricia Buck focused on four objectives: establishing relationships between Dadaab and U.S. universities to replicate the highly-coveted WUSC program (e.g., committed 4-year scholarship placements for Dadaab students to higher-education institutions abroad); publication of scholarly work; creating links between the Somalia diaspora (NGOs/CBOs) and the Dadaab community; and the creation of a joint proposal between CARE, Patricia Buck, and other relevant organizations for 2009 funding that focuses on a cultural exchange project between Dadaab's Somali community and the Somali diaspora.

9. During the sessions, the storyteller sits beside the group facilitator with the remaining participants forming a circle around the pair. The facilitator asks very open-ended questions that invite the storyteller to share whatever stories, experiences and thoughts she wishes. With the exception of additional prompting questions from the facilitator, the storyteller speaks at length (20-40) minutes, while other participants merely listen. After the storyteller has completed her story, other participants are invited to offer non-judgmental feedback, such as relating stories of their own of which they have been reminded by the storyteller's narrative. Participants may share for an additional 20-30 minutes after which the storyteller is invited to flesh out aspects of her story she has since recalled. Finally, participants may ask questions and generally converse for the remainder of the time. The session format is designed to evoke diverse stories as well as a sense of community through the creation of a shared space in which all participants have an equal opportunity to speak, listen, and share. Sessions are also safe spaces in that participants are free to tell their stories in as much depth and detail as they wish. All participants were compensated per session in which they participated. Each session in Dadaab was translated between English and Somali, audio taped, transcribed.

10. The group, co-facilitated with Ilana Adler-Bell, included female Form Four leavers with whom Patti and Rachel had worked as students in 2007. Together, we read and discussed Victoria Lee Barnes and Janice Boddy's (2003) *Aman: The Story of a Somali Girl* for the ways in which it related to and differed from students' life experiences.

11. Ballot questions in San Francisco, California and Portland, Maine that would have given legal immigrants the right to vote in local elections were defeated in 2010.

12. Though not identical in name or content, our organization of the sub-groups borrows heavily from Anderson-Levitt's (2003, p. 19).

13. We maintain a critical perspective on the terms Somali *traditionalism* and *enlightenment*, which we elaborate throughout the text. We reveal the contested nature of Somali traditionalism in Chapter 2, the meanings con-

strued by the term *enlightenment* in Chapter 3, and finally, our context-specific uses of liberalism and nativism in Chapter 9.

14.   In what follows we use text from these transcriptions exactly as they were uttered by the storyteller (in the case of the English speaking participants) or as they were orally translated into English. We have elected to make minor syntactic corrections for the readers' ease. However, we remain as close to the participants' authentic voices as possible. Given that the participant translators' English proficiency levels vary, in some cases this makes the text difficult to interpret.

15.   Pseudonyms are used throughout this study to protect participant anonymity.

16.   The practice is called infibulation in which the labia minora and the clitoris are excised and the outer labia are sewn together leaving a small passageway for urine and blood to escape.

CHAPTER 2

SOMALIA

Tracing a Contested Traditionalism

We employ the terms "traditional Somali culture," "traditionalism," and "traditionalists" throughout our examination of Somali women's schooling. In doing so, we draw upon a vocabulary widely used in both Dadaab and Milltown. In context, these terms are used to describe either a particularly conservative segment or aspect of the Somali population or to characterize Somali people and culture as generally conservative in nature. Each conjures a rootedness in the history of the Somali land and people and a determination to reproduce long-standing ways of being, thinking, and acting that stand in opposition to those introduced from the West. For our purposes, the danger of utilizing the terminology lies in conveying an essentialized understanding of Somali people and culture. Since we seek a very opposite end, we take pains to situate these terms within the particular time(s) and place out of which they have grown and evolved.

In 1991 Somalia's ruling regime suffered a crippling coup. In the years since, Somalia has gained worldwide repute as one of the most anarchic and violent lands in Africa. In popular media, the collapse of the Somali state is most commonly attributed to clan-based rivalry. While Somali society is indeed clan-based, the political instability of the state needs to be made conceptually distinct from the social organization of Somali people along genealogical lines. Given that kin-based Somali society sustained a general peace for centuries preceding colonial rule (Besteman,

Educated for Change?: Muslim Refugee Women in the West, pp. 35–62
Copyright © 2011 by Information Age Publishing
All rights of reproduction in any form reserved.

1999; Mazrui, 1997; A. Samatar, 1992), the insecurity that now character-izes the Somali nation is more fairly attributed to various domestic and foreign interests' exploitative use of clan.

In addition to clan, as in every society, Somalis utilize gender as a main principle of social and cultural organization. Similar to the narrative of clan rivalry, Western media largely construes gender salient tenets and practices as negative reflections on the traditions of Somali people. These portrayals emphasize the oppression of women as a function of funda-mentalist Islam (Badran, 2007). Mirroring the reductionism of clan-based explanations for civil disintegration of the Somali state, characterizations of gender inequality in Somali society by Western media presents an overly simplistic, homogenous socioculture gender order that does not account for difference in region, class, or clan and unduly dismisses the impact of foreign intervention and capitalist hegemony.

The notion that Somalia's civil war and the oppression of Somali women are both solely attributable to traditional cultural tenets and practices rests upon a myopic vision of Somali, and by extension, African history. Within Somalia, what constitutes tradition is neither primordial nor static, despite widespread representation to the contrary (see Burton, 1966; Hanley, 1971; Lewis, 1992, 1988, 1965, 1962). Global geopolitics of the colonial, Cold War, and post-Cold War eras further underlie widespread political instabil-ity, civil strife and human migration across the African continent. Somalia, which hugs the easternmost horn of Africa along the coasts of the Red Sea and Indian Ocean, is dishearteningly emblematic of the destructive influ-ence of these global struggles for power and self-enrichment. Beginning in the colonial era and carrying through the collapse of Somalia's indepen-dent government and into the Cold War, foreign interests have attempted to manipulate clan, geography and gender—often in the name of tradi-tion—in efforts to control Somali citizens. They have used schooling as a means through which to do so.

Somali traditionalism, as a discursive construct that bears material con-sequences, is neither exceptional nor essential, but rather shifts and changes over time in relation to several primary forces—customary law, or *xeer* (*heer*); kinship[1]; Islam; and the state. Colonialism, the expansion of global capitalism, and neocolonialism shape the definition and manipula-tion of tradition and related enactments of gender.

In conceptualizing traditionalism as contested, we situate ourselves with other contemporary scholars of the region (Besteman, 1996, 1998, 1999; Kapteijns, 1994, 1995; Rawson, 1994; A. Samatar, 1992, 1994; A. I. Samatar, 1994a, 1994b) who push back against the primordialist framing of Somalia as embroiled in tribal violence and Somali culture as particularly conducive to self-destruction. Instead, we argue that culture, like tradition, is dynamic and shaped in part by struggles over representation and governance. As Besteman (1999) notes:

> Culture affects and is affected by political struggles over signifying, representing, and providing meaning for identities. Groups of people incessantly shape and reshape their cultures and identities in dialogue with the state, the nation, and nation-state hegemonies. Historical memories, historical consciousnesses, and historical knowledges saturate these mutually constituting processes. (p. 11)

Given the salience of history in contestations of culture and tradition, we begin our examination with a brief look at social organization in precolonial Somali society before moving chronologically through state collapse. While we end our tracing of Somalia's sociopolitical history with massive refugee emigration from the country in the early 1990s, we acknowledge that the story of Somalia continues to be daily written. The unfolding of Somalia's contemporary tragedy remains relevant for the Somali refugees in our study through both the permeable Somalia/Kenya border across which bodies, ideas, and goods continue to flow as well as in the possibility of future repatriation.

Finally, we argue that education is a primary avenue through which different actors have tried to shape extant conceptualizations of Somali traditionalism. Given that the main project of the chapter is to show the contested and dynamic nature of traditionalism, for the sake of brevity, we do not provide a complete history of education in Somalia (for this, see Cassanelli & Abdikadir, 2007). Rather, we explore the ways in which a range of actors use the schooling apparatus as a tool in the reshaping of traditionalism across time.

Precolonial Somali Society

Despite assumptions of Somali homogeneity, precolonial Somali tradition was not monolithic, but varied regionally and according to primary modes of production. Nonetheless, each segment of society—the pastoral North and East coastal city-states and the riverine south, was stateless, shaped instead by the dynamic relationship between kinship/customary law and Islam.

The communitarian pastoralist mode of production defined life in Somalia's North and East (A. Samatar, 1992, 1994b) and appears most frequently in anthropological representations of the country (Cassanelli, 1982; Lewis, 1962, 1988). Lacking a central state structure, decisions were made by majority (male) rule (Afrax, 1994), and vast genealogical, or kinship, networks formed the base for the "meta-organization" (A. Samatar, 1994) of precolonial, pastoral life. According to Kapteijns (1994):

> Pastoral society forged a communal identity phrased in terms of kinship, an ideology that assigned each Somali to a certain patrilineal descent group (lineage, sublineage, major section, minor section, *jilib*, *reer*), to a specific age group, and to the male or female gender. (p. 214)

Kinship encompassed not only ties by blood (*tol*), but also ties by marriage (*hidid*) (A. Samatar, 1994).[2]

Two primary moralizing forces shaped life in precolonial, pastoralist Somalia: obligations to kin as prescribed by customary law (*heer*) and Islamic teachings contained in the Qu'ran and Hadith (Kapteijns, 1994, 1995; A. Samatar 1994; A. I. Samatar, 1994a, 1994b). Knowledge of both was transferred orally through informal modes of education. According to A. I. Samatar (1994, 1994b), the laws of kinship and Islam each provided a framework for regulating communal life and allowed members of society to resist feuds based solely on blood ties. He writes:

> Together, heer and Islam, in particular, gave the stateless Somalis a rightful political center of gravity capable of controlling capriciousness, managing intersubjectivity, and offering order and continuity. In short, Somalis of precolonial times might not have seen themselves as a nation, in the now familiar sense that nations are invariably associated with the state. However, they did have a moral commonwealth (or *umma*), despite the incessant feuding, constant competition over very limited resources, and gender inequalities. (p. 109)

Cassanelli (1982) describes how Islamic leaders in particular played a central role in fostering intragroup unity—what A. I. Samatar (1994b) terms *umma* (see Besteman, 1999 also). By making explicit the link between Islam and Somali genealogical structures, sheikhs united Somalis to a common history, just as they signified the religious import of Somali kinship networks (Besteman, 1999; Cassanelli, 1982). Specifically, Somali clans represent branches on a vast genealogical tree that links all Somalis to two common forefathers, the mythical *Hiil* and the prophet Muhammed (Mansur, 1995b).

The sanctification of kinship through religion, coupled with acknowledgment of shared origin and history among Somalis, resulted in the virtual fusion of religious and cultural identities (Cassanelli, 1982). Muslim ulema and sheikhs were, and continue to be, heralded as cultural guardians and intellectuals (Afrax, 1994). As Cassanelli notes, "If today one can almost automatically say that to be a Somali is to be a Muslim, historically it can be said that to accept Islam was to accept membership in a larger Somali nation" (Cassanelli, as cited in Besteman, 1999, p. 169). Thus, since precolonial times, Islam and the customary relations of kinship have together formed the basis for identification as a Somali (as opposed to a member of one particular kinship group).

Still, *heer* and Islam interact in distinct ways in particular historical moments to determine appropriate ways of enacting the Somali religio-cultural identity. In precolonial, pastoral Somalia, kinship and its related customary law played the primary role in governing social interaction. According to Kapteijns (1994):

> Members of Somali pastoral society were Muslims, and Islam constituted an integral part of their communal identity and unwritten constitution. How-ever, in relations with other Somalis, communal identity was primarily for-mulated in terms of kinship; although customary law was generally in accordance with Islamic law, it imposed many rules nonexistent in Islam and disregarded or sidestepped some specific Islamic legal provisions, such as those governing women's inheritances. (p. 216)

In the instance of inheritance, *heer* deactivated Islamic law, or sharia, (Kapteijns, 1995) which includes women as potential inheritors of land and property. Rather, kinship networks in precolonial, pastoral Somalia situated men exclusively as household heads and independent social units and, as such, were patriarchal by their very nature.

The implications of a patrilineal, patriarchal societal structure on women were profound and manifested in women's: ambiguous member-ship in and divided loyalties between birth and marital clan; inability to create independent households; and restriction from positions of power and authority in politics or religion (Kapteijns, 1994, p. 217). Given such, women could not participate in the definition or discursive interpretation of *heer* (or Islam), even as they remained subject to its rules and guaran-teed its protections (Kapteijns, 1995).

While disenfranchised, women remained highly valuable to pastoralist society for several reasons. To begin with, their productive and reproductive contributions to the highly labor-intense pastoralist lifestyle were necessary and recognized as such (Kapteijns, 1994, 1995). Second, in the exogamous marital structure characteristic of precolonial life, women embodied what were otherwise more intangible intraclan ties. Kapteijns (1994) writes:

> Because exogamy, from the perspective of the group, was to promote the likelihood of peaceful conflict resolution and economic resource sharing among groups competing for scarce resources, each married woman became a significant bearer of social capital in that she represented to both communities the rights and duties of reciprocal sharing. (p. 217)

Despite the economic and symbolic significance of women, however, pre-colonial, pastoralist life enacted a patriarchal gender order—even when Islam offered different possibilities, such as through gender-neutral inheritance laws. For Barlas (2002), the Qu'ran is polysemic and, as such, can as easily be read as a source of liberation for women as one of repression enacted in precolonial, pastoral Somali society.[1] The precolonial traditions from other regions of today's Somalia, however, constituted the balance between Islam and custom to different gendered effect.

In Somalia's coastal city-states, capitalist modes of production also contributed to the configuring of traditionalism and gender codes. While capitalism did not gain complete hegemony until after colonialism, a shift toward the market exchange paradigm emerged in towns in the years preceding imperial rule and impacted social relations accordingly. Town residents performed a newly constituted urban identity was less bound to the kinship structures that so defined rural life (Kapteijns, 1994):

> In contrast to the herders of the interior ... the largely coastal city-states forged a communal identity in which membership in a certain descent or ethnic group played a secondary role. Instead, the inhabitants of the city-state emphasized their civic identity, their citizenship in their town, with all that implied with regard to their way of life, behavior, dress, cuisine, religious observance, and so forth. (p. 218)

Likewise, adherence to Islam took a more prominent role in structuring town life, where its interpretation was said to be more textually accurate (Kapteijns, 1994). Urban areas such as Zeila, Mogadishu, and Brava became centers of formalized Islamic study (Cassenelli & Abdikadir, 2007). That a stricter interpretation of Islam was conducive to the increasingly exchange-based social relations in towns is not coincidental. Rather, Kapteijns (1994) explains that:

> by embracing Islamic law rather than the heer, a member of the urban middle class could avoid sharing his wealth with, or bequeathing it to, his distant male relatives and could instead privilege his nuclear family (both sons and daughters, men and women). (p. 219)

In town life, the accumulation of capital and shift to exchange-based social relations resulted in the increasing emergence of class, rather than clan, as the prominent marker of difference, just at it restructured the possibilities for gender relations.

Kapteijns (1994, 1995) describes how two distinct ways of being women emerged in precolonial city-states, determined primarily by class rather than clan affiliation. Middle and upper class women began the process of "housewifization" (p. 219) typical to bourgeois development the world over,

enacted in the simultaneous seclusion and increased emphasis on the beau-
tification of women. Preoccupied with self-care, household maintenance,
and small crafts, women of the upper and middle classes occupied a social
niche distinct from both their rural and working class, urban counterparts.
Women in the lower echelons of urban society worked for cash or exchange,
and as such, were less dependent on men than rural women of the time.
Though more autonomous in some senses, they faced marginal occupations
and life at the bottom rungs of urban society.

While the same structuring forces—Islam and customary law—defined
social organization in both urban and pastoralist, precolonial Somalia,
they were enacted to different effect. While this difference likely stemmed
from the distinct requirements of pastoralism versus market exchange
modes of production (as well as in response to different social threats), it
bore profound implications on gender.

Finally, before we shift to the impact of colonialism on traditionalism
(and Islam) in Somalia, the distinct social and economic realities of Somalia's riverine South bear attention. To this end, Besteman's (1999) ethnographic study of the Gosha people of Somalia's agricultural Jubba valley
is most helpful. The Gosha, or Somali Bantu, descended from slave populations brought to Somalia from across East Africa to work on plantations
farming cash crops for export. Despite their distinct historical experience
of race and class-based marginalization, which Besteman analyzes in
Unraveling Somalia, people of the Gosha likewise emphasized kinship and
Islam in their processes of identity formation and negotiations of belonging (Besteman, 1999). As such, Besteman credits Islamic sheikhs and local
leaders with the joining of ex-slaves and their descendants with mainstream precolonial Somali social organization. Besteman's analysis
emphasizes the heterogeneity—despite assumptions to the contrary—of
Somali society, and underscores the unifying forces of kinship and Islam
in social organization and identification for distinct subgroups. Besteman
does not, however, provide a gendered account of identity formation
among the Gosha, a task which falls beyond the scope of our work, but
would offer a valuable contribution to understanding the complexity of
precolonial Somali life.

Shifting Precolonial Traditions

Acknowledging that cash crop production and market exchange characterized precolonial economic life in Somalia's agricultural south and
city-states, respectively, pastoralism was, and remains, the country's primary mode of production. According to A. Samatar (1992, 1994), however, pastoralism is not a monolith. Different social and economic

formations underlie pastoralist practices and, given the simultaneous expansion of colonialism and rise of international trade that characterized Somalia in the nineteenth century, the paradigm of communitarian pastoralism lost much of its hegemony (A. Samatar, 1994).

The shift toward exchange pastoralism took root in Somalia before European colonial expansion, as we saw in Kapteijn's analysis of life in coastal city-states. With colonialism, however, these shifts became entrenched, as did the more novel centralized state structure (Kapteijns, 1994; A. Samatar, 1994). In the years immediately preceding and then during European settlement in Somalia, increasingly influential capitalist structures and policies resulted in the commodification of livestock; burgeoning of an urban middle class whose wealth derived from international trade; and the deepening of a class structure formerly absent in the hinterlands or less prominent in towns (Besteman, 1999; Kapteijns, 1994, 1995; A. Samatar, 1994). During the transitional period, structures of racial discrimination were intensified, with race joining class as a salient marker of difference. Besteman (1999) argues that the shift impacted Somali Bantus, whose rich agricultural lands in the Jubba valley were sought after and eventually co-opted by settler populations (p. 7). Shifting economic realities, in turn, impacted social and gender relations. According to Swift (as cited in A. Samatar, 1994, p. 70), traditional Somali social relations were unraveled by the commercialization of pastoral life.

For A. I. Samatar and others (see Afrax, 1994; A. Samatar, 1994), it was the reconfiguring of social relations—the supposed unraveling of precolonial tradition—that set up Somalia for its contemporary failure. Nonetheless, while losing dominance, precolonial tradition has been continually called upon, reinvented, and manipulated across time and in ways to suit particular social actors.

Educational discourse prior to the official partition of Somalia already blended an Islamic worldview with exposure to Western ideologies spread through trade relations. While formal Islamic education—in the form of rural *duksis* and urban centers of learning—fueled a religious revival that placed great prestige on Arabic literacy, so-called Western modes of thought, too, began to impact meaning making. According to Cassenelli and Abdikadir (2007), "On the eve of European colonization, new forms of Islamic and Western knowledge were diffusing throughout Somalia, *providing a set of competitive discourses about the modern world that would shape Somali public opinion for years to come*" (p. 92, emphasis ours).

The Colonial Period

By 1885, the territory that would later become known as Somalia was divided under British, French, and Italian colonial rule into five regions referred to as "Somalilands." The north was controlled by Great Britain; the east and southeast, which now make up Djibouti, by France; and the south by Italy. Colonial boundaries, which later translated into national borders as African countries gained independence and formed nation-states, were designed by and for Europeans without reference to preexisting ethnic or clan-based communities. Indeed, 3 million ethnic Somalis presently live outside of the borders of the Somali state in northern Kenya and the Ogaden region of Ethiopia (Hussein, 1997). During the colonial era, such externally imposed boundaries seldom remained static, but rather shifted in reflection of power struggles between European nation states. As an example, Italy ejected the British from Somalia early in the Second World War. The British retook their original area of occupation in 1941, adding all of formerly Italian Somalia to their territory. Eventually, however, Italy regained its sovereignty of southern Somalia in 1949 (Fitzgerald, 2002).

In their project of political and economic domination, colonial actors in Somalia, like their counterparts across the African continent, manipulated what they perceived as tradition towards their own ends. Under the British-designed system of indirect rule, colonialists began to take a stake in what traditionalism represented and how it was enacted. By using local leaders (designated or introduced by colonialists) to enforce customary law (as codified by the colonialists), indirect rule allowed the British (and later, other European colonizers as well) to: divide its subjects; develop a tier of native intermediaries to staff the lower levels of colonial bureaucracy; and elevate a group of selected chiefs or clan leaders whose own accumulation came with loyalty to the colonialists. Indirect rule further provided a means through which colonists could completely restructure economic and social relations under the guise of cultural continuity (see Young, 1994 and Mamdani, 1996 for more complete analysis of indirect rule). Most of the restructuring, though tailored to benefit indigenous—rather than colonial—elite, endured after Somali independence and continue to define contemporary life in the country.[1]

In the colonial period, therefore, for the first time the state became a major player in the invention and interpretation of tradition. By designating itself a moralizing force, the colonial state both used and wrote into policy the terms of kinship and, to lesser extent, Islam, even as the two remained the primary "constituents of the Somali superego" (A. I. Samatar, 1994b, p. 111). The more things appeared to stay the same, the more they changed.

Through Western eyes in Somalia, perhaps the most infamous reinvented trope of traditionalism is that of *clan*. As we have seen, in popular imagination both about and within Somalia, clan is discussed as a primordial identity marker and catalyst of the country's unraveling. However, as many scholars argue, this is far from the case; rather, clan best represents a contemporary "perversion" (A. I. Samatar, 1994a, 1994b) of the precolonial concept of kinship under the combined influences of colonialism, patriarchy, and capitalism (Afrax, 1994; Besteman, 1999; Kapteijns, 1994; A. Samatar, 1992, 1994a, 1994b; A. I. Samatar, 1994). According to A. I. Samatar:

> [Clannism] is the perversion of kinship through a decoupling of blood ties (particularly male lineage) from the great civilizing or universalizing factors of Somali culture: customary laws and Islamic precepts ... there is enough agreement to establish that the phenomenon is not only quite different from the kinship of old (as demonstrated by, among other things, the evaporation of authority of elders and veneration of *sheikhs*) but, in fact, is a manifestation of other things that have gone awfully wrong in Somalia. (1994a, p. 9)

For Kapteijns (1995), the major distinction between kinship and clannism is that while the former centers around the concept of reciprocity, the latter relies on "debt and dependence in a context of class inequality" (p. 258). While the former is inclusive and flexible, the latter, she contends, is parasitic. The clan-related divisions that haunt Somalia today, therefore, are not innate but socially constructed and brought to bear by particular contemporary factors and relations.

How did clannism, a social system likewise defined by descent, emerge from the kinship structure that for so long allowed Somalis to prosper peacefully in an otherwise hostile environment? Here we turn to analysis of colonial state policies and their deliberate manipulation of tradition. During the colonial period, the primary unit of social organization—the clan or kin group—continued to structure economic and political relations; however, clan groups began to control access to more than pastoral resources of land, water, and cattle. According to Kapteijns (1994, p. 220), the state sector and urban economy increased its wealth and power base under colonialism, spreading to once autonomous pastoral communities. Clan and clan leaders began to regulate access to these new forms of wealth and to the state itself, expanding the clan's traditional mandate exponentially.

In other words, the traditional unit of clan began to work in nontraditional ways: same concept, new meaning. Kapteijns (1994) describes the transition in the clan's role under colonialism in a quotation worth citing in its entirety:

> The old clan had been a community of producers whose economic means and social relations had been regulated in its name. The new clan, reimagined and reconstructed in the context of colonial rule, came to assert legal and political authority over individuals whose productive activities, wealth,

power, and prestige depended largely on a world outside the physical domain and control of the clan. The colonial state, in collaboration with new clan leaders, tried to mask the loss of autonomy of the clan by extending its legal and political authority to individuals who were members of the clan in only a very limited sense—for example, as the result of the accident of birth alone. The communal mode of production was dead, but the community was artificially kept alive and, through political negotiations and compromise between the new leaders and the colonial state, reimagined and reinforced. (p. 222)

Not only did the colonial state expand clan authority in novel ways, which were harmful to most of its members, it differently interpreted and enforced tradition in different places, splintering the national populace. In rural areas, customary law as codified by colonists and enforced by designated leaders held primary jurisdiction. As noted, these appointed "traditional" authorities often derived legitimacy not from the clans in which they came, but from their relationship with the state and concomitant access to state resources (Kapteijns, 1994).

In cities, however, European criminal law was enforced alongside the rule of Islamic courts. Somali merchants used sharia and criminal law to further entrench class divisions. Kapteijns (1995, p. 253) describes how lawsuits were increasingly filed against the debtors of urban merchants during this period. Further, she notes that by continuing to follow the inheritance laws of Islam rather than *heer*, urban merchants could guard wealth in their nuclear family rather than redistribute it among wider networks of kin. The dual standards set up to regulate Somalia's political and economic life resulted in an environment where behaviors acceptable in one place—and therefore among certain clan members—became unacceptable in another. Colonial legal policy at once enabled urban dwellers to develop identities based more prominently on class and Islam than clan (Kapteijns, 1994, p. 222), and reified blood-based social divisions in the pastoral regions.

With regard to encouraging urban, bourgeois development among certain Somali subjects, colonial policy went further than to simply manipulate clan and its relevance to distinct areas of Somali life. Kapteijns (1995) indicates how young men, now able to acquire wealth outside their kin networks, began to orchestrate independent marital arrangements that eschewed traditional requirements and obligations to clan. For example, in 1928 the government of British Somaliland enacted a new policy to "set limits to the free market competition for brides" (p. 256). The Native's Betrothal and Marriage Ordinance required youth to follow traditional marriage laws unless a woman came to the state to declare her traditional arrangement void. In that way, the colonial state created "a legal loophole that allowed individuals (women and men manipulating women) to bypass customary law (*xeer*) [and] … cautiously supported the urban trend towards bourgeois marriage of individuals" (p. 256).

While on the surface such a provision would seem to increase women's autonomy in relation to customary law and traditional male authorities, colonial governance, in fact, produced quite the opposite effect. According to Kapteijns (1994):

> The major political objective of the colonial administration … was the maintenance of law and order and the containment of social change in the interior. In general, therefore, its policies tended to reinforce kin group and male discipline over women. For rural women, whose goat and sheep husbandry was so crucial to the solvency (never quite attained) of the protectorate's administration, this meant that although the value of their labor to the state increased, their deepened dependence on men, who monopolized all major exchange activities, was taken for granted and reinforced by the state. (p. 224)

Thus Kapteijns (1994, 1995), who traces gender and social organization through the distinct periods of Somali history, argues that while precolonial Somali society was patriarchal, it acknowledged and valued the labor of women. Colonial and postcolonial society, on the other hand, entrenched patriarchy to a greater degree. Gordon (2001, p. 277) agrees, arguing that European imperialism both undermined existent sources for women's autonomy and augmented the authority of indigenous males.

Patriarchy was strengthened under colonialism when the introduction of private ownership over land and livestock in both agricultural and pastoralist societies further distanced women from money, authority, and decision-making power as men became sole deed and property owners. According to Gordon (2001):

> This now meant that men, not women could make decisions and profit from the sale or acquisition of family property. Women themselves became another form of property to be controlled as they lost effective control over their own labor. They had to work for their husbands in order to survive because they had no rights over wealth-producing property of their own. (p. 277)

As a result, women, who in precolonial times held strategic economic power, lost access to capital and command of their labor amidst shifts to an economic structure in which one's security increasingly relied upon the ability to acquire cash. Further, while colonial schools trained men to fill the lower bureaucratic ranks of the state, women were largely excluded from colonial schooling, enabling an urban middle class to develop around entirely male occupations. In a tactical move that would serve as a lesson for those who would later attempt to hold sway in Somalia, colonists used the provision of schooling to exploit markers of clan, geographical, and gender difference within the Somali society.

Among the Somali populace, schooling in colonial Somalia was far from uncontroversial. Just as in the years immediately prior to Somalia's partition, discursive competition continued to exist between Islamic teachings and Westernized models of education. Cassanelli and Abdikadir (2007), who emphasize distinction between the two models of thought, note that colonialists and Islamists vied for the "hearts and minds" of the Somali populace (p. 93). Significant resistance existed to what was seen as colonial school's efforts to prosthelytize, just as debates raged over the most appropriate linguistic medium for instruction in schools (Olden, 2008). Sayyid Muhammad's 20-year struggle (the longest such campaign in British colonial history) against the 1891 opening of a French Catholic missionary-run school in Berbera demonstrates the intensity of resistance to Western-style schooling. Given that missionaries dominated colonial schooling across the continent until after the First World War and that Somalis rejected mission-run schools to the extent that the colonial government banned them, Somalis' levels of formal education in British Somaliland lagged significantly behind those of other their counterparts in other British-run African colonies (Olden, 2008). Even after colonial authorities themselves assumed primary control over schooling, government-run education remained associated with the missionary model that preceded it, just as battles continued over whether the primary media of instruction should be Somali and English, as colonists preferred, or Arabic and English, as demanded by the Somali populace (Olden, 2008). Eventually, according to Cassanelli and Abdikadir (2007), colonial authorities began to incorporate Islamic religious leaders into their schools as teaching staff for recruitment purposes as well as the Arabic language (Olden, 2008)—tactics that proved more successful.[5]

Even with a more balanced approach toward the introduction of both Islamic and Western ideologies, however, schools remained heavily attended by elite, urban males. The first school for girls in Northern Somalia opened in 1947 with six pupils (Olden, 2008). In Southern Somalia, girls' schooling began in earnest in 1949, but was likewise sparsely attended (Cassanelli & Abdikadir, 2007). According to Dawson (as cited in Cassanelli & Abdikadir, 2007), "When independence came in 1960, there were 38 elementary schools for boys (enrollment 2,020), three for girls (319), twelve intermediate schools for boys (1,039), and two secondary schools for boys (70)" (p. 94).

Colonial officials likewise denied women political authority, only recognizing male leaders as intermediaries between colonial state officials and African populations. Thus, women were at once excluded from economic and political structures under colonialism and denied an alternative means through which to support themselves, increasing their reliance on men.

In the particular context of Somalia, the shift from communitarian pastoralist to capitalist modes of production devalued women in two significant ways (Kapteijns, 1995). First, as noted above, their labor was no longer considered central to the economic welfare of clans. Second, the priority newly placed on individual accumulation of wealth meant that communities began to intermarry more, in order to consolidate wealth in smaller groups (p. 255). This resulted in a shift away from exogamy, which, as noted above, gave women a symbolically significant role as intracommunal peacemakers.

Finally, the colonial state—in the name of their protection—began to at once sexualize and regulate women who were able to carve out niches for economic independence. Fearing a rise in prostitution, the colonial (and postcolonial) state sought control over the lives of financially autonomous urban women, a trend that emerges clearly in the first person accounts of Somali women including Aman (see Barnes & Boddy, 1994) and corresponded with the dictates of *sharia* as implemented in urban areas.

Thus, in a number of gender-salient ways the colonial state worked to enact new ways of being Somali while calling upon tradition and continuity as a guide. By manipulating the role and significance of clan in particular, the state laid the groundwork for the contemporary manifestations of elitism and a divide-and-rule policy. As the colonial structure began to unravel under the pressures of rising African and Somali nationalism, resultant manipulations of tradition did not. Rather, they continued to be molded by postcolonial elites toward their own ends. For its part, Islam and its legal doctrines continued to disproportionately impact urban, rather than rural, life in Somalia.

Independence, Nationalism, and the Postcolonial Period

After World War II nationalistic waves spread across the African continent, leaving European colonial states with the practical problem of how to best manage the increasingly inevitable shift to independence. Rather than withdraw completely, the continent's major occupiers, and in particular Britain and France, worked to conceptualize new arrangements in which their vested interests in colonial territories would remain protected to the greatest extent possible. The shift toward a protectorate model, in which European metropoles ostensibly worked with fledgling nations to build the necessary infrastructure for democratic governance and educate future citizens, became one pragmatic approach, popular (among Europeans) in part for the ways in which it enabled former colonists to plant the seeds for economic dependence and later neocolonial intervention.

In the case of Somalia, the transition toward independence, like colonialism itself, was bifurcated. In 1949, the UN General Assembly granted Italy (who, as noted before, had been ousted during the war by the British) permission to return to Southern Somalia and oversee a decade long trusteeship that would, by statute, end with the creation of an independent Republic of Somalia in 1960 (Tripodi, 1999). An advisory council comprised of three representatives (one from Egypt, the Phillipines, and Columbia, respectively) established itself alongside the Italians as the British military presence began to wane in the South. Tasked by the UN with preparing Somalia for independence through the development of institutions of governance, a vital economy, and a growing education system, Italy began a decade of transition with goals that mirrored those of the British in Northern Somalia.

Tripodi (1999) provides a thorough analysis of the decade of Italian Trusteeship on Somali soil, a period during which Italian intellectuals and bureaucrats had enormous influence in shaping Somalia's future economic, political, and educational policies, and, concomitantly, Somalia's manifestations of tradition. Somali intellectuals from various clan backgrounds were first educated in Italian-run schools in Somalia, later to be sent to Italy itself to attend institutions of higher learning. All of this, of course, was intended to help Somalia model itself after Italy while creating a sense of partnership with and indebtedness to their former colonial occupiers. Italy's role in demonstrating stability for Somalia is perhaps ironic given that, at the time, Italy was itself reeling from the end of a fascist regime and faced an economy too weak to lend the kind of aid other former colonists, including the British, were able to provide at the time.

While ostensibly moving toward autonomy, the trusteeship of Somalia, and later the new nation, faced considerable challenges following nearly 100 years of colonial rule. Like most postcolonial nations, Somalia's nascent economic infrastructure depended upon the self-interested largess of its former metropoles (Fitzgerald, 2002; Hussein, 1997). In addition to economic dependence, Somalis inherited social divisions that had become deliberately pronounced under colonial rule. The unified Somali nation was composed of clan groups from the culturally distinct regions of northern and southern Somalia, each of which had been differently positioned within the constructed social hierarchies created to serve colonial interests (Fitzgerald, 2002; Hussein, 1997). Further, Somalia appropriated a state-structured government modeled after those institutionalized in Europe and other Western nations that excluded women from participation in formal governance. Finally, according to Mansur (1995a, p. 107), the very notion of statehood did not resonate with the largely nomadic and clan-identified Somali people who "traditionally lack the state as a hierarchical power," despite a common language, religion, and culture. Over the decade-long effort to prepare Somalis for full independence, disparate groups were asked to forgo clan identity in favor of a Pan-Somali allegiance to nation.

In 1951, eight national political parties existed in Somalia, in addition to several regional ones (Tripodi, 1999). Prominent parties included the Somali Youth League (SYL), the Hisbia Digil-Mirifle (HDM), the Somali Progressive League, and the Somali African Union, each of which took different stances on the merits of Italian leadership as well as the prominence that clan should play in national politics. Of these parties, according to Tripodi, the Somali Youth League represented the "strongest declared pan-Somali movement," with a composition that was 50% Darod, 30% Hawiye, and 10% Digil Mirifle.

Italian leaders worked to transpose an electoral system on Somalia's geography and clan, testing the efficacy of Pan-Somali identification in 1954—the same year that the flag of the Republic of Somalia was first raised. The SYL, which fared well, maintained a platform suspicious of Italy, a fact that Italians on the ground counteracted with simultaneous efforts to work more closely with the SYL (in part, by sending its leaders to study in Italy), as well as to support consolidation of an anti-SYL coalition (Tripodi, 1999).

When independence finally arrived in 1960,[6] Somalia merged the regions formerly ruled by Britain and Italy into one nation-state.[7] In quick order, however, authority vested in the new democratic Somali state re-inscribed the existence of various distinct genealogical groups as clan associates further appropriated the political party structure. The Somali Youth League (SYL) continued to draw its strongest support from the Darod clan; the Somaliland National League (SNL) represented the Issaq clan; and the Greater Somali League (GSL) was comprised of members of the Dir and Hawiye clans (Lewis, 2002). Democratically elected administrations changed in quick succession in the years immediately after independence. However, postindependence elections were largely dominated by the SYL, resulting in the 1967 election of SYL member Abdirashiid Ali Shermaarke as president and the nomination of SYL Muhammad Abraham Igaal as prime minister. When Abdirashiid Ali Shermaarke was assassinated in 1969 by one of his guards, army commander Siad Barre, also of the Darod clan, assumed power.

While early postcolonial administrations took varied approaches to governance in Somalia, an overarching pattern emerged in which national leaders continued to manipulate clan, as an invented—or reshaped—tradition, to their own ends. Institutions of governance were harnessed to entrench elite privilege in the hands of few at the same time that national unity was espoused and propagated, as we shall see, through policy. Most contemporary scholars of Somalia attribute its eventual state collapse largely to the greed of elite state actors, and in particular, Siad Barre (see Afrax, 1994; Besteman, 1999; A. Samatar, 1994; A. I. Samatar, 1994a, 1994b).

Barre began what would become a 20-year stint at the helm of Somalia by immediately replacing the democratic governance structure with what he described as a system of scientific socialism backed by Soviet financing. Somewhat ironically, Barre's autocratic regime perhaps held the most potential to transcend the clan loyalties that had rapidly superimposed themselves upon the democratic governance structure. Initially, Barre's policies were in fact aimed at transcending clan. He dissolved the National Assembly, suspended the constitution, prohibited political assemblage, stripped traditional Somali leaders of authority, and dismantled clan-based water and grazing rights (Hussein, 1997). As we shall see below, Barre also used the provision of schooling to promote clan unification and Somali nationalist sentiments.[9] Through policy and a rhetoric of national unity, Barre claimed to espouse a pan-Somali identity, or *soomaalinimo*, a form of oneness which some (Rawson, 1994; A. I. Samatar, 1994b) regard as a natural extension of *umma*, the traditional Islamic conception of unity among Somali pastoralists.

In this way, Barre's state, like those of his postcolonial predecessors, embedded elements of Somali "tradition." According to Rawson (1994), "Underlying the structure of this postcolonial state were the foundational myths of Somali politics. What gave dynamism to that structure was the energetic quest of Somali elites for national unity and group identity" (p. 151). Among the populace, notions of pan-Somaliness that had already gained currency during the liberation movements in the 1940s-1960s climaxed during Barre's early years in power (Kapteijns, 1994).

Thus, like colonial rulers before him, Barre and the Supreme Revolutionary Council (SRC) that orchestrated the coup of 1969 also took an active role in conceptualizing tradition and shaping Somali culture. They used the state as a force with which to do so. According to A. I. Samatar (1994b):

> The state would become the pivotal mechanism for the overall development of society in the key areas of the economy, social life, and culture. More specifically, the declared ambitions of this highly active state were to guarantee everyone the right to work, strengthen principles of social justice, stimulate economic growth, establish orthography or the Somali language, clean up corrupt behavior, eliminate "tribalism," and conduct free and impartial elections at a suitable time. (p. 116)

In the 1970s, the scope of formal education grew dramatically as Barre introduced an integrated school system (United Nations Development Programme [UNDP], 1998) alongside mass literacy campaigns to promulgate the newly written Somali national language. Barre's extension of educational opportunity rested upon a vision of education that moved beyond clan (Abdi, 1998, p. 13; Laitin & Samatar, 1987; Markakis, 1987), as well as elite bias (Cassanelli & Abdikadir, 2007). In 1975, primary schooling became free and compulsory for children between the ages of 6 and 14 with lessons in Somali (Cassanelli & Abdikadir, 2007).

Barre, who pushed for gender equality as an aspect of his scientific socialist agenda, also hoped to envelop girls and women in the national move toward increased literacy. His efforts met with considerable success. By the early 1990s, a record 35% of girls were enrolled in formal schooling (UNDP, 1998). Indeed, the combination of mass literacy campaigns and the development of a written Somali language began to truly change the face of Somali society. While girls represented only 20% of primary school students in 1970, by 1979, that number had risen to nearly 40% (Cassanelli & Abdikadir, 2007). Further, according to the UNDP, Barre's literacy campaigns in 1973-1974 increased the literacy rates from 5% to 50% among those fifteen or older. The introduction of a written Somali language was significant as a "vehicle for nationalism" (Lewis, 1993). Abdi (1998) refers to the period as one of "social emancipation" (p. 334) for the Somali people, as the introduction of a Somali script aided the process of decolonization and fostered national unity.

Afrax (1994) highlights the ways in which the expansion of Western-style education was coupled with the propagation of enlightenment discourse and vocabulary (We see this even in Abdi's (1998) description of "social emancipation"). Despite the heavy suspicions colonial educators faced, according to Afrax, popular sentiment began to sway in favor of "modern," public education as early as the 1950s. He quotes one popular song composed by Abdillahi Qarshi in 1961:

Aqoon la'aani waa iftiin la'aane
Waa aqal iyo ilays la'aane
Ogaada ogaada dugsiyada ogaada
Oo gaada oo ogadaa
Walaalayaal oo adaa!

(Lack of knowledge is lack of enlightenment
Homelessness and no light
Be aware, be aware of schools, be aware
Be aware, be aware
Brother, be aware!). (Afrax, 1994, p. 245)

Words and phrases that, as we shall see in Chapter 3, pepper NGO advertisements and certain refugee descriptions of schooling in Dadaab, likewise feature in popular discourse in Somalia after independence. According to Afrax (1994), the expression "lack of education is lack of enlightenment" (p. 245) was common in the 1960s, just as the single literary journal of the period was called *Iftiinka Aqoonta*, or *The Light of Education*. He continues, "the words *education* and *enlightenment* were often used in the dissemination of modern literature" (p. 245). Nonetheless, and crucially, plays and other art forms that Afrax describes from this period, though clearly advocating public education, warn against straying too far from traditional ideals, including through marriage with Europeans or the manipulation of clan by educated elites for selfish, economic ends.

Disdain of both foreign influence and clannism emerged in Barre's original recognition of education's libratory appeal through socialism. He noted:

> The key ... is to give everybody the opportunity to learn reading and writing.... It is imperative that we give our people modern, revolutionary education ... to restructure their social existence.... This will be the weapon to eradicate social balkanization and fragmentation into tribes and sects. It will bring about an absolute unity and there will be no room for any negative foreign cultural influences. (Barre, as cited in Lewis, 1993)

From the beginning, however, many Islamic leaders were skeptical of Barre's version of socialism (Khazim, 2001; Ousman, 2004) and its educational policies, arguing that "socialist" education gave too little weight to religion, just as the choice for Somali's written script should have been Arabic (Cassanelli & Abdikadir, 2007, p. 102).

Nonetheless, Barre's goals for socialist change went beyond the scope of his educational agenda to include institution of state sponsored feminism and creation of policies that impacted the regulation of gender through customary law. These policies affected marriage, divorce, and inheritance laws by promising women increased, state (not kin)—backed individual rights (Besteman, 1999, p. 13). Barre even criminalized the form of female circumcision most common in Somalia, infibulation.

Thus, postcolonial leaders, including Barre, employed the notion of *umma* as the traditional backbone to justify existence of a nation-state, before using the state to in turn shape a new national culture. Riding the tide of national sentiment captured in his praise for education, Barre longed to gather all ethnic Somalis under the banner of the Somali state. In 1977, he initiated a military campaign to capture the Ogaden region, populated by ethnic Somalis, from Ethiopia. The burgeoning Somali nation could not, however, afford to blind itself to the "negative foreign influences" acting upon it.

Somalia was coming into its own as an independent nation as the Cold War ramped up and exerted its considerable influence over global geopolitics. As the U.S. and USSR jockeyed for strategic military and economic positions across the globe, Somalia turned to the USSR for aid in an attempt to reduce dependency on its former colonial rulers (Fitzgerald, 2002). The Soviets envisioned newly decolonized and thus economically and politically vulnerable African states as fertile ground for the spread of communism and Soviet power (Issa-Salwe, 2000). With strategic influence in Africa, Soviets hoped to break apart consolidated, Western influence in the region (Issa-Salwe, 2000).

Nevertheless, Somalia's aggression in Ethiopia angered Soviet backers, who were also allied with Ethiopia. Faced with Barre's refusal to back down, the Soviets withdrew support for the regime. Among other consequences, the withdrawal of Soviet support and the cost of the war sent educational funding plummeting (Abdi, 1998; Cassanelli & Abdikadir, 2007). By 1987, the rate of primary school enrollment for girls had fallen to only 6%, among the lowest in the world (UNDP, 1998). Sore from the loss of Soviet backing and facing an increasingly hostile northern neighbor, Barre looked to the United States for military training, aid, and supplies.

Given Somalia's strategic location near other Soviet supported regimes and Middle Eastern oil reserves, the United States was quick to respond to Barre's request for assistance. In fact, reflecting the Soviet and U.S. emphasis upon military might, Somalia soon experienced the largest buildup of armaments in sub-Saharan Africa and earned the dubious distinction as one of most armed countries in the developing world, second only to Iraq (Mansur, 1995a). Regrettably, the tenuous new nation could not withstand the rampant allocation of national resources toward armament and military action: The Ogaden War drained the national economy. In the face of widespread poverty and ill-timed droughts, Barre abandoned his own commitment to transcend clan. In desperate attempts to maintain power in the face of rising dissatisfaction with his rule, he fell back upon clan loyalties, a move which mirrored an underlying manipulation of clan found throughout the entire postcolonial period and in spite of nationalist rhetoric to the contrary.

Indeed, since independence, clan has functioned as a useful tool to manipulate for personal economic gain. Somali economic elites used the "idiom of kinship (and clan)" (Kapteijns, 1994, p. 227) to acquire capital and situate themselves in business circles, without reinvesting in the clan structures that originally propped them up. Likewise, state actors manipulated clan to acquire votes and sustain networks of patronage (A. I. Samatar, 1994a, 1995b). This latter manipulation was fully institutionalized by the 1980s with Barre's cluster of clients and family maintaining total power over the country. According to Besteman (1999):

Barre began to concentrate power in the hands of a small circle of supporters drawn largely from the clans of his father (Marehan), his mother (Ogaadeen), and his son-in-law, the head of the NSS [National Security Service] (Dulbahante) (all part of the Darood clan-family). (p. 15)

Those outside the Darod clan were increasing excluded from lucrative governmental positions (Hussein, 1997).

As time passed through the 1980s Barre's regime became increasingly repressive—killing or silencing political opposition—and exploitative of the Somali citizenry and the traditions that framed their lives through complete centralization of power in the close-doored state government (Besteman, 1999, p. 13). While Islam continued to serve Somalia as a unifying force and basis for self-identification under Barre's reign (despite a state push toward secularism (Ousman, 2004), his regime went so far as to attempt to control religious doctrine through arrest and execution of prominent Islamic theologians who opposed state policy (Khazim, 2001; A. Samatar, 1994). According to Cassanelli and Abdikadir (2007):

In retrospect, it seems highly likely that these events marked the beginning of a serious rift between the state regime and many of the country's Islamic scholars and educators, perhaps laying the foundations for the post-1991 Islamist movement in Somalia. (p. 102)

Indeed, the activism characteristic of current Islamic movements first appeared in Somalia in the 1980s when university graduates and scholars responded to Barre's repression with the formation of the Al Ittihad Islamic Movement (Ousman, 2004, p. 84).

Perhaps ironically, however, even oppositional political forces that developed in response to the repression of Barre, such as the Somali National Movement (SNM), employed clan to their own ends. The SNM, a largely Issaq movement who felt marginalized by the Barre government due to their clan affiliation, declared Somaliland an independent republic from greater Somalia. They did so with the ideological goal of a return to *umma*, or unity (see A. I. Samatar, 1994b, p. 123). However, according to A. I. Samatar (1994b), "Given the fact that one of the original defining features of SNM ideology was the principle of fairness and the rehabilitation of generosity (essential constituents of umma), it was troubling that eleven of the seventeen ministers and all four vice-ministers were from the Issaw community" (p. 123).

Thus, by this point in postcolonial Somali history, clan *did* in fact seem primordial in nature (Kapteijns, 1994, 1995), despite the impact of early postcolonial rhetoric to the contrary. Both Barre and the warlords that followed him deliberately invoked Somalia's history of strong kinship networks, reinvented them in the form of clannism, and justified this new creation through calls to supposed "tradition."

As we have seen, enactments of gender, too, faced enduring transformation during the postcolonial period, both expanding and contracting in response to different state and nonstate initiatives. The notion of gender equality—or at the very least, equal access to education—was, as noted, key to Barre's policy platform during his earlier years in power, even if the reach of state services remained limited in rural areas. Differential access to education for Somali women during the Barre administration emerges, as we shall see, among the refugee populations with whom we worked in Dadaab. Like women's education, emphasis on a socialist-informed, state sponsored form of feminism existed during Barre's early years, representing his state's theoretical commitment to gender equality even as it was both limited in scope and effectively stymied local efforts for nonstate affiliated mobilization among and by women (Lewis, 1993).

Finally, as we began to see in Kapteijns' description of urban, precolonial life, female cash earners in urban centers were increasingly repressed, in part justified by a push toward stricter morality and fundamentalist Islam. Hirsi Ali (2007) notes that as Somalia, and indeed other African nations with significant Muslim populations, faced weakening states, citizens began to mobilize around fundamentalist interpretations of Islam, with drastic impact on women's rights and social opportunities. Ali describes the rise of one particular Islamic movement during her youth:

> In Somalia the Muslim Brotherhood was cool. Siad Barre's dictatorship was anticlan and secular. The generation that grew up under his rule wasn't driven so much by clan: they wanted religion. They wanted Islamic law. The Brotherhood was above politics—and clan; it was fighting for God's justice. And it had money. Funds were pouring in from the oil-rich Arab countries to support and promote the pure, true Islam. (p. 126)

The increase in mosques, and more specifically, Islamist movements such as the Brotherhood, were at once a form of resistance to the corruption of Barre's paternalist government which manipulated clan to divide the population, a reflection of Barre's rhetorical push away from clan as a source of division, as well as the embodiment of a new vision of governance in Somalia in and of itself—a vision in which *sharia* serves as the legal underpinning for, among other things, relations between men and women.

As we have seen, Barre himself, aware of widespread swells of resistance catalyzed by increasingly popular Islamist movements, attempted to repress these movements and its members, through both threats and shows of violence outside of mosques around the country. In 1988, the

Somali National Movement from the Issaq clan also directly attacked Barre's regime. Barre responded with brutal violence.

Barre's repression set the stage for the eventual collapse of his government in 1991. Ensuing war and civil strife bore significant impact upon reconstructions of gender salient notions of tradition among Somalis.

State Collapse and Civil War

United in burgeoning common resentment, opposition groups, including the Hawiye United Somali Congress (USC), rallied and overthrew Barre on January 27, 1991. Along with Barre's regime, so, too, fell the cause for union among clan-based factions and a scramble for power ensued. Two leaders of the USC, Muhammad Ali Madhi of the Hawiye sub-clan Abgal and General Muhammad Farah Aideed of the Hawiye sub-clan Habir Gidir, simultaneously declared intention to rule. Fighting between supporters of the two political leaders brought thousands of daily deaths and the total collapse of infrastructure, services, and government.

During this time, the Somali Patriotic Movement (SPM), consisting of Darod clansmen, began attacking the weakening USC, exacerbating violence in Mogadishu and expanding warfare to outlying regions (Timmons, 2004). Abdi (1998) describes this period of chaos:

> With the collapse of the state, the only things Somalis could find in abundance were American- and Soviet-made assault rifles, artillery pieces, tanks, missiles, and fighter jets. (p. 335)

Africa Watch estimated that between 1991 and 1992 the fighting in Mogadishu caused about 14 thousand deaths and 27 thousand injuries (Fitzgerald, 2002). As the war escalated, a drought hit the East African region. With the economy grounded to a halt, opposing warlords of fractured regions gained control of food resources, which they employed to leverage power (Fitzgerald, 2002). By 1992, widespread famine left at least one-fourth of the population in danger of starvation and had killed approximately 25% of the children under 5 year of age (Fitzgerald, 2002; Hussein, 1997):

> Thus, many Somalis fell prey to the latest type of "clan leaders." These new war leaders, who built up their wealth and influence during the Barre regime, derive their current political power from the manipulation of kin identity, which they call "traditional." (Kapteijns, 1994, pp. 228-229)

Estimates from the late 1990s point to a school enrollment rate of only 13 to 16% for Somali children ages 6-12, again one of the lowest in the world (UNDP, 1998), while the contemporary schools that remain tend to be funded by Islamic or Arab aid organizations and use Arabic as the medium of instruction (Cassanelli & Abdikadir, 2007, p. 108). *Duksis* have faired better than government schools during the war, given that they are endowed with greater community investment.

Indeed, various forms of Islamism—some, though certainly not all, fundamentalist in nature—have flourished in Somalia after 1991, expanding to fill the vacuum of authority left by state collapse (Khazim, 2001; Ousman, 2004). Ousman points to the ways in which religious fundamentalism and calls to implement *sharia* nationwide served as a unifying ideology in the wake of civil war. Indeed, as of 2009, *sharia* is the law of the land, a tentative and recent compromise between the Transitional Federal Government (TFG), created in 2004, and the more moderate remnants of the Islamic Courts Union (ICU), which briefly seized much of the country in 2006. Together, these entities have formed coalition government that struggles to resist the action of more militant and rapidly expanding Islamist groups such as Al Shabaab, which are reportedly backed by Al Qaeda. More than 20 years after state collapse, violence remains commonplace in Somalia and the state is weak at best.

There exist myriad explanations for the Somali state's initial failure (for a thorough review of the literature on state collapse, see Kapteijns, 2001). Causation aside, the past two decades' massive instability has had profoundly gendered impacts. While young men were drawn into militias with their attendant drug abuse and numbing violence, girls and women's war experiences were similarly debilitating. The loss of men to war deprived girls and women of necessary security and protection. Somali scholar Mohamed (1997) writes:

> Contrary to men who were fighting to gain political power, to defend their clan, and/or "honor," women felt they did not have anything to do with the civil war and needed to cope with the loss of their husbands, fathers, and sons, their traditional "male protection." (p. 433)

Without male protection, throughout the war, rape and physical violence was used against women to humiliate rival clans (Gardner & El Bushra, 2004). "In addition to the fear of being killed or injured, starvation, injury, insecurity, and suffering the loss of loved ones, Somali women have become victims of everyday torture, sexual assault and rape" (Mohamed, 1997, p. 433).

The increasing prevalence (and acceptability) of rape, according to Afrax (1994), is one symptom of the manipulation of Somali culture and tradition by militias during the civil war period. He writes:

As the traditional moral code of right and wrong became reversed, what was once seen as offensive assumed a degree of acceptance or was even perceived as salutary. For instance, theft, lying, hypocrisy, rape and dishonesty began to be defined as indicators of *ragannimo* (manhood). (p. 248)

As their homeland descended into civil war, Somali men, women, and children fled by the thousands. Many in the northern regions headed to Ethiopia or Yemen. Thousands of southern Somalis made their way to the eastern border of Kenyan. It is in the refugee camps of Northeastern Kenya that we begin our ethnographic exploration.

Conclusion

Across time and region, *traditionalism* (as a discursive construct) has been shaped and reshaped through interaction between customary law, kinship, Islam, the Somali state, specific political actors, and the external forces of colonialism and neocolonialism. Somali traditionalism is neither exceptional nor essential, but rather shifts and changes over time in response to the aforementioned salient forces. Regardless of its dynamic nature, many scholars (see Afrax, 1994; Rawson, 1994; A. I. Samatar, 1994a) argue that strict adherence to the essence of Somali culture, or application of "actual" Somali tradition, could have prevented the country's tragic fate. While they acknowledge that traditionalism has changed over time, they define such change as generally negative and a catalyst of the downfall of Somalia. They glorify supposedly true tenets of Somali traditionalism, all of which have been "lost," "abandoned," or "distorted" throughout contemporary history and war. According to Rawson (1994):

The disintegration that they [militarization, elite competition, and misspent patronage] engendered might have been arrested if only Siyaad Barre had ceded to a council of elders and if liberty in discourse, movement, and commerce, so ingrained in traditional Somali culture, had become intrinsic to the political ethos of the Somali case. (p. 182)

Similarly, Ahmed Samatar opens his rich edited work, *The Somali Challenge*, with a mournful announcement at the death of tradition:

It is a major claim of this volume that the stock of tradition that calibrated the complexities of Somali character and behavior is under enormous battering, if it hasn't already been fully undermined. Consequently, the contemporary bloody decomposition of society is not a recidivistic reminder of an original sin particular to Somali culture; on the contrary, these events are witness to the denudation of a moral order, one sustained by kinship *heer* (customary code of conduct) and Islamic divinity and *qanoon* (law). (A. I. Samatar, 1994a, p. 8)

As such, for Ahmed Samatar (1994a, 1994b), Rawson (1994), and Afrax (1994), what is needed to restore order to the battered Somali nation-state is a return to the essence of Somali culture. Ahmed Samatar (1994b) believes that this cultural essence is comprised of three specific sources, "Somali kinship, Islamic teachings, and secular political theory" (p. 138). Through the fusion of these three cultural elements, a new, better state structure will come into being. In other words, A. I. Samatar calls for culture, informed by segments of religion and Somali traditionalism, in addition to secular political theory, to undergird a new state.

Samatar's vision, however, is not agreed upon by all, including the women described in Kapteijns' (1995) study who resent Kapteijns' scholarly efforts to learn about the notion Somali tradition. For these women, any quest to understand, and therefore glorify, traditional tenets and practices of Somali society represents an obstacle to female economic autonomy (p. 241). Kapteijns (1995) explains:

> For them, *hiddiyo dhaqan* [traditional society and culture] constitutes an ideological bludgeon, wielded by both men and women to deprive them of the fruits of their considerable social and economic contributions to the day-to-day survival of their nuclear and extended families. (p. 242)

For Besteman (1999) as well, who argues that race, class, and other social stratifications are as important to explaining the civil war in Somalia as clan, a return to traditional kinship structures does not provide the answer for peace—or stability—in Somalia.

We believe, as noted above, that traditionalism (or traditional Somali culture), though real in its ability to impact the lives of Somali citizens in discursive and material ways, does not represent something clear to which Somalis might return. Rather, we focus on what A. I. Samatar (1994b) calls the "interdependence of culture and governance" (p. 129) to argue that what constitutes tradition is both politicized and deeply particularized by region and era. Currently, the meaning of traditionalism as exercised in Dadaab is shaped by dictates of a fundamentalist interpretation of Islam, distinct from those at play during earlier periods of Somali history.

We have taken the time explore the sociopolitical history of Somalia in order to foreground exploration of diverse refugee experiences in Dadaab. In Dadaab, Somali *traditionalism*, as the politicized interaction of culture and religion, comes into contact with a unique set of external forces. In the case of the camps, the external paradigm, as propagated by the UNHCR and other transnational aid agencies, appears most strongly through the discourse of enlightenment. Enlightenment and its precepts, though present in the history of Somalia itself, are situated by aid workers and self-named Somali traditionalists as an ideologically polar opposite to essential Somali tradition. Refugees in Dadaab must negotiate this countervailing polarity to both survive under circumstances of acute duress and to make sense of what it means to be Somali and a gendered member of society. It is to the context of Dadaab that we now turn.

NOTES

1. While A. I. Samatar (1994b) conceptualizes *heer*, or Somali customary law, as synonymous with the rules and customs of kinship, Kapteijns (1994, 1995) highlights a distinction between heer (or *xeer*) and kinship. For Kapteijns, while kinship is a structuring ideology, *heer* is the customary law that, in precolonial Somali society, regulated its rights and duties (pp. 245-246). She defines *heer* as, "The idiom of discourse through which Somali pastoral society defined what was correct and incorrect social behavior, and the body of principles and procedures through which wrongs could be righted … an informal code of customary law that set standards for social behavior—standards that varied in detail from region to region and over time" (Kapteijns, 1995, p. 245). In this chapter we agree with A. I. Samatar (1994b) that *heer* and kinship are related, but lean toward Kapteijns' position for the ways in which it allows for a more dynamic and contested understanding of customary law.

2. As we shall continue to see, kinship in precolonial society is conceptually distinct from the colonial and postcolonial concept of clan, even though the words are often used interchangeably (Afrax, 1994; A. Samatar, 1992, 1994; A. I. Samatar, 1994a, 1994b; Kapteijns, 1994, 1995).

3. A debate rages over whether the Qu'ran in an inherently patriarchal text (Hirsi Ali, 2007) or is subject to multiple, even liberatory interpretations (Ahmed, 1992; Barlas, 2002).

4. Indeed, Ousman (2004, p. 67) argues that indirect rule as applied by the British laid the groundwork for the much later burgeoning infrastructure of Islamic militarism.

5. Colonial schooling was never seamlessly enacted in the Somali context. For a fascinating exploration of the resistance between British colonists and Somali religious leaders on the subject of education, see Olden (2008).

6. British Somaliland gained independence on June 26, 1960. Italian Somaliland followed quickly thereafter, gaining independence on July 1, 1960.

7. Large geographic areas with ethnic Somali populations, including the Ogaden region, remain part of Ethiopia or Kenya. Likewise, Djibouti has a French-speaking, ethnic Somali population.

8. In the years immediately following independence, postcolonial leaders worked to integrate the British and Italian educational systems, expand access to schooling in rural areas, and decide curriculum content and appropriate language of instruction. Still, formal education was very sparse in the 1960s, with only 25 young women in the country's four secondary

schools by 1963 (see Cassanelli & Abdikadir, 2007). Qu'ranic schools, or *duksis*, co-existed with formal state-run schools, though were far more widely attended. Nonetheless, however, gender disparities in public schools mirrored and in fact were influenced by gender disparities in the *duksi* system, where the male/female ratio was 6:1 in the North and 4:1 in the South (Cassanelli & Abdikadir, 2007, p. 99).

CHAPTER 3

"IF ANY CULTURE IS IN NEED OF CHANGE, IT'S SOMALI CULTURE"

Enlightenment and Girls' and Women's Empowerment in the Dadaab Refugee Camps

When Somalis reach Dadaab after what are often life-threatening treks across the desert, they enter a harsh physical environment and a radically new cultural and political milieu. The three camps that comprise Dadaab—Qaafis, Mooro, and Bartan—bring together an array of people from across the globe including Somali, Sudanese, Rwandan, Ugandan, and Ethiopian refugees; international administrators of supranational human rights organizations; Kenyan nationals who make up the bulk of the aid organization staff; Western researchers and interns; journalists; and the Kenyan police. The various stakeholders present are entangled in a large-scale polyhedral performance in which individual scripts are coded to ethnic, national, gender and racial identity and staged within what has cynically been termed "the international aid business." As the umbrella organization under which Dadaab's aid industry operates, the UNHCR plays a paramount role in the unfolding drama. UNHCR policy, as implemented through partnering agencies such as CARE, Save the

Educated for Change?: Muslim Refugee Women in the West, pp. 63–91
Copyright © 2012 by Information Age Publishing
All rights of reproduction in any form reserved.

Children, and the World Food Programme (WFP), regulates virtually all aspects of refugee life, including but not limited to: access to food, water, education, and health services. As a result, refugees' orientation toward the UNHCR's ideological underpinning, which, for the purposes of this project we term *enlightenment*, is highly relevant to their success in Dadaab—if not their very survival. Just as traditionalism assumes a particularized form Somalia, so, too, does enlightenment. The UNHCR's brand of enlightenment represents two strands of thinking married in UNHCR policy, rhetoric, and practice: universal individualized human rights discourse and humanitarianism. In Dadaab, as in elsewhere, these two strands have become intimately linked to the project of women's empowerment.

Camp Life

While the provision of humanitarian aid for Somali refugees was originally intended as a short term emergency measure, after more than 20 years and with no durable solutions in sight, the situation in Dadaab has become protracted. For refugees, life in Dadaab is a unforgiving existence. Located less than 50 miles from the Somali border, Dadaab occupies a swath of remote and sparsely populated semi-arid land. Average daily high temperatures range from 92 to 101 degrees and peaked at a blistering 118 during our initial stay. The topography is flat and sandy with minimum shade-providing scrub brush. Upon arrival, refugees are assigned to one of three camps, each separated by several miles of dirt road. During the rainy season, the roads, which are mere tire tracks in the sand, become passable only by double axle trucks. The four-wheel drive SUVs that the UNHCR and implementing NGOs use to transport staff cannot make the trip. The same is true of the sand road that leads from Dadaab to the nearest large town, roughly 30 miles away. There are two rainy seasons per year, each of which lasts over a month. Toward the end of our first stay in the camps, the rains were setting in and we needed to leave a few days earlier than planned in order to be able to make the journey while the road was still passable. Even so, we lost count after spotting 36 vehicles mired in the mud along the way.

In the camps, the sun beats down on the tin-roofed schools and aid worker housing. It is too hot to lie down during daylight hours because bodies trap extra heat against mattresses. For their part, the majority of refugees do not have tin roofs or mattresses. They live in dome shaped huts called *tukels*, which they construct from brush gathered in the surrounding "bush." The UNHCR distributes plastic tarpaulins to new arrivals and a select few families identified as being particularly needy. Otherwise, families are expected to purchase tarps in the local, refugee run markets. The plastic coverings are used to protect homes during the rainy seasons. Because there are not enough to meet demands, tarps fetch a good price in the local market. Because the families designated to receive tarps are often in the most desperate need, they tend to sell their tarps in order to purchase foodstuffs to supplement nutritionally inadequate rations. Receiving tarps also subjects vulnerable families to thievery, so it is often in their best interest to quickly sell their windfall. Small riots have broken out at the distribution of tarps because the process through which the neediest families are determined is rife with corruption. UNHCR or NGO agency staff asks residential block leaders to identify needy families. In turn, families that can afford to bribe leaders do so in order to get tarps. During distribution, those who have paid to be put on a list expect their tarps, as do those who might recognize their own greater need.

While tarps are scarce, the rainy season can be ruinous. In April of 2006, heavy rains brought devastating floods that destroyed over 600 shelters and left 3,000 refugees homeless. While mired roadways slowed food distribution, waters washed away what food refugees possessed. One of Dadaab's three camps was completely flooded, causing an international emergency and the relocation of an entire section of residential blocks. Because the Kenyan government forbids the creation of new camps, the UNHCR had to make use of a shadeless and remote location that could reasonably be considered an extension of the existing encampment. Officially deemed a new region of an old camp, the poorly positioned residential blocks have to go without a proximate food distribution site. As a result, every 2 weeks these residents are forced to walk two miles in the hot sun to get their food. Because the food sacks are too heavy and bulky for many of the malnourished refugees to carry, they end up trading a good portion of their rations to donkey cart purveyors, who drive the food to the homes.

Even prior to selling portions of their rations, however, the food given is inadequate. Every 2 weeks, refugees receive cereals (wheat flour, maize flour, and/or bulgar), pulses (yellow or green split peas and/or beans), salt, and vegetable oil, which together should equal a minimum of 2,100 calories per person per day. In reality, however, rations do not meet this target amount. Nor do they include meat, milk, fruit, or vegetables of any kind. In 2007, the World Food Programme (WFP) found that the rate of global acute malnutrition exceeded the 15% emergency threshold. The acute malnutrition rate among children under 5 years of age was 22.2%. Anemia rates are alarming high. A nutrition survey conducted in 2006 found that 78% of children under 5 suffer from anemia as well as 72.7% of women. The UNHCR maintains that in order to overcome these chronic rates of malnutrition, a complete package of assistance is needed. As it is, scarcities force refugees to sell portions of their food goods in order to purchase firewood, energy-saving stoves, and soap. There is also a need for complementary foods such as groundnuts that provide extra nutrients, supplementary feeding for children, and treatment for dangerously malnourished children. Walking through the camps, it is easy to see evidence of malnutrition. One of the most striking indicators of chronic food shortage is that the hair of many children and youth has turned white or yellow from lack of necessary nutrients.

Sanitation facilities are sorely inadequate at Dadaab. Water is also in scarce supply. Each individual receives an average of 16.32 liters of water per day, a level well below the UNHCR minimum health standard of 20 l/p/d (U.S. Department of State, 2010). Water allocations are available during specified hours and (female) children often miss school in order to fetch water for their families. Each pit latrine serves an estimated 230 people, again far more than the UNHCR standard of 1:14. To meet that ideal ratio in Dadaab, 39,000 new latrines are required (U.S. Department of State, 2010). In the meantime, 83% of Dadaab's families lack adequate latrine access (U.S. Department of State, 2010). With soap or water in scarce supply, it is not possible for refugees to maintain healthy sanitary practices. Accordingly, fecal born diseases are prevalent. During one of our stays, the beginning of the rainy season brought a cholera outbreak as stagnant puddles of water were used for bathing and laundry washing. Lacking sufficient or accessible medical facilities, cholera victims often die miserable deaths that could easily be avoided through administration of intervenous medications. It is further rumored that pharmacists dilute prescriptions in order to sell medication on the side.

With an estimated 97% of Somali women having undergone circumcision, problematic births are commonplace. Somalis practice *firuani*, the most extreme form of female circumcision in which the clitoris and outer labia are removed and the inner labia are sewn together leaving only a small hole the size of a grain of rice for passage of menses. While intercourse most often results in the partial tearing open of the vagina, the passageway remains too small for a fetus. As a result, obstructed labor is common. While the vast majority of births occur in the residential blocks with the assistance of Traditional Birth Attendants (TBAs), medical facilities see frequent emergency situations. Mothers who make the trip by donkey cart (for which they have to pay a fee) are often in dire need of emergency care. Not surprisingly, childbirth is the leading cause of death among refugee women of childbearing age. At Dadaab in 2009, the maternal mortality ratio stood at 298 per 100,000 births (U.S. Department of State, 2010). Neonatal mortality in 2000 was at a rate of 17 per 1,000 and stillbirths were at a rate of 37 per 1,000 (UNHCR, 2001).

Kenya and the UNCHR: Regulating the Liminal

Kenya began receiving refugees from neighboring countries in the late 1980s. Refugees first arrived from northern Uganda, followed by Ethiopia and, finally, from Somalia. Early on, Kenya handled the Somali refugee crisis on an individual basis and encouraged newcomers' integration into the national community through allocation of rights of movement, work, and education. As an emerging nation that had also undergone colonial occupation and struggled for independence, Kenya was reluctant to invite the UNHCR, a coalition dominated by erstwhile colonizers, onto its otherwise sovereign territory. Kenya's policy toward asylum seekers changed, however, when in 1990-91, roughly 400,000 Somalis crossed the Kenyan border through the towns of Mandera and Liboi, among others.[1]

Drained by resource demands that pushed past what its emerging economy could safely withstand and politically threatened by the sheer number of culturally, ethnically, and religiously distinct people, the government asked for external assistance (Kagwanja & Juma, 2008). Kenya coupled the ceding of responsibility for refugee administration to the UNHCR with a policy of refugee encampment. According to Kagwanja and Juma:

> Designed primarily to reduce the real or imagined threat that refugees posed to national security, the policy of encampment rested on two pillars: abdication of responsibility to humanitarian agencies, particularly UNHCR, and pushing refugees to the margins of society, away from the main economic activities in farmlands and urban areas. (p. 221)

Somali refugees, at the time of our study, were prohibited from leaving the camps to which they'd been assigned without a (rarely granted) pass from the UNHCR. Nor were they allowed to engage in agricultural activities or to enroll in the Kenyan public school system. Combined with the placement of camps in remote and harsh desert regions and the periodic closing of its border with Somalia, governmental officials avoid what they see as potentially destabilizing effects of Somali integration into the Kenyan national community.

The restrictive stance taken by the Kenyan government toward refugee integration mirrors that of countries of asylum in the global South more generally, where refugees are viewed with increasing hostility (Loescher & Milner, 2008; Loescher, Milner, Newman, & Troeller, 2008; Slaughter & Crisp, 2008; Troeller, 2008). According to Loescher et al. (2008), the shift from more open integration policies to containment has occurred in response to the negative impact of structural adjustment in developing countries coupled with the perception of diminished donor support and burden sharing from countries of the global North. Loescher and Milner

(2008) highlight the stated position of governments of the global South that they would be more amenable to hosting refugees if there existed a guarantee of similarly sustained donor engagement.

Instead, as forced migration scholars Slaughter and Crisp (2008) note, "the last two decades of the 20th century witnessed a growing sense amongst the developing countries that they were obliged to bear a disproportionate share of responsibility for the global refugee problem" (p. 126). Anxiety about the burden associated with serving as a host country to asylees and refugees is exacerbated by observation of ever-tightening asylum environments in countries of the global North, which impacts both rates of refugee resettlement and South-to-North immigration more generally. According to Troeller (2008), "One cannot underestimate the 'export value' and 'demonstration effect' of the growing tendency towards restrictive practices, both within the EU and in other regions, given global communications in an increasingly interconnected world" (p. 49).

While refugee containment in Kenya and other countries of the global South fails to meet basic standards of the 1951 and 1967 Conventions Relating to the Status of Refugees, the abdication of responsibility to the UNHCR gives the agency unusual autonomy in governing refugee life. In return for cooperation with Kenya's mandated restriction upon refugees, the UNHCR was ceded full responsibility for and authority over nearly all aspects of refugee care including declaration (or refusal) of refugee status[1] and provision of housing, food, education, sanitation, water, and a host of community services.

In the context of Dadaab and other protracted refugee crises, humanitarian services are enacted according to a "care and maintenance" model that eschews more politicized engagement or focus on durable solutions (Slaughter & Crisp, 2008). Within the parameters of this limited (and many would argue flawed, see Jamal, 2008[3]) model for camp management, the agency assumes the role of a pseudo-state (Slaughter & Crisp, 2008) in the lives of refugees. In her examination of UNHCR's gender based policies and practices, Baines writes:

> It is important not to under-estimate the tremendous institutional and discursive power UNHCR holds over refugees, the internally displaced and returnees under its care.... UNHCR is a large bureaucracy that limits refugee participation in the planning, implementation, and management operations.... As a result, refugee management more often resembles a form of discipline and obedience. (p. 8)

The UNHCR enjoys virtual sovereignty over camp life with few to no mechanisms for external monitoring or accountability (Loescher et al., 2008, p. 74).[4] Refugee studies scholar Verdirame (1999) writes that the UNHCR operates "with no checks on powers and, in effect, without legal remedies against abuses" (p. 65). To illustrate, Verdirame cites incidents in which the UNHCR imposed collective punishment on refugee camp populations, including a particularly notorious episode in Kenya's Kakuma camp. According to Verdirame, in retaliation for the destruction of a cluster of buildings used for food storage and distribution in Kenya's other significant, refugee camp, Kakuma, UNHCR cut off food distribution for 21 days. Verdirame writes, "It must be stressed once again that the people of Kakuma are completely dependent on food aid for their survival" (p. 74). After the incident, a refugee was accused of incitement and relocated to the Dadaab refugee camp. Under the Geneva Convention IV, Art. 33, collective punishment is denied even to occupying powers during times of war.

While the UNHCR has been known to abuse the power it enjoys over refugees, it is important to note that it also assumes primary responsibility for providing basic needs and protections to refugees when other state powers or supranational agencies fail to do so and that many refugees have expressed deep gratitude for the UNHCR's assistance (see Malkki 1995's study of Burundian Hutu refugees in Tanzania and as well as refugee responses in our study).

Further, in administering humanitarian aid, the UNHCR negotiates several inherent limitations, including that the on-the-ground realities it faces today in refugee emergencies differ dramatically from the post-World War II European context of its creation (Slaughter & Crisp, 2008). That the majority of refugee crises are concentrated in the global South while funding emerges primarily from the North also taxes the agency. The UNHCR must demonstrate its relevance to donors (Loescher et al., 2008), an all-too significant aspect of the agency's work given its sole reliance on voluntary funding. As a result, the UNHCR bears primarily responsible for refugee care, yet, is beholden to the states and state interests that created it and which often fail to prioritize refugee assistance among other foreign policy considerations (Loescher et al., 2008). The UNHCR must at once work to preserve its mandate of political impartiality and fundraise in ways that appeal to the interests of a select few wealthy states, or regional bodies, including the United States, European Union, Japan, Sweden, the Netherlands, Norway, the United Kingdom, Denmark, Germany, and Spain, which together contribute over three quarters of the UNHCR budget (Loescher et al., 2008, pp. 92-95). Unfortunately, the majority of protracted refugee crises have not historically ranked high among the interests of these states. To that end, the UNHCR operates with an increasingly tight budget even as it assumes an ever-widening slate of responsibilities.

As the resolve to provide humanitarian aid wanes, security concerns in refugee situations have become an area of increasing interest to states in both the global North and South (Loescher & Milner, 2008; Loescher et al., 2008). For the former, refugee populations, particularly Muslim ones, represent a potential pool for terrorist recruitment. For the latter, security concerns relate both to direct threats posed by militarized refugee populations as well as more oblique risks such as economic competition and shifts in sociocultural balances of power (Loescher & Milner, 2008).

In protracted and harsh situations that combine a loss of hope, scarcity of resources, intercultural inequality, abuses of power, and extreme environmental conditions, there is a constant worry that refugees will revolt. Administering agents as well as Kenyan officials fear refugee riots, terrorist activity, and military recruitment. Indeed, given a strong fundamentalist Islamic presence and proximity to Somalia, the international community identified the entire Northeastern Province as potential terrorist breeding grounds. Accordingly, Dadaab has been subject to gun sweeps, in which private dwellings are searched for arms. Cell phone networks are shut down when diplomats visit the area. Though not officially acknowledged by the U.S. government, staff members claim that U.S. military personnel and equipment have been sighted alongside Kenyan police and military forces within the camps.

According to UNHCR and implementing agency staff, however, the immediate threat on the ground is not terrorist activity, but rather, that the harsh conditions and lack of opportunity at Dadaab lure male youth back to Somalia in order to join militias. Warlords reputedly recruit youth by promising food and money. In many cases, impressionable youth hope to send militia salaries back to desperate family members remaining in Dadaab. According to one former agency director, beyond the material incentives of militia service, the sheer boredom of an ever growing pool of secondary graduates left with nothing to do acts as a pull away from camp life. While a vast number of incentive workers (teachers, counselors, and nursing assistants) are drawn from among educated youth, the supply of potential employees far exceeds the demand. The consequent fear of idle youth manifests in a number of extreme security measures. Refugees are only selectively (based on the purpose of their visit) permitted access to agency compounds, where they are greeted by armed guards at 8 foot tall steel gates. When outside of the fenced areas of agency compounds, all staff and visitors are required to carry walkie-talkies. Visitors are dissuaded from moving about the camps without an agency provided escort and are forbidden to stay overnight in camp-based compounds without special permission.

The convergence of concern and interest around security has translated into funding for certain UNHCR initiatives including Dadaab's new (and controversial, among the refugees) fingerprinting program. In the program, all refugee prints are entered into a databank and compared with those of Kenyan nationals. In the event that a match is found, the person in question has his or her refugee status revoked along with food, housing, medical, and educational services. Because food ration cards are distributed at the family level, the revocation of individual refugee status often impacts entire families. Ostensibly, the policy is meant to discourage ethnic Somalis who are Kenyan nationals from masquerading as refugees and, hence, increasing the burden of international aid organizations. It is also aimed at catching "recyclers," those who cross illegally back and forth across the border smuggling in goods for sale in the camps and claiming new food ration cards, also for sale. In reality, however, the policy does not take into account that many refugees seek false Kenyan citizenship documents in order to procure employment and freedom of movement. Further, official rationale for the policy ignores likely U.S. political pressure underlying the recent impetus to gather Somalis' fingerprints[5]

New policies, including fingerprinting, which are directed at Dadaab's primarily Somali refugee population are not surprising given that Somali refugees have long been perceived as high threats to security. The Dadaab camps were designated potential terrorist recruiting grounds following the 1998 bombings of U.S. embassies in Nairobi and Dar es Salaam, again after the 2002 terrorist attacks in Mombasa, Kenya (Haynes, 2005; Kagwanja & Juma, 2008), and more recently in the aftermath of bombings in Uganda. Kagwanja and Juma (2008, p. 219) argue that post-9/11 restrictions imposed by the U.S. government and reaction to increasing anti-Americanism following invasion of Iraq and Afghanistan now shape the treatment of Somali refugees more than humanitarianism. Soon after 9/11, Kenyan refugee policy fundamentally shifted from what Kagwanja and Juma (2008) term an "era of 'abdication'" during President Moi's regime to a more interventionist model heralded by the election of President Kibaki (Kagwanja & Juma, 2008). The Kenyan government began to enact policies that ensured maintenance of some influence over management of the refugee crisis. While Kenya delayed enacting a formal refugee policy for roughly 20 years after the first groups of refugees made their way to its borders, in 2006, the Kenyan Refugee Act was finally signed into law.

The Kenyan Refugee Act was designed to mitigate travel across the border and is widely viewed as a Western-backed security measure against terrorism and gun smuggling. Indeed, after 9/11, the second Bush administration pressured Kenya to pass an antiterrorism bill with wide ranging executive powers such as the Homeland Security Bill enacted in the United States. The Kenyan government refused to do after facing significant public outcry that the bill represented a violation of human rights. In a thinly veiled response, the Bush administration applied a travel warning to Kenya, thereby severely restricting tourism, one of Kenya's main income generating activities. While not explicitly complying with U.S. wishes for a terrorism bill, the long anticipated new Kenyan Refugee Law effectively met many of the aims advocated by the United States. It assisted Kenyan police and military to track the movement of suspected terrorists[6] near the border region. It is fair to speculate that passage of the law undoubtedly assures President Kibaki continued U.S. backing. Indeed, in 2007 Kenya was named one of 12 strategic military sites in Africa by the Bush administration, a designation that will generate aid and development projects, offer assurance of military support in regional conflict with Somalia, and monitor border activity. Meanwhile, in blatant disregard of international law, the new refugee legislation failed to provide refugees a means to naturalize into the Kenyan national community. Kenya currently remains under a U.S. travel warning. Given the July 2010 Al Shabaab bombing in Uganda, as well as the relatively porous border separating Kenya from Somalia, travel warnings in Kenya are not likely to be lifted in the near future.

Thus, while the UNHCR is powerful in regard to its ability to act with near sovereignty in the running of refugee camps, in the bigger geopolitical picture, regional and Western interests also play a significant role in determining refugees' fates. As noted above, influence is exerted largely through control of UNCHR purse strings and the practice of earmarking funding for crises of particular geopolitical significance (Loescher et al., 2008). The fallout of multinational maneuverings has meant that as of now, over 370,000 Somali refugees have been left in a state of perpetual limbo, denied the right to move, earn an income, or participate in the political process. The enactment of the 2006 Kenyan Refugee Law indicates that there is little hope for a change in status on the horizon. Verdirame (1999) writes:

> They [refugees in Kenya] are, in a sense, the human objects of a containment strategy to isolate and control displaced populations. Both UNHCR and the international community must sooner or later pay attention to the condition of *prima facie* refugees in limbo. For those residing in refugee camps, their lives are literally put on hold: they cannot move outside the camps; many cannot seek education beyond primary school; and employment is precluded because of their status. This situation of stagnation and dependence is deplorable. Moreover, it defies the standards set out in human rights instruments and international refugee law. (p. 63)

On the ground, the tone of policies enacted to contain Somali refugees is echoed in the words and behavior of individuals with whom we came in contact. When Somalis enter Kenya in search of asylum, they face a national populace that has grown increasingly intolerant of their presence. As one teacher we met at Dadaab explained, "it is time for them to go home." Whether in Dadaab or Nairobi, during informal conversations Kenyans repeatedly complained about Somali refugees. Another teacher at Dadaab declared that Somalis "have nothing to worry about." They are provided with free food, schooling, health care, and housing; services she and other Kenyans did not enjoy. In Nairobi, a taxi driver argued that Somalis, many of whom have settled illegally in the North Central district of the city, are responsible for a surge in the city's crime rate. Time and time again, Somalis were accused of drug and gun smuggling and characterized as sneaky and dishonest. Associations of the refugee population with violence and insecurity at the national level occurred in large part through their conflation with local ethnic Somalis and the historical strife that has left Kenya's Northeastern region unregulated. According to Kagwanja and Juma (2008):

> In the Horn, the "Somali refugee" quickly took on the negative stereotypical perceptions and marginality of the local ethnic Somalis, thus fashioning the dynamics of reception, protection and integration and hindering other forms of assistance. Specifically, the Somali refugees share the collective stigma attached to local ethnic Somalis in Kenya since the *shifta* (bandit) war in the 1960's. (p. 215)

In sum, distaste for Somalis held among the many Kenyan nationals with whom we spoke was instantiated in federal laws designed to manage (and minimize) their presence. Further, according to Milner (2008),

Figure 3.1.   Landscape just outside the gates to Mooro Camp (Buck & Silver).

Figure 3.2.   Typical refugee home (Kanyi).

Figure 3.3.   New arrival area during the rainy season (Kantande).

Figure 3.4.   Standard rations for one person (Buck & Silver).

Figure 3.5.   Line for food rations (Buck & Silver).

Figure 3.6.   Gathering clean water rations (Kanyi).

Figure 3.7.   Food unloaded (Adler-Bell).

Figure 3.8.   Food stuffs (Adler-Bell).

Figure 3.9.   Floods reach Dadaab camps on a twice yearly basis (Kanyi).

Figure 3.10.   Flooded home (Kanyi).

Figure 3.11.   Woman in flood water (Kanyi).

Figure 3.12.   Life in a flood zone (Kanyi).

Figure 3.13.   Agencies post educative signs throughout the camps (Buck & Silver).

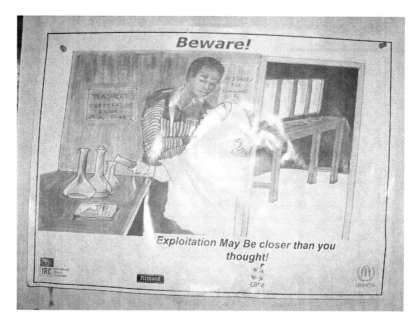

Figure 3.14.   Another cautions against teachers' abuse of female students (Buck & Silver).

Figure 3.15.   A sign warning against exploitation (Buck & Silver).

Figure 3.16.   More educative signage (Buck & Silver).

Figure 3.17.   Road from camps to Garissa Township (Buck & Silver).

Figure 3.18.   Night falls upon razor wire fence surrounding compound (Buck & Silver).

Kenyan politicians who do seek to advocate for refugee rights find themselves largely stymied. Left without a functioning government in southern Somalia and deliberately marginalized by Kenyan law, refugees are stranded in Dadaab where the terms of their everyday existence are defined by UNHCR policy and practice.

Enlightenment Discourse and the Politics of Cultural Change in Dadaab

   Rejection of Somali people and their cultural practices is not limited to Kenyan nationals. In Dadaab, international aid workers routinely cite traditional tenets and practices regarding clan, geography and gender to validate myriad camp-based initiatives aimed at creating sociocultural change in the refugee community. Evocation of an essentialized "traditional Somali culture" is commonly used both as a rationale for measures aimed at creating change, which manifest as calls for increasing Westernization, and justification for the failure to realize espoused measures of equality. Traditional Somali culture is alternately essentialized, demonized, and blamed in order to lend support for policy choices and justify perceived policy failures.

In our time at the camps, aid workers expressed a combination of disdain and sympathy (for Somali girls and women and ethnic minorities) in response to what they perceived as oppressive (often gendered) traditional cultural tenets and practices. During mealtimes, staff members often bemusedly told stories that feature ignorant refugee behavior or detailed programmatic efforts to transform refugee behavior. Forced early marriage and female genital cutting often struck the well-educated and mostly middle class Kenyan and international aid workers as particularly barbaric acts and deplorable violations of individual rights.[7] On one occasion an agency program manager got in a heated debate with several other aid workers about the best method to end female circumcision. While workers made the case that the practice could only be brought to a gradual end through education and awareness programs, the manager declared that, if it were up to him, he would use the police to enforce anti circumcision laws. He concluded the conversation with a climatic declaration that he hated the idea that any girl would undergo circumcision "under my watch." In another mealtime exchange, discussion centered on whether it was aid workers' mission to promote cultural change among Somalis. An aid worker from the U.S., who specialized in infant and child feeding, stated matter-of-factly that she had abandoned cultural relativism long ago. "If any culture is in need of change," she concluded, "it is Somali culture."

Indeed, we find that the UNHCR's agenda in Dadaab is not limited to care, protection and security. Rather, the organization manages refugee life with the aim to progressively move Somalis away from what are perceived as harmful life-ways dictated by a static traditionalism and toward an appreciation of "Western" tenets that sanctify awareness of individual rights and well being. In doing so, the UNHCR promulgates its own brand of enlightenment.

In the context of Dadaab, the term *enlightenment* is commonly used to describe the desired ends of refugee policy and practice. As a concept, the UNHCR's enlightenment agenda is at once traceable to the scientific and intellectual developments of the seventeenth century and takes on its own particularized meaning. Enlightenment in the Dadaab setting echoes Appadurai's (1990) conceptualization of an "ideoscape." He writes, "Ideoscapes are composed of elements of the Enlightenment world-view, which consists of a concantenation of ideas, terms and images, including 'freedom,' 'welfare,' 'rights,' 'sovereignty,' 'representation,' and the master-term 'democracy'" (Appadurai, 1990). According to Appadurai, while Enlightenment's "master narrative" assumed particularized forms in countries of the global North such as England, France and the United State, it retained a certain internal coherence that has diminished since the nineteenth century and with the emergence of globalization. What remains is a "loosely structured synopticon of politics, in which different nation-states … have organized their political cultures around different 'keywords' " (Appadurai, 1990, p. 297).

In Dadaab, where the UNHCR serves as pseudo or quasi state, enlightenment takes form at the braiding together of human rights discourse and humanitarianism. The arrangement of formal refugee leadership in camps, while not always meaningful in practice, reflects structures of democratic governance and individual rights, with elected block leaders forming councils and given decision-making authority. Each camp has an elected chairman and chairlady who in turn oversee the efforts residential block leaders. The UNHCR also assumes primary concern with refugee welfare, in part given a general negligence by other meaningful organizations of the international community as well as host states. UNHCR evaluations and reports are rife with calls for increased educational opportunities and access to the Internet in order to increase refugees' awareness of the larger world around them. CARE encourages economic self-sufficiency through micro-finance schemes that, if successful, plant a capitalist seed in camp economies. The National Council of Churches of Kenya touts reproductive and family planning even as it condemns early marriage and female circumcision. Through research and programming, aid agencies try to catalyze cultural change, keep idle youth busy and productive, and protect vulnerable women from regrettable aspects of traditional culture.

Signs speaking out for HIV/AIDS prevention and against domestic abuse, sexual exploitation, and forced marriage adorn the schools, offices and roadways. In less obvious but likely more influential ways, the UNHCR promulgates a human rights rationality indexed to Western democratic ideals. Through its choice of programming and implementing agencies, particular emphasis is placed upon girls and women's rights and vulnerabilities. The WFP, CARE, German International Cooperation Enterprise (GTZ-IS), Save the Children UK (SCF-UK), Norwegian Refugee Council (NRC), International Organization on Migration (IOM), UNICEF, Film Aid, Handicap International (HI), the Kenyan Red Cross, and the Nation Council of Churches of Kenya (NCCK) are all present at Dadaab. In their stated missions, each espouses a discourse of universal human rights and equality that echoes that of the UNHCR. In donor appeals, mission statements and programming, implementing agencies give voice to the idea that humanitarian aid is meant to provide scaffolding on which refugees can progressively advance toward greater autonomy, civility, choice, and self-reliance. For instance, Save the Children UK, a recent entrant on the Dadaab scene, specializes in child protection and schooling. Its mission statement reads:

The inspiration and vision for Save the Children came in part from the international children's rights movement begun in England in 1919 by Eglantyne Jebb, founder of the British Save the Children Fund. From this early effort in the hills and hollows of Harlan County, Kentucky grew a self-help philosophy and practice still at work today in more than 45 countries —providing communities with a hand up, not a handout.

This approach—working with families to define and solve the problems their children and communities face and utilizing a broad array of strategies to ensure self-sufficiency is the cornerstone of all Save the Children's programs.

In Save the Children's stated purpose, the notion that humanitarian aid should help those in need move toward greater economic self-sufficiency through participatory means is repeated and democratic and individualistic ideals are implicitly espoused. Perhaps most significantly, UNHCR policy emphasizes the agency's responsibility to protect human rights—and the rights of designated subgroups in particular. For example, UNHCR strives to meet protocol designated by the Convention on the Rights of the Child. UNHCR policy in recent decades, however, features a commitment to advancing women's rights with particular prominence.

In Dadaab, enlightenment ideology is most often evoked as an awareness of gender-specific rights, just as it is used to justify an array of policies and humanitarian efforts to reform what are presumed to be harmful gender practices. The emergence of gender in UNHCR policy occurred initially during the 1970s, when second wave feminists began to complain that the specific needs of women, who together with their children represent 80% of worldwide refugee population, were being neglected. Indeed, women were depicted as particularly vulnerable to oppression and therefore the most in need of enlightenment about their rights (Baines, 2004).

Specific mention and/or adoption of policy relating to refugee women occurred during the 1985, 1987, and 1988 UNCHR sessions. Each push of this period aimed to better incorporate women and their particular needs in refugee policy. 1989 witnessed creation of the Office of the Senior Coordinator for Refugee Women, charged with the task of "elaborat[ing] proposals for a policy framework to govern UNHCR's responses to the special needs and potential of refugee women, incorporating the women-in-development concept" (Women's Commission for Refugee Women and Children, 2002, p. 12). Other significant changes in the 1990's include formal adoption of a UNHCR Policy on Refugee Women in 1990 as well implementation of the Guidelines on the Protection of Refugee Women in 1991. As Women's Commission's Commission for Refugee Women and Children note, UNHCR policy during this period and the subsequent years was informed by the overall climate of the UN's

Decade for Women and its subsequent landmark changes, including adoption of the Convention on the Elimination of All Forms of Discrimination Against Women (CEDAW) and the Platform for Action created at the 1995 Beijing Conference.

On the ground, UNHCR policy on women and gender has translated into myriad programming initiatives, including but not limited to: implementation of gender-focused school recruitment projects, promotion of community education campaigns warning against gender and sexual based violence, creation of protection zones for women and children, increased access to reproductive health services for refugee women, development of requirements for gender equality in refugee leadership positions, as well as the prioritization of campaigns to sensitize aid workers around gender issues. In Dadaab, each of these efforts exists and each is articulated as a measure to further the cause of women's empowerment and stop existent harm.

The UNHCR and CARE offered bags of food and clean uniforms to families as incentives to enroll their daughters in primary school.[8] Qafis, Bartan, and Mooro each features an array of signage warning young girls and potential perpetrators alike of the dangers of forced marriage, domestic abuse, and female circumcision. Each of Dadaab's three camps likewise includes a "safe area," where female refugees and their children in particular danger of discrimination can take haven. (The degree of security around these safe zones, however, is limited). The NCCK and the Deutsche Gesellschaft fur Technische Zusammenarbeit (GTZ) offer lessons in reproductive health and direct reproductive care, respectively. Affirmative action policies demand that each camp has a chairlady in addition to a chairman, as well as a certain percentage of female participation in refugee structures of governance. Finally, all aid workers and long-term visitors to the camps must complete sensitization courses around issues of sexual exploitation and abuse before beginning their jobs. While each of these programmatic pieces faces significant limitation, as we shall see over the course of this study, they exist to forward the cause of refugee women's empowerment.

Thus, in Dadaab, enlightenment and women's empowerment are intricately linked; in fact, women's empowerment is the most potent expression of the enlightenment framework out of which the UNHCR operates. Reflecting the UNHCR's efforts to mainstream attention to women's rights in its programming, the implementing agencies are often careful to convey particular attention to women's needs. On the home page of its website and in countless print advertisements, CARE Kenya features the image of a woman from the global South, usually Africa, staring intently into the camera. Below a sentence reads, "I am Powerful." Beside her it reads, "She has the power to change her world. You have the power to help her do it."

The focus on women goes hand-in-hand with another shared vision among NGOs serving the Somali population: to foster change in traditional cultural practices. Film Aid's mission statement speaks to the desire to create change within an overall frame that affirms refugees' transcendent humanity:

Refugees too often go without education, a sense of community, a connection to the outside world and any type of mental stimulation or heart-lifting diversion.

The majority of refugees are women and children who have suffered unimaginable horrors, and have been separated from or lost their families. Many children have been born in the camps and it is the only world they have ever known. A generation is coming into maturity with few experiences that give them the self-esteem, knowledge and tools to become proactive, productive and participatory members of their community.

Intellectual, visual and aural stimulation are needs often overlooked in humanitarian responses where the first priority is naturally given to legal and physical protection, subsistence, and health care. As displaced populations languish in camps, the erosion of cultural norms and community environment further aggravates health and social problems. By packaging taboo subjects within entertainment, tough issues can be destigmatized. Film Aid's programs address critical social issues such as HIV and AIDS, sexual and domestic violence, reproductive health and family planning.

Film Aid's programs achieve both positive immediate change as well as an enduring long-term impact. In the short term, the refugees experience psychological relief from the harsh realities of the camps and obtain constructive knowledge and skills, giving them a greater sense of purpose and focus. In the long term, the films offer refugees a broader view of the world, an opportunity to imagine other futures for themselves and a vision for how they can make a difference in their communities.

Implementing agencies do not merely echo enlightenment and empowerment ideals as public relations strategies, however. Agencies at Dadaab offer a comprehensive set of services that, while too understaffed and underresourced to be as effective as staff might wish, clearly convey a Western worldview. Counseling programs aim at providing opportunity for personal growth and protection, healing from trauma, and prevention of disease. Community education features workshops on HIV/AIDS prevention, peace and conflict resolution, reproductive health, and the value of schooling. Nutritionists work with refugees to make the most out of meager rations. All of these programming efforts are packaged as benev-olent aid with an unspoken (to refugees) goal of drawing refugees toward ways of being that reflect Western cultural tenets and practices. Given that every facet of refugee life, including food distribution, water supply, sani-tation, housing, entertainment, and medical care is shaped by agency ser-vices, the appropriated ideals and language of enlightenment are a ubiquitous presence. Nowhere is this more true or intense than in the pro-vision of educational opportunity.

Empowerment Through Schooling

UNHCR policy markets education as a human right and a civilizing process. The educated women with whom we worked could all repeat from memory quotes about the power of education to enlighten and lift students out of ignorance taken directly from assigned school texts. Enlightenment ideals are readily evident in the rhetoric promulgated by the UNHCR and its implementing agencies. In its literature, CARE, which managed educational programming at Dadaab during the time of our fieldwork,[9] claims that education, "is one of the best investments toward fighting global poverty. By helping children gain the knowledge and skills to succeed, CARE helps lay the groundwork for healthier, more productive families, communities and societies." According to NGO dis-seminated rhetoric, schooling's potential to alleviate poverty is integrally tied to its ability to address the restrictive impact of traditional cultural practices upon girls' and women's rights. The following story found in Save the Children's promotional literature exemplifies the coupling of effort to achieve female empowerment with the need to change tradi-tional cultural practices:

> Florida awoke one morning in her village of Mtaja, Malawi, to discover that her grandmother had hidden her clothes. Her grandmother was deter-mined: she wanted to keep Florida out of school so that she would agree to get married. In Malawi, girls of 15 like Florida are often married off, espe-cially if their grandparents are elderly and poor, as hers are. Florida, then in grade seven, understood: she was another mouth to feed and her grandpar-ents had done so much to care for the family, especially after Florida's mother died and her father abandoned them. Florida was devastated, but with no other options she felt she had to accept the marriage proposal her grandmother had arranged.
>
> At school, however, the headmistress had other ideas. She notified the vil-lage's Bright Future Committee. Supported by Save the Children's sponsor-

ship program, Bright Future Committees encourage dropouts to return to school, while promoting community support of children.

Luckily, Florida had a friend who also wanted to help. She and the Bright Future Committee located Florida and her intended husband and talked to them about the situation. Then they talked to Florida's grandparents.

Florida is now back in school, attending eighth grade and living with her grandparents. "Thanks to my friend for reporting me to school," Florida said. "I am happy I am back. I will work hard so that I excel."

For Florida and girls like her, agencies promise that participation in schooling will bring happiness and self-sufficiency. Early in the development of the Dadaab camps, similar selling points were communicated to the refugee community at large through outreach programs at the block level. At the time of our study, as female enrollment continued to climb, perhaps beyond agency capacity, efforts to convince refugees to send their daughters to school were communicated in a one on one basis and within the curriculum. Students and parents were frequently reminded that schooling, "opens minds" and "eradicates ignorance."

In all, a women's empowerment agenda is central to UNCHR policy in Dadaab and intricately entwined with the concept of enlightenment. The enlightenment agenda is instantiated through deliberate pushes for girls' education, affirmative action, and the placement of public messages across the camp landscape. Due to their central positioning, these messages are difficult to ignore.

Conclusion

While infinitely complex, the Dadaab landscape is marked by two, dominating, ideological poles (traditionalism and enlightenment), which the UNHCR and its implementing agencies have actively worked to construct. Both poles take on particular, contextualized (time and space specific) meaning in the refugee camps. For its part, enlightenment is thoroughly institutionalized in ways that impact control and allotment of resources, resulting in a carefully inscribed power differential between the aid regime and refugees.

Rather than represent a simple choice for stakeholders, however, both polarities exert a "pull" and an accompanying set of positive and negative consequences of accommodation and resistance. Accordingly, refugees have to engage in a complicated cost-benefit calculation as they work to feed family members, sustain hope for the future, and develop self and community. For, while the disciplining power of the UNHCR and its network of implementing agencies is clear, it shouldn't be over-looked that, despite its remote location, it is nevertheless embedded in an age of flexibilization. As such, refugees often respond to Dadaab's polarized landscape not by choosing sides, but rather by moving intrep-idly between them.

NOTES

1. "Kenya's refugee population shot meteorically from a low of 16,000 in March 1991 to 427,278 at the end of 1992" (Kagwanja & Juma, 2008, p. 220).

2. This changed with the 2006 passage of the Refugee Law in Kenya. The bill states that the Kenyan federal government retains the right to grant refu-gee status. However, at the time of this writing it is unclear the extent to which this mandate has been put into practice. Possible changes are also likely to occur with the passing of the 2010 constitutional referendum, which provides for the legal recognition of Islamic courts, though at this time the effects still remain to be seen.

3. Jamal (2008) argues that "while the ultimate causes of and solutions to pro-tracted refugee situations are political, 'caring and maintaining' refugees until political conditions are ripe for a solution condemns millions to a state of unfreedom'" (pp. 149-150). Nonetheless, the substitution of humanitarian aid for more profound political engagement is a common strategy in the management of refugee crises (see Barber, 1997; Lischer, 2005; Loescher et al., 2008; Morris & Stedman, 2008; Terry, 2002).

4. The harsh conditions at Dadaab are further exacerbated by the denial of meaningful leadership roles at the camp. While the UNHCR employs block and camp leaders to facilitate interactions with the refugee popula-tion, these positions do not include power or responsibility to make policy decisions. According to Loescher et al. (2008), the exclusion of refugees from decision-making processes pertaining to them represents a major problem with the UNHCR more generally. While community meetings are often held to gather refugee feedback, in the end UNHCR and imple-menting agency staff make all critical decisions affecting camp life. At the same time that positions of power are withheld from refugees, agencies commonly make use of "incentive workers" to complete both mundane and in some cases skilled labor. Incentive workers earn a token wage that, while undeniably helpful in allowing workers to supplement meager rations, is well below wages earned by Kenyan nationals performing the same tasks.

5. We discovered upon our second visit to Dadaab in 2008 that the U.S. gov-ernment had temporarily frozen Somali resettlement to the United States in order to investigate allegations of DNA fraud, particularly in family reunification cases. An extensive fingerprinting campaign was discussed as one possible means to cut down on such fraud. In 2010, the U.S. again allegedly suspended refugee resettlement following an increase in violent activity by Al Shabaab in Somalia and East Africa more broadly.

6. In 2007, in a much-criticized move, Kenyan officials forcibly returned members of the United Islamic Courts who had fled to Kenya. Tipped off as to their location, the villages to which they were returned were subsequently bombed by U.S. backed Ethiopian forces. Several survivors were arrested.

7. Like Somalia, Kenya underwent a prolonged period of colonialism until independence in 1963. Its experiences under colonial rule as a settler colony were quite distinct from that of its north eastern neighbor, however. Britain maintained a singular, long-standing presence and successfully converted a majority of Kenyans to Christianity. As a result, Kenyan society continues to make use of many of the vestiges of the colonial era. It is a deeply religious nation, where the media, everyday conversation, and signs and symbols of daily life are saturated with references to Christian devotion. Kenyan schools, which are modeled after the British system, also reflect Kenyan colonial history. Lessons at the secondary level are taught in English with the effect that all educated Kenyans are fluent in English. Kenyan popular culture is also pervaded by Western media. Cinemas nearly exclusively feature Hollywood films while radios blast popular U.S. artists. Western-style clothing dominates Nairobi offices and nightclubs. In short, Kenyan culture reflects a much deeper embrace of Western culture than does Somalia's.

8. The policy of offering incentives to families who enroll their daughters first diminished and then ceased to exist as gender neared parity at the primary level.

9. Until 2010, CARE managed Dadaab's entire formal school system, from primary school through secondary. After nearly 20 years and in the face of an exponentially increasing camp population, in 2010, Windle Trust Kenya was given responsibility to manage secondary education in the camps. CARE continues to run schooling at the primary level in one of Dadaab's three camps, while the Association of Volunteers in International Service (AVSI) and the Lutheran World Federation (LWF) have taken over leadership in the other two.

CHAPTER 4

NEGOTIATING THE DADAAB LANDSCAPE

Refugees Respond to Polarity in Dadaab

While the influence of the UNHCR and its implementing agencies at the camp is significant, it is not singular. One of the ways that refugees respond to the UNHCR's empowerment apparatus is to self-consciously employ what has been deliberately termed a *traditionalist* perspective. As we've seen, traditionalism, as defined by refugees in the camps, represents only one of many discursive permutations under the same name over the course of Somali history. As elucidated in Chapter Two, the salient elements of traditionalism in postcolonial Somalia, though shifting in prominence, have included the Somali state, *xeer*, or customary law, and Islam. In the case of Dadaab, the UNHCR replaces the Somali government as a quasi state. Because Somalia was colonized by some of the very same nations that make up the UN and, perhaps more simply, because the UNHCR is not run by Somalis, a substantial segment of Dadaab's refugee population has developed a distinct oppositionality to the UNHCR's rule over the Dadaab region. This segment of the refugee population calls upon stringent interpretations of customary law, or *xeer*, and Islam to counter the desires and agenda of the UNCHR. As a result, traditionalism in Dadaab is in many ways tied to more fundamentalist strands of Islam than was the case in regions of Somalia and it offers a portent counter-

Educated for Change?: Muslim Refugee Women in the West, pp. 93–109
Copyright © 2012 by Information Age Publishing
All rights of reproduction in any form reserved.

manding worldview to the Westernism driving enlightenment and empowerment agendas.

Traditionalist pushback is often coupled with a vision of the UNHCR and its implementing agencies as proselytizing institutions. One student involved in our participatory research project also worked in an incentive position for the National Council of Churches of Kenya (NCCK). In his research he chose to investigate refugee perspectives on NCCK's activities in Dadaab. In his final analytic essay, he wrote of the research experience:

> I am purposely and deliberately told that I was fueled to spread Christian religious education. Very few people normally give consideration to my research. Those who give consideration to my research are the few who are educated and work with the organizations which operate in [the] Dadaab refugee camps. A mother says, "You came to teach us their customs and religions and diseases which exist in their myth and mysteries." (Excerpted from Student Research Report)

As the student's findings connote, self-proclaimed traditionalists often reject health and welfare related information conveyed by NGO incentive workers because of its association with the UNHCR and the West more generally. Knowledge viewed as scientifically derived (and thus objective) among the highly educated agency staff and incentive workers is dismissed by traditionalists as Christian propaganda deliberately designed to spread a Western worldview at the expense of Islam, Somali culture (*xeer*), and refugee lives. Suspicion about messages imparted by aid agencies, and especially NCCK, mirrors that held historically held by many Somalis in relation to missionaries as well as colonial administrators, both of whom were seen as prosthelytizing agents. In a more subtle way, the suspicion also echoes concern that Barre's postcolonial Somali state had the power to dilute crucial tenets of Islam and mute prominent Muslim voices in favor of more Western-style, secular national governance.

In the above excerpt, the "diseases which exist in the myth and mysteries" described by the traditionalist mother refers to HIV/AIDS. As part of its efforts in Dadaab, NCCK offers reproductive health workshops that promote condom usage as a form of birth control and preventative measure against HIV/AIDS. Condoms and birth control are strongly taboo in the traditionalist Somali community of Dadaab, as is public discussion of sexuality. Further, while rates of HIV infection in the camps are notably low[1] when compared to East Africa at large, agencies still place a good deal of emphasis on its prevention. Regardless, many traditionalists deny the existence of HIV/AIDS or believe it to be restricted to more promiscuous Westerners. In the latter case HIV/AIDS provides evidence of a failure of culture—of the consequences that can befall a society when traditional values are ignored—in favor of less prohibitive sexual mores.

For traditionalists, the notion that the UN and its implementing agencies are propelled by a missionary-like motivation completely undermines the credibility of institutional endeavors. In an interview conducted by another student researcher working on our project, an elder Somali man voiced his cynicism:

> Interviewer (I): Haven't you seen NGOs and community leaders are campaigning for the rights of the women and girls, like, "don't circumcise girls or don't oppress women?"
>
> Somali Man (SM): Yes, I have seen them. They are there, but they are doing [it] for their own interest not the interest of the girls or women…. There is the NCCK from the church of Kenya. They have hidden agendas. CARE also has many offices for such programmes for girls and women. Many other foreigners, i.e. White men and women. Some from the [Somali] community, they are doing [it] for their incentive [pay].

The elder in the exchange does not address the intrinsic merit of women's rights but, rather, dismisses outright all institutional activity as a reflection of self-interest on the part of White Christians and monetary remuneration on the part of incentive workers. He is opposed not to the content or concept of shifting gender practices per se—though that may certainly play a role—as much as what he perceives as unsolicited intrusion of a foreign agenda onto Somali ways of being. It is not surprising, then, that the programming sponsored by NCCK, with its explicit grounding in Christianity, meets with particularly strong resistance. Nor, is it expected that refugee incentive workers employed by NCCK often face harassment or exclusion from their communities.

Given apprehension of Westernization processes, traditionalists often do reject facets of social change associated with the West. Gender identity, the expansion of secular education, and increasing access to the Internet were three key areas of rapid social change occurring at the camp during our stay. Over the last few years, refugee-owned Internet cafes and businesses have opened in camp marketplaces. While for the most part girls and women do not use market Internet facilities, the cafes have become increasingly popular among male refugee youth who surf the web and watch movies after school. Indeed, the Internet represents one major venue through which refugees are exposed to different lifeways—both through news and access to entertainment industries across the globe—and as such, is viewed as a threat by many traditionalists. Toward the end of our 2007 stay in Dadaab, access to Internet service was expanding from the main staff compound to the sub-compounds at each of the camps. While refugee access would still be restricted, the expansion meant that a greater number of incentive workers would have daily access to Internet services. The expansion was widely discussed among refugees. A member of the participatory research project interviewed an elder Somali community leader on the increasing influence of the media in Dadaab. The leader summarized:

> [Life] is changing very fast and it is because of the availability of free education and a lot of media all over the region. I see [the influence of the media and the Internet] as being dangerous to the new generation in this region in a way that will result [in] them leaving behind their religion and cultural beliefs. I see [Internet users] as people who [are] lost from the right path and extremely contrary to our religion and cultural beliefs.

For this elder, the Internet presents a dangerous threat to cultural continuity and, as such, needs to be controlled or eliminated. Later in the conversation, he described his desire to partner with other elders to physically ban the Internet and other forms of media from the region. While it would be virtually impossible for traditionalists to ban the Internet, Internet café business owners and users face exclusion, shaming, and ostracization by traditionalists in the community. Once the primary decision makers of nomadic society, elder men have been disempowered by the Internet's uncontrollable ability to spread and sway youth. Accordingly, elders and others now employ more indirect—yet often equally powerful—efforts to exert social control. They do so by intoning an essential Somali culture they deliberately conflate with the observance of Islam. One young patron of an Internet café described the shaming he experienced daily to a member of the participant research team:

> Student (S):   What are the problems you face in your community in using the Internet?
> Internet User (IU):   I face very many problems. For example, I am abused, insulted, ignored, socially rejected or outcast and treated as [an] abnormal person.

Regardless of the protest his behavior elicited, the young man continued to visit the Internet café daily because, as he reported, he enjoyed increased exposure to global news, enhanced communication with friends, and the entertainment provided. Based on his findings, the participant researcher concluded:

Youth view the modern forms of the media as excellent development in the communication technology of the region and a sign of good hope in the future. Hence, they are happy about the installation of Internet, video, and cinemas…. On the contrary, the community elders[2] have a negative perspectives about the modern forms of media as something contrary to their religion and social cultural life. Since it is the ideology of the Western people, which is aimed to fight the Muslim world. It also wastes the time and money of the ignorant people (the youth) who think that they are civilized.

Like NCCK programming, for traditionalists the Internet represents an engine of Westernization that they are called upon to resist in order to preserve Islamic and Somali tradition.

Traditionalists also view efforts to affect gender equity with suspicion in part because the UNHCR and its implementing agencies clearly communicate their alignment with a women's rights (empowerment) agenda. Constance, a Sudanese refugee and member of the participatory research project, interviewed a traditionalist Somali man on the role of women in society. According to the informant, "In my culture a woman [is] a child with big foot…. Women is to bear only children nothing else to do more than. Woman is a hair of man." When Constance pressed him to elaborate on the implication of his view for a woman's right to education, he explained:

Each and everybody has to look for knowledge, but women can't rule men. Their right is [to] know if there is food or [there is] no food, but not to sit together with men and talk…. A woman contributing is nothing [in comparison] to [a] man's idea. Women can't lead a man. [That] is impossible to me.

The characterization of women as inherently subservient is commonplace in interviewers' conversations with traditionalists (as well as in other community members' representations of traditionalist perspectives).

As the interviewee's comments suggest, the construction of women as inferior frames traditionalist stances on a myriad of gender salient practices, such as female circumcision, domestic abuse, polygamy, early marriage, and schooling. Refugees of all ages are well aware of the presumption of women's inferior social status undergirding elders' prohibition of movement toward greater gender equality. One member of the participatory research team wrote (with regard to female circumcision):

The community has [a] long history of male domination of women. Female genital cutting was often justified on the basis of fear of prostitution if girls are not circumcised. These ideas still linger on. For example, 99% of 10-14 years old girls were circumcised/mutilated. Ninety percent of the mothers, they will never consider leaving their girls or daughters uncircumcised fearing their daughters will not be married and they will also lose their dignity in the society. The community portrays degrading and insulting stereotyping of uncircumcised girls.

As the researcher's words convey, Somali women's gender roles are deeply embedded in perceptions of longstanding cultural and religious tradition and creed. However in reality, gender roles in Somali society—as well as the relative power afforded women—have shifted dramatically over the course of history. As noted in Chapter 2, the significance of women as powerful, crucial members of society was well understood in precolonial, pastoralist communities where women symbolized intercommunal ties and scaffolded a family's means of production (Kapteijns, 1994). Women in colonial urban centers occupied very different roles and so, too, do refugee women in the Dadaab camps. That traditionalists' efforts to maintain the status quo in gender relations are as often attributed to the need to resist universalizing forces of Westernization as to the desirability of long standing principles of social organization reveals the significance of the UNHCR's impact on conceptions of tradition (in the form of inciting pushback).

The reactive dynamic of traditionalists' desire to maintain gender disparity is illustrated in talk about the appropriateness of girls engagement in formal schooling. Esther, a Form Four student, interviewed a male teacher in one of the camp schools. Although he professed to support girls' education, he described his parents' traditionalist opinion on the matter. "My sisters did not attend school because my parents didn't want her to follow the White peoples' way of life and also they didn't want her to go against their culture requirements through going to school."

Qamar, one of the few female Form Four completers to engage in the participatory research project, writes, "Most of the society/community will think that we are developing Western culture. They think if you support or talk about issues related to women and girls, you are totally against the [Somali] culture or the [Muslim] religion." They believe this despite the Qu'ran's textual promotion of gender equality in the form of the inclusion of women in inheritance laws.

In short, traditionalists draw upon an imagined version of Somali history, culture and ideology in order to stand in firm opposition to gender empowerment ideals, policies, and practices. All members of the Dadaab community, including aid workers, have to orient themselves accordingly. Among the aid community there is a constant struggle between those who hope to take what they view as ethical and legal stances against female circumcision and early marriage and those who wish to avoid the enforcement of policy that might inflame hostilities. For their part, refugees, and refugee women and girls in particular, face more personally consequential repercussions in their struggle to navigate the deeply divided landscape.

On the one hand, representatives of the UNHCR and its implementing partners serve as gatekeepers to employment venues, material resources, and educational opportunities. On the other hand, refugees have to live among traditionalist and family members and neighbors, who exert restrictive social control through exclusion, harassment, or even violence.

Despite the consequences, some stake out firm positions with regard to highly charged social issues. Others move more fluidly between stances, depending on shifting factors and self-interest. Some are grateful for the provision of particular social services, yet reject certain offerings in order to uphold traditional Somali practices. Many are willing to critique both the aid community and traditionalist Somali tenets and practices alike. Most appreciate increasing exposure to the world outside of the camps, even as they proudly maintain Somali dress and Muslim religious practices. In sum, the majority of refugees choose not to set themselves in opposition to the UNHCR and its agenda nor against traditionalist and traditionalism. Rather, most girls and women flexibly negotiate between the two dominating polarities at play. In so doing, they sometimes draw upon elements of *xeer* and Islam; at other times, they engage elements of enlightenment and empowerment frameworks.

Navigating Within the Middle Ground

Given traumatic experiences fleeing civil war in Somalia, the majority of refugees recognize that, despite limitations, life in Dadaab offers a sense of security and access to social services currently unattainable in their homeland. Despite the harshness of camp life and the social danger inherent in aligning with NGO agendas, refugees appreciate many of the services provided by UNHCR and its implementing partners. According to one middle-aged Somali man:

> [Although] we live in a trouble life, I think [between] Somalia and here in Dadaab, Dadaab region is best because there in Somalia there is war going on and there is no free education. But here, there is free education and security is up to date.

Indeed, time after time refugees explained that they remain in Dadaab in order to access free education, clean water, and security. As one Sudanese block leader reported (and many informants echoed), "My living environment is very hot and is difficult to live in, but we will have patience because we got many things that we hadn't when we were staying [in] our country like free education, peace, health care and also food." Refugees' statements of appreciation appear across generation, gender, and ethnicity. Many note that they might have returned to Somalia or sought alternative sites of hostel if it were not for "a way of pursuing education [for] the young generation" available at Dadaab. Somalis who complete schooling in Dadaab have educational qualifications superior to those of the vast majority of their fellow nationals who remain in Somalia, especially among women. Accordingly, as one student researcher summarized, "being a refugee did not waste the time of some individuals who have gotten free education up to [a] level they could not [in] their homeland." Similarly, although imperfect, refugees report that camp life affords a higher level of security than currently available in Somalia. Although rape and banditry presented significant problems in the early years of the camp's establishment (and certainly persisted at the time of our study), Kenyan police and agency workers have achieved a reduction in incidences of crime.

Appreciation for and critical evaluation of camp management are not mutually exclusive, as one Somali elder's succinct reply to a student researcher's questioning reveals. The elder explained:

> the life in the camp is not good because we are not given maximum free will to go to any other part of the country. We have got good security and education, which are not available in my war torn country.

While refugees critique the provision of services on many levels, most do not embrace a hard-line traditionalism. Rather, they reveal in-depth knowledge about the sociopolitical complexities of the region and creatively weave Western-derived human rights discourse with Muslim inspired ideals. Refugees are particularly resentful of the Kenyan government's policy to restrict refugee movement across the Kenyan-Somali border and within Kenya. Refugees of all classes, genders, ethnicities, and ages view the restriction of movement as an egregious human rights abuse.

Abdi, a student researcher, focused his project upon refugee perceptions of the ban on movement. His interviews, first with a 28-year-old Ethiopian woman and then 25-year-old Somali man, poignantly capture the refugee critique:

Abdi (A):	How do you perceive the restriction personally?
Ethiopian Woman (EW):	I perceive it as unfair action.
(A):	Why is it unfair?
(EW):	We were given eyes and limbs by God so that we can move and look for better life and future. But now we have been deprived of that natural right and kept as prisoners.

(A): Whom do you blame for this?

(EW): I blame both the Kenyan government and the UNHCR.

(A): If the restriction is placed by the government, why do you blame the UNHCR?

(EW): I blame the UNHCR because it is a refugee agency. This agency is supposed to advocate for refugees' rights, but it didn't.

(A): Why do you think the Kenyan government made the restriction?

(EW): It is meant to stop security threats and to ensure national interests.

(A): What does the government mean by security threats?

(EW): The security threats claimed are: smuggling of arms and opiums and also criminal activities.

(A): What about national interests?

(EW): According to the government, it is illegal for refugees to intermingle with Kenyan citizens and share the businesses and job opportunities.

(A): Has Kenya every experienced any threats of security from refugees?

(EW): I have never heard of such news, really. Even if some crimes have been committed by some individuals, it is not justice to punish the whole refugees. In any given community, there are crimes and even Kenyans do commit many crimes. I dare say it is a groundless phobia.

(A): Has the restriction affected you personally?

(EW): Yes, of course. Since I am unable to move anywhere and look for a way to my goal of higher education, I have succumbed to this miserable life and am compelled to marry. Now I am a mother of a child, a desperate mother and I will have more children to get more kilograms of corn. That is all.

(A): What do you suggest to solve this problem?

(EW): Oh! My suggestion doesn't help. I am a mere voiceless refugee. No one will hear and accept my suggestion. According to

> Kenyans' belief, I am inferior. I'd rather
> pray to my God to free me from this prison.

In her searing critique, Abdi's interviewee both reveals knowledge of the rationale and consequences of a restriction on movement and adopts a human rights discourse to mark it as an abuse. She positions the UNHCR as complicit in the abuse, given its assigned task of safeguarding refugee rights. Abdi's interviewee's appropriation of human rights language equipped her to offer informed critique of supposed security threats and Kenyan national interests. Her poignant appraisal of agency and governmental policy differs substantially from traditionalist concerns and represents an effort to make sense of and negotiate the context of Dadaab. Similarly, her invocation of gender distances her from traditionalist sentiments. For Abdi's interviewee, marriage and motherhood represent a disappointing outcome to which she had to "succumb" given a dearth of opportunities for education. Rather than passively accept her fate, however, she regards her childbearing ability as a compensatory (and survival) strategy to increase rations.

Abdi's second interviewe, who met with Abdi following the announcement of heightened enforcement of prohibitions against refugee movement between the three camps, demonstrates similar fluency in empowerment discourse and offers another critical reading of Dadaab's political landscape:

Abdi (A):	What tightened the restriction today?
Somali Man (SM):	They say it is because of insecurity.
(A):	What is meant by insecurity?
(SM):	I suppose it is a fear which arises from the present situation in Somalia.
(A):	Has the Kenyan government ever experienced danger from your fellow refugees?
(SM):	I have never heard such news. This claim of insecurity is just a pretext. There may be other fears apart from the dangers which come from only Somali refugees. If this large number of our people are allowed to move freely this would probably create pressure on the citizens, they will share their job opportunities.
(A):	Do you think this measure is fair?
(SM):	Absolutely it is unfair and it is against human rights. Here I want to uncover something, this treatment which is confined us in this camp is not applied in Kakuma (a camp in western Kenya that

houses mostly Sudanese refugees). This also shows me that religion also matters. Those of Kakuma have been issued ID cards apart from mandates they had which enables them to move. The majority is Christian and on the other hand, here the Muslims are the majority. So, it forces someone who thinks to ask a question of why Muslims and Christians are not equally treated.

(A): What do you think are the refugee agency's perspectives about the restriction?

(SM): The refugee agencies' perspectives are obvious; they like it very much because if the refugees are not kept in the camps, the flow of donation would stop, many projects would close down and hundreds of Kenyans would be subject to redundancy.

The young man interviewed by Abdi debunks the rationale offered for the restriction on refugee movement. He points to a nationalist desire to safeguard employment opportunities as the policy's impetus on the part of the Kenyan government. Like Abdi's first interviewee, his second invoked human rights discourse even as he claimed religious discrimination in comparative analysis with Kakuma Refugee Camp. In doing so, he critically appraised regional, national, and indeed international political contexts in which much attention has been placed upon relations between Christians and Muslims. Finally, he scrutinized the relationship between Dadaab's existence and the UNHCR's survival, highlighting the requisite of a refugee crisis for the provision of jobs for Kenyan nationals and procurement of funds for the UNHCR. His disdain for governmental and agency efforts was not based upon a desire for cultural preservation, but rather emerged out of a nuanced sociopolitical reading of the camp context.

In addition to the restriction on movement, the amount and type of biweekly food rations generated profound critique. Refugees lament the inadequate supply of food given the prohibition on agricultural production and herding. In order to supplement rations and diversify diets, refugees in Dadaab turn to the black market where rations can be sold for cash to purchase meat, dairy, or vegetables. Informal market zones skirt all distribution sites and attract Kenyan nationals from the region who come to buy low cost foodstuffs by the truckloads, transport them to other towns, and resell them at higher prices. While incentive workers or marketplace shop owners may supplement rations with meager incomes, a poor family of eight may sell the equivalent of two members' rations to procure milk for children. The following interview of a middle aged male refugee by a student researcher presents common critiques of food distribution:

Tenagne (T):   Is the ration you get from WFP enough to sustain life well in the camps? Why?

Informant (I):   No, the ration they give us is not enough not even to one person. We took it just only not to die. It is even very funny to be asked such questions. It is a joke for me.

(T):   Can you harvest or cultivate grains in the camps? Why?

(I):   No, I think the Kenyan government doesn't allow us to cultivate grains on their lands.

(T):   How do you describe life in the camps?

(I):   Life in the camps is very harsh. We cannot get enough food; we cannot get work; we cannot move from place to place as you want. I feel that I am in [a] detention center. The climate is harsh, there are a lot of hardships in the camps.

One afternoon, Rachel attended food distribution in Mooro with Hussein, a Kenyan-Somali manager at CARE. The Mooro food distribution center is a massive, open-air wooden structure near the CARE compound and secondary school. The space is divided by wire fencing into three sections: a waiting area, distribution lanes, and long exit hallway. Once through the stifling and labyrinthine waiting area, refugees who produce proper ration cards file into aisles according to family size. Along the aisles, incentive workers take turns scooping staple foods into the large sacs carried by refugees. The distribution process takes days to complete.

On that particular afternoon, an older Somali woman leaned over a small, lit stove near the entrance to the distribution center. Hussein explained that the woman was employed by the agency to demonstrate proper ways to prepare bulgar. He explained that many Somalis don't know how to cook the grain. During his explanation, an older Somali woman approached Rachel holding a small handful of it. With a pained expression, she spoke rapid and concerned Somali while gesturing demonstratively at her stomach. Hussein translated that people in the community claim bulgar makes them sick and admitted that, if he were a refugee, he too would sell rations to acquire flour, rice, or pasta. According to Hussein, bulgar and maize are made available in aid situations so that the U.S. government can subsidize U.S. farmers without breaking international trade law. At the same time, he noted that the United States stands apart from its European counterparts in the amount and frequency of food donations.

Agency representatives like Hussein are well aware of the widespread complaints surrounding food distribution as well as of the unregulated exchange that takes place in broad daylight outside of the distribution facilities. However, given that most major donor governments supply foodstuffs instead of cash, the WFP has little leeway in selecting what is provided refugees. Refugee preferences as well as strategic efforts to support local agriculture are only taken into consideration with regard to the small percentage of monetary donations.

During our time in Dadaab, rumors circulated that the UNHCR intended to distribute complementary food items, such as vegetables, in addition to standard bulk rations. The complementary distributions failed to materialize and came instead to symbolize oft-mentioned shortcomings of the agency: a tendency to tie up earmarked funding in bureaucratic red tape or lose it to institutional corruption. Indeed, interviews with refugees featured accusations of corruption and mismanagement on the part of both the UNHCR and its implementing partners. Such accusations spanned sectors and services just as they targeted refugee incentive workers. One charge centered on the allocation of water between residential blocks. In the following excerpt, a student researcher interviewed one Somali block leader on issues pertinent to CARE's Water and Environmental Sanitation (Watesan) sector:

Halima (H):	How do you see the role of the Watesan [sic] sector in giving water to the refugees.
Block Leader (BL):	Er, when you ask me how I see it, I have a problem in answering because there are different and opposing ideas that not only us but also the community we lead have about the agency, or … sector.
(H):	But it is this different attitudes I am interested in knowing.
(BL):	Well, first we are grateful to the sector for providing us with water and managing the water distribution. But we also hear and even witness a lot of mismanagement. Bad administration, I think is the cause.
(H):	What are some of this mismanagement you are talking about?
(BL):	There is water scarcity in many blocks. I am sure you have seen or have been told what is happening in blocks like D1 and D2. Sometimes people do not get enough water through day and night but on other times the taps run all night and stop in the morning and it is wrong to …
(H):	I am sorry to interrupt you, but why do you say it is wrong?

(BL):   Considering the security level in the camp, which even though it is better than it used to be, cannot be said is safe. It is wrong to let taps run at night and stop it at day time. This is so bad for women who fetch most water for their families.

 (H):   What do you think is the main cause of this scarcity and what excuse does the sector give to you as the community leaders?

(BL):   Us, the community leaders have had several meetings with the Watesan officials and they always promise to do something, but they never came round to significant actions.

 (H):   What do you attribute this inadequate water supply to? Poor administration or what?

(BL):   Yes, I believe poor management is the cause but there are also rumors that say [refugee] workers sell the petrol that is supposed to be used in the water engines.

 (H):   Are these just empty rumors or are there some facts in it? Any evidence you have for these allegations?

(BL):   I personally have never witnessed or seen a worker doing that so am not that sure; but, I do believe in these stories because I do not see how else can the water be scarce all the time.

Halima's conversation with the block leader demonstrates the ways in which refugees tenuously balance appreciation for and frustration with services provided in Dadaab. At the same time, it highlights the efforts of refugees, and in this case one refugee leader, to make sense out of water scarcity. When confronted with the inequitable flow of water from different taps, the block leader cited "mismanagement," "bad administration," and theft from incentive workers. Though he was unable to draw upon direct evidence to incriminate refugees of resource diversion, notions of mismanagement and corruption allowed the leader to understand the problems refugees experience in receiving necessary services and supplies.

What is of note for our purposes, however, is that displeasure with agencies stems from practical anxiety about the allotment of resources rather than from traditionalist concerns. Indeed, the majority of refugees navigating Dadaab's polarity seek out designated avenues to launch complaints and gain representation among the agencies. Rather than reject institutionalized outlets for participation, refugees, particularly those educated in Dadaab schools, voice their frustrations and accusations to agency staff in the language of empowerment and individual rights. In the above scenario, the block leader described having several meetings with sector officials. Indeed, agency staff in Dadaab spends a significant portion of work time in meetings with representatives from the refugee community—groups of elders, elected block leaders, or school Parent Teacher Associations (PTAs). Formal structures of governance in each camp include leaders elected at the block level as well as a head camp "chairman" and "chairlady." Block leaders and PTA members are unpaid volunteers. However, they nonetheless work to represent constituents on both logistical and cultural issues.

Not all groups who access agencies do so in order to register complaint. According to agency staff, school PTAs represent one of the most successful venues for participation in camp management and grassroots activism. Many cite PTAs as a principal engine for effecting increased participation rates in school among refugee girls. Parents in our study proudly recalled their work in school PTAs:

Student (S): For how long have you been working as PTA?
Parent (P): I work as a PTA for 10 years.
(S): Do you get salary for work as a PTA?
(P): No, I do not get salary, I am volunteer for the welfare of our children.
(S): Does the parent respect you?
(P): Yes, they respect me because I am working for the good of their children. I am also coordinating issues concerning their children from the teachers and parents.

In 2008, CARE staff showed us several newly built community secondary schools that PTAs and other refugee leaders constructed with their own energies and resources to accommodate the increasing number of primary school graduates whose exit exam grades do not qualify them for entrance in Dadaab's increasingly selective high schools, but who desire further education. In these community schools, refugees collectively hire and pay teachers, often graduates from official camp schools, from money pooled independent of from aid agencies. PTAs that work to achieve increased access to schooling for girls as well as the peaceful integration of ethnic communities often include members of mixed background and educational level. With the specific responsibility of mediating between traditionalist and agency interests, chairpersons are also influential members of the Dadaab community. Safi, a Form Four student, interviewed a former chairlady in Qafis about her term in office. Evoking human rights lexicon, the woman explained, "My role was to fight the right of refugee and tell their problem about the NGOs."

By acting as mediators, many of the PTA members, block leaders, and chairpersons counter traditionalist efforts to reject agencies out-of-hand. Indeed, not only do elected leaders express refugee concerns, but many also partner with agencies to share pertinent messages with the wider populace. Members of the refugee community strive to affect agency decision-making processes in which refugees typically have minimal control by participating in the structures of representative leadership. Despite efforts, however, such outlets for representation are often deemed ineffectual. One block leader reported that he had grown tired of what he declared to be "empty promises" from the agencies. When outlets provided for representation are found to be inadequate, refugees engage civically to claim rights, again using a language of empowerment. Communities converge to coordinate active political resistance, demand meetings with agency leadership, and even organize widespread strikes among incentive workers.

Our 2007 stay in Dadaab coincided with one such major strike in the education sector in which workers demanded better wages, claiming that agencies had gone back on an earlier promise to raise salaries. On account of the strike, all of the primary schools in the camp closed for a number of weeks. As tensions continued to escalate, incentive workers in other sectors joined the strike. The demonstration had tremendous impact on the functioning of the camps, as Kenyan staff struggled to compensate for the absence of incentive workers. Further, it attracted the attention of Kenyan national newspapers and the international media, including the BBC. In the end, several meetings and negotiations led to compromise and primary schools were reopened. In the interim, however, students missed several weeks of instruction and faced mandatory school attendance on the weekends for the rest of the term. The strike during our visit was not a precedent; rather, refugees in Dadaab have historically held several significant demonstrations for varying demands. Such political activism—buttressed by an appropriation of human rights discourse—represents one major tactic refugees in the middle use to navigate between polarities of empowerment and traditionalism.

Conclusion

Actors in the Dadaab refugee camps negotiate a landscape ordered by a countervailing polarity between localized, time-and-space specific brands of enlightenment and traditionalism. Refugee stances toward schooling serve as navigational touchstones—self-conscious efforts to stake out a location in relation to the dominant binary. For girls and women in particular, decision-making is painfully visible and high-stakes. Girls and young women's very enrollment in schooling represents a significant move away from mainstream enactments of Somali traditionalism in Dadaab and an embrace of gender change.

NOTES

1. According to the U.S. Department of State, the rate of HIV/AIDS among refugees in Dadaab is 1.2% (U.S. Department of State, 2010, http://www.state.gov/g/prm/142294.htm).
2. Student researchers used the terms *elder* and *traditionalist* synonymously. While the assumption that an elder will align with the traditionalist worldview reflects the reality that most of the older generation in Dadaab has not been able to access formal education and therefore tends to be less Westernized, it does not preclude the significant population of youth in Dadaab who also share traditionalist ideals. Nor, does it discount the much smaller percentage of elders who pioneered some of the activities associated with change in the camps, such as first enrolling their daughters in school.

CHAPTER 5

SOMALI REFUGEE GIRLS AND WOMEN IN SCHOOL

Marriage is optional. What's compulsory is education.
—Asha, Primary School Teacher and Refugee at Dadaab

[My family] doesn't want me to go to school. They see it [as a] shame [for] young girls to go out of the house.

–Somali Girl in Dadaab

NGOs in Dadaab enroll 39,550 students (CARE 2007) in six nursery, 17 primary, and three secondary schools (UNHCR 2005). Participation, performance, and retention levels within the camps, however, are deeply gendered. While nursery school enrolment through class three is 1.3 girls for every one boy, subsequent years witness a marked decrease in female participation. By Class Three, only one girl is enrolled per every six boys. Overall, the population of primary schools is 61% male to 39% female. The gap widens still more at the secondary level where only 19% of the student body is female (CARE 2007). Of the 40% of Somali children currently out of school, 70% are girls.

—UNHCR (2005)

In Dadaab, Somali refugees find hostel in a landscape dominated by the countervailing forces of enlightenment and traditionalism. As we have seen, regardless of sex, refugees' perspectives on schooling indicate the location they occupy in relation to the binary. For girls and young women, the act of enrolling in school has a similar, if more public and controversial purpose. As Asha's words suggest, for Somali girls and women, participation in schooling serves as a key marker of gender difference, negotiation, and change within the displaced Somali community.

Traditionalism and Girls' and Women's Schooling

The women in our study, who plainly advocated for girls' and women's education and made personal choices to reflect such a commitment, did so with a clear understanding that traditionalists strongly disapprove of their decisions. Nasro explained:

> Some community members have negative attitudes towards girls going to school, and they encourage our parents not to send us to school, but our parents are turning deaf ears…. Some are traditionalists and are strict to their culture. Some say school spoils culture. Some think school promotes pre-marital sex which is unlawful in Muslim religion.

Often traditionalism, illustrated in generalized attitudes regarding women's education, was articulated as *the* dominant perspective within the Somali community. As Ayaan, a Form Four student, wrote in an essay, "In our community they value marriage more than education. They believe that a girl should exercise early marriage so that they don't ashame their parents. The parents prefer boys [be] given more opportunity than girls." Ayaan's words suggest the main reasons why schooling is seen as a male prerogative has to do with expectations held for girls and women. Women are obliged to maintain virginity, earn a bride price for their families, and remain within the domestic realm first in their own families and later in the homes of their husbands. Given these prospects, the idea that a girl would venture out of the home and into school, where she would interact with boys and thus bring her virginity into in question, invites shame.

Anti-schooling attitudes were instantiated in the lives of community members the Form Four women interviewed during the course of their research. Indeed, the impact of early marriage practices on girls' enrollment levels is so well known there are references to it throughout the student-gathered data. The following is an excerpt from an interview with a Windle Trust student:

Interviewer: How does your husband, father, mother, sisters, brothers, and children feel about you going to

school? If they want you to go to school, why? If
not, for what reason?

Windle Trust Student: No, they don't want me to go to school. They
see it [as a] shame [for] young girls to go out of
the house.

Community members repeatedly identified early marriage as a barrier to
girls' educational access. Rashid, an advanced Windle Trust student,
interviewed a Form Four leaver:

Rashid: What do you think caused the low enrollment
levels among girls and women in Dadaab
schools?

Form Four Leaver: There are various reasons. Some girls are married in early age. Some parents see that it's
unimportant to educate girls. Some of them
believe if girls go to school they will adopt bad
behaviors.

Through student research, we discover that early marriage practices
both preclude many girls' initial enrollment and account for high dropout
rates among pubescent female students. One of the Form Four girls talked
with a father who had sent his daughter to school until she was marriageable, at which point he withdrew her:

Form Four Girl: Why do you like your daughter to finish up to
primary level?

Father: Because my daughter would be married [to] a
man who would be the person responsible for
her and he would work for her. She will remain
home as a housewife who can manage. Her
education [is] only her house and her children
i.e. reading information, checking her children's books (whether they learn or not), and
so on ... I believe women are weak by nature so
I prefer my daughter to stay at home [and]
keep her children as her mother [does].

As student research suggests, girls' and women's ability to attend school
is most often in the hands of older men in the community. In an interview
with the mother of a young woman who currently attends university,
researcher Dahabo engaged in the following discussion.

Dahabo (D):   When you were a child, who made the decision that you wouldn't attend school?

Mother (M):   My father had totally refused me going to school.

(D):   What was your mother's decision towards your father?

(M):   She was unhappy but she couldn't do anything about that.

Student researcher Kalifa spoke with another refugee who had been denied the opportunity to go to school. Madina is a young girl, aged 15, who lives with her parents. Her parents never took her to school and she stayed at home doing domestic work. Instead, Madina prepared food for her brothers when they came from school:

Kalifa (K):   Do you go to school? Why?

Madina (M):   No, because I am the only daughter in my family and I do the domestic [work].

(K):   Do all your brothers go to school?

(M):   Yes, they do.

(K):   How do you feel [that] all of your brothers go to school and you don't?

(M):   I feel discriminated [against].

(K):   Did you ever talk to your parents about taking you to school?

(M):   Yes, I talked them and they told that girls and women are supposed to be at their houses and not go out.

(K):   Did they ever tell the reasons as to why girls and women are not allowed to go out?

(M):   Yes, they told me that girls will bring a shame to the family.

In conversations between the female students and various community members, we learn about the ways in which power is maintained and reproduced within the community through evocation of traditionalism. We discover that decision-making power in the community largely lies with men, a reality of which female students are unanimously aware. The following interview occurred between Luul, a Form Four student, and a mother whose sons attended school but whose daughters remained at home:

Luul (L):   Why not girls?

Mother (M):   Because their father has refused.

(L):   What did you do when their father refused?

(M):   I could not do anything at all. On the other hand, there wasn't anybody else that I have told this issue.

(L): Did you discuss the matter with your neighbors?
(M): Yes, but it wasn't fruitful.

Still, the discourse of empowerment supplies a language with which members of the refugee community, especially girls, are able to complain about the inequities of opportunity afforded men and women. Student interviews with more traditionalist-identified families reveal that the discourse of civil rights and its concomitant conception of discrimination have permeated refugees' consciousness. Luul continued her conversation with the young mother:

(L): Who made the decision that you should marry?
(M): My parents.
(L): When you were married how did your family feel about your marriage?
(M): Despite my dismay they were very happy since they took a lot of cattle from the man they forced me with.
(L): How have you felt about this forced marriage?
(M): I really felt very bad and assumed that my parents sold me as a commodity for trade.
(L): Why have you been forced with your husband?
(M): I was forced because I was schooling and I was not ready to get married till I finish my studies.
(L): Which level have you reached before you dropped out school?
(M): I was standard eight and I was preparing for the national examination (KCPE).
(L): Why don't you pursue your education while you are still a wife of some body?
(M): I felt shy and I could not attend a class while everybody is aware of my status.
(L): Why don't you try to inform these problems to the agencies?
(M): I feel shy of problems being known to everybody.

Girls who have been denied an education framed their fate as representative of power abuses and injustice. While it is entirely clear that men in the community hold the majority of power, the discourse of rights at the very least provides a language with which girls are able to articulate lived inequities. Indeed, the prevalence of the idea that girls' opportunities and life courses are determined by men versus the idea that such decisions should be shared among mothers and fathers or be placed in the

Figure 5.1.   A typical primary school classroom in Dadaab (Kanyi).

Figure 5.2.   Student reading aloud (Kanyi).

Figure 5.6.   Female students develop close bonds (Kanyi).

Figure 5.7.   The number of female students drops precipitously at the upper primary and lower secondary levels (Buck & Silver).

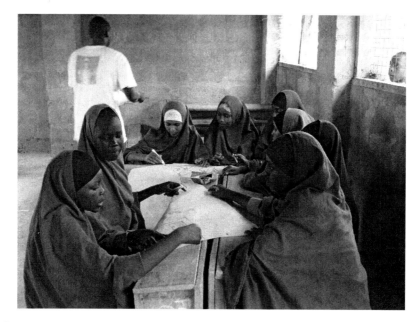

Figure 5.8.   Sex segregation within classrooms is commonplace (Kanyi).

Figure 5.9.   Upper secondary classrooms have few remaining female students (Kanyi).

hands of individual girls themselves animates interviews, girls' understanding of the context in which they live, and, indeed the camp itself.

A Community in Flux

Student writing and interviews feature disagreement over who should have decision-making authority in the family and community. Kalifa, the head girl in one Form Four class etched out the opposing positions:

> (Some believe) [w]omen's role is in the kitchen, [to] look after children and take care of her husband's property. Some insisted on that point while others think democratically, saying that women have the ability even to take part in politics and advocate for her rights.

Dahabo, a Form Four student, explained:

> the community has multiple perspectives about women's role in the society; some believe women's role is only keeping children and staying [home]; some other might have different idea and think they are supposed to do as men. They have the rights as men.

Another student noted:

> Mostly, in our culture a girl is supposed to be married at the age of 15 years. But these days girls are given the same rights [as] boys. Girls are also taken to school to be taught a lot and get an education like a boy. This gave room [for] a lot more girls to be in school and successfully helped them.... In today's society girls are more advanced than before. However, there are few people who don't [agree with] that.

In a more extended excerpt, Rashid, an advanced Windle Trust student who chose to research girls' and women's education for his individual project topic, depicted the divisive nature of the topic within the Somali refugee community:

> Many people disagree [with] sending girls to schools. [They] consider the matter from different angles: religiously and traditionally. Particularly, the Somali community practices the Islamic religion. They believe girls are fit to study at home in order to be well disciplined. They will also not get a chance to meet with the guys who [would] change their minds. These guys always convince the girls to follow them. Suddenly, you hear many daughters were taken away or were eloped. On the contrary there is another arguable issue that girls are trained in schools to adopt public speaking skills which totally opposes the Islamic religion. A Muslim girl is neither allowed to appear in front of a crowd nor is she permitted her voice to be heard publicly.

There are more issues that do not concern religion. Some people argue that girls do not deserve to get an education. Because when they adopt sharing the idea with men in schools, or they see other girls leading people and giving orders, then they will disobey their husbands and try to be the leaders of their families. This will result [in] family destruction. So, to avoid it, they better stay at home. The argument engulfs the whole community. There are three groups. The first one says, we do not want to abandon our religion and disobey a single order of it. The second one argues [that] we won't leave off our culture because we had been practicing on it for centuries and nothing had gone wrong with it. While the third group describes that girls get encouragement from the NGOs, which they [had] not gotten previously, so as to participate in community development and the economic recovery.

In the same manner, a lot of members in the society consider different issues. It is realized that women play a very important role in the community but when can this happen? Are we supposed to educate girls when they are young? They should also get support and encouragement from their parents. Then, they will become a crucial part among the community and participate in the economic growth. Initially, men used to work and earn the family needs but nowadays you see mothers working while fathers are jobless. Or in some cases you see both the father and mother going to work and earning enough money for the family. It will facilitate for them to develop small business, which may grow quickly and sometime later the family becomes independent. Girls who also complete their studies help their parents by doing different kinds of jobs. Therefore, it can be described as great factor that can develop their families and children. They like to go to schools.

Rashid, an educated man who did not hesitate to indicate a preference for girls' inclusion in schools, offers a sophisticated analysis that anticipates the various rationales underlying Dadaab's brand of traditionalism. In doing so, he intentionally disentangles religion and culture (or Islam and *xeer*)—two of the primary elements that comprise Somali traditionalism in all of its historic manifestations. His choice to distinguish religion from culture, so often conflated in discussions of what it means to be Somali, enables him to better understand the specificities of opposition to girls' schooling—be it that their mixing with boys in class represents a breach of Islamic sensibilities, a fear that potential challenges to male dominance in the home upsets cultural continuity, or simply that women's schooling exemplifies yet another detrimental neocolonial intrusion.

At the same time, Rashid acknowledges that in Dadaab, economic pragmatism has become a tremendously salient factor in deciding whether or not to enroll a daughter. For, in a context where a family cannot rely upon herding or legal trading as a way of life, they must turn toward new means of production to survive. One of these new means includes wage-labor with the NGOs, even if wages are barely a pittance.

Access to incentive positions demands education and, as such, the more educated and employable members in a family, the more likely said family is able to supplement rations, build a better shelter—in short, survive the harsh conditions of refugee life. The institutionalization of affirmative action in agency hiring policy underscores this point, proving that having educated girls can better position a family economically. Thus, as an educated male, a potential mediator, or at least translator, between traditionalist elders and the community formed around school, Rashid works to prove the very concept of traditionalism flexible, applied, context-specific, and adaptable.

Hassan, another advanced student who did research on women's and girls' education, spoke with Fardous, a secondary student. Fardous shared her views on community division. Hassan described:

> She [a community member who had not attended school] openly told me that some of them [community] who were educated were feeling happy because they knew that if a girl is educated, she will be able to help herself as well as [her] community. Although most of [the] community thinks that if a girl goes to school she will be destroyed or otherwise become a prostitute. Furthermore, her community said that "a woman should be in grave otherwise should be in custody of her husband."

As Rashid illustrates, discussion of girls' and women's schooling in Dadaab helps to gauge the spectrum of beliefs among Dadaab's refugees. For some, educated women are distinct economic (and communal) assets. Again, however, the discursive pull of the camps' particular construct of traditionalism emerges in the perception that girls' enrollment in school is a source of their degradation and defilement (both through exposure to Western ideas and at the hands of members of the opposite sex). Hassan and Rashid's writing also demonstrates, however, how well positioned both male and female educated students are to diagram Dadaab's complex, and often divided, sociocultural topography.

Families Divided

In their research, students found that divisions within the community were often mirrored in divisions within families. Students described situations where one parent, often the mother, wanted to send a daughter to school while the other, usually the father, refused. One interviewee reflected on her own family dynamic, "My mother was with me but she was powerless because my father is a dictator man, and you can't refuse whatever he tells you." Many other school-going girls explained how their mothers were able to persuade their fathers to enroll them. The following excerpt is from a conversation between Kalifa, a Form Four girl, and another female secondary school student:

<blockquote>

Kalifa:	When you were a child who made the decision that you would go to school?
Secondary Student:	My mother made the decision first to my father then he hesitated, saying he will never take his daughter to school because it is not important since she will get married. Then my mother, after a long discussion, told him that educating girls is like educating a whole nation.

</blockquote>

In a different conversation, Ayaan, another Form Four student, interviewed a primary school girl:

<blockquote>

Primary Student (PS):	Our tradition doesn't allow girls for education.
Ayaan (A):	Why? And what reason?
(PS):	Girls have to be married early so that the family [can] get bride price for their daughters.
(A):	How did your father overcome the Somali tradition?
(PS):	You know as time goes, tradition goes, so my father came to know the importance of education and later he agreed.
(A):	Has your mother had the same idea as your father?
(PS):	No, she had different idea from that of my father.
(A):	What was her idea?
(PS):	Her idea was girls for education and equal right-for both gender.

</blockquote>

While each of these conversations highlights families in which fathers were successfully convinced to send their daughters to school, according to participants, such a resolution was more the exception than the rule. Parents who do choose to send their daughters to school face harassment by opponents of girls' education. This is especially true for mothers who raise their children without husbands due to death or divorce. One Form Four student asked a mother about the "problems [she] faced from the community, family, and friends as a result of taking [her] daughter to school." The mother replied:

> Culturally, girls are not supposed to be taken to school, so when I decided to take my daughter I was abused and harassed. They kept on calling us "the

parent of the prostitute." Even our close family friend ran away. The whole community kept on telling us that we should remove her from school because it is shame for a girl whose breast have started appearing to go school. Instead, she should be married. On the way to school I am supposed to escort her so that she should not be beaten. Some people even throw stones in our compound.

During the time of our study, violence and complete ostracization of families of school-going girls were waning, as educating daughters had become more commonplace and, for economic reasons, increasingly practical. However, stereotypes about schoolings' negative impact on girls persist and with them very real barriers to girls' successful participation.

Obstacles to Academic Success

For girls who do enroll in school, attaining success is difficult. Boys consistently outperform girls in Dadaab. Female students easily articulate the ways in which traditional cultural tenets and practices form barriers to their academic success. Cultural and sometimes economic factors inhibit their ability to compete with boys on an equal playing field. In an interview, Rashid asked Ardo, a Form Four leaver, why she did not succeed in finishing secondary school at the top of her class. He summarized her reply:

There are many factors that contributed [to Ardo] not ... becoming number one. One, she said that she does a lot of household chores that she may even forget to study. She also said that it was worthwhile to mention that if [a] girl interacts or associates with [a] male teacher or student in order to gain knowledge or understanding a question, then, people will say she is a prostitute o[r] [in a] relationship with that person. Hence girls avoid interactions [with] teachers and male students. Therefore, in that scenario girls are confined in that culture vacuum. The girls also have low self esteem ... that they value themself very low or very dirty that they cannot do better than boys and they also have problems like menstruation period that they cannot come to school everyday as the boys do.... She told me that there are many factors [explaining why] the girls are poorly performing in Kenya Certificate of Primary Education (KCPE). This is because the girls do a lot of the household chores when they are staying at home and they don't get a chance to study. The boys are studying at home peacefully. In addition to that she said that girls are also getting married while they are in primary and become pregnant.... Early marriage is a threat to girl child education.

Rashid's conversation touches upon some of the cultural and institutional factors impeding widespread academic success for girls and women. Cultural barriers to girls' enrollment, retention, and performance in Dadaab include: the burden of domestic responsibility, restriction of movement, early marriage, female circumcision and related menstrual complications, minority status in the classroom, treatment by male classmates, and lack of widespread community support. While some girls do succeed and perform competitively with male counterparts, the academic performance of the vast majority of female students suffers. Differentials in educational participation and performance between boys and girls highlight tensions in the interplay between Somali culture and girls' schooling.

The Burden of Domestic Responsibilities

Girls and women unanimously cite domestic responsibility as a primary barrier to school participation and success. Although some girls note changing patterns, the burden of domestic chores in a family is borne almost exclusively by girls and women. The vast majority of school-going girls cook breakfast for their families before school, prepare lunch during the mid-day break, and return home in the afternoon to fetch water, make dinner, do dishes, wash clothes, set up sleeping areas, and sweep the family compound before being allowed to study. Their brothers and male classmates, on the other hand, are given considerable freedom to spend afternoons and evenings as they wish. A primary school student repeats an oft spoken lament about the disparity between boys' and girls' domestic responsibilities:

> There are quite [a] number [of barriers] I face, mostly being the housework. This is [such a] burden and [you] will see yourself busy the whole day and this will obviously effect my attendance [in] school and this is also another reason why girls perform poorly compared to boys. Because in our community, the Somalis, it is shame for a boy to do the housework while a girl is there, so boys will get the free time to revise for their books.... [L]ike even when it is school days I feel pity when I see boys revising and remaining in the school up to late hours, while me, as soon as the classes are [over], I will rush home to prepare supper or lunch depending on the time of the day. So this is also lowering us as girls and it is very hard to change because this is the way of life of our community.

In addition to maintaining the domestic sphere, war-driven demographic shifts have necessitated that women supply an income, often as single heads of households. Newfound positioning as breadwinners, however, does not preclude women's exclusive responsibility for domestic work. As a result, mothers often work incentive jobs at the agencies or run small businesses in camp markets while daughters are increasingly accountable for cooking, cleaning, wash, fetching water, and childcare. Gardner (2004) writes of a similar situation among those who remain in Somalia:

> Where there is access to schooling, the true cost of the change in gender relations at [the] family level is paid for by daughters, for whom the chance of even attaining primary level education, already low before the war, significantly diminishes when their mother is the breadwinner and needs their assistance in the home. (p. 106)

According to one long-standing primary school teacher, female students in Dadaab between Classes Four and Six often drop out of school in order to supplement family incomes in the markets or to attend to younger siblings as their mother works outside of the home. Despite pressure from school staff, families in such situations name economic desperation as the impetus behind withdrawing girls from school. Payoff garnered in the long run from investment in girls' schooling cannot stave off immediate financial crisis.

Another strategy that families often use to cope with profound responsibility at the household level entails that the eldest daughter remain at home to care for her family while her younger siblings enroll in school. Such pattern of sacrifice among eldest daughters simultaneously guarantees immediate domestic assistance and maximizes a family's investment in education. Notably, many successful female students with whom we spoke benefit from this situation and, not necessarily having to cook and clean when they return home from school, are enabled supplementary study hours. Both of the two 2007 female WUSC recipients and many of the likely candidates in the upper levels of secondary used an exemption from household chores to focus exclusively on schoolwork. Given the increased probability for a girl to perform competitively when given time to study, such strategy represents a calculated effort to ensure future financial returns.

The headmaster of one primary school said that female students often do chores until midnight, at which time they collapse from the combined fatigue of school and housework. In such cases, girls may not have time to revise schoolwork in the evenings at all. Despite school personnel's cognizance of the responsibilities most girls face outside of the school sphere, girls reported often being punished by teachers for tardiness or failure to complete homework. At the same time, they described being chastised at home if they return later than usual in the evenings due to afternoon lessons or study sessions. As the primary school student interviewee describes above, many mothers believe that their daughters loiter in the market or outside of school in the afternoons rather than come immediately home to prepare supper.

Restriction of Movement

Even when or if girls finish domestic work in the evening, they are forbidden to leave their homes at night. During one focus group, participants described how girls' school marks are lower than boys because of domestic work as well as because of girls' inability to attend night prep sessions. They explained that boys often gathered in the evenings at school to collaborate, share ideas, and tutor each other. One teacher shared that in the months approaching the KCSE, boys often sleep at school to ensure a late night of studying where there is electricity and where male Form Four leavers often return to tutor their younger counterparts on challenging subjects. Girls, on the other hand, do not have time to collaborate and remain at home at night. Focus group participants explained that restrictions on nighttime movement in the camps exist largely as a precaution against instances of rape as well as due to culture condemnation of girls' free movement outside of households.

Without electricity at home, the majority of girls do not have sources of light by which to study after dark. Instead, they share kerosene lamps with their entire families who often lack financial means to fuel them unnecessarily. According to the girls, solar lamps or even rechargeable electric lamps provided by the agencies would allow them to revise at night after completion of household work without burdening family resources. For the time being, however, acquisition of lamps is largely class determined, and, as a result, girls who can afford them tend to out-perform girls who cannot.[1] Given their ability to move freely, boys in similar financial situations often pool resources to buy a lamp as a group. In such a case the lamp is left in a central location at which the boys gather to study. Girls, on the other hand, have to procure the means alone. Finally, given the limited number of books per classroom and the requirement that students share, girls are often unable to access books at all in their homes at night.

Early Marriage

Labeled a cultural requirement by some and an economic necessity by others, forced early marriage, as noted above, dramatically constrains girls' participation in schooling. Indeed, many informants designated it as the primary barrier to girls' education despite its illegality in Kenya and centrality in NGO campaigns against gender-based violence. The financial viability of early marriage is guaranteed by the future husband's payment of a bride price to the daughters' parents. For her part, the newlywed girl must join the husband's family and assume responsibility for his household. Once married, she can be required by her husband to withdraw from school or face shame and difficulty in school once pregnant. One interviewee described:

> Forced early marriage has led to the termination of so many young ladies and boys from school. When young ladies become pregnant their hope of attending classes declines as they feel ashamed of their classmates who fingerpoint them and assume as they are the laughing stock of class. Moreover, when the young boys marry at tender age they would be forced to cater for their family bill. Therefore, they are supposed to win the daily bread of their family which becomes impossible if they are in school.

Still, married boys are far more likely to remain in school than their female counterparts. As another student explained,

> Girls who are married get poor performance in exams [because of their] chronic absences in the school. Besides that, girls who are married are not given the chance to read their books and [are] always busy cooking the food, cleaning the compound, fetching water and also beautifying [for] her husband.

One teacher informed us that expectant and nursing girls at his school are exempted from certain school activities. Others, he explained, are only able to attend classes three days a week if their children fall sick. While camp schools such as his try to accommodate these students, academic performance among mothers undoubtedly suffers.

Since 2006, refugees have been subject to Kenyan law that declares forced marriage of a girl under 18 illegal. Equipped with such knowledge, many girls try to thwart parental attempts to arrange marriages while they remain in school. These attempts are not always successful. Sahra, a Form Four girl, related the story of her former classmate:

> From the beginning of the year 1999, I even remember an uncountable [number] of girls become school drop-outs when they were told to get married [to a] man. For instance the lady [with] whom we use to sit in one desk has left school after meeting pressure from her father when a man who wanted to marry her came to their house. After a few days the father told his daughter that you will no longer be in school and talk as boys do. You will get married to a man who came to me and is very much ready to arrange engagement for you. ["]My daughter, be happy and feel free. School has no value for you and it will only waste your time. The man is very rich and you will have a bright future with him.["] When she told me this as she was [crying]. After a long confusion and frustration I decided to include [myself in] the issue. We have gone to the police as to inform that issue to the local government. When her father accused me that I am igniting a fire between him and his daughter and my father told me that you should not interfere in an

issue which is not yours. The lady was married there and she left her school on that day.

Sahra's example is illuminating in that the girls attempted to employ Kenyan legal structures to resist a father's arrangement. Despite the unsuccessful result of their efforts, Sahra's story illustrates a shift in the ways daughters are able to respond to situations of early marriage, particularly in order to protect educational prospects. Just as girls themselves try to resist marriages, NGO education personnel maintain an informal policy to actively follow-up with female students who appear to be slated for early marriage. One acting headmaster explained that if a girl is suddenly absent from school, the classroom teacher informs the headmaster or deputy headmaster to investigate the situation. If suspicions of early marriage prove valid, the headmaster writes a letter to the education supervisor who in turn sends an NGO representative to the family for follow-up. Occasionally, as in Sahra's example, Kenyan police become involved and arrest the parents. Many such instances of intervention from the school community have successfully thwarted marriage and resulted in girls being allowed to remain in school. Successful examples become (in)famous and are often called upon to symbolize shifting community practices.

"Shyness" and Minority Status in the Classroom

In interviews with school personnel and teachers, girls were frequently described as "shy" and "tentative" class participants. While boys are aggressive and active learners, girls' shyness was cited with frustration as an impediment to academic success. For their part, girls took differing stances on the assertion of pathologic female shyness. Many Form Four students denied feeling timid in class and instead reported active participation, often debating with male classmates and even teachers on issues of gender. In particular, Form Four women excitedly recalled conversations and classroom debates on gender roles during the unit on Marjorie Oludhe Macgoye's (1986) novel *Coming to Birth*. They explained that debates reveal to their classmates, who feel like brothers, that they are equal learners and leaders. Many focus group participants shared how males and females in class help and tutor each other, sitting "side by side" over a math book. Finally, girls in the Mooro focus group explained that they like to compete with boys in class for marks, with the goal to one day surpass them in achievement.

At the same time, other interviewees expressed frustration at the treatment of girls in class as well as disappointment at hindrances to girls' competitiveness. The same group of Mooro students who focused upon their active class participation and eagerness to answer questions aloud admitted that other girls feel shy when called upon. These girls (some of whom were in the focus group itself) were reported to answer required questions but only reticently and sometimes while holding a book in front of their faces for fear of being laughed at by boys. According to the group, however, boys never laugh at each other.

Regardless, girls' purported shyness was attributed to cultural expectations for women's public behavior, the dramatically disproportionate number of girls to boys in the classroom, as well as the ways in which such numerical disjuncture favors boys' ability to participate. One morning, Rachel observed a Form Three math class. During this particular session the teacher explained geometric proofs to the class, asking questions intermittently during his lecture. While girls, who, as in all classrooms, sit entirely segregated from the boys in the front left corner, answered questions quietly under their breath, male students raised their hands, swayed them back and forth and beckoned loudly for the teacher's attention. Though Rachel noticed the teacher made a point of addressing both male and female sections of the classroom, only boys shouted aloud answers to his first series of questions. Finally, the teacher called upon a girl by name. As she began her explanation, male students projected their answers loudly over her. Quickly, the teacher faced the boys and announced, "You are not her," before he pivoted back to wait for her reply.

The class continued on as such until the teacher put a sample problem on the board and asked for a student to come up, solve it, and report steps taken to the class. An outspoken boy in the fourth row raised his hand and was called on. When the boy "taught" the class, he seemed to exclusively direct explanation to the boys and ask questions only of male students. In this case, despite the teacher's attempt to create space for girls' active class participation, male students partially thwarted his efforts through interruption, laughter, and ignoring their female classmates.

Female Circumcision and Resulting Menstrual Complications

Finally, the vast majority of girls interviewed reported tremendous pain during menstruation as a result of infibulation. Restriction of the vaginal opening as part of the female circumcision procedure practiced in Dadaab obstructs the flow of menstrual blood during a woman's period, resulting in painful blockages and infections. Due to the severity of pain, many girls reported remaining at home from school for up to one week per month and, as a result, miss one quarter of academic instruction. As Ayaan described:

> FGM[2] has a very [big] impact on us generally as girls. Because during menstruation period, girls cannot learn because of joint pain, back pain and also abdominal pain. Because of all these problems, girls don't attend during lessons and because of this they get lower marks than boys. During menstruation period they feel stress, hence [they] don't understand the lessons as per the boys.

While many female students announced that they did not plan to perform the same form of circumcision on their daughters, an estimated 90% of the girls and women currently in camp schools undergo infibulation and therefore likely experience painful menses. The very few who do not face constant harassment and teasing by peers.

Female Students' Understanding of Schooling in the Dadaab Context

Despite the controversy school enrollment stirs and the significant challenges and risks girls and women face as students, study participants spoke enthusiastically about the benefits associated with schooling. During our stay in Dadaab, we organized a focus group of female primary school teachers. In that meeting, Asha, who was significantly older than most of her female colleagues and one of the very few women we met at the camp to have been educated in Somalia, explained to the assembled group that her mother had sent her to school because she considered schooling to be an avenue of empowerment. In a lengthy soliloquy, Asha described what her mother had said to her when she enrolled in school, "I'm not an educated person, so I would like you to be the light of the future.... Encourage the rest of the women." According to her mother, as an educated woman, Asha could "turn around and teach other people and it would spread."

During that morning's gathering, in which a group of twelve Somali female educators sat in a circle to share perspectives and ideas, Asha seemed to realize her mother's wish. She talked at length about the value of girls' education as an avenue of empowerment, assessed the cultural and financial obstacles that girls and their families face in accessing educational opportunities, and concluded with an affirmation conveying the unqualified priority of girls' education. *"Marriage is optional,"* she asserted matter-of-factly. *"What's compulsory is education."*

In our work, we came to see that, like Asha, Somali female students and teachers at Dadaab are fully committed to the notion that schooling provides girls and women with greater life opportunities. Women expounded upon school's ability to equalize relations between men and women, offer an escape from ignorance, and provide a sense of discipline and order. They spoke glowingly of the first few girls on their blocks to bravely don the distinct school uniform and make the highly visible, daily trek down the sun baked, sand pathways to the school compound. When brought together to talk about school, groups of secondary students inevitably listed the names and current status of predecessors who had recently graduated. One might offer that Fawzia, who completed Form Four in 2004, was married with two children. Another would remember that Maryan was in Canada with Khadro on WUSC (World University of Canada) scholarships. And, that Nimo works for CARE as a translator. The women also relayed regrettable stories of close friends with whom they had started out in primary school but who had since been withdrawn by family members in order to be married.

Female students were curious about our levels of educational attainment and marital status. When Rachel told a gathering of Form Four girls that she had completed university, a silent pause was finally broken by a young woman appointed head girl of her class. Apparently struck by the closeness in age between Rachel and all of the gathered Form Four students, Kalifa reassured her classmates that, though not as far along the educational pathway as Rachel, their status as Form Four women still represented an accomplishment. "It is different for us," she noted and went on to list the obstacles women at Dadaab face that "slow their (school) progress." Heads nodded in agreement and another participant asked when Rachel planned to marry and have children. Rachel responded that she did not know when or if she would marry or have children. Again, women's heads nodded. Another from the group spoke up to say that she would "complete her studies" before turning to marriage. Heads nodded a final time in agreement. Attending school provides women with an alternative to early marriage and childbearing.

In their conversations about education, female students easily described the meaning they find in education. Without fail, discourse about school was peppered with generalized assertions correlating education with knowledge and worldliness and evoking a symbolic battle against ignorance. One woman in an upper intermediate English language class declared that "Education is key [to] the world." A girl making her way through primary school employed ornate language to capture her ardor. "It's impressive and delightful…. It's the one that's important to the entire life of person. Ignorance is blind, so education opens to the light." Suleha, a Form Four student, explained that school "helps me to become a responsible person, and it will take me from dark room to light room because education is like light."

When asked to speak in greater length and detail about the place of school in their lives, the women's descriptions fell into several subdomains: they believed that participation in schooling enhances the realization of basic civil rights, moral and character growth, and economic opportunity.

Civil (and Human) Rights

As many of the above narrative excerpts reveal, female students frequently allude to the notion that schooling provides knowledge of and greater access to civil rights. In one interview, a Form Four student asked another woman enrolled at the secondary level what the difference was between herself and "a lady who has never gone to school." The woman responded that:

> There is great difference between me and her simply because I know the world around me, express my ideas and advocate for my rights whereby somebody who has never seen the four corners of a class lacks all these privileges.

Unwittingly, in her adapted metaphor, the interviewee communicated the idea that, for those trapped within the confines of the camp, education itself represents access to the world. Through schooling women learn about the larger world, including the various roles women play in different communities, nations, and cultures.

In our meetings with Form Four women, they routinely questioned us about the rights we enjoy at home. They wondered if we are able to choose our marriage partners; if we can work in traditionally male occupations; if we can speak our opinions freely. They asked whether there are any female presidents of Muslim countries and if we thought Hillary Clinton had a chance of being elected president of the United States. With pride, they presented their knowledge of women in the wider world. They asked our thoughts on Ellen Johnson Sirleaf, the first female president of an African country (Liberia), and listed, as if by habit, the names of accomplished women they had learned of in their classes, including those prominent in Kenya's struggle for independence. And, they spoke with emotion about the sense of entitlement education provides as well as the reactionary fear the threat of educated women sparks in the community. As one female interviewee explained:

> Parents have negative attitude toward educating girls because they view school as a place where [a] girl spoils and gets [the] bad manners of going against their parents will.... They also fear that, if girls are educated, they

will know their rights and they will not accept anything which will make them suffer.

Many hoped their own access to education would allow them to become lawyers in order to fight against such restriction of women's rights within Somali culture.

The women's desire to use their education to push for greater rights within the Somali community mirrors data they gathered in their research with school community members. In one interview, a Form Four woman asked the mother of a school girl what she hoped for in her daughter's future. The woman responded:

> She said she wants be a lawyer, she is studying law so that in the future she fights for [the] rights of others and also educate people about their rights so that they should not be exploited by people of higher rank.

Just as was the case in our conversations with Form Four women themselves, the concept of rights dominated community members' consciousnesses, "I have learned so many things ... e.g., my rights—women rights, human rights." In another interview, a parent used the notion of rights to justify her decision to send her daughter to school despite community members' objections, "Girls are suppose to be educated because they are the majority who suffer, so they should know their rights and also fight for the rights of their fellow girls."

Among the women with whom we worked, knowledge of the concept of human rights was not simply abstract or theoretical. Rather, they spoke with facility of specific examples in which they believed their rights were violated. During a focus group with female primary school teachers, we asked what they would change in the camps if they were in charge of the agencies. They responded that they would have freedom of speech, "even among the police." In the conversation that followed they gave multiple examples of rights violations experienced at the hands of Kenyan police, whether personally or as told by other refugees. In one story they described a man "in trouble with the police." When the man had tried to explain his version of events to the police, the police officer retorted, "You are a refugee. You do not have freedom of speech. Be quiet."

In another instance, Roda, a Form Four leaver at the top of her class who had recently learned that she had earned a scholarship to a university in Canada, relayed a personal experience. Having scored well enough on the KCSE to make the first cut in the competition for limited scholarships to Canada, CARE and Windle Trust personnel had arranged for her to take a bus to Nairobi in order to sit for the TOEFL exam. During the ride, the bus had been stopped for a routine police check during which Roda was identified as a refugee, removed from the bus, and sent back to Dadaab despite carrying an official CARE letter authorizing her to travel outside her camp. Roda expressed deep frustration and despair when recalling this event, and she, like the other focus group participants, shared the goal to one day live in a "democratic country" where freedom of speech and movement, among others, are safeguarded.

Moral and Social Character Development

In addition to serving as a process through which women gain knowledge of their rights and develop a voice with which to demand their observance, female students at Dadaab view education as a moralizing force. For female students, education provides access to an alternative belief system as immersion in the schooling process shapes one's ways of thinking and being in the world. In a focus group of secondary girls in the Bartan camp, Leyla explained that being educated meant that she had learned that reasoning and discussion, rather than the exercise of forceful authority to solve problems, led to better solutions. She explained that her mom used to beat her younger brother when he'd spend his days watching TV in the market. She reported telling her mother that beating the boy wouldn't stop his behavior, and then sitting her brother down with the request that he think about his future, as he could one day "be a pilot or a driver." "What was he getting from TV?" He said, "Nothing." She told him that he needed to go to school. Now, he is enrolled in upper primary and always thanks Leyla for her intervention. As she explained, knowledge of such preferable strategies differentiates her from average Somali girls:

> There's a difference between a village girl and me. I can direct my mother. Then, we discuss, sit together, discuss, and have solutions…. It's a productive thing…. Education is about relationships. You have a theory. I have a theory. One idea is not better than the other.

Another young woman explained simply, "I have learned … in order to understand what is bad and what is good." Amina echoed the sentiment, "I stay in school because I want to increase my educational level and to differentiate between good and bad." Through school, students gain a particular lens through which to view the world. Women's additional observances on the subject suggest that the moralizing power of schooling is all encompassing in that it shapes not only one's vision of the world, but also molds the very form of students' beings. After Safi, a Form Four student, asked a primary school student why she and her friends attended school, the girl replied, "In order to gain knowledge and become a responsible person in society."

As female students' words suggest, school has the power to mold students in certain ways. Suleha, a Form Four woman, responded to the question if her role had changed since being a student, "Yes because I become responsible person in my family and community, because they [are] happy about me, and I help them by creating awareness." Schooling was talked about as a veritable supernatural force acting against destructive ignorance. Hawalul described, "I went [to school to] eliminate the ignorance and in order to be able to read and write." Or, as one primary student explained, "I am learning because I want to eradicate ignorance that harms the body more than cancer." Finally, in an interview with an adult female student, Yasmeen, a Form Four researcher, asked, "Why did you make the decision to go to school?" The woman replied, "I reached the decision because I wanted to be out of ignorance to read, write and become a responsible person."

Contributing to the Economic Development of Their Communities

For women in Dadaab, schooling also has the ability to produce citizens who add value to their communities. Concrete linkage between education levels and employability for incentive work at agencies such as CARE, UNHCR, and WFP points to the ways in which educated girls and women are almost guaranteed to play significant roles in sustaining their families financially. In Dadaab we met many girls who provide for their families. Nimo is a 21-year-old Windle Trust upper intermediate student, Form Four leaver, and incentive worker employed by CARE as an English/Somali translator. Nimo's father was killed in Somalia. As the sole breadwinner in her family, Nimo has provided for her mother and siblings since completion of Form Four and has single-handedly financed the construction of two houses on her family's compound. Composed of muddung and roofed with iron sheets, Nimo's home is one of the nicest in her block.

As a result, assertions that "school made me useful person" or "[school] has transformed me in to a useful person in the community" echo throughout student interviews. Zainab, a Form Four student, explained, "I also like school because it is like a factory which made useful ladies out of girls."[3] The language of "usefulness" employed by the girls is linked to expressly economic purposes. Along with ties to industrialization and hence, Western economic structures, the women described learning to behave as productive, Westernized industrial workers. Shakur explained:

I stay (in school) in order to have a bright future. I like the role it plays. It has transformed me into a useful person … I have learned hard work and punctuality since school is where we have rule and regulation.

The ability to act as workers holds the promise of membership in a different sort of world than the one they occupy as dependent and vulnerable refugees. Indeed, girls anticipated the ability to actively contribute to their community and family livelihoods. Ayaan explained that she attends school "in order to get education and to improve the living standard of my people." Another secondary school student shared that she and her peers hope to get jobs as incentive workers after completion of school since, as one female refugee reported, contribution of a monthly salary, however small, is like "reimbursing your family" for support through schooling. Another secondary school girl looked forward to being able to sustain her mother financially since, "She is the one that bought for me the books and the pen."

Female Students' Position in the Struggle

School-going girls in our study are inspired to strive for personal academic success as well as to increase access to schooling for women and girls generally. One of the ways school-girls justified their continued progress was by viewing themselves and other educated members of the community as enjoying higher social status given greater worldliness, skills, and sophistication. As a complete package, schooling offers moral, economic, and civil advancement, access to which brings a status stratification in which uneducated Somalis are distinguished from educated ones. According to one primary student, school "makes the difference between the ignorant and the elites." As a result of its formidable influence as an enlightening (and distinguishing) force in their lives, students spoke with consequence about their backgrounds prior to enrollment in Dadaab schools. Hawalul, an upper intermediate Windle Trust English student, remarked, "My average day like before coming to Dadaab was next to nothing as I never knew and had no education background." One parent explained that pre-arrival she "was just a nomadic and [her] family were pastoralists." The phrase "just a nomadic" echoed among student answers to the question of their family origins.

Through schooling, women in our study came to see the Somali community as divided into two groups: the lesser, uneducated citizens and the more desirable, educated ones. When asked about the difference between a girl who had never attended school and herself, Haali elucidated that "the non student … is those people who are not learning anything, and sleep [in] the market like vagabond children of barbaric [parents]." She continued to describe overall change in her community as a result of educational offerings in Dadaab:

> Before when we [Somali refugees] are coming here [to Dadaab] nobody knows the benefits of school and today everybody knows the benefits of the school … because the people of before were ignorant and the people today are adapted the world and developing step by step in knowledge.

Implicit in such stratification is the positioning of self as leader in the process of "eradicating ignorance" within the Somali community. The particular goal "to eradicate ignorance" appeared in nearly every interview with a school-going girl. Similarly, teachers in a focus group characterized their motivation to teach, "so as to educate the ignorant people in my country." One primary teacher in particular explained, "All of the Somali people are ignorant. But some are now educated." If given the opportunity to repatriate, "We [herself and other educated women] would tell them [Somalis who have remained in Somalia] what is war and what is peace." Part of such process includes the cessation of female circumcision as a community practice. Considering education as a tool for the eradication of ignorance—and educated women as actors in the processes of personal and community transformation—frames women's and girls' understandings of their own participation in schooling.

Even as women describe schooling as an empowering force, they adroitly adopt the language of rights to critique the lack of educational opportunities and resources afforded to girls' schooling in the camps. According to one group of students, 2005 was the first year in which girls were awarded some of the WUSC scholarships; two of the roughly 40 awards were given to girls. As a result, some secondary school girls with whom we spoke found it difficult to maintain morale when they saw so few tertiary scholarship opportunities given to female peers, feeling instead that they were "struggling for nothing." However, they explained that if more opportunities were provided girls, they would feel renewed perseverance. Female students' access to scholarships is crucially important for, as was explained to us, if you do not receive one of the few afforded opportunities for tertiary education, there are little to no options left except to loiter in the market or, "become another mother." Instead, every informant wanted to further her education to seek PhDs, MDs, and other worldly experience.

In a separate instance, we discussed possible stipends for participation in our research with Form Four women. While Windle Trust students' research formed a component of their required English curriculum, Form Four women attended workshops and completed interviews on a volunteer basis during their month-long school holiday. After learning about female students' acute need for lamps, we suggested provision of solar lamps to each Form Four girl in exchange for her contribution to data gathering. The Form Four women seemed pleased with the idea until they learned that solar lamps were temporarily out of stock and would not arrive to the camps until June. Urgently, they explained that receiving lamps in the summer would be of no use to them as it was too near to the KCSE date. Rather, they asked to be given cash to buy their own electric lamps, which could be recharged at school during daytime hours. Finally, they wanted to know if they would be provided a certificate to include in their CVs. Throughout the process, the students revealed a weariness of promises for resources and ensured that, if provided, stipends would be of direct use to their study processes and therefore, chances of obtaining scholarships.[4]

In addition to critiquing a lack of resources, students critically analyzed classroom dynamics and offered suggestions to better support girls' education. The following excerpt is from an interview of a primary school girl by Bashir, an advanced Windle Trust student:

Bashir (B):   Are you a school girl?
Student (S):   Yes I went to school when I was 9 and I am now in level five of primary education.
(B):   What do you hate most in school?
(S):   Classroom participation. As compared to boys is something that is disappointing because girls are fewer than boys in the class, so sometimes you see yourself feeling shy and probably not taking part actively in the participation and discussion in classroom. I sometimes ask myself, "if you were a boy, would I have participated well and done well since I could share my views with very many boys who are my classmates[?]." And, I also thought that a separate school for girls can also be effective.

Other students critiqued teachers' regulation of female students' tardiness given their awareness of the tremendous domestic responsibilities such students carry. In their writings and conversations, girls adeptly analyzed the reality of girls' education in Dadaab and easily articulated structural improvements that would better support their efforts.

At the same time that female students strategically critique the lack of educational opportunities and resources afforded to camp schooling, they maintain that access to schooling will allow them to create newly imagined futures for themselves, their families and their communities. They envision themselves as change agents in dreams of a better future. During a focus group at Qafis Secondary School, we asked why each participant attended school. While the possibility of a WUSC scholarship stood out as central in girls' motivations, one student noted, "we want to empower women to have equal rights for women." Another desired to "be a doctor and care for my people," while still others hoped to become nurses, teachers, professors, and politicians. One respondent revealed her goal "to solve the problems in my country." As a role model, she referred to a Kenyan female Mau Mau fighter pivotal in the struggle for independence from British colonialists. All of the girls seemed to know of whom she spoke and nodded emphatically in agreement. Female students frequently identify role models in female political activists in Kenya, Africa, and the world at large. Jawahir, a participant in a focus group at Bartan Secondary, shared that she and her classmates see women the world over making a difference and hope to have similar positive impact. When Patti asked specifically which women they look up to, the group talked about a female minister of the Kenyan parliament as well as of women more generally who hold graduate degrees. According to Jawahir, female students in Dadaab likewise desire graduate education in order that they might one day actively participate in politics and leadership.

As they dream of possible future contributions, female students take the time to advise peers and in doing so, actively foster shifts in gender practices. Shamso, a Form Four student, wrote in her analytic essay, "I would have liked to give brief advice to those girls who marry in earlier ages and become drop-outs to stop and continue their education until they finish." She then repeated the oft-echoed edict, "They say if you educate a girl you have educated the whole nation." Another informant described conversations she had with girls out of school, "I always advise them and tell them how education is important to an extent where some of them took my advice and enrolled [in] school at old age." Esther, a minority student of Christian background, decided that, after witnessing her Somali friends suffer from harmful effects of circumcision, she wanted to fight against the practice "for her fellow girls." Finally, one mother described why she agreed to let her daughter attend university.

> I took my daughter to school because I was even taken to school so I know the importance of educating girls. I also took my daughter to school because I want her to change our society and also be self dependent even if she will be married in future.

After being asked what expectations she has of her daughter after she finishes her studies, the mother replied:

> I can't really say but I hope [it] is going to be important person in our society and help eradicate illiteracy, ignorance of our society. I hope she will help her fellow girls who are bound by the chain of culture.

Using the language of empowerment and participation in schooling, girls (and often their mothers) dream of—and take active steps in—re-envisioning what it means to be a Somali woman.

Changes Engendered From Women's Schooling

Interviewer: Has your role in the family or larger community changed since being in Dadaab? If so, how?

Student: … Now I have a very important role both in the community and in my family.

The expanding number of educated women in the camps coupled with their increasing earning power signifies a substantial population with new prospects, powers, and possibilities. Accordingly, women's schooling both fosters and indicates gender change within the larger Somali community at Dadaab. These changes manifest in relation to structures of decision-making authority, early marriage, women's leadership, relations between girls and boys, and the division of domestic responsibility. As Asha, the primary school teacher depicted in the chapter's opening, summarized, "Now a days there is great change. These days you [a Somali girl/woman] can challenge your father." She continued to say, as if to an imagined father, "'In the future, I will obey you [and get married] but now you need to listen to me.'" Another primary teacher explained, "Now things are changing, instead of a father giving his lady to a man … he says his lady will learn … take her to school. She will go to the U.S., Canada."

To illustrate the shift in dynamics between fathers and daughters (largely engendered through the influence of schooling), Asha shared a recent example of a primary school student in her block whose father forcibly tried to marry her. According to the story, the girl reported her situation to the education supervisor, which eventually resulted in the arrest of the girls' parents. After some struggle, Asha explained that the father "gave up" and now the girl is a successful student in Form Two. When asked if the father eventually supported his daughter's education, she replied affirmatively and described how he buys her uniforms and books. Asha finished by recalling what she advised the father, "Support her today so that tomorrow she will support you."

Roda, a successful Form Four leaver and WUSC scholarship recipient reiterated the shift in practices of early forced marriage:

In fact early marriage does happen in camp but [it is] rare [as] compared to past time when we were new [in Kenya]. A father used to call his daughter and say I want to marry you to this man. If she rejects she'd be beaten. As people get educated and learn more about the rights of women and children this has reduced.

A third teacher summarized, "It's very rare. "Nobody can be forced these days."

As women take stands against early marriage in favor of further education, new possibilities emerge for women in leadership roles. Form Four student Yasmeen wrote in an essay:

> Going to school may change the role of women in society because of women are [an] example in society. They educate their children, alert women in society of the importance of education. This creates change. Their role of being housemaid or housewife throughout their life [changes] and this up lifts the role of women in society.

Curious as to perceptions around the permanence of such changes, we asked women whether shifts in gender roles occurring in the camps would endure a return to Somalia. One woman replied simply that "now they're educated," and therefore changes made in Dadaab would indeed last in Somalia. Female teachers described seeing women for the first time in the Mogadishu parliament. They even recalled that a woman had run for president of Somalia in the last national elections. While she faced significant resistance and lost the race by a landslide, her very candidacy signaled a transformation in perspectives on gender roles among a significant portion of the Somali electorate.

Shifts fostered and indicated by girls' schooling also manifest at the domestic level. Khadra, an upper-intermediate Windle Trust student interviewed a primary school girl:

Khadra (K):	How did your parents feel about you going to school?
Primary girl (PG):	My parents are really happy [about] my education because they have seen many who have learnt and now engaged as incentive work and helping their parents.
(K):	Do your parents treat you the same as your brother? If so, how?
(PG):	Yes, my parents treat me the same as my brothers, because they buy for us the same textbooks, same number of exercise books.

Not only are some parents reported to view sons and daughters equally, others have modified division of domestic responsibilities in the household to lessen the burden on girls. Ayaan interviewed a lower primary girl:

Ayaan (A):   What is role of the boys before 2000?
Primary Girl (PG):   They were only going to school and played foot-
ball sometimes fetching.
(A):   Has their role changed now?
(PG):   Yes, we have same role and we divide the equally
and do together.

Gender change among the Somali refugee community in Dadaab is not absolute. While, at the time of our study, the majority of families still required that girls bear the brunt of domestic duties, others had begun to divide responsibility between sons and daughters. And, while possibilities for community leadership opened up for some women as early marriage was postponed for further education, many felt that such change brought newfound difficulties.

Conclusion

In the Dadaab refugee camps, Somali female students grapple with the myriad challenges and newfound possibilities engendered through access to schooling. Just as enrollment in school signals their (and their families') orientation to the polarity, female students' meaning-making reflects newly contextualized ways of being Somali women in Dadaab. For, just as female students define themselves differently from their counterparts who remain at home, they also employ discourses of empowerment learned at school to contest the power dynamics that shape the Dadaab landscape.

NOTES

1.   Windle Trust Kenya started a program in 2008 that lends lamps out. Groups of girls rotate the lamps amongst themselves over the course of a school year. The program also works to ensure that every Form Four girl has regular access to a lamp over the course of her last year in school. Windle Trust hopes that the lamps will better enable young women to study from home at night after the completion of domestic work.

2.   Female genital mutilation (FGM) is the term preferred by most aid workers and adopted in turn by many refugees in Dadaab to describe the practice of infibulation. We follow Nnaemeka (2005) and others who prefer the term female circumcision for its closer relation to the language used in practicing cultures.

3.   Mahfouz's (1991) short story, "Half a Day," describes school as a "factory." "Half a Day" is taught as part of the nationalized Kenyan curriculum dur-

ing secondary school (and thus to all high school students in Dadaab). Likely, the use of this expression by a study participant is a reference to Mahfouz's story.

4. After discussion with students and education sector personnel, cash stipends were provided Form Four participants. The students compiled earnings to purchase rechargeable lamps as proposed.

CHAPTER 6

"THE CULTURE WILL CHANGE AS THE WORLD CHANGES"

Using School to Navigate the Global Era

> *(Since being in Dadaab) we have adapted with*
> *another culture.... We do the house together with our brothers since*
> *the world has become global village.*

—Suleha, Form Four Student and Refugee at Dadaab

Despite geographic isolation, limited Internet access, and a largely homogenous camp population, Dadaab is, as Suleha noted, part of the "global village." The camps, like Kenya and East Africa at large, are subject to the transnational flows that help define our current global era. Journalists come and go, punctuating periodic floods and droughts. The grinding strife in Somalia brings waves of desperate newcomers even as "recyclers" and traders move surreptitiously back and forth across the desert border. International aid workers arrive for short stays in order to offer expertise in particular areas of emergency management. While in the minority, refugees from a range of East African countries establish ethnic neighborhoods replete with restaurants, churches, and small markets. Young Somali couples can make clandestine trips to the Ethiopian village where a photographer will take their picture within a heart shaped backdrop. Somali women, driven from their own communities due to perceived misbehavior, often find hostel in neighboring minority blocks. Young Kenyan professionals, funded by a donation from Nike, organize soccer and volleyball matches among male youth. Western researchers and interns, sometimes donning traditional Somali garb in order to garner acceptance, also ebb and flow.

The varied currents of human bodies carry equally diverse knowledge and belief systems. An expert in urban planning comes from Norway and spends three months working with refugees to establish drainage systems that prevent catastrophic flooding during the rainy seasons. A veteran Ghanaian aid worker fresh from a post rehabilitating child soldiers in Sierra Leone offers insight on salient child protection issues. Members of NCCK lead trainings in family planning and HIV/AIDS prevention. For a small fee, refugees can watch Western films on small computers in privately owned computer cafés in the marketplaces. The Dadaab economy also reflects the diversifying impact of globalization.

Although the Kenyan government forbids refugees from farming or raising livestock and heavily regulates trade practices, nevertheless, a vibrant economy has developed in the camps. Members of the Dadaab community establish intricate networks of monetary exchange. Money spent by aid workers and refugees in refugee owned businesses feeds an informal economy that flows through a Somali banking systems called the *Hawala*. Refugees use the *Hawala* or taar to receive remittances from relatives who live abroad and grease the wheels of trade across the Somali border and throughout the camps.

The worldly diversity that characterizes Dadaab is especially apparent in its remarkably well run, yet deeply under resourced school system. Dadaab's schools serve as physical, intellectual, and economic centers of diversity. The average secondary classroom contains between 30 and 30 uniform-clad students seated tightly together along rough-hewn wooden benches. School uniforms are simple: blue slacks for boys and blue ankle length skirts for girls. Boys wear white shirts; Somali girls wear white *hijabs*. Each morning and at the end of the lunch hour, a teacher stands at the school's front gate to ensure that the shirts of arriving boys' are tucked neatly into their trousers. The structure of school buildings, which feature concrete floors, spare wooden beams, and rusted tin roofs, varies little between camps. Half walls are constructed of thick metal sheets or collages of flattened tin from cans that once held food rations. Images of U.S. flags appear on the cans, reminding students and teachers of the origin of much of Dadaab's donated foodstuff. Screened windows bridge the low metal walls and the eave of the roofline. An occasional breeze through the gaping windows offers some relief from the oppressive heat. A large blackboard hangs at the front of each classroom. Teachers are equally likely to be female as male, though male students comprise the vast majority of a given classroom, leaving a few desks at the front right corner for female students. Though the ratio of boys to girls in secondary classes is strikingly disproportionate, that classrooms are not sex segregated is a key marker of shifting gender relations occurring at the camp. School provides one of the few forums outside of the family where girls and boys interact. The majority of students are Somali Muslim; Dadaab primary schools are 96.9% Somali while secondary schools are 97.1% Somali (CARE Kenya, 2007). Accordingly, school grounds feature mosques for both girls and boys in addition to a low-lying water tap for the practice of ritual ablution. While Somalis are in the majority, the student body is not homogeneous. Sudanese, Ethiopian, Eritrean, and Ugandan students, among others, intersperse with Somali counterparts at shared desks. The physical closeness of Somalis with non-Muslims also establishes a new precedent. Traditional tenets, which often view non-Muslims as unclean, discourage Somalis from touching those outside the religion. Female members of minority populations complain that they cannot walk safely through the marketplace without covering their hair and, after using a water tap, witness Somali women washing the areas they had touched with soap. But, in the schools, proscriptive interethnic and interreligious practices fade. Minority Christian girls sit alongside Somali friends. Some wear the standard white *hijab* in order to fit in more seamlessly. Others prefer only loose, simple scarves, a compromise between full coverage and allowing hair to show plainly. Christian girls also wear skirts, though they tend to fall mid calf rather than extend to the ankle. Some Christian girls don short-sleeved shirts baring arms in order to better cope with Dadaab's heat.

The demographic make-up of faculty also contributes to school diversity. Secondary teachers and the vast majority of administrators are Kenyan. Most are Christians; some are ethnic Somalis with Kenyan citizenship who hail from the Somali dominated Northeastern Province of Kenya. While the majority of primary school teachers are refugees paid meager incentive wages, secondary school staff is composed of certified teachers compensated with salaries comparable to the Kenyan national average. As a result, the camps draw teachers from all parts of Kenya.

Classrooms in Dadaab bring together women who are otherwise unlikely to meet. During our initial meeting with female Form Four students in Qafis, we asked each participant to share her family's background. Their stories reveal a range of class, geographic, and educational family histories. They described their mothers' roles in the family before immigrating to Kenya and in doing so, revealed the existence of disparate gender practices even prior to deterritorialization. Three families had lived in Mogadishu. One woman's father worked for the government, another's parents were both in business, and one mother had been a

nurse. Three families hailed from Kismaayo, two of which were pastoralist. The third had made their living in the marketplace. One woman's
family had lived in rural northern Somalia. Two families had been farmers in tiny villages near the coast. We even met one young woman whose
mother had obtained a university degree in Somalia.

Students also represent diverse class and clan backgrounds—both in
Somalia and within the camps. While most refugees lost significant portions, if not the entirety, of their assets during the civil war, class differences, which are inextricably tied to clan, still cross borders and become
reinscribed in Dadaab. Those with previous education or valuable skills
are quickly employed as incentive workers earning wages and important
contacts within the aid community. Those with family members abroad
are likely to receive remittances allowing them to supplement food rations
and purchase school supplies. While those students who are able to enroll
in school undoubtedly reflect the more privileged strata of refugees, the
fact that schooling is provided as a public service means that a far broader
contingent of youth are able to attend. As a consequence, schools bring
together youth who might otherwise be distanced by class and clan.
Instead, they become a tightly knit cohort of friends and peers who move
together through years of intensive study.

Diversity and cultural change are also affected through the curriculum,
which exposes students to new skills, ideas and worldviews and provides historical contextualization of current world events. By scaffolding students'
acquisition of English and Kiswahili proficiency, schooling supplies common languages with which students can dialogue across their differences.

Schools symbolize Dadaab's status as a member of the global village.
When asked about the role of education in their lives, students echo an oft-
repeated adulation, "School is key of the world." Of course, for others,
schooling's articulation with the larger world outside of Dadaab threatens
established authority and custom. As we described in Chapter 5, female
students—who employ Dadaab's enlightenment ideology to justify their
attendance, offer critique, and make requests of power brokers—whole-
heartedly embrace school's role as a vehicle of globalization.

Among other purposes, young female students utilize schooling as a
space and process through which to seek exposure to and build community across difference. As in their talk about what it means to become educated in general, in coming to terms with the differences they encounter
in school, young women selectively draw upon enlightenment ideology to
imagine new ways of being Somali women and members of the Somali
and global communities. However, in distinction from rhetoric used to
justify school attendance, in developing orientations to diversity, the
young women express more nuanced identities. While retaining a self-
perception as a new type of Somali women, they root their identity work

squarely within Somali culture. In doing so, they forcefully shed light upon ground typically obscured in the dominant discourse of polarization and illustrate ways of being "modern" and worldly Somali women.

Gender Diversity: Learning With Our Brothers

> Relationships with boys have both negative and positive effect on girls. Positively, she can gain support and interaction from him and also can lead to marriage. But negatively, it can lead to her to be cheated and impregnated easily and this leads the girl to have a fatherless child. In conclusion, I think relationships with boys are not something to be forebidden[.] I know I can defend myself.
>
> —Zainab, Form Four Student

Given the value placed on an unmarried woman's virginity, gender segregation outside of the domestic sphere is strictly adhered to by most Somalis in Dadaab. Women and girls bear significant responsibility for the maintenance of their virginity and are expected to restrict public movement. Tremendous stigma exists around premarital sex and out-of-wedlock pregnancy. Women accused of either face ostracism from their family and wider community. As Shamso described, "Relationship with boys is something very contrary to Somali culture. Girls who have boy friends are rejected in the community. They are also isolated from the society." Accordingly, every effort is made to minimize the risk of sexual relations. Situations that require extrafamilial gender mixing, such as rations distributions, incentive jobs, and schooling, are often born from demands or opportunities specific to the Dadaab context.

Because schooling not only requires, but promotes public interaction between male and female students, those young women who pass into secondary have to carefully balance successful participation in school—which involves active engagement in the classroom—with the cultural prerogatives of gender segregation and patriarchy. The young women in our study shared different experiences and strategies for engagement with male students. They described their classmates' use of idioms of family to normalize relations and situate themselves within traditionalist expectations. Some women explained that it was not uncomfortable to attend school with boys because they had done so with the same male peers their whole lives and male classmates had become "their brothers."

Taking a more pragmatic approach, other students explained that when interacting with male classmates they simply "adapt" to their surroundings and strategically employ newfound relations for homework assistance. Male students have exponentially more time to spend on schoolwork outside of school hours. Mathematics is particularly difficult for young women who do not have the luxury of study time. As a result, they often ask male peers to tutor them on homework during early mornings or school holidays. Kalifa, a Form Four woman, discussed this predicament in an interview with a younger female student:

> Kalifa: How do you see sitting in a classroom with boys or in other words how do you see learning with boys?
> Student: I see it as normal so long as I can learn with them. Moreover, if they even help me in my weakness like in mathematics.

Observation of increasing interaction caused one young primary school headmaster to note, "Relationships between girls and boys are changing because now they are working together in school, sharing classrooms, and even sometimes sharing desks!" He explained that newfound communication garnered through schooling spills out to the larger community and transforms marital relations at large. Yasmeen voiced similar sentiments in an essay, "Relations with boys [is] normal and better because interaction will take place in school and more students will [know] each other hence [the] creation of good relationship."

In addition to relationship or community building, girls also credit engagement with boys with a newfound ability to debate, compete, and exchange ideas—all forms of interaction typically condemned by traditionalists. Sahra asked a primary school student to describe her experiences in school. She replied, "I experienced different things like sitting in class with boys listening [to] explanation from one person exchanging ideas." In a focus group at Bartan, Rachel asked a group of Form Four women what it was like for them to learn with a disproportionate number of boys. One participant explained, "We have an adaptation method. We challenge each other." She continued to describe how, when reading novels in class, the boys "support" male characters (and their male classmates) while the girls "support" female characters (and female classmates). An example they provided was the relationship between Paulina and Martin in MacGoye's (1986) *Coming to Birth*. In the story, Martin repeatedly abuses his young wife Paulina who moved from a rural Kenyan community to join him in Nairobi. In one instance, Paulina, who has never before lived in a city, gets lost on her way home from the hospital where she had just miscarried and wanders in search of her husband for two days and nights. Inflamed and embarrassed in front of his neighbors at her absence, Martin responds to his wife's return by severely beating her. Secondary girls in Dadaab recalled how they condemned Martin's violent behavior in class debates while males unequivocally defended him. By the time students reach Form Four and have spent 12 years with the same classmates, many female students claim that they no longer hesitate to insert their often differing opinions. Furthermore, such publicly voiced disdain of practices endemic in the community—such as domestic abuse—signifies cultural and gender change engendered through schooling.

Not all of the informants' depictions of engagement with boys were positive, however. Young women reported that male peers often tease them if they offer incorrect answers. Aman, a primary school student who often visited us at the CARE compound, described how young men harass young women if they see a spot of blood on their clothing during menstruation. Aman condemned such teasing as humiliating and, although distribution of free sanitary products helps mitigate the situation, female attendance at school during menstruation diminishes nonetheless. When asked if boys face consequences for such harassment, Aman said no and explained that if a headmaster were to hold the boys accountable, the students would simply beat him on the way home from school. Catherine, an upper intermediate ELL student from Sudan, interviewed a Sudanese girl who had dropped out of primary school. After asking the former student how she "interact[ed] with boys in the school," the girl replied, "it was very hard because I do not share any other things with them." Luul, a Form Four student, disclosed, "I don't like singing in front of boys while in class." Somali interviewees frequently mentioned their disdain for singing and dancing requirements as well as in-school sports activities.

For her part, Kalifa viewed interaction with male students as a distraction to her studies:

> Also the relationship with boys that is one thing [in which] I will never [be] involved. That is, I have negative attitude towards such thing since I am always concentrating on my studies. That is, I have no chance for entertainment.

When asked about CARE's intention to open a girls' boarding secondary school in Bartan, respondents seemed extremely excited at the prospect of focusing exclusively on academics rather than negotiation of the social sphere. Despite admission that such a school might result in reification of more traditional marital arrangements, as boys would no longer interact with girls in an academic environment, one education supervisor extolled the boarding school plan. He explained that not only would girls no longer worry about boys, they would also face minimal domestic responsibility. In the context of Dadaab, the supervisor furthered, single-sex education would acknowledge community wishes and signal schooling's compatibility with Islam.

In their varied appraisals and approaches to attending school with young men, the women in our study intermix sentiments that echoed

Dadaab enlightenment rationale, acknowledge challenges traceable to traditional perceptions of women as intellectually inferior and unclean, and evoke the commonplace understanding that gender integration is acceptable within family to normalize the co-ed classroom. In doing so, they call attention to the expansiveness of ideological territory present in Dadaab. Rather than pull merely upon the dominant polarities of enlightenment and traditionalism, they treat the entire Dadaab landscape as fertile ground to foster and support complex and dynamic identity work. A similar, multipronged strategy is evident in the young women's developing orientation to ethnic diversity.

Ethnic Diversity: Learning With Minorities

Interviewer (I):   What do you learn about in school?
Shamso (S):   I learn to interact [with] people of different cultures, religions, ethnicities, and traditions and [to] live with them in harmony.
(I):   What do Somalis and other minority groups say about schooling in Dadaab?
(S):   They appreciate by saying education eradicate misunderstanding and brings co-operation among the community.

During our time in Dadaab, we sought to garner multiple perspectives on camp life. These included the voices and experiences of ethnic minorities. In order to protect the safety of minority refugees, as well as to respect cultural preference, agencies divide residential blocks by ethnicity. Each of the three camps contains minority blocks referred to as "Little Ethiopia," "Rwanda," or "Sudan" and officially labeled according to ethnic designation, such as E1 (Ethiopia 1), R II, and S1. During interviews and informal conversation, minorities shared painful stories of intimidation and violence at the hands of their Somali neighbors.

Leah is a Christian, minority woman who lives with her children in Dadaab. Both Leah and her husband are employed as incentive workers at the agencies. After flooding destroyed her house in December 2006, Leah moved her family to drier ground in another of Dadaab's three sub-camps. Her husband, however, was forced to remain behind in order to keep his job. When possible, he travels during weekends to visit his wife and children. While Leah likes that the new area lacks mosquitoes and flies, she lamented the hour-long walk her daughters had to make to and from school. To assist them, she described waking up at 4:30 am to prepare breakfast. While a shorter route exists between her compound and the secondary school, Leah's daughters take the long way to avoid having to walk through several Somali blocks.

Leah invited us to visit her one afternoon in her brother Gabriel's household. She and Gabriel spent many hours with us, offering up their only stools in a small, modest room with dirt floors and a bed palate. On that day, Leah wore a sleeveless dress and a shawl around her shoulders. A small scarf covered her hair. Much of the afternoon's conversation highlighted the difficulties she and her family face living as ethnic minorities and Christians in Dadaab. Leah described being jeered at and called "satan," "pagan," or "prostitute." She claimed that Somali children learn anti-Christian invectives in *duksi*, the neighborhood Qu'ranic schools. An official mediator for community issues, Leah spends her days traveling between blocks and often works in Somali sections of the camp. She explained that she covers her hair, arms, and legs at work to avoid harassment, even though the climate is dreadfully hot. Despite the effort to accommodate Somalis dress preferences, Leah has learned to no longer ask for water when working in Somali blocks because she noticed that people would throw away their glasses after she sipped from them.

As we listened to Leah's stories, a young woman who looked about seven months pregnant came in and out of the room, quietly presenting us with cold water, juice, and complete meal of goat, *ugali*, the Kenyan staple-food of boiled maize meal, and *sukumawiki*, a bitter leafy green. Given the omission of greens and meat from refugee rations, the family's invitation to share food was extremely generous and kind. Rahma, the woman who cooked and served the meal, was not of minority background; rather, she looked Somali, yet wore a loose, short-sleeved muumuu and kept her hair uncovered. Without prompt, Gabriel explained that Rahma, his wife, is an orphan from Somalia who came to the camps and lived with a Somali family until her foster father made sexual advances. Rahma abandoned the family and met Gabriel, whom she married. She was pregnant with their first child. According to Gabriel, the woman had since been banned from the Somali community and wore a *niqab* to the market in order to hide her identity. Since their marriage, both he and Rahma had been repeatedly attacked, as had their compound. However, he proclaimed definitively that it was better to "die together" than be separated.

Rahma is one of the many women of Somali origin to whom we were introduced that live in minority blocks. According to Elemo and Getachew, two male, Ethiopian incentive workers at CARE, many Somali women are "prostitutes" who live unofficially quarantined in minority sections of the camps and fear for their lives. Elemo and Getachew explained that oftentimes the women, who begin as sex workers, end up marrying Ethiopian or other minority men, have families, and adopt a Christian lifestyle. They also noted that, if the women do venture to the market, they don *niqabs* in order to conceal their identity.

Elemo and Getachew, both Christian, also described the challenges they face as Ethiopians in the camp. Ethiopian women, they explained, constantly fear attack in the marketplace if they do not cover. They also lamented that, while Kenyan police stations are intentionally located close to minority blocks, they often feel physically unsafe, particularly during the 2007 Ethiopian invasion of Somalia. Given longstanding tensions between Ethiopia and Somalia, flair-ups between the two countries bear directly upon intracamp relations. Even without specific political impetus, Elemo and Getachew cited cultural and religious differences as the source of discrimination.

A member of the participatory research team interviewed a fellow Ethiopian refugee:

Tenagne:	Do you think your life is secure in the camps? Why?
Ethiopian Informant:	No, since we live with Somali majority and local Kenyans Somalis we feel insecure because most of the time they abuse us. They intimidate and discriminate [against] us because of our religion and culture. Therefore, if something bad happens we feel that they might harm us.

Reports of discrimination, marginalization at the hands of Somali community leaders, and imposition of Somali, Muslim cultural practices on minority populations echo through conversations with minority refugees. Francis, a Sudanese ELL student, interviewed another Sudanese woman in her block:

Francis (F):	What made you to become a minority in refugee camp?
Sudanese Woman (SW):	It was due to war in my country and after I fled I found myself a minority.
(F):	How did the majorities feel about you?
(SW):	The[y] feel good, since it is an easy way for them to impose their culture on me and their way [is] proud…. I am not feeling good.

Allegations of mistreatment include discrimination in the workplace and in the allocation of agency resources. While such assertions do not necessarily target entire organizations or their staff, some minorities believe they have been denied promotion or disproportionately excluded in the distribution of non-food items and educational scholarships. They note the significant number of local Somali Kenyans on staff at the agencies and that Somali refugees fill the majority of community leadership and incentive positions. One story of discrimination relayed by a Kenyan staff member went so far as to declare that a Sudanese clerk at one agency was falsely accused of stealing in order to cover up an embezzlement scam on the part of a Kenyan Somali staff member. While we cannot speak to the truth of these allegations, the pervasiveness of such reports reflects a widespread distrust between Somalis and ethnic groups in the minority at the camp.

Minorities also complain that Somali peers and teachers harass their children. Leah reported that minority children had recently been attacked on their way home from school. She said that in response to the incident, as well as to the string of others that had occurred in her stay at Dadaab, she holds her children back from school for two or more weeks during which she personally teaches them. After she feels the conflict has blown over, she allows them to return to school at the urging of her husband. Nonetheless, she claimed that her children have been beaten and that her primary school-aged children often dread school and beg to stay home. Despite the pain she feels in returning them, she believes schooling represents their only hope for a better life.

Gabriel shared Leah's assessment of schools as a violent place for minorities, describing that, even as a teacher in the secondary school, he does not feel respected by Somali students. In fact, he announced that students do not respect any Kenyan or minority teachers; rather, they "need them for the information." Gabriel recalled a time he prevented one Kenyan teacher from being beaten by students for refusing to let them use books on an exam and another when he stopped a teacher from being attacked on her walk to the CARE compound. Gabriel said that no minority students or teachers use school restroom facilities for fear of being followed and teased. He said that if, in order to assimilate, minority students use a jerry can, they are asked mockingly, "What are you, Somali? A Muslim?", and, if they do not, [they] are labeled "dirty."

Leah and Gabriel's recollections provide one version of a complex, highly charged and multisided account of Somali-minority relations in Dadaab. Regardless of whether their assertions are true, the perception that minority children are harassed in school drives a large number of Ethiopian children to drop out or never enroll in camp educational programming. Many opt instead to home-school. An interview with an Ethiopian man again illustrates such a situation. He explained:

The teachers who teach in nursery classes are Somalis and they teach and explain to students only in Somali language or English or other language. Therefore, this leads to our children to become confused and feel alienated and rejected. In my view, our children are discriminated [against]. Secondly, our children are forced to wear the uniform like Somali children wear according to their culture and religion. This also neglects the other culture. Thirdly, if our children do not wear like Somali children, they will be beaten by the children. And, this is one main reason why my child withdrew from school. The other problem is that my child was given a religious name "Fatuma" and this annoyed me and created psychological problems [for] me and my child.

In his assessment, the interviewee deemed schools more psychologically harmful to his daughter than beneficial. Most primary schools in Dadaab do feature Somali instruction in the lower levels, just as primary schools across Kenya begin instruction in regional mother tongues before phasing to English. According to Elemo and Getachew, informal schools have been created in Ethiopian and other minority blocks in order to offer an alternative to Somali-dominated schools. Other private schools are also run in the markets. However, these schools are not credentialed, so their graduates lack certificates relevant for employment in Kenya and remain ineligible for incentive work.

Ethnic discrimination in Dadaab is acutely gendered. That Christian women do not traditionally cover is a source of contention, and while many women have adopted the practice, others resist such assimilatory measures. Many maintain a public/private distinction, veiling in public spaces and uncovering when safely within minority blocks.

While the majority of accounts we heard regarding discrimination came from minorities themselves, one interview features a Somali student's appraisal of the situation. Hassan, an advanced Windle Trust student and member of the participatory research project summarizes his interviewee Fardous' poignant assessment of minority students' experiences in school. According to Hassan, Fardous:

openly told me that [minorities] look different in class. This is because they don't interact with Somali student. They sit alone in class. She thought that the reason was religious differences and cultural background. In addition to that she said that, since all Somalis have [the] same religion and culture, they consider other religious sectors to be dirty and people to be astray. Therefore, they don't want to associate with other faiths, and in that context they are segregated. Although those minority have their own thoughts and beliefs that hamper them [from] socializing with other communities.

Agency staff assessed the situation with similar candor. One staff member in the Education Sector admitted that more should be done from an institutional standpoint to support minorities in schools and in the camps at large. In the meantime, however, he explained that a dearth of resources and small staff already work overtime to accommodate the majority. Another teacher noted of female minority students:

> For the minority groups, their situation is worse. They are discriminated against firstly because of their differences in religion and culture from the Somalis and secondly because of their gender. Being a non-Somali and a woman is double misfortune in Dadaab.

Certainly, harassment and discrimination toward minority communities is not endorsed or practiced by all Somalis in Dadaab. Nor do members of refugee minority groups contend that all Somalis are bigoted. In her depiction of Somali-minority relations, Leah made a distinction between Somalis from Mogadishu and Somalis from "the bush." Leah and her family had originally been placed in the Thika camp outside of Nairobi where, she reported, the Somali refugees were highly educated and from Mogadishu. According to Leah, given their urban background and professional status, they lacked the bigoted qualities of those in Dadaab. Similar distinctions are made among on-the-ground staff and refugees who view more educated, urban, and middle-class Somali as less traditional than their rural, uneducated counterparts.

One afternoon during the teacher strike, we visited a primary school in Qafis. Because only headmasters, deputy headmasters, and watchmen were present on school grounds during the strike, we were able to benefit from a few rare hours of the administration's undivided attention. At one point in our informal question and answer session (which was directed both ways), an older Somali man pulled over his mat on the ground to join the conversation. We learned that this man was a member of the school PTA, an avid proponent of girls' education, and an enthusiastic supporter of the United States.[1] The man proudly shared that he had studied in Spain and demonstrated his proficient Spanish. After the impromptu performance, he sat down and posed a round of questions about life in the United States. Specifically, he wanted to know how resettled Somali refugees fare in the U.S. as compared to other immigrant groups. "Were they prospering? How were they getting along?"

Patti explained that although we are friends with many Somali women, we could not make comparisons between experiences of different refugee populations because the U.S. community in which worked has an almost exclusively Somali refugee population. Rather than make a comparative analysis, Patti shared that Somalis in Milltown enroll in the public school system, live and work alongside diverse counterparts, and have opened new businesses including a Somali restaurant and halal market. When she

began to candidly report and critique some of the racist elements in Milltown that also shape Somalis' resettlement experiences, the man interrupted her to note quickly that "Somalis are not African but are more like
Arabs even though our skin is black." He continued to explain that Africa
consists of "Cushites, Nilotes, Bantus, and Semites" before concluding
that Somalis are more like Semites and Cushites. According to the man,
Somalis act like Arabs and Ethiopians despite looking Black in appearance. This was not the first time we'd heard such a distinction. In fact,
some Somalis in both Dadaab and Milltown often labored to differentiate
themselves from Kenyans, Somali Bantus, or African Americans. Others,
like the young headmaster in Qafis, seemed to disagree.

The difference in perspective between the two men demonstrates an
inherent diversity among Somalis as a whole. While the older man
appeared to situate himself as racially distinct from Africans and thus
closer to Europeans and Americans as part of a larger discursive effort to
celebrate the West, for unknown reasons, his counterpart dismissed his
racialized world vision.

In order to explain such intraethnic diversity, Nimo, a young Somali
woman who translated for us, credited the availability of education. When
Patti asked Nimo about minority life in Dadaab, she responded, "(Minorities) really struggled in the beginning. Somalis didn't even know they
were also people, but after education things have gotten much better for
them." She finished by announcing that Ethiopian and Sudanese women
can now walk safely in the market uncovered even as there remain many
older members of the community who are displeased with such behavior.
Nimo's comments raise questions about whether students generally share
her vision of schooling as a space and process through which students
learn to accept ethnic diversity. More to the point, her comments invite
further analysis of whether close interethnic relations between Somalis
and ethnic minorities are perceived as a product of students' alignment
with Western enlightenment ideology or, alternatively, a reflection of a
long standing way of being Somali that exists in distinction from familiar
images of Somalis as religious separatists.

In our work with the male and female members of the participatory
research project, we found that, while students exhibited openness to
egalitarian, interethnic relations and associated schooling with such openness, they did not credit enlightenment forces with affecting greater multiculturalism. Ahmed Hussein researched relations between ethnic
communities in Dadaab. In his analytic essay, he addressed difference by
theorizing the relationship between religion and culture. Ahmed Hussein
wrote:

Refugees are all Africans. They have more similarities than differences. There are five ethnic groups in the camps. For instance, the Somalis who are the largest population in the camp, and Oromos, Sudanese, Gambelas, and Eritrians. The communities above do not have the same cultures and religions. Somalis have the belief that their culture is their religion. This means that what their culture states is what they took from their religion as a reference. There are very little things that their culture teaches and not in their religion. For instance, FGC [female genital cutting) is a cultural practice of the Somali community. They mostly carry out this practice but their religion does not state FGC but *Sunni* type of circumcision. They have adopted and decided never to leave this practice as its one of the fundamentals of their culture. Oromos are almost the same as Somalis. The two even intermarry one another. They differ during ceremonial activities. The rest of the communities are totally different from Somalis. They have their culture separate from their religion. There are so many things that their culture teaches but their religion does not mention. Sudanese trim their faces and remove their lower teeth as a way of undergoing circumcision.

In his analysis, Ahmed Hussein focused on unifying notions of Africanness while at the same time called to task the notion that Somali culture and religion are inseparable. In doing so, he suggested that female circumcision is a cultural, rather than religious, practice common among certain non-Muslim groups. He went on to note that Oromos are so similar to Somalis that intermarriage is common, yet the fact that some differences do exist clarifies that complete cultural conformity is not an end goal among Somalis. Implicit within his statement is syllogism that: if circumcision is a cultural practice, and cultures vary in acceptable ways, then circumcision does not need to follow only one form. Though convoluted, Ahmed drew upon the image of a diverse Somali culture in order to justify changes in long standing Somali practices indexed to traditionalism. Significantly, he did not couch his argument within enlightenment discourse. At no time did he mention Western texts that speak out against circumcision or note that Westerners no longer practice female circumcision.[2] Rather, he restricted his supporting evidence to empirically derived knowledge garnered through exposure to a variety of Africans and Somalis.

While Leah and Gabriel's stories highlight the challenges minority youth face in school, Nimo's assertion indicates a vision of schooling as a change agent that brings about cultural harmony. Leah's oldest daughter's experiences in school demonstrate the veracity of both perspectives. Esther was one of the top contenders for a WUSC scholarship and socializes easily among the group of (otherwise all Somali) Form Four women with whom we worked. During our time with the young women, Esther shared books, desks, and pens with her best friend Suleha and other peers. Esther was praised by the group for having acquired fluency in

Somali and openly inserted her opinions in group discussions. On our last day with the group, we held a small celebration. As the women passed around a tape recorder, certain class members volunteered to sing traditional Somali songs and poems. One sang the Somali national anthem and another chanted well-known folksongs. One woman translated the words into English while her friend embellished upon their implicit meaning. After each performance, the women rewound the tape recorder and laughed jovially when they heard their voices played back. During the celebration, Patti asked Esther if she wanted to add anything to the tape. Her classmates turned to her and enthusiastically encouraged her to sing something from her country of origin. As the group faced her in silence, Esther recorded a traditional Acholi song and explained its significance. When she finished, her peers clapped in praise.

Certainly Esther's secondary school experiences were not uniformly smooth and celebratory as was that particular afternoon; rather, she negotiated a delicate balance as the sole representative of difference in her peer group. At times she defended such difference. At others, she made efforts to downplay the ways she might stand out. Esther questioned Somali friends on how they can wear thick, polyester *hijabs* in such heat and announced proudly that schooling with Somali peers had motivated her to become an activist against female circumcision. All the same, after assurance from us that she was welcome to explore minority women's experiences in school for her research project, she chose all Somali informants whom she was able to interview proficiently in Somali.[3]

One morning, as we prepared to leave Esther's Form Four class, we wrapped ourselves in the loose scarves we wore under Dadaab's direct sun. Shamso immediately announced, her voice full of praise, that we looked beautiful covered and should always wear scarves to "hide ourselves from the boys." In excitement, she offered that she and her friends would return the next day with two real *hijabs*. Esther quickly retorted that *hijabs* would be too hot for us and that we were just fine as we were. Shamso never returned with the promise *hijabs*, though she did persist in encouraging us to seek out Somali mates.

Shamso's pride in Somali ways of being did not translate into critique of Esther's however, at least in our presence. For their part, Somali girls saw school as a place to learn about difference. Shamso interviewed an 18-year-old parent and former student. When she asked her informant to describe her experiences in school, the woman replied simply, "I have interacted [with] so many people and learned their culture, behaviors." Hawalul wrote that she stayed in school "In order to learn. I learnt [about] different people within the school." Similarly, Nimo asked a primary school girl, "How does going to school help/assi[s]t you?" The student answered, "So many ways. In terms of communication, community integration, participation, and decision making." Students described learning "interaction and interrelationship," just as they valued school for the ways in which it enabled socialization with refugees from other ethnic-linguistic community otherwise segregated from them.

One upper intermediate ELL student painted a rosy picture of schooling in Dadaab, "All majority and minority groups in Dadaab were schooling in same schools and same levels together, and, they share everything at school; and, they were happy about the opportunity." A Sudanese block leader, when asked about obstacles he faced in Dadaab, replied:

> Yes, we met many challenges. Like, if the other communities, especially [the] Somali community, see our girls who are wearing their traditional clothes, they used to insult and throw stones and, of course, they couldn't understand what they were saying because they didn't know anything about this language. But now, we learnt more about with each other. They can understand us and we can understand them and we deeply entered with each other.

While the block leader's analysis of linear transformation from misunderstanding to harmony can be read as a strategic response to a Somali interviewer's questions, the interview itself signals that school attendance has been discursively coded to the celebration of diversity.

Somali students value the skills they built in school and described them as crucial in their efforts to develop as global citizens. Suleha, a Form Four student and close friend of Esther, wrote of her time in school, "I have experienced knowledge, new friends, how to stay social and how to behave in society. [The] classroom environment is peaceful where learning is going on smoothly." Just as Suleha learned how to "behave in society," a Form Four leaver shared, "There are many things that I liked about school. I liked some subjects such as English and History. I liked to stay with students of different nationalities and races and that helps live with various societies." Zainab likewise answered a question about how her family's religious practices differed from those in non-Somali communities by writing, "We are similar in the practices but how we do [them] is the difference—example, the non Somali communities in Dadaab also pray but their way of praying is different from our way." Rather than problematize difference in religious practice, Zainab chose to emphasize commonality, a position distinct from that of many traditionalists in the camps.

Relations between Somalis and various minority communities in Dadaab have a tenuous history and, at the time of our study, faced undoubted tension. However, our work with a variety of students confirms that a general sentiment championing harmonious inter-ethnic relations exists among students. Interestingly, however, talk about developing relations did not attribute the growing appreciation for multiculturalism to Westerners or Dadaab's enlightenment ideology. Rather, students related personal experiences of friendship and mutual appreciation between diverse students as the source of improving relations. While students unquestioningly saw school as a key space within which their positive experiences across difference occur, they did not qualify constructive interethnic relations merely as a manifestation of enlightenment. Rather, they framed multiculturalism as a natural outgrowth of closer proximity and familiarity as well as a reflection of longstanding heterogeneity within Somali culture itself. This counters the view of Somalis as separatist and homogenous held by many in the mainstream media and aid communities.

Role-Models and Resources: Relations With Kenyan Teachers

Given a dearth of resources and surplus of low-cost refugee labor, the majority of primary school teachers in camp schools are Somali incentive workers. Although most lack training in teaching methods and many have not completed secondary school, refugee teachers provide a less expensive alternative to hiring national staff at the primary level, just as they enable instruction in the Somali language during early grades.[4] At the secondary level, however, the demographic makeup of school staff shifts dramatically as agencies recruit teachers certified in national teaching colleges or universities to prepare students for competition on national exams. Given the relative poverty and low educational levels of Northeastern Province, most secondary teachers hired at Dadaab travel from provinces outside of the region to teach in the camps. The vast majority are Christian, in their 20s and 30s, and, as a result of rules barring families from accompanying aid workers to Dadaab,[5] are either unmarried or live apart from their families. As a result, refugee students come to know a population of young, educated, and financially independent Kenyan women at secondary schools. In positions of relative power and authority, female secondary teachers serve as role models for many girls who seek them out for advice in traversing the distinct spheres of schooling and traditional culture.

In an interview, one male teacher explained, "Teachers give advice to girls about school performance and also help her when she is stressed by social problems at home … especially the female teachers. They have a time in which they talk to girls and discuss female issues." Indeed female teachers, referred to as "Madams" by their students, are described with respect among informants. In Qafis, one girl explained of student interaction with female Kenyan teachers, "We have a good relationship. We talk about girls' issues. Factors that affect our academic performance. They talk to us against early marriage and encourage us to study to the highest level we can." Mooro students expressed regret that there were not more female teachers in their secondary school.

Teachers reiterate such characterizations, sharing the ways in which they help girls balance the multiple expectations placed upon them. In an interview, Jane, an English teacher, described the issues girls seek her out to discuss, "The issue that really bothers the girls is how to overcome their prevailing circumstances in their role as refugee women and excel in studies at the same time—to maximize the little time they have." As the male teacher alluded above, "Ladies Clubs" are set up in each secondary school for groups of (primarily) Somali female students to confer with Kenyan female teachers on the at times problematic interface between cultural expectations and academic pressures. Jane explained that such forums allow students and teachers to strategize ways girls can, for example, best use their after-school time for both domestic responsibilities and homework. Resources provided by NGOs specifically for girls, including sanitary supplies, are also distributed at these meetings.

Some female teachers become academic coaches for the few girls who make it to secondary school, following their students' successes after graduation as well. Jane explained, "I encourage the girls to work hard to overcome the stumbling blocks. I especially encourage them to put more effort in the sciences." Roda, preparing to resettle in Canada for WUSC, shared that she traveled to Mooro to meet with Dorcas, a former teacher who had recently transferred from Qafis. Roda made the journey to visit her and described how Dorcas advised her to work hard in Canada and try to focus on education. Roda paraphrased Dorcas's counsel, "All other things other than education—marriage, children—are there for you. The only thing that needs to be struggled [for] is education." As academic advisors, Kenyan teachers advocate for girls who face barriers to educational success including propositions for early marriage. Ruth talked about how girls often approach her with news that they have been promised to a man by their fathers. By reporting such propositions to touchpoint teachers, female students take the first steps to shift their fates. For, as we have seen, with girls' permission, Kenyan teachers can set into motion efforts taken by school and agency personnel to thwart or postpone marital arrangements. Accordingly, teachers often bridge gaps between refugee students and agencies.

Perceived difference shapes and even defines teacher-student interactions. While such difference is employed strategically so that Kenyan teachers can advocate for their students against cultural practices such as early marriage in ways that Somali teachers may not, religious difference is also cited as a barrier to closer teacher/student relations. As Jane noted,

"I have a cordial relationship with the girls though not very perfect. This is because of religious differences." While Jane problematized religious difference, Windle Trust teacher Molly described how, through patience, constructive comparison, and being a good listener she has been able to overcome cultural barriers with her students:

> Initially, girls were introverted and apprehensive about talking to a non-Muslim, but I cultivated a friendly atmosphere by being less formal and prodding into controversial issues like marriage in a light way. I also talked about myself, though careful not to expose my personal life too much, and by so doing, developed a trust. With time the girls, though one by one, started opening up. It was so moving to hear issues girls go through at the expense of culture and religion. For the Somali women, it is about early and forced marriage, FGM and its effects, and a culture generally bigoted against women.
>
> In view of all this, I was propelled to be a counselor though it is not in my JD [job description]. Although I have been trained as one, I find it hard to give definitive answers especially where religion is concerned. But I try to be there for the girls. Listening is therapy to them but I also encourage them especially to pursue excellence in studies. Generally, I have realized that just giving them special attention boosts their self esteem.

Teachers also align themselves with the cause of women's education in the community at large, often explicitly adopting a language of empowerment and equal opportunity. Such efforts are particularly salient given that the Kenyan teachers themselves represent one of the first generations of Kenyan women to be educated en masse. Relative gender parity in primary schooling is a recent phenomenon in Kenya, boosted by the implementation of free primary education in 2003. Young women's participation at the secondary level, however, varies drastically by province. While Nairobi has seen female enrollment in Form Four exceed that of males, regions evaluated in Northeastern Province face a 1:3 participation ratio (Forum of African Women Educationalists [FAWE], 2001). Further, boys are disproportionately represented among top national examination scorers, holding 77% of the 100 top KCPE positions in 2006 (Kenya National Exams Council [KNEC], 2006). Regardless, achievement of gender parity has been a primary goal among service providers in Kenya, including FAWE.

In light of national pushes for girls' education, from which many Kenyan women have benefited, teachers in the camps often employ personal affirmative action policies by tutoring or supplementing resources for female students. Molly explained:

> I must confess I am biased towards girls in the camp though I try not to openly show it to avoid making male students feeling less wanted. I always give extra attention to girls in my class by giving extra coaching, giving more resources e.g. books and pens, being more friendly etc. However, when awarding marks, I treat them the same as boys to avoid making them (girls) feel less capable.

Further, Molly liaises with secondary school teachers to identify girls particularly well positioned to compete for WUSC scholarships. Molly's advanced English classes are filled with Form Four leavers who attend in order to prepare for the TOEFL examination. As a result, she is well positioned to bolster the efforts of outstanding female students. One such student is Halima, the sole female participant in Molly's advanced English class deemed eligible for a highly competitive scholarship. In the ensuing time between the completion of secondary and her scholarship interview, Halima attended Molly's class, worked an incentive job, and spent her spare time preparing for the crucially important TOEFL exam and interview. After Jane and Molly identified Halima as particularly competitive for the scholarship, Molly spent significant portions of her free time tutoring Halima in English listening, her area of weakness, as well as effective interviewing strategies. Molly also challenged her to study hard and constantly revise her work. Through her own efforts and Molly's encouragement, Halima excelled on the TOEFL practice exam, out-performing all of the male contenders from Dadaab. After Halima succeeded in obtaining the scholarship, her father invited both Jane and Molly to their family compound to celebrate. Molly described:

> Her family gave Jane and I a treat. We were invited for a sumptuous lunch in their house, which we took the Somali way—sited [seated] on a mkeka (mat) and eating from one large plate (all of us). The father is an *Imam*-leader in charge of a mosque but he loves and treats his 3 daughters fondly. Through interpretation by Halima, he told us he was glad we were friends with the daughter and were keen on her learning, and that we instilled good morals in her. He thanked me for trusting her ... and for extra coaching. We in turn thanked him for choosing to educate his girls and being keen on their excellence in it and for supporting them in every way. The mum was too excited that her daughter going to Canada. It was my best day in Dadaab.

That Jane and Molly, two Christian Kenyan women were invited by Halima's father into their home is significant in a climate of often tenuous relations between Christians and Muslims, Kenyan nationals and Somali refugees, traditionalists and aid workers. Further, that the two were personally thanked for promoting girls' education and for instilling good morals by a sheikh bears note. Halima's father's ability to simultaneously represent Islam, support the secular education of his three daughters, and gloss religious difference for shared morality symbolizes the diverse and shifting interpretations of Somali culture in the context of Dadaab. At the same time, Halima's achievements through schooling brought together different ways of being and fostered meaningful exchange and interaction between people in vastly diverse social locations.

In all, young Somali women's relations with Kenyan female teachers are a significant source of support. Kenyan women serve as role models, advisors, and advocates. Given their own struggles to seek higher education and the independent bend living in Dadaab requires from its young staff, it is likely that most female teachers consider traditional Somali cultural tenets and practices to be both highly influential and an oppressive force in young women's lives. They also commonly give voice to enlightenment rationalities that position schooling as a civilizing force for Somali students. Female students are undoubtedly aware of their teachers' perspectives and are likely to agree on many points. We also noted, however, that not only do students hold different opinions and priorities than their teachers, there is great variance in perspective among female students themselves. Accordingly, it became clear that in their relations with teachers, young women are not looking to assimilate Kenyan women's ways of being. Rather, they look to their teachers to assist in navigating the diverse terrain of Somali culture.

Seeking Relations With International Visitors

Given its status as an emergency operation, reliance on donor funding, as well as proximity to the Somali border, Dadaab receives international visitors from a range of governmental and nongovernmental organizations. Visitors seek different levels of access to refugees themselves. Particularly with those visitors or staff members who spend extensive time in the camps, refugees often build strategic relations in efforts to learn about other ways of being, access new outlets for needs claims, and insert critique of camp structure or policies.

Many students or young, educated members of the refugee community perceive access to visitors from the global North as an opportunity to pursue further education abroad. The vast majority of students with whom we spoke desires tertiary education outside of Dadaab and preferably, outside of Kenya. Shamso interviewed an 18-year-old parent and former student. She asked the woman, "What is your educational motivation?" In answer to Shamso's question, the woman noted simply, "In order to get further, study abroad." That access to educational opportunity represents a potential ticket out of the camps is significant. Demand for scholarships, however, far exceeds available opportunities. As a result, students seek out visitors to learn about education in other parts of the world and build potentially fruitful relations.

Female students' queries about public schooling in the U.S. are gender salient, particularly given that they have heard from friends and relatives of school's compulsory nature. Pertinent questions include: How does it work for all children in a family to go to school? Who bears primary responsibility for domestic chores if all daughters, including the eldest, attend school? How do girls perform as per boys? How do educational standards in the U.S. compare with those in Kenya and more specifically, is the national curriculum of Kenya more demanding in terms of mathematics? Students seemed pleased that all daughters in a family are required to attend, that girls and women in the U.S. tend to outperform boys, and that such programming as free meals for low-income families exist to mitigate the burden of feeding large families of school-aged children. They also appeared skeptical that schooling in the U.S. is as demanding as in Kenya; rather, they had heard rumors that math in the U.S. is optional. For WUSC scholarship recipients who await departure, questions of interest pertained to common practices among North American university students: Are undergraduate students often married? Would we recommend getting married as an undergraduate?

In another instance Patti asked Roda, a female 2007 WUSC scholarship recipient, what she was most looking forward to in North America. Roda replied, "learning, studying hard, getting degrees—Masters." She continued to explain that "learning in America is very different than in Africa because people in Africa have to struggle very hard, work very hard. Money is a problem." She asked Patti if the same holds true in the United States. After Patti's explanation of the advantages and challenges of federal loans for students in the United States, Roda inquired whether loans were forgiven in the case of death. Roda also wanted to know what types of jobs are available to students, each of which she assessed in its (in)compatibility with her religious practices. Roda used her interaction with Patti to learn about and begin planning for her future in the West. Such planning necessarily entails careful analysis of the interplay between traditional gender practices and new goals. Through dialogue she explored ideas to strengthen or relinquish as she forged a new way of being an educated Somali woman in the diaspora.

Relations with outsiders provide a means to learn about diverse gender practices more generally. On one of our last workshop days with the Form Fours, we asked the women to respond to two essay questions. The first asked that they explore if and how going to school has affected their thinking about certain gender practices, including marriage, relations with boys, female circumcision, and dress. The latter asked that they draw upon their interviews and experience doing community-based research to describe if and how education has affected the ways members of their community perceive the same practices. After writing the prompts on the board and discussing them, Rachel asked if anyone had any questions. Kalifa raised her hand and announced simply that they would like Rachel to share her individual perceptions on each of the above topics before they began. Heads nodded around the class as everyone showed keen interest in her perspective. Though we had made explicitly clear from the beginning of our time with the Form Fours that they were always welcome to ask any questions, the group chose to wait until this moment, when Patti was absent, to request a complete appraisal of gender practices by Rachel who is closer in age.

Rachel began by explaining the difficulty in asserting a "U.S. perspective" on any topic given existence of many diverse communities and experiences. Rachel shared that while some in the U.S. certainly marry early, others do not and that many people live with partners outside of marriage. Shamso interrupted at this point, asking simply, "Well, how many [relationships] have you had?" After Rachel answered honestly, Shamso wanted to know if her most recent relationship was with an age-mate. Someone else looked up to inquire if Rachel currently had one boyfriend or two. (Assumptions of heterosexuality were explicit).

Kalifa, with a concerned look on her face, asked suddenly, "So then, if people who are not married stay together, what happens if someone gets pregnant?" Rachel, repeating the difficulty of generalizing, noted that there are diverse possibilities in such a scenario. After listing a few, Rachel shared a story of her close friend Simone who had gotten pregnant at a young age and decided to raise the baby. The class did not appear particularly surprised by the story until she explained that Simone had brought her son Daniel with her to university where she enrolled as a full-time student. Rachel remembered how Simone carried Daniel to the college dining hall in the evenings. At the notion of a student-mother, many class members shook their heads vigorously and voiced "tsk tsk" noises. In response to the shows of dismay, Rachel asked if such a scenario, or for that matter premarital sex, often occurs in Dadaab. Suleha jumped in to say, "very rarely—very, very rarely and it is very bad." When Rachel asked what happens if an unmarried woman gets pregnant, Kalifa replied simply, "She will be left alone to take care of herself." Unsure as to whom exactly Kalifa described would be left alone, Rachel waited until someone explained that sometimes the grandparents take both new mother and baby in. Esther added that in such a situation the girls' brother has to go out and find the baby's father and demand that he marry his sister. If the father refuses, the brother then has to kill him. Kalifa added that the brother alone does not take such action, rather, the father or another elder spearheads the intervention.

Shamso, ready to move on from this line of discussion, asked what Rachel's parents would say if she moved in with a man before marriage. Students were visibly shocked when Rachel explained that she already lives apart from her parents. Concern and disbelief registered on many faces when Rachel shared how she had initially moved to a different state for university. Kalifa asked incredulously, "What about your parents? They are just left alone?" When Rachel replied that fortunately, they are both still healthy and work full time jobs, Kalifa refuted, "What about later?" Again, when Rachel explained that such a scenario would be addressed when necessary and that she hopes to eventually live closer to her family, Kalifa continued to shake her head. Rachel agreed that elder care could stand improvement in the U.S., though explained the strain a full-time job places on a person's ability to care for relatives. When nursing homes were broached in conversation, the group frowned and continued head-shaking. Esther was the only student who had heard of nursing homes and seemed to fathom the situation, albeit with curiosity.

At this point Kalifa again took the lead, asking Rachel who was responsible for domestic work in her childhood home. Rachel responded that both of her parents worked outside of the home, both were breadwinners, and both contributed to the domestic work, though her mother did more in the home. Kalifa responded incredulously, "Your father cooked?" When Rachel nodded, Kalifa fired back, "So you would just sit there while your father cooks?" Rachel replied that in such a case, her father might cook but she would clean the dishes or alternatively, her mother might cook, her father clean, and she would do the laundry. The group exploded into laughter at this point and announced that such would be "very shameful here." Esther and Ayaan conciliated that "you make an arrangement with someone you marry and so it is okay." Rachel nodded and furthered that she would in fact only marry someone with whom acknowledgement of shared domestic duties is clear. Kalifa looked up critically and exclaimed, "You won't cook and clean for him, but he brings home the bill!" After a few more questions, mostly which probed at perceptions of premarital sex among Americans without actually mentioning the word "sex," Shamso announced abruptly that it was time to stop questioning and start responding to the essay prompts.

In the above conversation, the students used Rachel's presence in the classroom to ask questions about different ways of being young women in the world. Students sought to hear about, comment upon, align themselves with, and at times distinguish themselves from other forms of gender performance. Our presence, and in this moment Rachel's, signified difference that was measured up against traditional practices common in

Dadaab. And while some—such as favoring independence to marriage while young and seeking further education—were relatable, others—including parenting as a student or allowing husbands to cook—were not. Similarity and difference were dialogically carved out against a background of change and multiplicity in ways of being. Dialogue itself signified engagement with difference made possible through refugee life and camp schooling.

Beyond being interested in gender practices among women of other cultures and religions, students in Dadaab asked for reports of how resettled Somalis experience life in the United States. In particular, students were interested in Somali women in the U.S.'s efforts to mediate differing gender expectations. Jawahir asked in a focus group at Bartan Secondary what resettled women's lives are like in general. Deko, who awaited departure on a WUSC scholarship, asked if, "it is true that in your place you can wear whatever you want?" She followed her question with admission that she worried about what kind of reception she would meet when wearing a *hijab* in Canada. Would she constantly have to explain herself? "Do people there know Islam?" Deko wondered.

As noted, another common strategy of relationship building with international visitors in the camps includes using their perceived status to seek address of specific needs and problems. Women and girls in the camps seek out visitors in efforts to locate new avenues to manage often deeply personal and gendered issues. Specifically, women and girls look for touch points outside of the Somali community to help mediate pressures facing them from within the community. In doing so, they employ strategies similar to the report of problems to Kenyan teachers. However, in engaging with foreign visitors, they try to supplement, or even bypass, structures established by Somali community organizations and local agencies in the address of pressing gendered issues. In the next chapter we provide a detailed account of one young woman's effort to avoid her own circumcision by seeking Patti's assistance. Though successful in the end, Aman would likely have been circumcised without the social capital made available through alliance with a White, international visitor.

During each focus group we held in Dadaab, we shared our e-mails and local phone numbers in case participants wanted to follow up on discussion points or needed to reach us. After meeting with Qafis primary school teachers, Patti received a call from Muno who asked to meet privately. On the appointed afternoon, Muno, who was clad in *hijab* and *niqab*, looked carefully around to assure that she and Patti were alone before beginning to share her story. Once certain, she lifted her *niqab* and told Patti how she had been raped as a primary student and consequentially dropped out of school. Rather than stop studying, however, she had spoken with the CARE education supervisor who in turn made extra efforts to obtain books for her so that she could sit for the KCPE exam. Nonetheless, Muno remembered not feeling well on the test day and performed poorly. Missing the entrance requirement for secondary, Muno again turned to the education supervisor who was able to secure her teaching job in a primary school. With the expanding number of Form Four leavers in the camp, however, Muno felt nervous about being replaced. The education supervisor who had helped her in the past no longer worked in Dadaab. His successor was a Somali Kenyan man with whom Muno did not feel comfortable sharing her problems. As a result, she appealed to Patti for help in the form of a scholarship. Muno specifically asked Patti to orchestrate something for her while maintaining confidentiality.

Like many others, Muno looked to Patti as a sponsor for further education. In her particular case, such an appeal replaced efforts to follow established mechanisms for help. Not only did Muno not want to share her history of rape with a Somali man, she also knew that such a report of gendered struggle would likely not set her apart from the hundreds of other qualified students in need of further education. As a primary school teacher who did not attend secondary, Muno lacked access to female Kenyan teachers. Instead, Muno assumed that Patti would be sympathetic to gender issues, endowed with easy access to resources, and willing and able to go above the heads of existent structures to champion a cause. Muno's situation was not unique; rather, White visitors are often besieged with requests for sponsorship. Strategic partnerships with Western visitors are particularly useful for the many Somali women who tend not to seek help from other Somalis in order to avoid judgment and community exposure.

It is crucial to note, however, that while some women appreciate and view relations with Western women positively, others are rightfully skeptical of Westerners presence in the camp. Certainly, a range of political viewpoints and agendas for being in Dadaab are represented among visitors to the camp. Given the constant presence of international visitors yet enduring inadequacy of resources and stymied possibility for exit, refugees express frustration at perceived inaction. One day at the end of a focus group discussion, we asked the gathered group of secondary students if they had final questions for us. Hawo announced that she did indeed have a question. She described how from her early days in school, she had memories of researchers coming into schools, taking notes, and carrying around big books, yet after such interactions she and her fellow students never again heard from them nor knew what happened to the acquired information. She wanted to know if and how we planned to differentiate ourselves from such a model. We agreed that she made a very good point and planned to follow a research paradigm in which analysis emerged through continued dialogic engagement. Further, during our time in Dadaab, Patti began to make arrangements for sustained partnership with CARE as an educational consultant. Beginning in 2008, Patti spearheaded a project geared specifically at the creation of new opportunities for refugee girls and women. We explained this to Hawo and the group. Hawo's question echoed in another student's inquiry, "How will you represent our stories?" Finally, students are quick to question us on why Canada offers educational scholarships with resettlement opportunities while the U.S. does not. While they recognize the U.S. as a leader in general refugee resettlement, they feel frustrated that none such opportunities are merit-based or linked to education and often say so to American citizens in the camps.

Relations with international visitors provide refugees further exposure to different ways of being and in doing so, ask students to compare, critique, or reify various Somali ways of being. Further, such relations are often employed strategically for advocacy within the camps, particularly in gender salient ways. Refugees use connections with Westerners to seek supplementary resources and critique perceived dearth of opportunities or exploitation experienced at the hands of other Western visitors. Significantly, those refugees granted meaningful exposure to visitors are drawn almost exclusively from among the educated, English speakers: The father of a young woman whom we assisted in her efforts to apply to U.S. universities noted that it was his daughter's enrollment in school had made our burgeoning friendship with his daughter possible.

> After educating our children for so long, now that we look at others who are in the village ... and we appear different among the refugees. Those, you White girls from U.S., we would never, it might happen that we would see each other. It's out of the knowledge that we educated our daughters that we have seen even you people.

Rashid acknowledged how his choice to pioneer education for his daughters, which, in addition to the salaries he now receives from two who have graduated, enabled his relationship with us that without an educated daughter, simply would not have been possible in the context of Dadaab.

Conclusion

Through embrace of difference, multiculturalism, and an expressed desire for global citizenry, students come to view themselves as a newly evolving type of Somali woman. In their dialogue across difference, they highlighted various facets of Somali culture. Such appraisal was not uniform but rather individualized as each student crafted her own dynamic understanding of what being a Somali woman means in Dadaab. The young women's processes of identity formation employed various means of reaching out across difference. They built relations with ethnic minorities, Western visitors, male students, and Kenyan teachers.

Taken together, young women use schooling as a space and process through which to become knowledgeable of and connected to a larger world beyond Dadaab.

NOTES

1. The timing of our first visit to Dadaab corresponded with the U.S. funded occupation of Mogadishu by Ethiopian troops as well as the U.S. bombings of rural Somali communities. As a result of such intervention as well as other U.S. foreign policy decisions including the invasion of Iraq, many refugees in the camp were sharply critical of the United States. Two American researchers who made frequent visits to the camps explained that the level of anti-American sentiment was increasing. At the same time, it was well known that the United States sponsored by far the most refugees for resettlement, just as it provided much of the food stuff distributed as rations. Oftentimes, refugees critical of the U.S. dreamed of resettling there. As a result, opinions of the United States in the camps were deeply mixed.

2. Until as recently as the 1940s, scientists in Europe and the U.S. recommended clitordectomy to curb perceived "hypersexuality" in women (Boyle, 2002; Gruenbaum, 2001; Lane & Rubinstein, 1996; Parker, 1995).

3. On our second visit to Dadaab, after Esther had graduated from high school, we noticed that she was more outspoken in her critique of certain practices common among many of her Somali neighbors, including discrimination, just as she spoke more proudly and openly about her Christian identity. As it was no longer necessary to attend school daily as a minority (but rather she spent her days working among the primarily Christian aid worker community), she seemed to experience a bit more leeway in voicing her opinions. Esthers careful presentation of self demonstrates an adept negotiation of context—a social survival mechanism in Dadaab.

4. At the time of our study, demographic makeup of primary school teaching staff was undergoing significant change. Increasing numbers of Form Four leavers were chosen to replace original hires for primary positions, bearing significant gendered consequences as the vast majority of graduates were male while many original teachers were female Class Eight leavers. CARE's Education Sector was also making a concerted effort to send Form Four Leavers to regional teacher training colleges on scholarship in efforts to improve the standard of primary education in the camps. Again, such held gendered consequences, as the vast majority of teachers with KCSE scores high enough to be eligible for college were men.

5. CARE recently amended the rule declaring Dadaab as a "no-family post" to allow female staff members to bring dependent children. According to

CARE management, such represents an institutional effort to recruit and retain more women on staff. During our time in Dadaab, each camp compound housed one or two mothers and their children. For the most part, however, NGO staff used their time off to visit family across Kenya. At CARE, most workers were allotted two weeks off per eight while teachers followed the school calendar and had three, one month holidays during the year.

CHAPTER 7

DIALOGUES OF CHANGE

One blisteringly hot morning, Patti, Rachel, and Windle Trust teacher Molly walked along the sand road from the CARE compound in Qafis to the secondary school where they were scheduled to meet with Form Four students. As they walked, Patti felt a hand slip into hers. She turned to peer a 16-year-old girl. Aman wore a dark colored *hijab,* which was standard dress among women in the camp, as well as the less commonplace *niqab.* The effect was to cover all but her sandaled feet and pleadingly determined eyes. Aman held tightly to Patti's hand and leaned in toward her ear. Firing few words with great precision, Aman explained that she needed help to thwart an impending circumcision. Her aunt was coming from Somalia to drag her "to the bush." Her mother was sick and could no longer stop the aunt from acting. Could Patti please contact a protection officer at the UNHCR? She urgently repeated her block number as if to brand it in Patti's mind. "Please. Please."

Trying to avoid dramatic gestures that might rouse attention, Patti returned of Aman's grasp, "Come with us," and steered her through the gates of the schoolyard. Once inside, the two found a deserted bench and sat to talk.

"I wish I was Christian," Aman began. Her pronouncement struck Patti as the recklessly brave words of a teenager. "Christians don't circumcise their daughters and girls can be educated and have careers." She retold her story with greater elaboration: Aman's mother was ill with a mental disease. She sat all day staring off and did not speak. She no longer helped the family to cook, gather water, or care for the children. She longed for her eldest daughter whom she had thought was dead.

Educated for Change?: Muslim Refugee Women in the West, pp. 175–200

Recently, she had heard that the 18-year-old was recently seen crossing the desert from Somalia en route to the camp. As a result, she had gone to a man in the town of Dadaab who frequently crossed the desert to trade goods. She had paid him to take her with him on his next journey. Now, she waited to depart, but mentally, she had already left Dadaab. Her mind wandered in the desert searching for her lost daughter.

aunt was also in the desert and also on her way to Dadaab. She had heard that the mother was ill and that her nieces had not been properly circumcised. She was ashamed and was resolved to amend the situation. She had sent word that she would arrive shortly. The aunt was a midwife who performed the ritual procedure on girls throughout the community. She knew that the girls did not wish to be circumcised but, nevertheless, she communicated her plan to bring Aman and her younger sisters to the bush against their will. She promised that it would not be avoided.

As Aman unraveled her story, Patti interjected questions and comments. How old were the sisters? Aman was 16 and a Standard 7 student. One sister was 13 and was also enrolled in primary school. The others were only 5 and 6. Patti remarked that Aman's English was excellent given her grade level. Aman smiled with evident pride at the compliment. She described her dream to excel in secondary school and one day to migrate to Canada on a WUSC scholarship. In preparation, she had developed the habit of asking her teachers for a new English word to practice everyday. In this way, she had won the teachers' favor and acquired proficiency long before her peers.

Aman explained that her father had died when she was young. Since the onset of her mother's illness, Aman and her sister had taken care of the four younger siblings and attended school. When girls are circumcised, she explained, the blood cannot pass every month like it does for uncircumcised girls. "It backs up and gives cramps. Makes girls sick," she said didactically. "You miss school and fall behind. That is why I don't want it. I want to go to school like Christian girls."

Given her mother's condition, Aman was now unprotected against her aunt's wishes. Older women harassed her family at the water taps in efforts to pressure compliance. She was teased by peers at school. Given such treatment, Aman had taken to hiding behind the veil.

Patti promised to look into the matter and asked Aman to meet her the next morning.

Patti first approached James, the head of CARE's Gender and Development (GAD) sector in Qafis camp. As anticipated, James was deeply skeptical and concluded that Aman had "probably already been circumcised and is lying [to Patti] to better her chance for resettlement." At Patti's urging, James reluctantly agreed to investigate the case nonetheless.

Aman and Patti met several times over the next 2 weeks. Aman's persistence did not diminish. At their second meeting, Aman explained that James had found her and referred her to the Voluntary Counseling and Testing Center (VCT). She was excited and encouraged. She thanked Patti repeatedly for her interventions. James had written Aman a note and instructed her to give it to Maryanne, a Kenyan and the head counselor at VCT. James had strictly instructed Aman to ensure that the letter travel directly into Maryanne's hands.

A few days later, Aman and Patti met again. Aman had a stricken expression. As instructed, she had walked to the VCT to book an appointment with Maryanne. However, Maryanne hadn't been available. A male Somali incentive worker in charge of scheduling had coerced her to hand over the letter. After reading it, the man scolded Aman harshly and told her that it was a very shameful thing she had done to report her case. He finished by warning Aman not to tell anyone else about the situation.

After establishing that Aman wanted to continue to try and meet with a counselor, Patti, Aman, and Aman's younger sister walked over to the counseling facility. They found Maryanne in a staff meeting. Aman, seeing the face of the incentive worker with whom she had originally spoken, shrunk back and away from the door. Patti asked Maryanne if they could set a time to talk. As if in response to Patti's request, the male incentive worker announced that Aman's case had already been "handled." Patti met Maryanne's eyes and shook her head gently to indicate that it had not. Maryanne stood and led Patti and the girls around to the outside of the building. The area reeked of urine and the sand reflected the blinding glare of the noonday sun. Quickly scanning Aman and her sister, Maryanne announced: "you two don't even look related." The girls fell silent and their eyes fell to the ground. Looking back at Patti, Maryanne instructed them to return a few days later during a 2 hour window of time when she might be able to work them into her schedule.

In the interim, Patti spoke with the head of the GAD sector who, in a now familiar refrain, told her that the entire situation sounded "like a hoax." Maryanne missed the next appointment. The next day, Patti located Maryanne at lunch. Maryanne explained that her schedule was, "In šā' Allāh" (God willing), and told Patti to come to her office again the next day.

The time of Aman's aunt's arrival was drawing closer. Patti gave Aman a cell phone so that Aman could reach her in case the aunt arrived in Dadaab. One evening, Aman called Patti and anxiously reported that her aunt was scheduled to return any day and that if nothing were done, she would be circumcised in secret within a week of her aunt's arrival. Patti urgently sent an e-mail to all those from whom she had sought assistance: CARE management, GAD sector representatives including James and Maryanne, and UNHCR protection officers. More time passed with no response.

On the evening before the aunt's scheduled arrival, Patti fielded increasingly panicked calls from Aman. Patti went to the UNHCR only to learn that both protection officers were away for the weekend and their assistant was busy in the field. Patti returned to CARE and found David, the program support manager for all of CARE operations in Dadaab, who promised to organize a problem-solving meeting the following morning. While David scheduled the gathering, Patti heard back from a UNHCR representative who agreed to go to the block and look for Aman. Before the end of the evening, Patti called Aman to inform her of the plan and to tell her to come to the Qafis CARE compound in the event that her aunt arrived.

In the morning, Patti received a panicked call from Aman. The girl's aunt had returned to the camps. No one from the UNHCR had come to help her and she had been turned away from the CARE compound. Unable to locate appropriate CARE staff, Patti called the UNHCR protection office and spoke to a secretary who agreed to forward the message to the field officer. She told Aman to find the UNHCR field office in Qafis. Urgently, Patti secured transportation to Qafis and began to search for Aman. Unable to locate her or a UNHCR protection officer, Patti moved quickly to the CARE compound to find James. Though James was out of his office, Patti ran into Alex, a European UNHCR field worker. Patti was relaying the story to Alex when James appeared.

James announced that he had just visited Aman's residence. Shaking his head at Patti, he declared that he was "sorry," but while at Aman's, he had met the aunt who not only denied ever being in Somalia but also accused Aman of lying. James reported that, when prompted by her aunt, Aman admitted the story was false. During James' description, Alex asked incredulous questions and demanded to know how James could believe Aman's confession when it occurred in her aunt's company. In response, James announced that he knew of every uncircumcised girl in Qafis, and furthermore, could identify a girls' status by her walk and behavior. He had no doubt that Aman had already been circumcised.

Shocked, Patti demanded to know Aman's whereabouts. James looked around in confusion. "She must have returned to her home." Patti found her crying on the walk home from CARE and brought her back into the compound where she discovered that James had left. Alex interviewed Aman about the details of the situation and asked if she would be comfortable with a physical examination to prove the validity of her story. Though clearly fearful, Aman agreed and was soon transported to the Qafis hospital where the head maternity nurse performed an examination and verified Aman's uncircumcised status.

Upon hearing the news, Alex assured Patti that in 1 hour a UNHCR vehicle would arrive with police escort to deliver Aman to her block where she could gather her siblings and supplies. Three hours later the car came, and Patti and Aman were driven to the edge of Aman's residential block. Neither the UNHCR protection officer nor the police escort volunteered to follow Aman to her compound but rather announced their intention to wait in the vehicle. Afraid that Aman would be harassed or hurt, Patti accompanied Aman through the block.

Inside her family's compound, Aman's mother sat, as reported, on a stool and stared into space. Aman spoke to her in hushed tones but elicited no response. As crowds of women and children gathered, Aman and her younger brothers and sisters, ranging in ages 5 to 14, exited quickly with only an old mat, a few cooking pots, a jerry can, and a small plastic bag of clothes. The UN car then delivered Aman and her family to the protection center, a fenced in area with rows of dried dung homes covered by tin roofs. As it started to rain, the protection officer announced that she, and therefore Patti, needed to return to the NGOs at once. The children remained in the protection area with no food or lamps for their first night alone.

In the morning, Patti returned to find Aman and her sister preparing breakfast over a small fire. Relieved that they were okay, Patti learned that neighbors in the protection area had donated firewood and flour to the family. In the following weeks, Save the Children was handed the case and ensured that the family was given food, a new ration card, as well as supplies to care for themselves. Fearing harassment, Aman had to withdraw from school for several months. The family was routinely visited at the fence of the compound by family members who scolded her for her behavior and told her that, one day, she would be circumcised.

Reportedly, the harassment Aman faced at the hands of Somali community members eventually receded. Her mother came to join the children within the protection area. When an older sister arrived from Somalia, the family was moved out of the protection area and into a new camp. All of the family's children were re-enrolled in school and Aman writes occasional e-mails to let Patti know that she is doing well and continues to study hard in order to secure a college scholarship.

Aman's story seems to have ended well in that she has thus far avoided circumcision and does not regret her decisions. Yet, hers is also a cautionary tale. While Aman was determined and uncompromising, her actions were widely discussed and stirred significant controversy throughout the camp system. In the process of fighting for what is ostensibly a legally protected right not to be forcefully circumcised, she was accused of lying and largely dismissed by the aid community. She withstood fear, isolation, and self-doubt; at age 16, she took on the care taking responsibilities for her entire family and withstood blatant harassment. Other young women with whom we worked did not share Aman's unmitigated courage or her blatant rejection of key aspects of Somali culture and tradition. Rather, Aman's story is the exception that proves the rule. Her discursive rejection of Islam in favor of Christianity, avowed desire for equality of opportunity for men and women, and depiction of Somali culture as uniformly "backward" stood apart from the more nuanced language and practices of peers.

The fact that change is happening within the Somali community at Dadaab and throughout the diaspora is widely understood by refugees and aid workers alike. As we have seen, change revolves around gender as a central principle of cultural and social organization. While most women do not embrace gender change to the degree that Aman does, they all acknowledge its salience in their lives and work proactively to make sense of their positionality within a dynamic period of Somali culture. In our work with the Form Four girls, we observed that, although girls did not share a single voice with regard to their opinions and positions on symbolic indicators of sociocultural change—such as circumcision, marriage, authority, and schooling—they did collectively craft and draw upon a set of discursive strategies or logics to justify their perspectives and choices.

Something Old, Something New

Unlike Aman, none of the Form Four women with whom we work expressed a desire to be Christian, assimilate to Western ways of being, or break dramatically from well established Somali cultural practices and tenets. While young women often aligned with the language of enlightenment to provide a rationale for their participation in schooling, rather than signaling a simple "colonization of the mind" (Wa Thiong'o, 1986), their praise for education as a civilizing force communicates a deeper, more nuanced understanding of their circumstances and possibilities for change. The majority of the women in our study talked about their participation in schooling as an emergent practice that, while new and unique, is nevertheless a legitimate way of being Somali and Muslim. More than just aligning with enlightenment, female students claim schooling as a medium through which they craft ways of being open-minded and wise Somalis. They see their participation in schooling as the key mechanism through which they can gradually expand options for Somali women. New options are, at once, modern and represent reenactments of well-established values and beliefs. Somali women sculpt lives that are distinct response to current realities of yet echo motifs of religiosity, modesty, and gendered familial expectations.

Form Four women developed overlapping strategies for carving acceptable, new ways of being Somali. One of these approaches is to distinguish culture from religion and mark those practices they hope to change as cultural in order to avoid the appearance of irreligiosity. Another strategy is to make the case that those ways of being required by formal education are compatible with desirable elements of Somali culture. Finally, the women point to the necessity for limited cultural change, especially with regard to gender norms, given particular possibilities and constraints of refugee life in Dadaab.

Distinguishing Culture From Religion

In their relayed stories and individual standpoints, participants commonly claim an ontological division between immutable religious doctrine and (time and place) dependent cultural constructs. In the women's narrative description of their lives, they implicitly define culture as a collection of convenient adaptations to ever changing environmental circumstances and conditions. Accordingly, cultural practices are viewed as functionalistic exercises that often become obsolete across time and place. Accordingly, in order to make a case for a particular type of change, the young women often characterize traditional practices as anachronistic rituals that have outlived their instrumentality. As young, educated Somalis whose habits are less entrenched than those of older community members and whose life experiences expose them to different institutions, bodies of knowledge, and belief systems, the women position themselves as credible agents in the identification of necessary points of cultural change. Simultaneously, they either maintain that the cultural change in question does not represent a break from Islamic religious doctrine or discursively tie proposed new ways of being Somali to older, established religious tenets and practices.

In our discussions about whether Islam's place in their everyday lives is subject to change, study participants stress continuity. When we asked upper intermediate Windle Trust students to describe if and how their religious practices had changed since arrival in Dadaab, one student replied, "These practices cannot be changed. It's an obligatory duty." Another echoed her sentiment, "We [haven't] changed these practices since we came to Dadaab and we have never changed these practices ever on the Earth." Form Four students reiterated the sanctity of religious doctrine. One student said, "They remain the same and will continue to remain the same." With the same tone of insistency another woman exclaimed, "No change at all and it will remain the same." Indeed, in countless focus groups and interviews students pledged to safeguard Islam's central role in their lives and adhere as closely as possible to Qu'ranic teachings.

Alongside their repeated re-inscription of Islam's immutability, women justified support of particular changes in cultural expectations and practice. In a focus group, Molly asked Form Four leavers to define *religion* and *culture* and explicate their relation to one another. She paraphrased the women's response:

> Culture is a peoples' way of life; customs, beliefs, and art. Religion is belief in a supreme existence and activities connect with the worship of that Supreme Being. The Somali culture is deeply rooted in Islam. However, the two differ in some aspects—there are cultural practices especially those concerning women that are contrary to Islam e.g. on circumcision.

As Molly's summation of the women's words conveys, even though Somali culture has roots in Islam, educated girls and women differentiate between practices associated with the worship of Allah and those deemed singularly cultural, sanctifying only the former. The students communicate that significant cultural transformation could occur *without* compromising Islamic devotion and, in certain cases, might demonstrate a more complete adherence to the Qu'ran. As one student wrote, "Some of these [gendered] practices were generally prohibited without any good reason or belief but it has now changed as people came to know they do not violate the religion." Many in the refugee community, for instance, argue that girls' participation in camp schooling embodies, rather than contradicts, Qu'ranic teachings. Still others condemn female circumcision as an expendable cultural practice.

Despite the ease with which some students verbally contrast Somali culture and religion, in reality lines separating the two spheres are blurred, shifting, overlapping and subject to individual interpretation. For example, both proponents and opponents of female circumcision drew heavily from the Qu'ran. In the Dadaab Refugee camps, the vast majority of young girls (around 97%) are circumcised, even as NGOs take firm rhetorical stances against the practice. Though effective prevention of circumcision on the part of NGOs is hindered by reluctance to alienate traditionalist segments of the population, campaign strategies include, but are not limited to: sponsorship of anti-FGC dramatizations on International Women's Day; instruction on *Against the Pleasure Principal* in the Form Four Curriculum[1]; workshops outlining the consequences of FGC to a woman's health; and propagation of anti-FGC messages on t-shirts and signs in both English and Somali. CARE's GAD sector dedicated an arm to the prevention of Gender Based Violence (GBV) for which "touchpoint" persons are spread throughout the camps. Despite NGO efforts, student participants were clear that, unlike early marriage, the prevalence of FGC has far from abated in Dadaab. They explained that traditionalist refugees respond to circumcision in residential blocks by simply relocating the practice "to the bush."

In discussion and writings, girls reveal exhaustive knowledge of the consequences of female circumcision. They share personal experiences of missing class due to excruciating menstrual pain, echo public health warnings about the transfer of HIV/AIDS through circumcision razors, and lament the hazards childbirth often presented circumcised women. However, they vary in their stances on circumcision. While some students dismiss female circumcision as a harmful cultural practice, others defend it in the name of religion. In their meaning making, girls who take anti-circumcision positions employ a discursive distinction between culture and religion in order to condemn the practice without signaling compromised religious sensibilities. With the singular exception of Aman, no Somali informant in our study seemed comfortable amending religious practice. Rather, for students, rejection of female circumcision requires demonstration of its insignificance to Islam. Qamar, a student researcher and advanced Windle Trust student, compiled her research on forms of violence against girls and women in an analytic essay. Like many others, she makes explicit what she considers the religious irrelevance of female circumcision:

> But the worst of all the types of circumcision women and girls undergo is a type known as F.G.C., *which has no point in any religion*. It involves cutting and removing some parts of women's reproductive organs. [Some people] claim women are bisexual; others say that it will increase women's desire which is directly opposite what is there; others say they do this for health reasons, of which they say uncircumcised girls and women are unclean and smell. This claim is untrue as all people keep clean and prevent themselves from smelling of sweat and dirt by washing. In fact, girls and women who have [been circumcised] suffer [from] F.G.C. related problems: acute urinary retention, urinary infection, abnormal menstrual discharge, and foul-smelling odor. [Emphasis is ours]

In a similar vein to Qamar, Kalifa shared:

> This is something I want to abstain from, [as] FGM has impact on somebody's health and wellbeing. *It is not a religious but cultural practice* and [it is] not only me who has seen its impact but also the community at large. (Emphasis is ours)

Similarly, Shamso notes: "FGM is a wrong concept believed and inherited from the older people. It also have a negative impact on Somali girls." Finally, Jawahir explains, "the Qu'ran only requires male circumcision." According to Qamar, Kalifa, Shamso, and Jawahir, the dispensability of female circumcision stems from its cultural and traditional, rather than religious, rationale.

Somali writer Saida Hagi-Dirie Herzi made famous the argument that FGC is a cultural practice as opposed to a religious one in her short story "Against the Pleasure Principle." Banned in Somalia and first published in the *Index on Censorship*, "Against the Pleasure Principle" features Rahma, a young, pregnant Somali woman, as she anticipates accompanying her husband to an Ivy-League University in the United States. Rahma's mother attempts to dissuade her daughter from the move for fear that American doctors lack experience in childbirth with circumcised women. She arranges for a group of Somali women who had lived abroad to recount to Rahma the reactionary responses of Western doctors to their circumcised bodies. However, rather than convince Rahma, these recollections, coupled with memory of her own circumcision experience as a child, fuel a profound questioning of Somali culture. As one character in the story wonders:

> Why did her people do this to their women? Hundreds of millions of women the world over went through life the way God had created them, whole and unmutilated. Why could her people not leave well enough alone? It seemed to her, at least in this case, that man's attempts to improve on nature were a disaster. (Herzi, 1999, p. 248)

Herzi (1999) offers a searing critique of female circumcision on the basis of its consequences to a woman's sexual pleasure. Rather than a religious practice necessitated by the Qu'ran, her protagonist understands infibulation as an attempt to safeguard a woman's virginity for the sake of a male partner. According to Zabus (2007, p. 155), Herzi "ventriloquizes" through Rahma and, in doing so, shows "an awareness of Muslim jurisprudence, whereby excision is *makrumah*, that is, permissible or recommended but not *wajib*, that is, obligatory or required. She presents infibulation as an 'ugly custom borrowed from the ancient Egyptians'" (p. 782).

In the end, Rahma resolves never to circumcise her own daughters. She wonders, "How much longer … would the women of her culture have to endure this senseless mutilation?… She had always hated circumcision. Now she hated it more than ever. No daughter of hers would ever be subjected to it." Rahma's announcement is particularly portentous for the ways in which it breaks from the practice's generational transmission chain (Zabus, 2007). Certainly, knowledge that students read "Against the Pleasure Principle" as part of the Form Four curriculum fuels accusation among traditionalists in the community that school is incompatible with Somali culture and, as noted by some, "ruins women and girls."

However, Somali female students' endorsement of Herzi's message was not ubiquitous. Many refute the assertion that circumcision is simply a product of culture, defending it in the name of Islam. Form Four student Luul wrote:

> Large numbers in our community do this practice [circumcision] in today's society that we live in. It is a practice which has been inherited from our forefathers. *FGM is the act of a religion* which must be fulfilled by the parents in a healthy manner. This must be done carefully [and] may not harm any organ in the body in consideration to that. [Emphasis is ours]

Luul's justification for circumcision as an act of religious devotion includes a call for sterile practice, revealing her familiarity with anti-FGC arguments. Indeed, informants who defend FGC do not deny its consequences; nor, are they less educated than Shukri, Kalifa, Shamsa, and Jawahir. Rather, they at once label female circumcision an Islamic prerogative and, as Luul recommends, support precautionary measures such as the disposal of razors between patients so as to curb health risks. Another student, Zainab, explains that "FGM is female [genital] cutting and … when it is seriously cut, it will effect the female in her future. But, I support when it is done as per required." Like Luul, Zainab recognizes potential complications associated with the procedure, yet maintains that circumcision is a requirement for Somali Muslim girls. Among the Form Four informants, Yasmeen was the most ardent supporter of FGC.

Yasmeen generally remained quiet in our meetings with the Qafis Form Four girls. Her writings, however, revealed a conservative bent. According to Yasmeen:

> *The issue of F.G.M. is both a traditional and religious process* and I think it is right to be practiced because [the] traditional is the backbone of society and every society has got its own tradition and must be practiced. I hope school doesn't [have] any impact on it since school does not interfere with traditions and practices of the society. [Emphasis is ours]

Even as Yasmeen warns against the infiltration of school-based knowledge in the arena of tradition, she supports girls' schooling, and accordingly, an end to early marriage. In order to at once reject the tradition of early marriage and uphold the practice of circumcision, Yasmeen symbolically separates culture from religion, and depicts the latter as impenetrable to change. Similar to her peers who take anti-circumcision stances, such a discursive distinction allows Yasmeen to establish a personal balance between continuity and change encouraged within her new environs.

In their efforts to craft novel enactments of Somaliness, educated girls and women endorse (or condone) reform in gender practices when such change can be perceived as a cultural rather than religious modification. In cases when the young women support circumcision, they attribute the necessity of the practice to religious doctrine.

Even as women call for change in cultural practice, however, rather than doing so in bold, outspoken ways, they tend to stake out modest positions that represent peaceable compromise. Again, this approach is illustrated in the women's discussions about acceptable forms of circumcision.

Zabus (2004) describes three primary types of FGC (p. 112):

> First, *sunna(h)*, which involves the removal of the prepuce or hood of the clitoris; second, excision *per se*, also called clitoridectomy, which involves the removal of the clitoris itself and all or part of the labiae minorae, leaving the labiae majorae intact; and third, infibulation or suturing, which consists in "the removal of the whole of labiae minorae and majorae, and the stitching together of the two sides of the vulva, leaving a very small orifice to permit the flow of urine and menstrual discharge." (Lightfoot-Klein, 1989, p. 33; Thomas, 1987, p. 16, emphasis is the authors)

Infibulation, or *firuani*, is the technique predominately employed in Somalia and Dadaab. However, students who deem FGC to be religiously mandated vary in their commitment to infibulation as best practice. At the same time, among women who label circumcision a cultural practice, many desire a degree of continuity just as they fear that complete rejection of FGC would render their daughters unmarriageable. For both groups of students, *sunna* represents an appropriate compromise.

Molly held a focus group with Form Four leavers in which she asked participants of their future intentions regarding circumcision. Halima replied:

> I don't want to bring harm to my child's health thus deny her rights but at the same time, I don't want to totally desert my culture, so I will settle for a compromise, that is the *sunna* type of circumcision.

Halima's articulation at once draws upon enlightenment discourse in her reference to "rights" and to traditionalism in her need to avoid what would feel like cultural desertion. Molly summarizes other participant's responses:

> Almost all [participants] said yes. Few were undecided. Those who said, "yes" will use the *sunna* method, which is accepted in Islam. It does not have negative health implications unlike other methods; e.g., the traditional *firuani* which the ladies think is cruel.

Roda, who tentatively advocates a compromise position similar to Halima's notes:

If I have daughters, I cannot circumcise in [firuani] way. Circumcision is a religious act, from the prophet. Not infibulation—maybe clitoris should be pierced so that blood comes out. Pharoah introduced infibulations. He used to kill male children. For every child he killed, he infibulated (a girl) to reduce the sense of women, so they don't feel like they want to have sex.

In her nuanced analysis, Roda locates the origins of infibulation in Pharoic Egypt and in a racist attempt to reduce the size of the Semite population; at the same time, however, she declares female circumcision religiously significant. Distinguishing between forms of circumcision allows Roda to make sense of the contradiction and choose *sunna* as an appropriate compromise. While Roda does not believe that female circumcision prevents a woman from engaging in sexual activity per say, she deems such functionalist analysis of the practice irrelevant to its symbolic significance.

In sum, educated young women both critically assess the significance of female circumcision and pay heed to its consequence in women's quality of life. They take a range of stances regarding the continuance of the practice—or some form of the practice—and on circumcision's salience in construction of what it means to be a Somali Muslim woman. Whether or not students condemned female circumcision, however, a strategic separation of culture and religion allows them to make sense of circumcision as a potential area of gender change in Dadaab and to etch out new, yet redolent ways of being in and seeing the world as Somali women.

The Compatibility of Schooling and Somali Ways of Being

One afternoon we met eight Form Four girls for a focus group discussion in Bartan camp. Surrounded by beakers and books in the school's chemistry laboratory, conversation turned to what it is like to be an educated Somali girl in Dadaab. Hawo summarized simply, "It doesn't mean we don't know our culture." To illustrate, she shared that Somali girls are not allowed to play sports outside. Though she neared completion of 12 years of formal schooling, Hawo "dresses the way her community allows … not playing outside, not intermixing with men." Jawahir echoed Hawo's point, eyeing her peers and announcing on the group's behalf that "They love Islam and wouldn't play outside"—to do so would be "totally haram!" Indeed, NGO efforts to form sports leagues among Somali female students have been largely unsuccessful—protested by parents and boycotted by students. Despite such restrictions, Jawahir explained, "religion also states you [as a girl] are supposed to be educated." Accordingly, female students with whom we worked argue that school attendance is compatible with Somali ways of being female. In the highly visible arena of dress, for instance, students signaled an unwavering commitment to the maintenance of traditional standards.

During our conversation, Sahra, a Form Four completer, outlined the parameters of appropriate dress in Dadaab, "[The] majority of women in Dadaab dress in accordance to the recommended Islamic code. We cover our bodies except the face and hands. Dresses should be free and long. The head is covered in a *hijab*." Indeed, all of the Somali refugee women and girls that we met in Dadaab donned traditional clothing. Only women in the non-Muslim minority communities varied clothing styles and, as described, often endure significant harassment as a result. According to Zainab:

> Dress is a mode of wearing clothes; dressing [is] something which does not depend on education. Dressing is stated in my religion. Even if I gain the highest standard of education, I think [I] would dress as the religion states, as I am educated and learn religious education in school.

Like Zainab, when asked about whether or not education had influenced her perspective on certain gendered practices, Kalifa responded, "I still have my dressing style and I am content with it whatever the circumstance, since it is religious." Yasmeen similarly explained:

> Going to school discourages earlier marriage and makes people understand about knowledge and its importance; hence this can create [an] elite society. On the other hand, school does not affect one's style of dress.

In their marked commitment to traditional (and purported religiously prescribed) modes of dress, school-going girls demonstrate that participation in formal education does not conflict with ways of being Somali. For their part, NGOs in Dadaab work to signal compatibility through provision of appropriate school uniforms as well as through the construction of separate mosques and water taps on school facilities. While Dadaab students acknowledge that Somalis in the diaspora are known to modify their dress, they reify the symbolic significance of Islamic identified dress in the camp setting. According to Nimo, while, "these days it seems it [dress] is changing because of cultural assimilation and I anticipate that it will continue changing," for her, such change was unacceptably irreligious. "The ideal dress for a woman is the one that is recommended in the religion that covers the whole body and is again loose when worn, because it is recommended in the religion of Islam." In the face of perceived change, female students reject shifting standards of dress in order to support the notion that secular school attendance does not necessitate a rejection of Muslim ways of being.

Young women's observance of traditional Muslim dress practices comprises a highly visible and material marker of the seeming compatibility between Somali ways of being and participation in Western, secular schooling. Women's efforts to demonstrate compatibility between established ways of being Somali women and school attendance are also evident in the women's less tangible work to envision future selves. In the traditional organization of Somali society, women's major contribution to family, clan, and community occurs through marriage, child rearing, and domestic labor. The act of marrying itself represents an opportunity to forge or strengthen bonds between clans. Clan-exogamous, cross-cousin marriages[2] unite couples from distinct clan lineages, and in doing so, create symbolic for partnerships between groups (Ahmed, 2004). Girls are typically married in their early teens, and by the age reached by many Form Four students in Dadaab, have already borne multiple children. Within marriage, a woman's value is in part determined according to her ability to birth and raise children, especially sons. Female students in the camps, therefore, chart new terrain whereupon increasing access to higher education delays reproductive responsibility. In efforts to reconcile schooling and marriage, they frame the former as a requisite that postpones, rather than precludes, the latter. As such, education does not impede their ability to meet the symbolic standard of Somali womanhood. Form Four student Ayaan wrote in a personal essay:

> Going to school does not have very big impact on marriage because after school they can get on marriage and then can have children, if God gives them as a gift. Though in our culture and tradition, a girl must be married immediately when she reaches 15 yrs old, it has changed these days. I, personally, marriage does not have [an] impact on my school because it's my wish and choice to get married and can plan it easily in the future to come, In šā' Allāh.

Building upon the understanding that marriage is not, in fact, threatened by schooling, female students emphasize education's significance in their present lives. During the aforementioned focus group in the Bartan school chemistry lab, Hawo explained that reaching Form Four had involved tremendous sacrifice and she was committed to seeing her personal and economic investment through. Hawo concluded that, like her peers, she would marry only after exhausting possibilities for further education. In response, Patti asked if the girls' families were in support of their plans. Leyla answered simply, "Who can force us now? We're given to freedom." Fadumo explained that in the past a girl might have been told, "You will become the mother of twenty children." Now, however, she could counter, "I have my own work-plan. Let me exhaust these hours for learning." Implicit in Fadumo's statement is acknowledgment that later hours would be spent raising children. However, looking imploringly at her peers and the two of us, Fadumo inquired, "A baby—what will a baby bring you? But education!" She drifted off to allow the group to imagine possibilities. She concluded by voicing the oft echoed regret that "if a girl marries [before being educated] she is just thrown away." Rather than reject marriage, Form Four students in Bartan framed it as a future requirement.

Like Fadumo, female students with whom we worked uniformly condemn early marriage, an umbrella term used to refer to the marriage of a child under the age of 18. According to Otoo-Oyortey and Pobi (2003), "Most early marriages are arranged and based on the consent of the parents and often fail to ensure the best interests of the girl child. Early marriages often include some element of force" (p. 8). In Dadaab, early marriage represents the single most formidable obstacle to girls' schooling and, as elsewhere, often evokes economic rationalization. Poor parents with few livelihood options earn monetary compensation for the transfer of their young daughter to a husband's household. Backed by school personnel, however, female students are increasingly able to refuse unfavorable marriage arrangements without consent of family and community.

Just as school-going girls demonstrate an unwavering commitment to education and condemn early marriage, they reify the importance of (delayed) marriage in a woman's life. During one afternoon in Qafis, Form Four student Shamso asked why Rachel was not married. She insisted that, unlike herself and her peers, Rachel was ready. According to Shamso, "you have finished university; you can get married now." As Shamso offered to find Rachel a suitable Somali marriage partner, other students made "tsk tsk" sounds, laughed abashedly, or rolled their eyes. Ayaan, placing her arm around Rachel, protested Shamso's prescription and announced that Rachel had yet to complete graduate school. She then accused Shamso of already having had babies. Suddenly quiet, Shamso aborted her persuasive mission. Unsure of what to make of Ayaan's comment, which Shamso appeared to take as an insult, Rachel let the conversation drop. The next day, Shamso, flanked by friends from the group, approached Rachel to apologize for her suggestion. After Rachel assured her that there was no problem, Shamso eyed her peers and, with a smirk, announced that Ayaan was in fact a mother. Ayaan laughed and looked away.

As far as we were able to ascertain, neither Ayaan nor Shamso had ever been pregnant. Rather, Form Four women proudly distinguish themselves with pride from the vast majority of their peers who a forced to withdraw from school on account of early marriage or pregnancy. More likely, Ayaan and Shamso were trying to embarrass each other through teasing about promiscuity. Out of wedlock pregnancy highly shameful and even dangerous for Somali women in Dadaab—particularly for girls allowed by circumstance to continue their schooling—and the situation is reportedly rare. Ayaan and Shamso's presence in Form Four attests to their ability to avoid early marriage and unintentional pregnancy as much as to their prioritization of education. Therefore, through accusations of motherhood, Ayaan and Shamso questioned each other's commitment to the project of education as well as adherence to the expectations for unmarried Muslim women. At the same time, however, both girls envision themselves marrying and starting families soon after completing schooling. While for Shamso, Rachel's unmarried status after obtainment of a university degree was problematic, for Ayaan, it signaled a commitment to still further education rather than any questioning of or disinterest in the practice of marriage itself.

In fact, Qafis Form Fours frequently teased Shamso for her professed eagerness to marry immediately after secondary school. While everyone in the group planned to marry eventually, Shamso was unique in her pressing desire for a romantic arrangement. For the others, education's guarantee of economic stability and potential avenue of escape from Dadaab stood paramount. As long as they remain eligible for further schooling, they, like their counterparts in Bartan, make academic achievement a more immediate priority. As Kalifa summarized simply, "My attitude is that I will marry when I finish my studies so long as I achieve my goals."

Students also insist upon the compatibility between pursuit of an education and the expectation that they become mothers. They justify their enrollment in schooling as a strategic delay in childbearing in service to their eventual ability to transfer acquired cultural and social capital to their children and to serve as mothers to the imagined Somali nation at large. Women and girls commonly evoke the proverb "to educate a girl is to educate an entire nation." In an essay, Zainab expresses the desire to universalize primary education so that all girls might actively engage in community building as parents:

> If I were in a high position, my authority could say for a girl to be married, she should finish at least primary school and reach a good level in her religion education so that she will train her children and uplift the living standard of the society.

Zainab argues that, rather than contradict her responsibilities as a Somali woman, schooling facilitates her ability to take part in the "uplift" of society at large.

Roda, a Form Four completer, told us her family's story to underscore the importance of a mother's educational attainment. Roda explained that in order for her younger sisters to attend school without the distraction of domestic responsibility, Roda's eldest sister remained at home with their mother. Now that Roda had finished schooling in Dadaab, she encourage her sister Hanan to enroll. Hanan, however, refused to join primary school as an adult. When Patti asked Roda if Hanan was married, Roda shook her head and explained, "She doesn't want to marry. If she marries while in refugee camp, she'll have children and have to bring them up but she doesn't know anything. [She] is not educated." Reportedly, Hanan not only sacrificed the opportunity to become educated so that her sisters might serve as assets to the Somali community, she also elected not to marry and bear children out of a similar desire to contribute to the betterment of the imagined Somali nation. Hanan's refusal to marry speaks to the increasing value placed on maternal literacy at the camps. Given that most women of the previous generation were not exposed to formal education, expectations like those held by Hanan result from the newfound access to schooling. In Hanan's and others' examples, rather than contradict ways of being Somali women, engagement in schooling enables female students to demonstrate a commitment to pioneering a new way of being daughters, sisters, wives, and mothers.

The Camp Context Requires Change

Educated women and girls in Dadaab support facets of cultural change on account of a pragmatic appraisal of camp life. They argue that contextual contingencies impel strategic shifts in gender expectations and performances. Indeed, the overall refugee community's increasing receptivity to girls' participation in schooling stems in large part from economic expediency, as two income earners facilitate a household's survival in a way that one cannot. Just as traditionalist members of the community attribute cultural concessions to context, so, too, do school-going girls. They consider particularities of camp life in their assessments of traditionalism in order to argue that, with regard to certain practices, the Dadaab context demands change. As noted, the act of marriage plays a crucial role in the social organization of Somali communities. According to the traditional paradigm as practiced in Somalia, marriageable young girls, often in their early teens, are exchanged for a series of bride payments usually in the form of livestock. While women do have some rights of refusal, these marriages are often made to significantly older men in polygamous arrangements. In Dadaab, however, the traditional model for marriage is no longer as commonplace. Restricted livelihood options hamper Somali men's ability to afford bride prices for multiple wives. Even when initial payments can be met, the difficulty of sustaining large families on limited rations means only the wealthiest refugees can afford the four wives sanctioned by Qu'ranic law. Instead, in the context of camp life monogamy emerges as the only realistic option for most.

When we asked female students which of the two marital arrangements (monogamy or polygamy) they would choose if given the option, the vast majority favored monogamy. Nimo explains:

> I have preference [between] the two, I would prefer monogamy because in monogamy—the income directly goes to one family; the chances of my husband absenting from home will be limited. That means he will always be available; the chances of (us) getting infected will be limited; the love, trust and honesty to one another will be very high since there is no one sharing with you.... Most educated girls are monogamist and they don't want to hear of polygamy. Most uneducated girls feel that it is good to be in polygamy because they will have children [that] are brothers and sisters to their [own] and will be in an extended family who will in turn help them in doing some work.

In her reply, Nimo employs an evokes economic rationale to substantiate a preference for monogamy. She also called attention to the risks of partner sharing with regard to HIV/AIDS and other sexually transmitted diseases. Although the rate of HIV/AIDS in Dadaab is comparatively low, students draw upon NGO-sponsored public health campaigns to voice disdain for particular gendered practices. At the same time, Nimo's answer reveals her desire for a love marriage, unsurprising given that she and her peers meet with idioms of monogamous, romantic love through school and increasing access to the global media. Rather than emphasize the latter, however, Nimo frames her preference as an economic strategy equal in its pragmatism to her uneducated peers' reliance upon polygamy for the division of labor. Far from an offhand rejection of traditional ways of being, Nimo's choice represents a rational response to shifting circumstances in which small families prove both easier to maintain and more sustainable.

Like Nimo, Roda desires monogamy yet acknowledges the limited parameters of her preference:

Roda: Polygamy is not changing. The only restriction—every man would be happy to have four wives—the only restriction is in this camp people can't support four wives.

Patti: And the women? Do they want polygamy?

Roda: It is a decision for the man.

Patti: If you were deciding?

Roda: She would have preferred monogamy. If her husband doesn't have any other wives he will treat her well, give her all the things, like money.... If he marries another, she will be

> jealous. Fighting even happens in the camps [among wives].... If I could have the decision, I'd want a man with no wives.

Roda is cognizant that any widespread shift toward monogamy stems in large part from context rather than a fundamental change of worldview. Nonetheless, she embraces monogamy for the financial stability it offers women. She, too, hopes for the exclusivity of a love relationship, yet is careful not to reject the possibility of a polygamous arrangement. Paying heed to traditional gender norms, Roda creates a space to critique polygamy while recognizing that she might not be in a position to avoid it. Interestingly, Nimo differs from Roda in that she feels the increasing level of education in the camp changes the terms in which married couples make decisions. According to Nimo:

> [In] my opinion, I think it is both men and women [in the position to choose] in this modern world for educated persons. But, in the olden days, as I heard, I think it was the husband. But now, women are [included] in the decision making process, and if that doesn't happen, than I have the right to move out of that marriage.

Nimo asserts her support for paradigmatic shifts garnered from refugee life and commits herself to monogamy, even if it means ending a marriage.

Attention to intramarital relations highlights changes engendered by a refugee crisis. Demographic consequences of war necessitate that women take on roles previously reserved for men, both within and outside of the home. In light of increased responsibility, educated girls hope for marriage arrangements in which they will share decision-making authority with their husbands. It is widely known that educated women are likely to claim a voice within marriage. Accordingly, many men hesitate to marry educated women for fear that they will "be less willing to work and more likely to debate," strategies of household management. Yasmeen, a Form Four field researcher, interviewed a secondary school boy. Although the interviewee pledged his support of girls' education as well as an intention to educate his daughters in the future, when asked whether or not he would marry an educated girl, he responded emphatically, "No!" When Yasmeen asked why, he explained:

> Because women who have gone to school are dictators and may compete with the husband, they know their right[s] and may not obey some of the husband's instruction. The women who have gone to school normally go to work, hence, they may not fulfill their role as wife. Women who have gone to school may detect your affairs with other women, hence, they may have control over you as a husband.

While one CARE manager refuted the assertion that educated women are regarded as less desirable marriage partners, the Qafis Form Four women seem familiar with the sentiments revealed in Yasmeen's interview. Ayaan, after hearing of the interview, nonchalantly noted "They won't marry us because they can't get us under their control." Zainab agreed, adding, "they want to hand you the budget, not have you be able to count the budget yourself!"

Even as rumors that men prefer uneducated women circulated, many students believe that, in reality, men value the increased capacity of educated women to buttress family welfare in the camps. Certainly, the advantage of two economically viable adults in Dadaab is undeniable. While many mothers with little to no experience of formal schooling run market stalls or other small businesses, educated women are eligible—and indeed, prioritized—for incentive work at the NGOs. Through education, therefore, girls and women prepare to take jobs in the formal sector and assume increased decision-making authority in reciprocal and respectful marriage partnerships. Nimo describes just such a desire:

> In my upcoming marriage, we [will] have no roles that are separate to one only. Each of us will do the work without any discrimination. In case of one of us not knowing some work, the other is next to help and teach.

More than a personal preference, Nimo's model for marriage represents a strategy for survival in Dadaab. Accordingly, her ideal husband would be "God-fearing (a Muslim), educated, loving, monogamist, honest, respectful, and hardworking." She deems a prospective partnership with an uneducated man to be problematic. Roda recalls when a peer from Dadaab married an uneducated Somali man living in Nairobi. Roda asked her friend how she intended to "talk" to him. When nearby boys overheard the conversation and reminded Roda that the girls' fiancée was neither blind nor deaf, Roda announced:

> Uneducated men are worse than deaf and blind ones. I don't think I can understand an uneducated one. Somali men are different than the others, like Americans or others. Somali men think ladies have no intelligence, intellect, they treat her like a small child. Educated men understand, talk to them, etc.

Educated young women at Dadaab expect to be allowed to contribute financially and intellectually to family welfare just as they hope male partners will pragmatically respond to camp context by desiring educated wives. Students respond reflectively by advocating for transformation of marriage practices.

Complications and Exceptions

Though patterns emerge in the young women's strategic negotiation of gender change in Dadaab, women's positions on complex issues are not always consistent or moderate in nature. Aman's campaign to thwart her circumcision described in the chapter's opening powerfully illustrates one radical course of action. Nor are commonly accepted arguments for particular ways of being simple and straightforward in women's minds. Just as educated girls work to demonstrate the compatibility of schooling with Somaliness, there are moments when they acknowledge contradiction and wonder aloud about the consequences of the changes they witness and embrace. Secondary school graduates granted admission to Canadian universities through WUSC, for instance, grapple with the reality of an ever-delayed age of school completion. Newfound access to tertiary education complicates a framework that positions schooling as a time-limited postponement of marriage.

We asked Roda, who at the time awaited departure from Dadaab on a WUSC scholarship, whether or not she planned to marry. Roda replied, "Maybe after I see the four corners of the university classroom. Then, I can think about that." Roda's evocation of the symbolic significance of a classroom's four corners echoes throughout many female students' justifications of schooling. Poignantly, she added "university" to the typical four-cornered classroom girls often hope to see and, in doing so, extended the postponement of reproductive responsibilities through the completion of university. Even as she commits herself to higher education, however, Roda expresses uncertainty about her future marriage prospects, "here if a girl goes beyond 20 she will be considered old. Everyone will ask you."

At the time we spoke, Roda was 22. Her entrance into a 4 year university and the subsequent possibility to enroll in graduate, law, or medical school demands a much more significant delay of marriage if she were to remain single while a student. In a culture where girls are considered old at 20, such an extensive postponement could call Roda's marriageability, and by extension any schema arguing the compatibility of education and marriage for Somali women, into question.

Like Roda, Dahabo, the only other girl to receive a WUSC scholarship in 2005, grappled with future uncertainties and worried about the logistics of delaying her marriage. During one conversation she asked about the prevalence of marriage among undergraduate students in Canada and whether or not we recommended such an arrangement. On a different day she inquired about the length of time required to become an MD in Canada or the United States. The question represents Dahabo's larger effort to envision a future for herself that incorporates new academic and career goals with the realization of gender norms she had long expected to meet.

Dahabo dreamt of becoming a doctor since first excelling in primary school science. After hearing of the lengthy process required to obtain an MD, however, she worried aloud about logistics. She explained that she was already 22 years old and, since "women only lived to be around forty," the 12 or so years required to complete medical school and a residency were simply too long, particularly if she were to remain unmarried throughout the process. Balancing the options and calculating timing, Dahabo announced mid-conversation that she was newly interested in pharmacy. For Dahabo, pharmacy presented a more reasonable compromise between her love of science and her desire to marry sooner rather than later. Though limited opportunities for postsecondary education mean that very few students find themselves in the same position Dahabo and Roda do, efforts to reconcile increasingly lengthy school careers with marriage will only gain significance in the future.

Expanding avenues for higher education provided by WUSC scholarships represent one of many challenges to patterned meaning making among female students. At the same time that newfound educational prospects complicate the terrain for gendered negotiation, individual girls act out behaviors that contradicted their espoused perspectives. Dahabo's preparation for resettlement demonstrates such contradiction.

As noted, Dahabo spent the weeks and months preceding her departure inquiring about life in Canada. She wanted to know if Canadian (Christian) women would recognize and be familiar with *hijabs* on their Muslim counterparts. We noted that female Somali students in Dadaab maintain a strong commitment to maintain Islamic dress. Accordingly, Dahabo announced that she would maintain proper religious standards once in Canada regardless of the degree to which residents in Canada understood her choice. She assuredly announced her intention to circumcise her daughters and, as noted above, believed that circumcision was a necessary precaution to deter women from prostitution. In general, Dahabo positioned herself more conservatively on the continuum between traditionalism and change. Toward the end of our time in Dadaab, however, Dahabo asked to borrow our digital camera for a night in order to photograph her family. She wanted pictures to bring with her to Canada. We agreed and the next day found Dahabo, who is particularly computer savvy, busily uploading her frames on an NGO computer. She invited us to come and look at the pictures and proudly gazed over our shoulders as we scanned the photos.

Rather than pictures of her mother and sisters, however, the vast majority of photos depicted glamorous shots of Dahabo and her friends in varying combinations. In each picture, the group was unveiled and modeled styled hair, thickly applied foundation and white powder, and dramatic eye makeup. Appearing almost bleached, the girls smiled broadly or eyed the camera seductively. Surprised and unsure of how to react, we nodded at Dahabo who laughed lightheartedly.

In the pictures, Dahabo and her friends transgressed from traditional ways of dressing in what appeared to be a performative and overt display of "Western" sexuality. Significantly, they removed their veils and wore makeup, both of which are highly unacceptable in the context of Dadaab. They also deliberately bleached their skin. However, their activities occurred in the private context of Dahabo's home. In public, Dahabo never failed to maintain the standards expected of her as a Muslim Somali woman. Instead, her pictures contrasted the ways in which she carried herself daily and reportedly intended to carry herself in Canada. The pictures were likely to be kept private and shared only with close female friends who, like us, she assumed to be sympathetic. Dahabo's efforts to relegate experimentation to the private sphere brings to mind Hawo's similar declaration that, while she maintained appropriate dress when in public, she saw no problem with wearing Western clothes if safe among women and removed from the public, masculine gaze. According to Hawo, if she and her classmates were in a private space without men, they would "just play and relax." Looking toward us, she noted that "she could even wear our clothes!" and ran a hand up her leg to indicate a miniskirt.

In their contrast from the language and choices made, Aman, Roda, and Dahabos' examples illustrate that most young women elect to occupy the middle ground between the polarities of traditionalism and enlightenment. Aman, in fighting for her perceived right to remain uncircumcised, risked her own and her families' safety and reputation. Most young women elected to quietly succumb to the practice while expressing a desire to modify the practice for their own daughter' sake. Roda, in postponing marriage until the completion of tertiary education, pushed the boundaries of an espoused compatibility between engagement in schooling and expectations held regarding marriage and child rearing. In doing so, Roda perhaps exposes the pragmatic nature of the young women's claims of compatibility, as most women longed for the opportunity to study abroad awarded to Roda. At the same time, if only in its singularity, Roda's case highlights a new norm being established at the camps where women marry at older ages in order to complete secondary education. Finally, Dahabo's hidden longing to take on some of the aesthetics associated with Western women signals that her espoused conservatism is likely context dependent and, hence, flexible. While in Dadaab, Dahabo and others voice a narrative of reasonable compromise in order to reach a balance between the familiar and the new, mollify traditionalist anxiety and the pull of options afforded in the name of enlightenment. In the process, they develop a localized rendition of Somali womanhood.

Conclusion

As the first generation of girls to receive an education in most of their families and the community at large, the Form Four women with whom we worked are on the frontline of carving out the parameters of a new womanhood. Paradoxically, through the very act of identifying those ways of being that they deem acceptable, the women put in relief new ways of being which are gauged too extreme. Dadaab schools serve as spaces in which female students work to imagine new ways of being Somali in the context of refugee life and, simultaneously, mark the parameters of unacceptably radical change. Individually and dialogically, the women carve out perspectives regarding what amounted to (un)acceptable degrees of transformation in traditional gendered practices such as dress, marriage, women's roles in society, and female circumcision. Through dialectic acts of meaning making, girls and women stake out moderate positionalities on an imagined continuum between cultural continuity and modification, between articulated polarities of enlightenment and traditionalism.

Most young women sought to uphold certain Somali cultural tenets while they acknowledge and support adaptation of others. And, while a few chose radical paths, the majority braid enlightenment discourse with well established Somali cultural tenets and practices to construct unique ways of being. In their identity work, cultural change is neither linear nor a default result of schooling, as emergent traditionalists would argue. Rather, students use schooling to enact particular ways of being educated young Somali women in Dadaab. In doing so, they employ three main discursive rationales: distinguish between religion and culture; posit compatibility between school and Somali ways of being; and emphasize the pragmatic necessity to adapt to localized constraints and possibilities.

For the vast majority of students, similar patterns of negotiation are likely to characterize their continued efforts to complete schooling, marry, and begin to establish adult lives in Dadaab. For others, as we explore in subsequent chapters, the opportunity to resettle in a wealthy, Western country will drastically change the parameters for making sense of gender change.

NOTES

1. Instruction in Dadaab secondary classrooms follows the standardized national curriculum of the Kenyan Institute of Education. Form Four stu-

dents in Dadaab, like their counterparts across Kenya read: Marjorie Oludhe Macgoye's (1986) *Coming to Birth*, William Shakespeare's (1987) *The Merchant of Venice*, Naguib Mahfouz's (1991) "Half a Day," and Saida Hagi-Dirie Herzi's (1999) "Against the Pleasure Principle."

2. Traditionally, marriage in Somalia was "clan-exogamous, cross-cousin" (Ahmed, 2004, p. 51), meaning that marriage was encouraged between cousins who were children of a brother and a sister. As children of a brother and sister, the potential couple would likely come from different clans, fostering alliances across lineage (Ahmed, 2004).

CHAPTER 8

BRIDGE

From Dadaab to Milltown

After the 1951 United Nations Convention Relating to the Status of Refugees, several countries (and regions) from the global North, including Canada, the United Kingdom, Australia, and the United States, formally committed to prioritize refugee resettlement. Accordingly, while the vast majority of Somalis in Dadaab remain in the camps in protracted crisis, some are selected for resettlement in third countries by the UNHCR. Resettlement slots are highly sought after and selection processes are rife with accusations of corruption. For a sense of scale, in the years 2007 and 2008 respectively, only 3,000 and 5,000 Somali refugee applications were approved for resettlement to *all* major refugee-hosting nations, including: Canada, Australia, the Netherlands, as well as the United States (U.S. Department of State, 2010). Refugees chosen for resettlement in the United States must meet several prerequisites before travel, including the completion of cultural orientation sessions sponsored by the International Organization for Migration (IOM).

In this bridging interlude, we provide a portrait of cultural orientation sessions and describe the ways a countervailing polarity is again used to understand upcoming life in the United States. In the cultural orientation sessions, however, the universality of human rights gives way to their instantiation in U.S. law. In music theory, the term "bridge" refers to the passage in a score that connects two distinct sections. Here we briefly stray from our discussion of women's schooling to provide a contextual bridge

Educated For Change?: Muslim Refugee Women in the West, pp. 201–220
Copyright © 2012 by Information Age Publishing

linking Parts 1 and 2 of our story and, correspondingly, two of the major phases of a refugee's life post exodus from Somalia. While many refugees spend stays of varying lengths in third or fourth countries between Kenya and the United States, the vast majority of women with whom we worked did journey through Kenya to the United States. As a result, we portray such a trajectory to illustrate the basic contours of a U.S.-bound refugee journey.

Refugee Resettlement in the United States

The United States has relocated refugees to its shores for more than 50 years, although regulatory ceilings regarding resettlement were not statutory until the passing of the Refugee Act in 1980. According to the Federation for American Immigration Reform (2004), "the 1980 refugee legislation was enacted in part in response to Congress's increasing frustration with the difficulty of dealing with the ongoing large-scale Indochinese refugee flow under the existing ad hoc refugee admission and resettlement mechanisms." As mandated by the Act, each year the President, under the auspices of Congress, designates the annual quota of worldwide refugee admissions to the United States. During 2004, for instance, the final ceiling for refugee resettlement was at 70, 000 spaces, 30,000 of which were allocated to refugees from Africa specifically. While the number of refugee applications approved for the U.S. in 2004 was approximately double that of 2003 or 2002, tightened security as a result of September 11 continues to affect the processing of refugees to the United States and, consequently, numbers from 2004 still remained significantly lower than those preceding 2002 (Rytina, 2005). In 2007, the ceiling remained 70,000 with only 22,000 allotted to refugees from Africa and notably, while the ceiling was raised to 80,000 in 2009, African newcomers were only allotted 12,000 of the 80,000 spaces (Martin, 2009).[1]

Of the 52,835 refugees[2] admitted to the United States in 2004, 13,331, or 25.2%, were from Somalia (Rytina, 2005). According to 2004 Yearbook of Immigration Statistics, 47,726 Somali refugees have arrived in the U.S. between the fiscal years of 1995 and 2004, making Somalia the primary source of resettled African refugees in that period (Office of Immigration Statistics, 2006). Of the 117,152 Africans represented in refugee arrival totals between 1995 and 2004, Somalis represent 40.74% (Office of Immigration Statistics, 2006). In more recent years, migration statistics from the Horn of Africa look quite different. Of the 74,602 refugee resettlements to the U.S. in 2009, only 4,189 were Somalis, representing a mere 5.6% (Martin, 2009). (In 2007, Somali resettlement accounted for 14.5%) (Martin, 2009). This shift reflects a change of the nature of crisis in Somalia and its surrounding countries of primary asylum from one of acute emergency to a more protracted refugee scenario, a declined interest in conflict in the Horn in relation to other regions, as well as delays in the resettlement process from East Africa due to security concerns.

The process of getting from Kenyan refugee camps to the United States is a complex and often grueling one, characterized by many as tremendously stressful. From initial registration and interviews in countries of primary asylum such as Kenya, refugee files traverse a string of governmental departments, nongovernmental organizations, and embassies before a visa for travel is produced. The U.S. Citizenship and Immigration Services (USCIS) and UNHCR begin the progression of refugee processing by embarking on "circuit rides" through refugee camps and other areas with high concentrations of refugees to conduct interviews and designate a refugee's priority rating. In these USCIS or UNHCR interviews, refugees have to prove credible fear of return to Somalia and are often required to retell painful and traumatic stories multiple times. In order to determine eligibility for resettlement to the United States, refugees are placed on a continuum of priorities currently ranging from P1 to P4, which establishes their precedence among the thousands of annual applicants.[3] According to the USCIS, Priority One refugees include:

> UNHCR or U.S. embassy identified cases: persons facing compelling security concerns in countries of first asylum; persons in need of legal protection because of the danger of refoulement; those in danger due to threats of armed attack in an area where they are located; persons who have experienced recent persecution because of political, religious, or human rights activities (prisoners of conscience); women-at-risk; victims of torture or violence; physically or mentally disabled persons; persons in urgent need of medical treatment not available in the first asylum country; and persons for whom other durable solutions are not feasible and whose status in the place of asylum does not present a satisfactory long-term solution. (USCIS, 2006)

Priority 2 includes members of certain groups within a nationality identified to be at collective risk. Somali Bantus have been designated as P2s and were given priority for resettlement as a group from Kakuma. Priority Three consists of parents, spouses, and unmarried children of refugees, asylees, and other legal permanent residents already admitted to the US (USCIS, 2006).[4] Finally, the categorization of Priority 4, which is currently only open to Bosnians, includes grandparents, grandchildren, married children, and siblings of refugees, asylees, U.S. citizens, and other legal permanent residents in the United States.

While criteria for resettlement have been standardized in an effort to prioritize the most "vulnerable," refugees in the Dadaab camps tell stories of corruption and neglect by UNHCR caseworkers. The notion that resettlement slots are "sold" by UNHCR workers to wealthier refugees frames such accusations, and several families explained to us that although they had been selected for resettlement, they remained in Dadaab because another family bought their names and traveled in their place. In such reports, buyers need not necessarily be refugees but might be Somalis of Kenyan nationality or even Kenyans pretending to be of Ugandan descent. One mother of a secondary school student explained that her neighbor, an elderly man, was selected for resettlement to the United States. During his medical screen, however, he tested positive for tuberculosis. While the neighbor was treated medically, follow-up x-rays required for health clearance were continually postponed. Finally, after a year of treatment, he was x-rayed again. His tests came back negative for tuberculosis; however, he was no longer able to resettle since his place had been sold during the delay. The mother explained that her own family had been cleared for travel to Australia; soon after she learned that another family had taken their names and was already gone.

By the late 1990s, allegations of corruption leveled at the UNHCR reached management, and subsequent investigations by the United Nations in Nairobi as well as the UN Office of Internal Oversight Services (OIOS) were conducted. While the former were inconclusive, the latter uncovered evidence that UNHCR employees were indeed selling resettlement slots for between $3,000 and $5,000 U.S. dollars. Corrective measures included removal of staff from the entire protection and resettlement departments in Kenya's UNHCR office. According to IRIN Humanitarian News and Analysis (2002):

> Other remedial measures already taken included the creation of a "transparency committee" composed of UNHCR protection staff, officers of embassies representing the resettlement countries, NGOs, and representatives of civil society organizations. The refugee agency said it was also carrying out frequent security spot checks of operations in Nairobi, and strengthening the training of staff in fraud awareness and prevention.

We draw attention to such history of corruption for a number of reasons. First, Horst (2006) notes that various actors refer disparagingly to refugees in Dadaab as "cunning crooks." Perhaps ironically, in order to access resettlement opportunities, refugees traverse a system that, at least in the 1990s, requires some cunning to successfully negotiate. Further, as refugees position themselves in relation to an ideoscape of polarity, their experiences with structures and policies born from enlightenment ideology were often characterized by frustration, deceit, and corruption. Analysis of the ways in which some refugees harbor anti-Western sentiments must, therefore, be viewed at least partially in light of such experiences.

After resettlement selection is made, a refugee's files are prepared and processed by international and U.S.-funded NGOs in East Africa. The vast majority of refugee applications from across East Africa reach Nairobi at some point in the process and, according to a staff member at IOM, about 80% of the 10,000 refugees processed through Nairobi are Somali. For U.S.-bound refugees, two agencies in particular, the Joint Voluntary Agency (JVA) and IOM, couple to prepare refugee files. Once such preparation is completed, JVA "conditionally approves" them until the refugee or refugee family completes four final steps required by the U.S. government. These steps do not necessarily have to be undertaken in any particular order, but they include a medical examination, security clearance, sponsorship assurance, and completion of a cultural orientation course.

The comprehensive medical examination required for resettlement is completed by a physician at IOM and includes a physical examination, blood test, and x-ray. Other drug screening procedures such as urine and saliva samples may be requested at the doctor's discretion. Only three medical conditions bar or delay travel to the US, and, according to an IOM staff member, they include being deemed: "violent or out of mind,"[5] addicted to drugs other than to *miraa* or *khat*,[6] or in need of treatment for tuberculosis or any sexually transmitted disease other than HIV/AIDS. HIV/AIDS does not disqualify or delay travel to the United States, although after diagnosis, counseling is provided and the refugee is asked to sign a waiver used to set up treatment options in the United States. The U.S. policy around HIV/AIDS is more liberal than those of other refugee receiving countries such as Canada and Australia, which retain the ability to deny entrance on the basis of a positive HIV diagnosis. Other conditions such as hypertension and diabetes are taken note of and occasionally require a supplementary appointment, though tend not to delay travel.

The security clearance of refugees occurs actually within the United States and includes a background and name check. For males age 15 and above, an SAO or Security Advisory Opinion is also required. Refugees are not provided many details on this aspect of the process and, most likely, exact requirements for security clearance shift in correspondence with U.S. policy around national security. Sponsorship assurance is required of P3 refugees and asks that relatives in the U.S. sign a waiver verifying that the refugees bound for resettlement are the same family fir which they applied. In signing, they also guarantee to partner with a local resettlement agency in sponsorship of their incoming relatives. Finally, cultural orientation (CO) entails attending and completing a 5-50 hour[7] course which formally introduces refugees to varying spheres of U.S. national life. Cultural orientation has occurred at 53 different refugee processing sites in 28 countries across East, Central, and South Africa. However, of the 80,038 refugees participating in cultural orientation between the years of 1994 and 2005, 52% were Somali (IOM, 2005). As a result, the majority of CO sessions occur at the IOM transit center in Nairobi or in Kenyan refugee camps.

Cultural Orientation

Cultural orientation programs for U.S. bound refugees are planned and implemented by IOM, which receives 80% of its funding from the U.S. Department of State's Bureau on Populations, Refugees, and Migration (BPRM). While IOM also runs cultural orientations on Canada, Australia, and the United Kingdom, the introductory courses to the U.S. are state-sponsored forms of U.S. public education—the first a refugee will receive. As a result, how refugees are introduced to the relationality of U.S. law to the counterveiling polarity experienced in the camp can be understood as both indicative of expectations placed upon newcomers to the U.S. as well as fundamental in shaping refugees' initial conceptions of their relationship to the U.S. nation.

According to its mission statement, the purpose of cultural orientation is "to prepare refugees for their first few months in the United States. In particular, to enable refugees to become self-sufficient as soon as possible" [sic] (IOM, 2005, p. 2). The CO curriculum is framed around *the Welcome Guide* developed by MAEC of Applied Linguistics[8] within the United States, and covers such topics as basic U.S. history, employment, education, housing, health services, laws, and culture. Although the *Welcome Guide* provides the orientations' basic framework, courses are constantly under revision by CO instructors as well as in accordance with suggestions of partner resettlement organizations and former CO participants now living in the United States. Individual instructors also shape pedagogy, inserting their own teaching methods and designing unique activities to best convey information to the particular groups they teach. During the two 3-day cultural orientation courses that we were able to attend, the instructor, an Ethiopian refugee living in Kenya, used his background in education to develop engaging, participatory, and group-based activities. All CO instructors are either refugees themselves or Kenyan nationals, and they speak a wide range of languages. Although our instructor was proficient in Somali, he led the classes in English with the accompaniment of a Somali translator.

While CO's official mission is framed around survival and self-sufficiency, another primary emphasis of the program voiced explicitly, and interwoven thematically, is the idea of "lowering expectations." Intended to disrupt notions of the U.S. as a land paved with gold in order to ease refugee transitions, class sessions provide an intense dose of realism about life in the U.S. as one demanding hard work with few rewards. Promulgated by the almost religious mantra of "work to succeed," refugees become well versed in the American dream narrative as they also receive an initial glimpse into the nearly impossible task of supporting large families on minimum wage jobs. Finally, potential areas of conflict between ways of being Somali in Africa and what is deemed the "American" way are illustrated and addressed in order to avoid potential problems or legal ramifications. In all, the CO curriculum, while largely aimed at improving chances of success among refugees, introduces the U.S. nation's regulatory relationship to Somali culture and hints at newcomers' restricted participation in U.S. society and economy.

An Ethnographic Glimpse Into Cultural Orientation Sessions

If you start here, you have to learn it all again there.

—CO Participant

It's a competitive society, so you will be entering into that competition.

—Teferi, CO instructor

The IOM transit center in Nairobi contains a handful of breezy, clean classrooms adorned with maps of the United States, U.S. flags, and laminated color photographs of snow-covered houses and suburban streets. Rows of wooden chairs are evenly divided into two sections by an aisle. During the sessions we attended, participants included refugee men, women, and children aged 15 and above who had managed to live undetected among Kenyan nationals of Somali ethnic descent in the Somali section of Nairobi.

While the vast majority of Somali refugees in Kenya live in Dadaab, some, including participants in the cultural orientations we attended, bypass or escape from refugee camp life, opting instead to live undocumented in Kenyan cities. Ability to make such a choice is determined by a number of factors including: presence of family and community contacts already established in urban centers as Kenyan nationals or undocumented residents; existence of family members in the diaspora who send remittances; and social positioning in Somali society before the dissolution of the state. As colonial partitioning resulted in the existence of a significant population of ethnic, Somali, Kenyan nationals, refugees entering the country or looking to escape life in refugee camps can sometimes identify a safety net among Kenyan relatives or clan members.

Other refugees begin in camps and eventually transfer to more permanent settlements in cities. Class is a significant determinant of such possibility, as even minimal resources can allow families to begin rebuilding lives in large urban centers such as Nairobi and Mombasa. Finally, families in refugee camps might send one family member to Nairobi to attempt to find work and send income back to Dadaab.

The almost exclusively Somali area of Nairobi known as North Central is characterized by an extremely high population density in which multiple families share apartments, often sleeping in rotating shifts throughout the night and day. However, North Central is also an economically booming area, with bustling streets flowing with vendors who sell goods imported to Kenya from Dubai primarily through the black market. Vibrant colors of fabric hang from booths while electronics, jewelry, shoes, and clothes pile high on tables set up for both Kenyan nationals and Somalis to peruse. And, like much of Nairobi, traffic clogs the main streets of North Central as passengers fill *matatus*, Kenyan public transportation vans, to come to the area. The existence of a worldwide Somali diaspora facilitates the success of the North Central marketplace. Somali refugees in Kenya form business links with other Somalis in the Middle East. And, already resettled relatives in the U.S. send remittances that grease the wheels of commerce. Communication and frequent transport occurs between North Central and the refugee camps, in Dadaab. Refugees from North Central who resettle in the United States, including those we met at IOM, are often P3 cases who obtain their status from family sponsorship.

At the particular cultural orientation sessions we attended, participants settled into a sex segregated seating pattern. Males dominated one section of seats, females the other. Standing at the front of the room, Teferi, the instructor, began by asking everybody to introduce themselves and say what they hoped to be or do in the United States. One by one, male followed by female members of the four or five large families represented in the classroom stood up to represent their aspirations. Laughs and side conversations provided the background for lists of careers and life goals. One young man wanted to be an engineer, another simply to "be educated." Some of their responses indicated they had spoken with family members already settled in the U.S. about the sorts of jobs in high demand. Several women announced that they wanted to be nurses or nurses' assistants. By contrast, one older patriarch in his seventies stated that he wanted "to go and rest." Without offering feedback to initial responses, Teferi asked the class to break into large groups and list twenty facts that they already knew about the United States. Again, their answers reflected the hopes, dreams, and expectations of refugees awaiting resettlement, and included such diverse responses as: "a peaceful country," "many sports," "very cold," "a world superpower," "a democratic country," "a multicultural country," "a strong economy," and "good, high quality education."

Teferi, gathering the class together again, reviewed each assumption, asserting its validity: "Yes, it is a peaceful country;" "Yes, very stable;" "Yes, very good economy;" "It is the richest country in the world." "60% of the richest people in the world live in the U.S." "Yes, it is multicultural. You can find people from all over the world living in the U.S. and being Americans;" "There is no discrimination by law;" "The riches of the country reflect the riches of the people, that is true." During this introductory activity, Teferi established a pattern of directing his comments toward the male side of the room, a habit that continued throughout the duration of the session; he also situated the bubble of expectation regarding life in the United States, at the center of the curriculum. Over the course of the next 3 days, he would systematically work to burst this bubble by foregrounding the economic and cultural challenges Somali refugees face in the United States. Inherent in such characterization of U.S. life was a recalling of the polarity present in Dadaab; this time, however, U.S. law and free-market capitalism corresponded with full realization of enlightenment ideals. On the other end of the spectrum, Somali culture and livelihood strategies were described as largely incompatible with U.S. life, and therefore in need of transformation.

A large part of the cultural orientation sessions focused on employment concerns: why work is so crucial; how to get a job; how to interview; and, what kinds of jobs are available. To begin the discussion on employment, Teferi asked students to again break into groups and answer the question: "What kind of jobs do you think you can get in the U.S.?" As the groups responded, Teferi wrote their answers on a board in three distinct categories, ranging from "lower kinds of jobs," to jobs that "might require a skill," to "professions which require long term training." As participants relayed job titles, Teferi ascribed them a category. "Truck driver," "butcher," "worker in animal husbandry," "tailor," "interpreter," "construction worker" and "business owner" required some skill and training. "Doctor," "Pilot," "Pharmacist" and "Professor" required long term training. "Hotel worker" and "farmer" were designated as low skill jobs. Once all potential jobs had been categorized, Teferi explained that "Column One" represented the point from which most newcomers to the U.S. might expect to start their life in the United States, while "Column Three" required extensive planning, dedication, and schooling.

The establishment of a dichotomy between skilled and unskilled labor in the column scheme provoked a conversation about the deskilling many refugees face upon entrance into the United States. A man who had been a pharmacist in Somalia asked: "I've heard that if you are skilled here, you may have to start over there. Is it true?" After Teferi affirmed that recertification is a very real possibility that would have to be sustained by temporary work in entry level jobs, the same man sighed and said "If you start here, you have to learn it all again there!" Acknowledging the almost certain deskilling of Somali professionals after migration to the United States, Teferi asked the group to consider their own assets in an effort to highlight everyone's employment potential and innate skills. For this activity, class members broke into pairs and were asked to write down the skills they had at the moment. Many class members appeared confounded and emphatically bemoaned a lack of relevant skills for employment in the United States. One young man exclaimed: "We are refugees here, we don't do anything!" Another added, "We're not learning. We're not going to school!"

These statements and the experiences that underlie them highlight refugees' tentative, shifting and dependent relationship to the state. As Priority 3 refugees, members of the class had largely belonged to the middle and upper classes in Somalia. This meant that the older men in the class as well as those family members already resettled abroad had previously enjoyed a privileged position within the Somali nation that entitled them access to the credentials and training through schooling that reproduced their status and power within the Somali national community. That same privilege worked against them when rebels sought to violently depose the established governing class in Somalia. Those who were able to safely flee the country with family members were then once again privileged given their class position in Somalia. Once in Kenya, they were able to capitalize on family and communal connections among Somali Kenyan nationals in order to live outside of the refugee camp and to earn a living on the black market in Nairobi. However, in order to be chosen for resettlement in the United States, this population of entrepreneurs presented themselves as desperate, helpless, and traumatized in their USCIS interviews.[9] Now, faced with the immediate challenge to incorporate into an unknown U.S. community, class members needed to compose yet another narrative of self while they remained in transition as undocumented Somalis outside of the refugee camp system in Kenya. Well aware of the danger in admitting engagement in productive economic activity while in Kenya, it took much cajoling on Teferi's part to pull class members into the discursive space that shaped consideration of newcomers' life in the United States. After assurance that their status as designees for resettlement would not be compromised by anything said in the classroom that day, one class member tentatively began to list his experience and skill as a crane operator. Teferi responded quickly with a demand that the man adjust his thinking about what his status position in the U.S. might entail.

Let me ask you something. What can I do with this in the U.S.? What if another person has the same skills but speaks English, who will get the job? What if there are no cranes in the place you're going? What can you do better than others? Everybody has not one skill but too many skills! You don't have to fix your skills!

As the refugees began to embrace a shifting set of expectations about the ways in which they would prepare for and be allowed to participate in the U.S. versus the Kenyan national community, Teferi and the cultural orientation curriculum revealed a fundamental contradiction. Those with professional skills gained from education in Somalia and those with skills gleaned from job experience in Kenya are expected to start their lives in the U.S. at the bottom of the economic and social latter and work doggedly toward economic independence, even as the opportunity to do so is highly restricted. According to this logic, in order to succeed in the U.S. refugees must pull themselves up by their bootstraps, think creatively, and dream large—yet the ability to get profitable jobs in the first place demands English fluency and is often limited by racism and anti-racism sentiment. After noting that the type of entry level jobs presented in "Column One" would most likely be their first jobs, Teferi said:

But that doesn't necessarily mean that you have to do this for life ... some may want to be doctors.... But you need to plan.... But the first skill you need is to be able to speak and understand English. That's why you need to attend ESL (English as a second language) [classes].

While refugees under twenty are permitted, if not required, to enter the public school system, adult education emerged as both crucially important and a hindrance to employment. As Teferi succinctly stated, "Employment must take priority over ESL." This contradictory notion of education's priority yet practical impossibility in their new lives was woven throughout CO session, and was echoed in the American dream rhetoric at large. For, as one man aptly asked, "If I go straight to the U.S. and I want to go to school to learn, how do I support myself?" Teferi responded, "If you want to go to university, you have to pay for it yourself ... [before then] you should convince yourself to start at zero. You have to be willing to take any job." Even if jobs exist that "they can do better than others," refugees must be willing to temporarily shelve their aspirations and accept some of the least desirable positions often relegated to immigrant newcomers.

The CO curriculum crystallizes such contradiction with a sample budget activity. The class was asked to break up into family groups and then sort themselves into potential workers and nonworkers based on age. Most of these families had over six members in attendance, many with up to 10 or 12. The class then came up with a list of probable expenses on the board. Realistic estimates of rent and electricity were provided each family based upon statistics of the particular city to which they were going and the number of rooms they would need, with two or three children sharing each room. Food, telephone, and other projected expenses were estimated and balanced against the projected $8/hr wage of each potential worker for a 40 hour work week. A final expense identified by refugees themselves, sending money to their relatives in Africa, was noted as contingent upon their ability to afford the rest.

Not surprisingly, very few families were able to balance their budget. One older man noted, "I am shocked, when I counted, I was shocked." Another woman aptly added from the back of the classroom, "Where's the opportunity?" Teferi asked the class what else they could do to ease their financial constraints. Conclusions included bargain shopping (to the great disdain of one older woman who refused to imagine buying secondhand goods in the United States), working overtime, taking on two or even three jobs, foregoing educational goals in the short-term in order to work, and including women and elderly men as potential money earners. To conclude a conversation that had introduced what would amount to a fundamental reorganization of families, gender norms and practices, and the structure of community at large, Teferi concluded, "Those who work, and work hard, will make it."

Already, however, students recognized restrictions to their ability to do so on a number of levels. One woman, perhaps in her mid-30s, who later shared with us that her youngest child is epileptic, asked Teferi how she would be able to go to work if her child became sick. Teferi replied that she would find someone to baby-sit, or pay for childcare. When she followed up by asking who pays for such services, he responded pragmatically, "You do." In this case, notions of personal responsibility and individualism emerged as fundamentally problematic for single refugee parents just as they do for long-term residents in the United States, as balancing full-time employment and single parenting without outside resources proves a nearly impossible task.

Another woman, probably in her late sixties or early seventies, spoke out, asking, "Old women like me, old grandfathers—What kind of work can I do?"

Teferi replied, "What are your skills? After some prompting, she answered, "Childcare, cleaning, working, plants and flowers."

Other people in the class corroborated that mothers have a lot of innate skills, particularly around childcare and cooking, which Teferi explained were essential to advertise. Despite the fact that exclusive reliance upon such skills largely restricts women's work to low skill jobs in the private sphere, often as domestic help or maids for White, middle-class families, such discussion was intended to assure every working age adult that there would be an available niche for them. Before the conversation turned course, however, the original woman added, almost rhetorically, "but what [about] when I get really old?"

Finally, one man asked whether or not he could walk to his job. Teferi replied, and we paraphrase, "Do you have time to?" And then the oft-echoed remark, "Time is money." Such repeated emphasis on the monetary value of time—so much so that schooling and English language learning must come second—underscored the entire discussion. As one older man noted poignantly, "I know you cannot sleep there, you must work!"[10]

The unquestioned emphasis on work for both survival and success denies the fundamental reality of globalization's effect on the diminution of entry level jobs in the United States, that refugees have to compete against fluent English speakers for a shrinking pool of jobs, and that they are subject to long standing realities of racial discrimination in the United States. Refugees in the cultural orientation sessions alluded to such realities, demonstrating that they had already been warned of the dearth of jobs by previously resettled family and friends. To these queries Teferi replied again with an unwavering rhetoric of personal responsibility:

> Personally, I think it depends on you. You have to be proactive. There are some people who are not like that.... There are jobs out there but you need to go out and look for them.... You have to have an attitude whereby my first job is to find a job.

The contradiction between an ethos of personal responsibility and a lack of opportunity, which framed discussions of employment in the cultural orientation sessions, were echoed in conversations on participation in the civic sphere. From the outset, students spoke to the notion of participatory democracy. In another class activity that asked students to list five things they wanted to know about the United States, one of the groups inquired "How [they] get their freedom from Washington." Both the concepts of freedom and democracy were key to refugees' knowledge about civic life in the United States, and both seemed particularly meaningful given the denial of complete protection and freedom from the Kenyan, Somali, or colonial states. As one refugee put it, "It's a democracy, of course I'm going to fight for my rights." In referring to American democracy, refugees aligned themselves with discourses of enlightenment and envisioned proudly claiming deserved rights.

In the cultural orientation sessions, however, dialogue concerning governance in the U.S. rested upon its regulatory power over the Somali population and, concomitantly, upon the numerous ways in which Somalis were poised to breech U.S. cultural expectations as regulated by the legal system. Teferi warned of the illegality of chewing *khat* or *miraa*, the practice of polygamy, and wife and child beating. Discussion of individual rights similarly positioned Somalis as making unacceptable demands upon the U.S. national community. Students were given a handout that contained six boxes of cartoons depicting different everyday situations. Teferi asked refugees to discuss whether the characters illustrated had "the right" to do what they were doing. One cartoon featured a burglar crawling through a window with a policeman waiting to arrest him. A dialogue bubble above the burglar read, "I have the right to know why I am being arrested." The remaining pictures depicted characters claiming a false right. One box pictured a neighbor playing loud music while claiming the right to entertainment; another showed a line of vicious dogs barking at the heels of a woman while a man yelled that it is his right to have a pet. A reckless driver claimed the right to drive as he wished; a drunk man in his car defended the right to continue drinking and, finally, the last picture depicted a caveman and cavewoman, with the man beating the woman and claiming the right to be in charge of his own cave.

In the ensuing discussion, class participants positioned themselves and were positioned by the instructor in relation to the various pictures. Everyone agreed that the illustrated pet owner did not have the right to bring his ferocious dogs onto the street. Participants, noting that drinking alcohol is forbidden in Islam and that the Kenyan government recently passed an initiative outlawing drinking and driving, had no problem acknowledging that the man drunk in the car was clearly in the wrong. Critique of the final picture was more complex and invoked a long, heated debate among members of the class and Teferi on the practice of wife-beating among Somalis. Many of the more outspoken men vocalized their understandings of the merits of wife-beating in order to preserve a hierarchy of authority and garner respect in the family. One woman, the only one in the class clad in a *burkha* rather than *hijab*, countered by conveying her understanding that Islam forbids wife and child beating. However, for the most part it was acknowledged among class members that wife beating was, regardless of personal stance, a pervasive practice in their community's expression of Somali culture. Teferi, sensitive to the time constraints of the session, drew this discussion to a close with a didactic assertion that in the U.S. domestic violence is illegal and members of the class needed to begin envisioning alternatives to it. That such a debate was catalyzed by an illustration clearly intended to look barbaric and primitive eluded discussion.

While discussion of U.S. laws that prohibit traditional practices among Somalis was undoubtedly meant to inform refugees headed to the U.S. so that they might avoid "getting into trouble", the discussion also revealed a regulatory relationship between the U.S. government, law, and the population of Somali newcomers. At the same time, the conversation reified a structural polarity between the enlightenment ideals assumed to be actualized in the United States and those of traditional Somali culture.

The framing of U.S. and Somali culture as diametrically opposed, and potentially in conflict, also characterized the unit devoted to orienting to the cultural sphere of U.S. national life. While conversation about cultural difference was woven throughout the entire orientation, one afternoon in particular was set aside to introduce elements of U.S. culture deemed fundamental. In order to foster discussion of culture and cultural difference, Teferi asked the class to break into groups and make lists in response to the questions: "What is culture? What is different about Somali culture?" Each of the group's answers repeated and reinforced one another and shared an emphasis on those aspects of Somali culture most blatantly incongruent with U.S. culture. Rather than noting the importance of establishing community and bonds of reciprocity in Somali culture, the key tenets of Somali culture attendants chose to list included: polygamy, female circumcision, wife and child beating, patriarchy, separation of duties in the household (with men as the sole breadwinners and women running domestic life), respect of elders, dowry, young marriage, separation of gender, nomadic and pastoralist lifestyles, and the use of clans as a mode of social organization.[11] While the list represented the points of views of those most vocal in class, who were for the most part men, women in the class often nodded in agreement.

In response to such projected cultural incompatibility Somali newcomers were, again, instructed to reform their ways of being. Teferi noted that, while in Kenya or Somalia the father of a Somali family served as the head of the family unit who exercised unquestionable authority over women, children, and adolescents, in the U.S. such dynamics *will* shift. This shifting, he elaborated, is due in part to the reality that women may have an easier time finding work in the United States. Speaking of the need for men to compensate in the domestic sphere when women work outside the home, Teferi warned, "You exchange roles! Otherwise life could be difficult if you don't want to do this." Having established its pragmatic benefit, Teferi went on to link the transformation of gender roles to the legal status of women in the United States. Again, he distributed a handout featuring a cartoon illustration. Clearly extreme in its depiction, this document pictured a scantily clad woman in a small, fitted tank top, tight pants, and high heels waving farewell as she exits a living room where a man, baby strapped to his back, toils on his hands and knees to grind corn. A dialogue bubble above the man's head read, "This is North America!"

As the class filled with laughter, loud discussion, and disdainful head-shakes, Teferi asked people what they saw and how it made them feel. One young girl, rolling up her paper tightly, shook her head back and forth and said "It is not good." Directing his question to the men in the classroom, Teferi asked, "What will you do if this happens?" One man replied simply, "I will leave her and the kids." Not responding to the comment or the hush that fell over the room, Teferi explained that elders (males) will lose their authority in the U.S. as family members begin to do things without first asking for permission. One young man noted that such men "will become like a woman." Teferi abruptly countered, "What is the difference between men and women anyway?" A voice from the class cried out, "God made them different." At this point, everyone in the room was very attentive; many fidgeted tensely or leaned forward toward the front of the room. Teferi, having formed his rebuttal, pointed out that the Somali parliament now has women in it, that girls can be smarter than boys, and that refugees must accept these realities. Signaling a close in such open classroom discussion of Somalis' perspectives on the illustration, Teferi stated matter-of-factly, "in the U.S. they (women) *are* equal."

Teferi proceeded to systematically analyze the identified tenets of Somali culture and point out their illegality in the United States. While some of the topics, like the one on domestic abuse, sparked debate among class members, others, such as female circumcision, were more unanimously defended.[12] As one young woman stood up and said, "This is good for us. This is what we want." Regardless of its content, each discussion ended with Teferi's pronouncement that the practice must be discontinued.

Interwoven with the threat of punitive repercussion for failing to change were subtle messages regarding the promise of cultural hybridity—the promise, that is, of maintaining those values and practices that would help Somalis to survive in the United States. In a brief conversation on elder care, Somali culture was presented as a positive force that, when incorporated in U.S. life, had the potential to enable families to imagine a wider span of options. The discussion occurred after one woman in her seventies raised her hand and noted she had heard that in the U.S. elderly relatives were sent away to homes. Teferi admitted that while the practice of sending older relatives to nursing homes was prevalent in the United States, refugee families would not have to do so if they continued to foster strong community networks of support. The support provided by extensive yet close associations of relatives and friends would enable families to care for elders at home and, at the same time, reinforce and re-instill Somali concepts of community in the United States. Nevertheless, the overriding message Somali refugees faced in the 3 day orientation to life in the U.S. was that the U.S. national community and Somalis maintain two distinct and opposing cultures that have high probability for conflict. Given the marginalized and disempowered position of Somali newcomers, who neither speak English nor possess those skills in demand in the local labor market, the brunt of such a clash will fall upon the newcomer population and, as such, it is in Somalis' best interest to change and adapt. The most salient and immediate change upon which the CO session focused was in the realm of gender norms and expectations. In its discursive positioning, the CO curriculum: (1) cautioned Somalis to enact change in gender norms and practices in ways that introduced tension and fear on the part of class participants, (2) situated the U.S. government as a moral arbiter, and (3) caricatured Somali men as oppressive patriarchs and Somali women as passive victims of oppressive cultural practices, from which entrance into the U.S. promised deliverance. Such tension over gender meanings immediately catalyzed an oppositional relationship between Somalis' and the U.S. government and broader national community.

While it is crucial to note that the contours and discussion points of cultural orientation sessions we participated in were different than they might have been had the course been conducted with refugees from Dadaab—many of whom would already have been educated in the Kenyan system and therefore familiar with shifting gender responsibilities and practices—the presentation of Somali culture and U.S. national life as diametrically opposed probably would have still framed discussions geared toward orienting refugees to the United States.

From Kenya to the United States: Final Steps and International Travel

After refugees have completed the cultural orientation sessions, cleared final medical examinations, and received security clearance and sponsorship assurance, their forms are sent back to the JVA which requests visas from the U.S. embassy. The visas are then sent to IOM to arrange and post-U.S.-bound flights. Before the family can actually leave East Africa, however, certain final steps must be taken. The principal applicant must sign a promissory note guaranteeing that s/he will pay back all airline tickets. Another document must be signed agreeing to no longer chew *miraa*. Each traveler must take provided anti malarial and anti amoebic medications 2 days before departure.

At last, refugees are travel ready, facing their new lives with only two allotted bags of 23 kilograms, one carry-on of 5kg each, as well as their travel package of required documents provided by IOM. Escorted to their flights by IOM representatives, the families leave Kenya, many never to return, bound first to Europe where they will again be met by IOM representatives, and finally to their connecting U.S. flights. Upon arrival at a U.S. port of entry, refugees fill out applications for employment, complete authorization documents, and get fingerprinted. Finally, after landing in their particular city of resettlement, they are met by their new U.S. resettlement agency.

The U.S.-based resettlement agencies are nongovernmental organizations that work to aid refugees in initial phases of resettlement, specifically the first 30 days, by acting as what Teferi termed "advisors and cultural brokers." While they do receive some government funding, these organizations are nonprofit and often religiously affiliated. While services provided by each organization vary from state to state, in general each resettlement agency provides temporary housing, food, money for transportation, bedding material, some clothes, a primary medical checkup, as well as up to 2 hours a day of English language instruction free of charge. They also provide another cultural orientation for refugees within their first month, introducing specific local laws. Finally, resettlement agencies assist refugees in filling out social security cards, registering children in public schools, and opening a bank account. At the end of the initial 30-day period, resettlement organizations guide refugees towards other community organizations as well as general social services and welfare programs. After 8 months in the United States, refugees stop receiving any special assistance, are required to begin repaying the cost of their airline tickets from Africa, and, after 1 year, are both privy to the entitlements and subject to the expectations of U.S. permanent residency. It is at this point in the process of resettlement that many refugees choose to move to another location in the United States. For several thousand Somali refugees, this site of secondary resettlement is the northern New England community of Milltown.

NOTES

1. On the other hand, slots allotted to refugees from the "Near East/South Asia" rose from only 9,000 in 2007 to 39,500 in 2009 (Martin, 2009). Primary refugee producing countries in this region from this period were Iraq, Burma, and Bhutan (Martin, 2009).
2. Distinguished from an immigrant, a refugee is defined by the U.S. Immigration and Nationality Act as, "an alien outside the United States who is unable or unwilling to return to his or her country of nationality because of persecution or a well founded fear of persecution on account of race, religion, nationality, membership in a particular social group, or political opinion" (USCIS, 2003).

3. In 2004, a total of 75,536 applications were filed for refugee admission to the U.S. worldwide (Rytina, 2005).

4. The P3 categorization also includes unmarried children above 21 as well as parents of children under 21 who are already U.S. citizens (USCIS, 2006).

5. The phrase "violent or out of mind" was used at their cultural orientation session by the instructor Teferi to explain conditions barring travel to refugees. The reasons for his slightly disturbing semantic choice may include attempts to simplify language for translation and understanding. While Teferi was most likely referring to schizophrenia, we are not sure exactly which diagnoses of mental illness bar travel, or whether or not treatment and reexamination are provided as options. Most likely it is case dependent and up to the discretion of the reviewing doctor.

6. *Miraa*, or *khat*, is a mild amphetamine taken by chewing on its leaves. While in general alcohol consumption is quite low in Somali communities (though this is changing, anecdotally, by young Somali men who report increased use of moonshine in Dadaab), *miraa* is extremely popular and easily accessible in Kenya, where it is legal. It is illegal to chew *miraa* in the United States (for the active alkaloid cathinone found in it), however, and before being allowed to depart for the United States, refugees must sign a waiver agreeing to discontinue the practice. According to U.S.-based refugee advocates, a certain amount of leeway exists in which to argue that a refugee using *miraa* may not have known of active alkaloids present, or may have used older *miraa*, making its consumption a nondeportable offense. *Miraa* use certainly presents an area of contestation in U.S. courts today.

7. Course length is determined by the context of particular refugee groups as well as "student numbers, implementation logistics, competing training needs, and cost-effectiveness" (IOM, 2005, p. 2).

8. The U.S. *Welcome Guide* was produced by MAEC for Applied Linguistics in consultation with the U.S. Department of State's Bureau on Populations, Refugees, and Migration (IOM, 2005).

9. One instructor at IOM explained that one survival skill acquired by refugees in their experiences of state-lessness includes the ability to adapt to certain perceived expectations of them when demanded. As refugees are repeatedly asked to tell their stories, identify themselves, or justify their presence in various interviews, they learn to frame or present themselves in particular ways. For instance, he instructed the refugees in his cultural orientation sessions to approach job interviews in the US exactly opposite to the ways they treated their UNHCR and USCIS circuit ride interviews, in which it was beneficial to look ragged, destitute, or hopeless. Instead, he said that at job interviews they should look put together, clean, and well dressed, as well as educated.

10. This observation becomes particularly poignant when juxtaposed with another older man's earlier description of his personal goal in the U.S. as "to go and rest."

11. That the more contentious cultural factors were listed first—wife beating, polygamy, female circumcision, gender inequality—is not necessarily coin-

cidental and most likely reflects an expression of resistance against Teferi and the U.S. state for which he is speaking. The choice of cultural characteristics could also be seen as symbolic of an effort to emphasize things deemed distinctly "Somali," particularly given that each of those practices had already been touched upon or alluded to as no longer permitted in the United States.

12.   Of course, dissenters might not necessarily feel able or comfortable to speak. In general, however, there was overwhelming support of female circumcision expressed, even among the younger girls sitting in one corner of the room.

CHAPTER 9

THE UNITED STATES
AND MILLTOWN

Traditionalism, Liberalism, and Nativism

Every weekday morning during the course of our study, between 35 and 50 East African, mostly Somali, refugee men and women bore the extremes of northern New England weather on their to walk to the modest cinderblock building that houses the Milltown Adult Education Center (MAEC). Many traveled several blocks from the aging, subsidized housing complexes where their families had been placed upon arrival in Milltown.

Somalis are attracted by several of Milltown's qualities. With an estimated population of 30,000, it is significantly smaller and thus more manageable than the metropolises of Atlanta, Minneapolis, and Columbus, Ohio, which have been used as primary sites of resettlement. Milltown has a low crime rate and affordable housing. The quality of its schools and social services are among the highest in the nation. Since 2001, well over 3,000 Somali newcomers have made their way to the city, where they live among the working and underclass descendents of French Canadian migrants. French-Canadians made their own transnational journey to the area during the industrial revolution. The twenty-first century landscape of the city still echoes the earlier immigrants' story of incorporation.

In the late 1800s, Milltown took shape as a textile manufacturing center dependent upon the labor of French-Canadian newcomers. A grand

Educated For Change?: Muslim Refugee Women in the West, pp. 221–244
Copyright © 2012 by Information Age Publishing
All rights of reproduction in any form reserved.

and ornate cathedral, the largest in New England, dominates the skyline and continues to offer services in French. An active Franco-American historical center memorializes a period of industrial productivity and French Canadian cultural influence. Down the street from MAEC stands *Le Palais de Sports*, a local skating facility recently renovated in order to attract a minor league men's ice hockey team from Canada.

At the time of the study, the markers of twenty-first century globalism were increasingly laid upon the aging structures of nineteenth and twentieth century industrial and cultural order. Typifying the stories of many New England cities, Milltown's once booming industrial economy declined precipitously in the post industrial era and finally ground to a virtual halt in the aftermath of the passage of the North Atlantic Free Trade Agreement. Storefront shops once left hauntingly empty, their "mom and pop" proprietors having surrendered to the introduction of big box stores on the outskirts of town, were re-born as *halal* meat markets and mosques. *LeBlanc's* hotdog stand, a local landmark, flanks an African store carrying *hijabs*, henna, and the low lying, ornate couches that line the living rooms of many Somali homes. In City Hall, Somali translators are hired to work alongside city and state employees bearing French surnames in order to facilitate the provision of social services to the community's newcomers. Spacious apartments, originally designed to accommodate large Catholic families, perfectly suit the average Somali family of seven.

Each morning, Ayaan, a Somali woman and MAEC student who has lived in the U.S. for 19 years, drove roughly half a dozen women from a subsidized housing area located in the outskirts of town to MAEC. A bumper sticker affixed to her minivan reads: "You better say your prayers before your prayers are said for you." It is unclear whether Ayaan appreciated the irony of her appropriation of such Christian inspired moralism to express Muslim religiosity; still, the act symbolizes the entwinement, blurring, and paradoxical entrenchment of markers of U.S., French-Canadian, and Somali cultural sensibilities that routinely occurred in Milltown.

The differences in the Dadaab and Milltown landscapes speak volumes about the changed lives of those Somalis who make their way from the hot, dry and harsh desert conditions of northeastern and eastern Africa to the temperate climate and relative wealth of the northeastern United States. The permanence of the latter's structures punctuates migrants' change in status as they move from a protracted emergency situation, in which they are literally prohibited from laying down roots, to an area where they are expected, even pressured, to find a way to integrate, become economically self-sufficient, and thrive for generations to come. The supragovernmental organization (UNHCR) upon which refugees have depended for years, and that holds near omnipotence over refugee lives in Kenya, has negligible powers within U.S. borders. Once prohibited from exiting designated camp territory, raising livestock or planting crops, or building permanent structures, Somalis in Milltown now routinely interact with civil servants—teachers, case managers, cultural brokers—eager to weave them into neighborhoods, schools, and workplaces.

In addition to shifts in land use and temporality, over the years we observed physical changes in many of those with whom we worked. We also noted distinctions in affect and the topics of concern upon which women dwelled. Once thin women became plump; missing teeth were replaced by startlingly white dentures; glasses came to frame faces that once squinted with futility over workbooks. In Dadaab, girls and women talked about a lack of resources, a dearth of food and jobs; they inserted requests for tarpaulins into every chance conversation with aid workers. With a glint of desperation in their eyes and an underlying assumption that White Westerners could access resources for them, they spoke to Patti about the need for more postsecondary scholarships for those few girls able to make it through secondary school. In Milltown, desperation is replaced with an ironic abashedness about weight gain. And, women wonder aloud about the young Somali girls and boys who do not perform in school. Why do they not try harder? Why do they not respect their parents and teachers? "They do not remember. They do not know how much we have suffered to get here. Here, it is all handed to them, not like before," a 30 year old mother of six lamented.

Life in Milltown is certainly different than in Dadaab. Despite dissimilarities, however, both locations share much in common. Somalis in Dadaab and Milltown both face resentment from the host population. Though widely known as a proud and independent people, in both locales Somalis have to adapt to environments in which they are largely excluded from positions of power and made dependent upon others for their very survival. In both Christian-dominated contexts, as Muslims they are in the religious minority. Many of their cultural traditions are viewed, at best, as quaint anachronisms and, often, as outlandish violations of human rights. In both places, they are compelled to experience the homogenizing force of globalization as they interface with power structures saturated with Western-derived cultural tenets and practices.

Paradoxically, so, too, are they entangled in the diversifying impacts of globalization. In Dadaab, aid workers and researchers caution one another to practice cultural sensitivity in their work with Somalis. Western women in particular are expected to make accommodations in dress and behavior in order not to offend Somali sensibilities. Aid workers turn a blind eye to illegal circumcision and early marriage practices in order to maintain peace in the camps. Somali is the language of instruction throughout primary school classes. In official meetings between aid worker staff and Somali community leaders, men gather in a circle while women sit in the outskirts. Aid workers relax in a refugee-operated restaurant featuring Ethiopian and Somali dishes. In Milltown, educators and service providers attend professional development workshops in which they are instructed about the particularities of Somali culture. Female teachers are cautioned not to expect Somali men to shake their hands and urged to allow female and male students to segregate themselves in the classroom. Food in the school cafeteria is labeled to indicate whether items contain pork. An existing ban against headwear was amended to allow for scarves worn as an expression of religiosity. In both places, Somalis have opened businesses that serve Somali cultural sensibilities: *kikois* (men's wraps), Somali *injera* (an unleavened bread), camel's milk, and *halal* (prepared in accordance with Islamic law) meats are readily available.

As an additional commonality, for the most part both locales provide Somalis greater access to a range of services, including health care, education, food security, and psychological counseling. In both places, Somalis' newfound access to Western style secular education introduces novel perspectives on gender, multiculturalism, and social mobility as well as unprecedented language and technical skills, even as traditional elements of Somali cultural tenets and practices maintain their force of influence.

In short, both Milltown and Dadaab are cauldrons of cultural complexity, friction, overlap, and compromise. Newcomers' presence in the U.S. national community requires adaptation and evinces tension and struggle on the part of multiple actors. For Somalis themselves, entrance into the United States, and the Milltown community in particular, represents neither a wholly new nor an entirely familiar experience.

Indeed, for Somalis, life in both Dadaab and Milltown finds order in the tense opposition of worldviews. While the overarching polarity between Dadaab's enlightenment and traditional Somali cultural tenets and practices dominates the Dadaab landscape, Milltown is a media saturated, multiethnic American city with striaded socioeconomic class system in which multiple worldviews are relevant. In what follows, we examine the nuanced "intertwining" of the varied interests, experiences, accommodations and constraints brought to bear by the introduction of Somali newcomers to the Milltown community. In our examination, we elaborate on what are highly localized resonances of social, cultural, political, and economic dynamics of global scope. We begin by sketching out two opposing responses to the flow of immigrants from the global South, and Somali immigrants in particular, that have occur at the national level. One of these views, the liberal discourse on immigration, represents a manifestation of North American secular humanist political tradition that seeks transcendence of barriers of race, class, gender, and national belonging. The second, American nativism, reflects an equally historically steeped reaction to pluralism. Originating in the religious fear-mongering response to Irish immigration of late nineteenth century, American nativist sentiment has a long and sordid history animated by subsequent and unending waves of immigration to the United States. After outlining national responses to immigration, we reflect and particularize the story within Milltown itself, identifying reinscriptions of liberal discourse on immigration, nativist sentiment, and traditional elements of Somali cultural tenets and practices.

Response to Immigration at the National Level

As is widely known, over the last century the U.S. and other nations of the global North have experienced an increasing flow of immigrants from the global South. According to the U.S. Census Bureau, in 1910 a mere 2.1% of the U.S. foreign born population emigrated from Latin America or Africa. By comparison in 2007, 57.9% of immigrants were from Latin American or African countries (U.S. Census Bureau, 2010). Recent newcomers' status as racial, language, and religious minorities, introduce a particular set of challenges to the incorporation process.

As we have seen, in regard to Somalis, the U.S. has the most generous immigration policy of all Western industrialized nations. However, the relative openness of U.S. policy does not mean that Somalis are welcomed with open arms. Indeed, post-9/11, the number of immigration opportunities has dwindled and, increasingly, newcomers face a decidedly unwelcoming reception from nativist elements of the U.S. national community. In her examination of discourse that has emerged in response to immigrant activity along the U.S.-Mexico border, Lytle (2003) notes that border crossers are commonly referred to as "border violators" and "criminal aliens." Such chauvinistic talk is coupled with heightened regulation, both official and vigilante, of the border under the auspices of a war on drugs.

> Therefore, the way that the War on Drugs has transformed border spaces and filled prisons has fueled the general panic about race and migration that is simmering in the United States. It is the collision of discourses of the criminal alien with the incarceration structures of the War on Drugs during this specific period of racial panic that has awoken the vigilante spirit along the U.S.-Mexico border at the turn of the twenty-first century. (p. 8)

As the race-laden fear Lytle describes suggests, opposing representations of newcomers are rooted in particular utopian visions of U.S.

national identity. Nativist political philosophy imagines a homogeneous, White Anglo-Saxon nation-state and thereby perceives the immigrant (racial and religious) other as a threat to national well-being and as undeserving of protection or inclusion (Chavez, 2001; Higham, 1955; Katerberg, 1995; Perea, 1997; Vecoli, 1996). Anti-immigration discourse highlights the cultural and political differences between a normalized image of an American and that of newcomers. Negative press highlights that newcomers from the global South tend to have lower than average income and educational levels as compared with more long term U.S. citizens (Borjas, 1990; Burke, 1995; Kemnitz, 2006; Thomas & Murr, 1993). Those within the current demographic of newcomers from the global South are also perceived to be less familiar with meritocratic and democratic governance traditions, an impression that raises concern about the continued wellbeing of structures of reward, discipline, and governance in the global North. In talk about the compatibility between particular cultural practices and the forms of governance that lend order to American institutions, the perceived threat represented by Muslim immigrants in particular is stressed. While "the danger posed by foreigners to American values and institutions," Vecoli (1996, p. 13) writes, has been a constant theme throughout American history, since 9/11 xenophobia has been focused on a presumed incompatibility between Islam and liberal democracy (Fukuyama, 2006).

The media serves as a vehicle for fear mongering both through established news outlets and individual utilization of the internet. While Fox TV is widely known to disseminate a conservative politics and reactionary position on immigration, more mainstream outlets are increasingly falling on the ratings-garnering, chauvinist bandwagon. In a recent critique of CNN coverage of immigration, Fairness & Accuracy in Reporting (FAIR) maintains that Lou Dobbs, who offers "consistently alarmist" coverage of immigration, "isn't the only CNN personality uninterested in nuance or immigrants' rights perspectives" (FAIR, 2006). According to the press watchdog, long time anchor, Jack Cafferty, has "launched into a scornful tirade that seemed to even threaten violence against the peaceful protesters":

> Once again, the streets of our country were taken over today by people who don't belong here.... Taxpayers who have surrendered highways, parks, sidewalks and a lot of television news time on all these cable news networks to mobs of illegal aliens are not happy about it.... America's illegal aliens are becoming ever bolder. March through our streets and demand your rights. Excuse me? You have no rights here, and that includes the right to tie up our towns and cities and block our streets. At some point this could all turn very violent as Americans become fed up with the failure of their gov-

ernment to address the most pressing domestic issue of our time. (FAIR, 2006)

Cafferty went on to suggest that the government stop the buses transporting protesters and demand that occupants show their green cards. FAIR (2006) writes:

> It's troubling that Cafferty seems entirely ignorant of the fact that under the U.S. Constitution, everyone in this country, whether documented or not, does indeed have rights—or that illegal immigrants pay billions of dollars in taxes each year.

The report goes on to highlight the slanted perspective of CNN journalist after journalist, concluding that the portrayal of immigration as a "problem" is more the rule than the exception at the network (FAIR, 2006).

The media is also an outlet through which nativists express fear regarding the supposed Islamic threat to U.S. democracy. Walker (2007) describes how a recent *Los Angeles Times* op-ed (Pipes, 1999) states, "Some Moslems living in the U.S. advocate a violent overthrow of our democracy in favor of a theocratic Islamic state" She continues:

> In fact, democracy in Moslem countries is rare. An Islamic government is an autocratic theocracy by definition and practice, since Islam does not recognize the separation of church and state. Many Moslems are not only unsupportive of free speech but actually condemn it—as Salman Rushdie can attest. (Walker, 2007)

Similarly, in response to his own rhetorically posed question, "Will Muslim immigration destroy western democracy?" a blogger writes,

> The problem with Islam is that it teaches loyalty to the Muslim Ummah (nation) first. For them, the world is divided people [sic] of many religions who happened to live in different countries. For the rest of us, the world is divided into different countries who happened [sic] to have people of many religions.... Thus accepting Muslim immigrants means accepting people whose loyalty will not lie with the host country. If the numbers of Muslims are small, the problem is not serious. But with their high birth rates, a tipping point will be reached in which the viability of the western nation states will be compromised. (Heavy Handed Politics, 2006)

Not surprisingly, given the amorphous demonization of immigrants from the global South, and the more pointed characterization of Muslims as terrorists, anti immigrant sentiment translates into a commonplace harassment of Somali immigrants by individuals, the press, and the government. The most virulent expression of anti-immigrant sentiment comes from individual acts of hate speech disseminated via the Internet. One well-known blogger begins his diatribe with an appeal for sympathy for a population of Native Americans displaced by the introduction of Somalis to "their neighborhood." From this expression of apparent cultural sensitivity, the author reels off a list of (in some cases blatantly unfounded) characterizations winding toward a final, full-blown nightmare scenario in which Somalis wage war against American from within the country.

> Somalis, who are culturally violent, took to drug running and sending money to Al Quaeda. The FBI has shut down some of their money wiring activities, but the situation has caused a great deal of negative social change. Most Indians had to move out for fear of the constant shootings. Local stores had to put up glass in front of cashiers, because the Somalis spit at the cashiers. People complain about their lack of hygiene (they don't shower their bodies, only their feet) and high rate of tuberculosis. On 9/11 the high school had to be shut down, since Somali teens cheered and American kids fought back, creating a riot. They had a riot a while ago wielding machetes at police. When war comes to America, we know who we'll be fighting in the streets, just watch the movie "Blackhawk Down." Why are our enemies living here? (Francis, 2003)

In addition to individual bloggers' portrayal of Somalis as violence prone, diseased, drug users and gun dealers, the Federal government is also widely perceived as a source of disparagement. The use of law enforcement against Somalis often occurs for transparent political gain rather than as a genuine concern for security or the well being of Western democracy. In Seattle, federal, state and local officials performed a highly publicized series of raids in the Somali community, ostensibly targeting a drug ring funneling funds to terrorist organizations. The raids, which found neither drugs nor money, occurred just as Bush went public to defend illegal wiretaps (Hill & Docekal, 2006).

The press exacerbates the government's politics of fear. In his examination of the conservative press's coverage of Somali immigration, Britt Robson (2001) argues that Somali newcomers have unjustly been accused of knowingly funding Al Qaeda activity:

> In the days following the November 7 raids, newspapers nationwide reported that the Al-Barakaat money-transfer service had funneled "tens of millions" of dollars to Al Qaida. Twin Cities readers learned that Al-Barakaat, based in Mogadishu, Somalia, was by far the most popular money-transfer firm for local Somalis, and that the metro area is home to approximately half of the 100,000 Somali refugees living in the United States. In short, it seemed as if millions of dollars—maybe tens of millions—had been flowing from local refugees to bin Laden's coffers every year. Perhaps not coincidentally, the Star Tribune reported that at a subsequent town meeting

on terrorism held at Bloomington Jefferson High School, an audience member received scattered applause when he 'questioned the loyalty of Somali immigrants.

Unlike Dadaab, in the United States, anti-immigrant sentiment is not countered by a significant universalistic human rights discourse. Further, in contrast to former colonizing countries, in the U.S. there is little awareness of, or sense of responsibility for, the nation's interconnectivity with the struggles of those from the global South who make their way to U.S. soil. In her examination of Sikhs' entrance into the English nation-state, Hall (2002) maintains that Anglo-Saxon English women and men feel a sense of racial superiority intimately tied to English citizenship. However, this sense of innate ascendance is counterbalanced by a guilt around having oppressed former colonial subjects that finds outlet in a liberal discourse of individual human rights.

In the United States, there is a similar sense of Caucasian preeminence expressed as a cultural conservatism, but there is a lack of equivalent consciousness, at least as expressed within mainstream media, about the U.S.'s involvement in the destabilization of nations in the global South. Weighed against rhetoric in the United Kingdom, the liberal orientation toward newcomers from the global South from within the U.S. features less concern for the remedying of previous human rights violations and a more self-conscious interest in the assertion of pluralist ideals. In holding virulently to the proposition that it is quintessentially "American" to provide equality of opportunity, in America the proimmigrant, enlightenment polarity is expressed with an air of self-conscious generosity. Positioned on a moral high ground, Americans situate immigrants from the global South as a needy, less advanced other in need of the help provided by superior U.S. institutions, resources, and cultural ways. In exchange for the promise of equal opportunity and a tolerance for benign forms of cultural difference, the liberal perspective communicates an expectation that newcomers learn the dominant language, work toward economic self-sufficiency, and integrate into the sociocultural fabric of the national community.

The liberal perspective framed a recent report on immigrants' opinions about life in the United States, in which Farkas, Dufer, Johnson, Moye, and Vine (2003) argue that immigrants are "thankful and appreciative" for the opportunity to live and work in the United States. Immigrants' sentiments, they claim, are "anchored in the view that the U.S. holds the comparative advantage over their home countries, and these are not limited to economic considerations" (p. 28). Indeed, the authors call repeated attention to newcomers' esteem for the United States.

The focus group conversations with immigrants would typically follow this pattern: an initial outpouring of affection for this country would be followed by candid talk about the nation's shortcomings and would end with a bottom line assessment—its problems notwithstanding, there is no place better than the U.S. in which to build their home. (p. 28)

In his examination of the significance of immigration in the early formation of American national identity, Vecoli (1996) writes:

The notion of America as an asylum for the oppressed of the world has exerted a powerful influence on [American] minds and hearts…. And let it be said that it was flattering to the national ego that the United States was the Promised Land to the poor and persecuted of the old world. (p. 12)

In his account of more recent history, Chavez (2001) demonstrates that Americans continue to uphold a relatively generous immigration policy as a bulwark of the national self-image. Describing media portrayal of Vietnamese immigrants of the 1970s, Chavez writes:

Refugees came to symbolize how we thought of ourselves as a nation that helps the world and the uprooted in their times of need…. By generously receiving Vietnamese refugees, America was acting in character, at least the part of our national identity that welcomes immigrants. (p. 84)

Commonplace liberal portrayals of newcomers as industrious, vulnerable, and appreciative, and Americans as generous caretakers, stand in opposition to an equally familiar nativist image of newcomers as lazy, devious, and ungrateful. Lytle (2003) describes this phenomenon as the "criminalization not only of migration, but of migrants" (p. 2).

In the face of sociocultural pluralism, the liberal political tradition promotes individual rights as the avenue to equal opportunity. In this context, liberalism translates into a discourse that foregrounds the contribution newcomers make to the U.S. economy, celebrates U.S. self-characterization as a nation of immigrants, and boasts that equality of opportunity afforded by the U.S. social and economic system distinguishes it as a morally advanced nation. While anti-immigration discourse focuses on immigration as a drain upon our economy and a threat to our civil order and cultural unity (see Chavez, 2001). Liberal discourse suggests an exchange in which the U.S. extends welcome in return for gratitude and service. In this arrangement, the U.S. appears as an accommodating host while maintaining its position of power and ownership. Those who welcome immigrants and refugees often expect newcomers to shout the loudest about the freedom and opportunity that life in the U.S. provides and, then, to get to work. Given extant relations of power, this schema presents a seemingly fair trade: the U.S.'s existing assets (social order, services, educational opportunity) in exchange for immigrants' and refugees' efforts to become American through obsequiousness, accommodation, and labor.

Just as the conservative media disseminates anti-immigrant sentiment, so, too, do the progressive media promote the liberal perspective. In 2004, PBS offered a series titled, "The New Americans," which traces the experiences of several groups of newcomers. The stories feature a question and answer section that broaches "common misperceptions regarding immigration and its effects on American society" (ITVS, 2004). One multiple-choice question inquires about the national origin of most immigrants. The correct answer, Asia and Latin America, is set against presumably more frightening options including the Middle East and Africa. Another question clarifies that less than one percent of the world's emigrants come to the US, apparently dispelling the image of America as a mecca, of sorts, for the world's terrorists and gold seekers. The underlying point is further supported by a question about the reason most (75%) immigrants come to the United States, which, we learn, is to join family members already here. Finally, the myth-dispelling questions are also geared toward evoking sympathy. We discover that in southern California an average immigrant makes $8,500 a year and sends 31% of it home to support less privileged family members (ITVS, 2004).

The *New York Times* (*NYT*) also features stories that evoke compassion. One notes the rising numbers of immigrants who, in response to an increased presence of border and national guard agents, lose their lives as they try riskier ways to get across the border (*NYT*, 2007). *The Times* also features a story that follows three undocumented sisters for a week. These stories highlight the women's increased standard of living in the U.S. while simultaneously noting that the new standard is still far below that of the average American. Further, the women face the daily danger of being exposed and repatriated. Despite such challenges, the women manage to raise children who earn A's and B's in school, maintain jobs, and send money to relatives in their nations of origin. A final human interest story features a federal crackdown on employers who hire undocumented workers, thereby leaving families desperate for income and fearful of deportation (*NYT*, 2007).

Expressions of proimmigrant sentiment particular with regard to Somali newcomers likewise mirror liberal immigrant discourse writ large. Advocates for Somali newcomers invoke equality of opportunity, patient tolerance of difference, and compassion toward the needy as fundamental values that define the American national identity. Sounding a pragmatic bell, they argue that newcomers stimulate economic growth, enrich communities with culturally distinct foods and celebrations, and remind overscheduled Americans to reprioritize family, community, and friends. PBS recently featured a story on the desire of Somali immigrant youth in Minneapolis to give back to Somalis still trapped in their home country. One Somali adolescent is quoted as saying:

> "People think you become American and you forget your culture," she said. "But you have to remember there are students in Somalia, where everything is war-torn, yet they're still seeking an education. And here, we complain if we have to do homework while our favorite TV show is on." (Ginther, 2006)

The Times also published the story of a Somali man whom the government neglected to inform that he had been granted political asylum. Thinking that he could not travel abroad legally, the man left the safety of U.S. shores in order to attend his mother's funeral in Kenya. When he tried to return using forged documents, he was detained for a month even though, in fact, he had long ago been granted legal asylum (Smothers, 1997).

Individual editorials expressing liberal sentiment similarly highlight immigrant vulnerability as well as the ways in which newcomers enrich US life ways. Anthropologist Kathleen Hall Jamieson sponsors a blog dedicated to answering political questions. On the blog, she addresses a question regarding Somalis and welfare posed by a fellow academic in Ohio.

> My students are under the impression that when a new refugee/immigrant enters the country they are given thousands of dollars, a new car, exempt from paying taxes and preference when it comes to housing and college. Could you clear this issue up for me?

> Thanks for your question, Tina. On July 17, I spoke with a representative at the Department of Health and Human Services who said the "rumor" that refugees receive cash, a car, and preference for housing and college was "totally false." The following day I spoke with Abdirizak Farah, a Somali refugee and an employee of the City of Columbus. Mr. Farah said point-blank, "I did not receive a penny from anybody when I came to this country."

> While Mr. Farah may not have received any money when he arrived to the United States, some refugees do receive minimal financial and medical assistance. The Department of Health and Human Services oversees The Office of Refugee Resettlement (ORR), which "provides funding for refugee services programs through state governments as well as through NGOs." The ORR also organizes transitional cash assistance programs, health benefits and a "wide variety of social services" for refugees.

> The rules governing how much individual refugees can receive in cash assistance is determined by the state governments. Many states, including Ohio, establish cash assistance for refugees that is no more beneficial than welfare. Refugees are given the opportunity to attend public high schools and col-

leges, and must pay federal income taxes on the wages they earn in compliance with the law. (Hall Jamieson, 2007)

As we have seen, in Dadaab the polarities of traditionalism versus enlightenment are marked by conservative Somalis on the one hand and humanitarian aid workers on the other. In the United States, ironically, dominant traditionalist discourse expresses a strongly anti-immigrant, anti-Muslim, anti-Somali perspective. In Dadaab, enlightenment voices articulate a universalized human rights discourse. By contrast, in the United States, such ideals are given expression via a liberal ideological framework in which talk sympathetic to newcomers highlights the value added to the nation both in economic and cultural terms.

Narrowing the Lens: Milltown

In Milltown, the overarching nativist and liberal polarity structuring U.S. response to immigration is reproduced in local discourse on the newcomer Somali population, while taking on its own, contextualized quality. Somali newcomers to Milltown enter an environment in which even seasonal visitors from nearby New England states have long been referred to as "from away." At the time of the study, which coincided with the first few years of Somali presence in Milltown, locals' fierce independence, famous reticence, and wariness of strangers, was coupled with a generalized sense of desperation due to recent regional job loss. The Maine Department of Labor reports that between 1993 and 2005, the Milltown area's population of 36,000 lost 1,685 trade-related manufacturing jobs (PICA, 2007). This loss struck the death knell for a textile industry in long and steady decline. Between 2001 and 2003, approximately 1,200 Somali refugees came to Milltown (Maine State Planning Office, 2005). By 2007, that number had reached over 3,000 (Nadeau, 2007).

Locals immediately worried aloud that Somalis introduced an undesirable burden upon scarce resources. In May of 2001, only months after the arrival of the first wave of Somali newcomers, the undercurrent of resentment in the community bubbled forth. The city sponsored a public forum regarding what was commonly referred to as the "Somali situation." The local paper described the event: "About five hundred, mostly Whites, filled the Milltown Armory Tuesday night to listen to the city's panel of immigration experts—from State Department of Human Services officials to representatives from Catholic Charities and the Somali community itself" (Taylor, 2002, p. C1). The majority of questions broached that evening focused on the distribution of social service benefits between refugees and native residents, as well as the migration's impact on employment levels in the area.

In addition to logistical questions, intolerant sentiments were voiced both subtly and explicitly. Skepticism about the new Somali refugees permeated the Milltown community. In the fall of 2002, within weeks of moving to Milltown herself, Patti spoke with an elderly man at a local laundry about the situation. He described the "primitive" practices of newly arrived Somalis, whom, he reported, moved into government-provided housing that featured new oak cabinetry. "They removed the cupboard doors so they could raise chickens in them!" he exclaimed. He concluded, "This always was a good place to live, not anymore. That's all over now." Over the next few years, we encountered the oft-repeated rumor about chickens being raised in cabinets, along with other equally disquieting ones that conveyed a widespread perception of Africans as culturally backward and as a drain upon an overly generous state and local welfare system.

The resentment flowing through Milltown surfaced publicly again in the fall of 2002 with the publication of the mayor's controversial letter, entitled, "Maxed Out." In his letter, the mayor asked leaders of the Somali community to "stem the tide of migration," in order to lessen the economic strain on Milltown. He wrote, "Please pass the word: We've been overwhelmed and have responded valiantly. Now we need breathing room—our city is maxed out physically, financially, and emotionally" (*Portland Press Herald*, 2002). The controversial rhetoric of the mayor's letter put Milltown in the national spotlight, receiving coverage in various newspapers and media sources around the country, including the *New York Times, Washington Post, CNN,* and *National Public Radio.*

The letter also attracted the attention of national White-supremacy groups, including the National Alliance and the World Church of the Creator, which planned and held a controversial hate rally in Milltown on January 11, 2003. One such event speaker characterized Somalis as "the enemy" who, if given the chance "will probably slit your throat" (Democracy Now, 2003). More frequently echoed rhetoric described Somalis as leaching off the welfare system or taking already scarce jobs from locals (Bouchard, 2002; Democracy Now, 2003). A hugely successful counter rally occurred at the same time. In this latter event, various Somali, local, and state leaders offered words of praise for the newcomers and called attention to the responsibility of long term members of the community to extend a welcoming hand. The former Milltown Mayor announced, "We are many, we are one—one community that welcomes all. We say 'no' to hatred. We say 'yes' to safety. We support full membership in the community for everyone" (SPLC, 2003). Together, they described an imagined future in which Somali newcomers were fully incorporated into the local schools, neighborhood, and marketplace.

The two gatherings symbolize a starkly divided community. On the one hand there are those reacting in fear and aggressive intolerance to newcomers from the global South. Local academics, liberals, and members of the public sector charged with serving the newcomer population articulated a more welcoming position. They hoped newcomers would lend vibrancy to the economy and culture. They longed to open doors of opportunity and celebrate Milltown as a city united in its increasing diversity.

Aligning With Liberalism: Milltown Educators Welcome Somali Newcomers

Like educators throughout the national scene, during the period we conducted fieldwork in Milltown public educators in Milltown aligned with liberal frameworks in designing educational policy and practice in relation to Somali newcomers. In the K-12 system, advocacy for newcomers took shape in response to the punitive accountability scheme implemented through the federal education legislation entitled No Child Left Behind (NCLB) Act. NCLB mandated that various subgroups' test performance be tracked. If a particular subgroup; that is, based on race, ethnicity, socioeconomic status, and language use; failed to meet universal standards or, subsequently, to achieve adequate yearly progress toward those standards, an entire school would be publically declared a "failing" school. The legislation places schools and district with English Language Learning (ELL) populations in an untenable situation because once a student has attained fluency, he or she is no longer a member of a language minority subgroup. Consequently, it is impossible for the subgroup to ever achieve the standard as defined. Several Milltown schools with Somali immigrant students quickly found themselves on the list of schools failing to meet adequate yearly progress based on the performance of their language minority subgroup. In response, Milltown educators spoke out on behalf of Somalis, who, as ELLs, were the subgroup identified as preventing local schools from meeting standards. Referring to the recent failure of three schools to meet standards for adequate yearly progress, the superintendent of Milltown schools asked rhetorically, "How would you feel if you were in China for two years and you sat down to take a Chinese test in Chinese?... We want the rules to be fair" (Washuk, 2007).

Educators critical of NCLB were joined by Milltown city administrator who critiqued federal disinvestment in the public sector. In a report to the state congressional delegation, he writes:

That (legislative revisions to NCLB have not occurred) is certainly disappointing particularly in light of what has occurred with Montello School, a public school which has produced a "Teacher of the Year" in Donna Tardif and has been recognized nationally for its partnership with Geiger and it's "Night of the Stars" program which recognizes the best writers/illustrators in each class. In 2005, 900 attendees celebrated 92 students' written work. From 2001 to 2005, the percentage of students' writing at grade level *increased by 23%* in Grades K-3 *and 17%* in Grades 4-6. The idea that Montello school faces the distinction of being a "failure" given its extraordinary work with first generation refugees who are often socially and academically challenged, seems to fly in the face of why NCLB was created. (Nadeau, 2007, Emphasis in original)

The director of K-12 ELL programming in Milltown joined Nadeau in making a case for increased federal support. In an appendix to his report, she writes:

NCLB states that students must be tested and held to the same standards in math as their English speaking peers as soon as they enter the county. In reading there is an one year grace period. Thus, if a 12-year-old, comes to us from another country with no prior schooling, after one year, he/she is expected to meet the same standards as English speaking peers in reading, writing and science. Because Maine has among the highest standards in the country, we have students "failing" who in other states would meet standards. While this is problematic for all students, it is particularly unfair to ELLs. Finally, once students become English proficient, they are removed from the ELL "subgroup." This means their scores no longer count in measuring the effectiveness of the local ELL program. (Nadeau, 2007)

Educators' efforts to advocate for their ELL clientele demonstrate an alignment with liberal belief that the public sector should be strengthened and utilized to facilitate greater integration and access to equality of opportunity for immigrants. The same alignment that characterizes the public education system at large in Milltown, typifies the position of those adult educators serving ELL students and study participants with whom we worked in Milltown.

Long term educators and leaders of ELL programming at Milltown Adult Education and Learning Center (MAEC), Sue and Jacqueline, echo liberal sentiment regarding their largely Somali clientele. Sue is the head of personnel, fund raising, and programming for both adult basic education and ELL at the MAEC. As the teacher with the most seniority and in whose classroom ELL students spent considerable amounts of time (often multiple hours on a daily basis), Jacqueline, too, made a strong impression upon the student body.

For Sue and Jacqueline, liberal discourse offer both a language in which to respond publically to strident, local anti-immigrant sentiment and a framework to structure everyday governance of the rapidly expanding adult education program. Sue and Jacqueline see the MAEC as carrying forth a proimmigrant agenda in the face of local, nativist anti-immigrant sentiment. At a celebration of student achievement at the MAEC, Jacqueline spoke to an assembled crowd, "Those people who say our students are lazy should come in any day and watch them. They work for hours every day to learn English, and it is not easy to learn a language." While Jacqueline's words of praise implicitly countered derogatory characterizations of Somali refugees prevalent in the community, both Sue and Jacqueline also explicitly push back against racist, anti-immigrant sentiment in Milltown. Both attended the large counter rally against the hate group that came to Milltown in 2002. (The main organizer of this counter rally was a popular teacher at the MAEC until the summer of 2005). They are also frequently quoted in local, regional, and national media covering the story of Somali resettlement, where they always offer words of admiration and empathy regarding newcomers. As reported in the local newspaper, Sue described Somalis as "among the most interesting, engaged and appreciative students [Sue] has met." She continued, "These immigrants, who have come from terrible situations in their home country, can begin to build their lives here … every student she's worked with wants a job and wants to learn English so that they can get a job" (Washuk, 2006).

As long-term members of the Milltown community, Sue and Jacqueline's viewpoints are sensitive to the workings of the larger community and lend a nuanced reading of the particularities of educating newcomers in Milltown during the current time period of rapid community change. Both Sue and Jacqueline are deeply engaged in the civic sphere of community life and are well versed in the worldviews and proclivities of fellow community members. From this position, they enjoy a "bird's eye view" of the environment into which the resettled newcomers enter, and have insight into the developing relations between the newcomers and other members of Milltown's largely working class, White, politically conservative and Catholic community.

While Sue and Jacqueline make their allegiance to newcomers evident, they are also sensitive to the perspective of members of the White working-class community, which is often identified by the media as the source of anti immigrant sentiment. Sue is careful to point out that the vast majority of those who attended the rally and continued to be involved in an advocacy coalition that subsequently formed, "do not represent your average Milltown resident. Most are from out of town." In a depiction of the racial and ethnic tension that flow through Milltown, she stated:

I am not going to talk badly about Milltown because it is the same every-where. When you bring a group of people into a community who are differ-ent, people have a hard time with it. They want them all to be the same and when they see how they are different, different skin, different clothes, differ-ent food, what have you, they want them to change. I deal with it myself. We all do. The same rules just have to apply to everyone, that's all. That's what I think.

As adult educators, Sue and Jacqueline are called upon to serve members of both the White working class and newly arrived refugee communities, and they speak regretfully about the decrease in working-class White stu-dent enrollment following the influx of Somali students at MAEC. Sue reports that, before withdrawing in large numbers from classes, working-class Whites have become resentful of the sheer number of newcomers enrolling at the MAEC. White students feel pushed out of the very class-rooms they have occupied for years both physically, by the sheer number of new students making use of the facilities, and symbolically, as their interests and needs are no longer reflected at MAEC of the curriculum. As Sue explained, "it is easier for the middle class to embrace newcomers because we are not poor and scrambling for the same finite resources."

As her words suggest, Sue believes that the best way to balance diverse students' varying interests and needs is through assurance of fair access to opportunity. For Sue, the classically liberal orientation to the challenge of grappling with difference offers a manageable and fair solution: apply the same rules and processes regardless of difference. Accordingly, Sue and Jacqueline attempt to produce hardworking, economically independent citizens who will compete on a level playing field with their working- class White counterparts.

The educators' wish to transform newcomers into desirable community members is responsive to the heightened hostility nonassimilationist immigrants and refugees are likely to face. The everyday practices and interactional dynamics between students and teachers within the MAEC conveys the message that in order for students to gain equal access to eco-nomic and social opportunity, they not only need to learn to read, write, and speak English; they also need to learn to behave like workers and desirable neighbors. Implicit in the liberal promise of equality to which Sue and Jacqueline subscribe, is the conviction that, in order to enjoy its rewards, immigrants should assimilate to the demands of the local eco-nomic and social sphere. According to this reasoning, immigrants and ref-ugees must change culturally-informed values and routines in order to mirror the grateful immigrant of liberal imagination. As Sue once suc-cinctly captured her mission, "My job is to teach them (refugees) to be Americans."

Sue divides her work time between the search for funding to address growing program needs and the development of mechanisms for formalizing a school environment that brings together community members with starkly different expectations and desires. During our time at MAEC, she spoke of the need to counter the continued use of "African time," to which she attributes students' frequent tardiness and absence. Sue's efforts to facilitate the transformation of newcomers into desirable workers and community members takes many forms. She works to secure grants and take advantage of a service-learning partnership with a local college in order to gather the resources necessary for newcomers to acquire communication skills. She tries to supply students with watches and proper interview attire. She seeks funding for a course in preemployment in which students are introduced to vocabulary that conveys workplace expectations about punctuality, alongside terms for the hierarchy of power, such as "boss," "employee," and "time clock." At one point, she proposed that students wear color coded tags that would signify their class schedule so that they might be admonished if found in the hallways when they ought to be in class. She monitors the hallways herself, coaxing entry level students into short conversations in English, loudly praising the "quick learners," and berating (sometimes jokingly, other times not) those who were frequently late or absent.

Jacqueline's leadership in the classroom expresses a similar liberal orientation to schooling. She, too, is assertive in her efforts to regulate students' use of time and language. Students are required to sign in and out of her classroom daily, and she forbids non-English language use. She explains that her approach is geared toward preparing students to acquire habits necessary to obtain and keep jobs. She positions herself as a pseudo-employer responsible for inculcating her charges with workplace practices and values. While there are roughly seven classrooms available for use, "Jacqueline's room" dominates the landscape of the ELL program and serves as a homeroom of sorts. ELL students work individually in Jacqueline's room, cycling out at different points of the day for direct instruction sessions from other ELL teachers. Jacqueline's room features a large, rectangular table. Students fill the chairs around the table as well as the small desks scattered in the room's pockets of free space. Each student has his or her own assignment to complete, workbook to finish, or old textbook to read as Jacqueline circles around the room correcting, directing, praising, and scolding.

Jacqueline not only helped students with language and literacy acquisition but also instructed students on "proper" manners and codes of conduct. She often scolded students for having drinks in class, talking too loudly, writing in books, or displaying behavior or conversational dynamics she deemed inappropriate. On one particular morning, Fathia, who until this moment had been working by herself, called Jacqueline over to ask for help with her work. Jacqueline, who had been with another student when Fathia called, reprimanded her for interrupting. "When a tutor [is] working with students their time is valuable. It is very rude, very rude." Fathia responded several times, "Okay teacher, I am sorry."

On this occasion, Jacqueline used Fathia's request for attention to convey a lesson on proper interactional dynamics between teacher and student. Yet in our work with Somali women in and out of the school environment, we consistently noted the employment of overlapping and collaboratively constructed oral narrative form. Judging from this observation, while Fathia probably addressed Jacqueline in a way that she would have spoken to any one of her family members or friends, Jacqueline made it clear that these informal, or more typically "Somali," conversational dynamics were simply not appropriate in the classroom.

In her mention of time as valuable, Jacqueline re-invoked the ever-present notion that time in the U.S. has monetary value. This principle also resonated in the use of attendance logs: The many students who received state aid were required to record hours of school attendance in order to maintain eligibility. Jacqueline supplemented such authentic documentation with forms that mimicked time sheets used in the workplace.

The English-only language rule limited some of the newer English learners from communicating with one another either about personal matters or schoolwork. One morning as Rachel entered Jacqueline's room to greet students, Jacqueline communicated Sue's newly enacted rule that "if students speak Somali, they go into the hall."[1] On another morning, Jacqueline chastised a student for speaking Somali by saying, "English is green. The Somali language is worthless in America."

Mirroring the actions of a workplace manager, Jacqueline regulated the sorts of language and behavior condoned within the classroom. Another morning Rachel was working with Saba, who painstakingly copied word for word out of a book so she would have a duplicate to take home and study. To expedite the process and save Saba the pain of hand-copying the entire chapter, Rachel asked Jacqueline if she could photocopy the sheet for Saba. "No!" Jacqueline responded emphatically, as she then informed Rachel that Saba needed to copy every word she could because her writing is "what's the worst."

On a different day, when our ESOL class was having a seminar-like discussion on the situation in Sudan, Jacqueline walked in to use the copy machine in the room's corner. During our class's conversation, Fathia had been participating verbally, while simultaneously finishing an assignment that she had started in a workbook. Though we had decided not to say anything and allow Fathia to continue with her independent work, Jacqueline, interrupting the discussion, demanded that Fathia stop, pulled the book away from her, and left the classroom. Anyon (1980) writes,

> One characteristic of most working-class jobs is that there is no built-in mechanism by which the worker can control the content, process, or speed of work. Legitimate decision making is vested in personnel supervisors, in middle or upper management, or, as in an increasing number of white-collar working-class (and most middle-class) jobs, by bureaucratic rule and regulation. For upper-middle-class professional groups there is an increased amount of autonomy regarding work. (p. 71)

Jacqueline's interactions with students replicated such power relations between employers and employees. Jacqueline, acting with a large measure of autonomy, overrode the students' abilities to decide which learning styles and schoolwork activities were best for them. Students were given little latitude to determine how they would spend their time at school.

Because they were attuned community members, Sue and Jacqueline's decision making in regard to educational practice was deliberately responsive to local contextual factors. They justifiably worried that their students would not find success in the economically struggling city. Sue and Jacqueline felt an urgent need to prepare students to meet the challenges that faced them: to compete in the economic sphere and find acceptance in the social. Their desire to change students' culturally derived ways of being emerged out of an earned appreciation for the misgivings newcomers faced within the larger community, and reflected on-the-ground realities associated with the schooling of newcomers in the current neoliberal and global era.

Traditional Somali Cultural Tenets and Practices in Milltown

In Milltown, resettled refugees have relatively little direct authority in the shaping of community ethos, policy, or practice. While local anti-immigrant, nativist sentiment often articulates its worldview in reaction to traditional Somali cultural tenets and practices and Liberal discourse positions itself as meeting the needs of newcomers in order to promote integration and honor diversity, in fact Somalis have minimal direct influence over the workings of the larger community. They comprise just 10% of the entire population. Few are eligible to vote. As language minorities they have little access positions of power and status. Rather, decision-making power, whether expressed through access to leadership positions, social capital, the simple right-to-vote, or the threat of collective action/ protest, remains largely in the hands of the White citizenry.

While the structuring polarities of Liberal discourse on immigration and nativist sentiment shape the larger public or civic sphere in Milltown, Somalis traverse a more complicated landscape that at once includes the public, civic domain and the private sphere of family and Somali community life. In the latter, traditional Somali cultural tenets and practices comprise a significant force that still holds sway in the lives of its members. The following newspaper excerpt details a Milltown imam's reaction to another Somali resident's community activism:

> Omar Ahmed, a tweedy, genial man in his fifties with a scholarly-looking beard, speaks English well, and is a welfare case manager for the city. He had an idea about how to break through to the Americans: he would write a play—in Mogadishu, he had been a teacher and a playwright. In 2003, a Milltown theatre company agreed to produce his latest work, called "Love in Cactus Village," which Ahmed had translated into English. It was the story of a rural Somali girl who defies her father's wish that she marry a rich man. Ahmed described the play to a local reporter as his way of thanking his new neighbors for their hospitality toward him and his fellow-Somalis.

> Ahmed had other motives as well. "I wanted to convince the local people that we come from somewhere, that we had universities, that we don't just come from the bush," he told me. "We have such a rich literature, which has survived from our oral traditions. It's so important not to lose our culture. Only a very minute amount of our literature was written down, and even that portion was destroyed in the war. Even our national museum was destroyed, and wild plants are growing there. You can go see."

> Ahmed's play was well received by Milltownians but the local Somalis found it controversial. Even though most of the roles were played by Somali students from Milltown High, few Somalis attended the performances. And their absence revealed at least as much about the Milltown Somalis as anything shown onstage did.

> "There were so many different objections," Ahmed told me. "People said, 'They will see us as camel riders, camel herders.' But it's true—we have a feeling for animals." The imam of the local mosque demanded that the town ban the play, because it had men and women performing on the same stage. Theatre itself is haram—forbidden—according to a certain interpretation of the Koran. "These people are saying, 'We cannot have theatre,'" Ahmed said, in exasperation. "I say, 'How can we live?' Other Muslim countries—Indonesia, Egypt, even Saudi Arabia—they have theatre." (Finnegan, 2006)

In this example, divisions within the Somali community emerge clearly; as in Dadaab, the conservative or traditional perspective remains well represented. Milltown's imam expounded upon Islamic religious doctrine in an interview with Finnegan and *The New Yorker*, detailing which jobs in the local economy were considered *haram* (forbidden according to Islamic law). "If you're a drinks waiter, you're poisoning people — that's *haram*. But if you're just clearing dishes it's O.K." He went on,

> People in Somalia like plays and concerts. But every concert is no good, especially when they talk about love and sex. You are waking up the population. Big band is not allowed in Islam. The big drum, saxophone, trombone, xylophone—Satan created those things.

In addition to delineating tenets of Muslim religiosity, the same imam has been found to reinscribe traditional aspects of Somalia's racialized class structure. A Bantu man residing in Milltown described his friend's reception at the local mosque:

> Sheikh Mohamed works as a cashier at Wal-Mart. He is lithe and frank, and his English, which he learned in the camps in Kenya, is good. He did not seem afraid to speak up for himself. But he found the insults and racial slights that the Bantus experienced in Maine—from other Somalis—to be unrelenting. A Bantu friend of his had gone to the Milltown mosque to pray, "and they told him to come back with six guys to wash the mosque. For free! They still think we work for them!"

Traditionalism has certainly influenced Somali community members' lives across gender, class, and race distinctions. Finnegan reports:

> There has been a distinct shift, in the past few years, among the Milltown Somalis, toward stricter religious observance. Women who never wore hijab in Somalia—where miniskirts were once popular in the cities—told me that they always do in Maine. Prayers and fasting have, by all accounts, become more common.

Many understand the bolstering of traditionalism among Somalis in the U.S. as a response to the threat that they will lose their culture and religion in the new environment unless they work proactively to protect it (Berns McGown, 1999).

Conclusion

National and local response to newcomers' entrance into the U.S. national community illustrate that, as members of the global South enter the cultural, economic, and political space of the global North, disparate understandings and practices come in contact with one another and do so across a range of venues. In this chapter we have looked first at how the power relations extant in the U.S. as a whole play out in microcosm within Milltown and, even more specifically, at the MAEC. We note the continued pull of traditional Somali cultural tenets and practices upon Somali newcomers. In all, disparate world visions and ideologies come together in a complicated improvisational production shaping the emergent realities of Somali newcomers' lives in Milltown. As we explore in the next three chapters, Somali women's participation in schooling reflects the complexity of local social relations between members of the Milltown professional class, White working class, and resettled Somalis.

NOTE

1.   Despite Jacqueline and Sue's recommendation/rule, we made the decision to continue to not only allow Somali in our classroom but to also incorporate it in our actual curriculum. Even more, the women themselves continued to speak Somali both in hallways, during breaks, and even quietly in Jacqueline's class. While we occasionally heard scolding from Jacqueline or Sue, we quite often continued to hear Somali conversations occurring between students.

CHAPTER 10

SOMALI WOMEN IN U.S. SCHOOLS

From mundane enactments to grandiose displays, Milltown's diverse actors alternately and strategically intertwine, juxtapose and elide the particularized languages of liberalism, American nativism, and traditional Somali cultural tenets and practices. As a microcosm of the surrounding community, MAEC operates as a discursive field in which disparate ways of knowing and acting in the world exist in understated tension (Weedon, 1987). At MAEC, the prospect of outright interethnic conflict, open discussion of cultural difference, or mitigation of power differentials is smoothly diverted. Myriad skills, knowledges, experiences, and habits are neatly set aside through the institutionalized veneration of reading and writing, English proficiency, and patience for repetition. Within the bounds of their common low status, ELL students are differentiated from one another according to perceived intellectual facility, punctuality, obedience, and tenacity. Taking their places at the desks and tables of MAEC, Somali women engage the localized liberal and traditional ideologies as they plunge headlong into a strange, and an often, disempowering world.

Many of the women with whom we worked at MAEC navigate the fraught terrain through a concerted effort to align with local expectations of them as newcomers. They express deep gratitude for all the resources made available in the United States, and they work diligently to transform themselves into valuable (i.e., English speaking, financially independent, and appreciative) community members.

Educated For Change?: Muslim Refugee Women in the West, pp. 245–254
Copyright © 2012 by Information Age Publishing
All rights of reproduction in any form reserved.

During the summer of 2004, Patti spent her days volunteering as a participant researcher and tutor at MAEC. She passed her first few weeks tutoring in Jacqueline's classrooms. While there, she met Amina. One morning, Patti worked with Amina and two other women. The four shared a workbook and took turns reading aloud a brief passage that introduced members of a White, heterosexual family. Halting her reading, one of the women leaned toward Patti. Looking into the adjoining room at a bearded man who worked attentively in his own workbook, the woman whispered in a conspiratorial tone, "That is Amina's husband."

Patti looked at the man and then at Amina in surprise. She had been in the same room with both Amina and the mysterious man for days on end and had never seen them come within several feet of one another or acknowledge each other's presence. Amina pursed her lips in an uncharacteristically demur smile and then looked down at the table top. Patti had seen younger Somali men and women talking, even working side by side together at MAEC and, to an even greater degree, within the local and middle and high schools. Amina, though, was older and of another generation. As these thoughts moved through Patti's mind, Amina looked at her. They exchanged smiles.

"He is cute," Patti offered, raising her eyebrows suggestively. Amina smiled more deeply. "He looks very smart, like you."

"Yes, good, smart man." Amina concluded the exchange and the four women returned to the passage at hand.

After Patti had tutored for several weeks, Sue encouraged her to start her own entry level class. Sue handpicked a small class of six women, all of whom spoke only a few words of English. They could state their names, addresses, the number of children in their family, and the U.S. city from which they had moved to settle in Milltown. The women huddled around a disproportionately large table within a small back room. Patti had brought a paper grocery bag of random objects and held it out before Amina, the woman closest to her. Amina looked quizzically at Patti and with slow motions reached her hand into the bag. All along, she watched Patti, squinting her eyes as if to ask for assurance. Patti nodded encouragingly; yes, she had hoped Amina would pull something from the bag. Out came a toothbrush. Amina held it up before the others, "Prush," she said. Patti nodded and said, "Brush. Toothbrush." She pretended to brush her teeth. The women laughed. Amina smiled widely, revealing a gap where her front teeth had been lost. She glowed with appreciation and humor. "Toothprush?" she asked.

"ToothBrush."

"Toothprush."

"Tooth B B B B Brush."

"B B B Brush."

"Yes. Yes. Exactly! B B B Brush! ToothBrush."

"Toothbrush!"

The small room erupted in cheers, clapping, and laughter. Amina beamed.

Amina never missed a class. She arrived early, greeting Patti warmly, and helped to set up the classroom. The summer wore on as she tried new words, laughed at how awkward they felt in her mouth, and learned quickly. Her attention never seemed to wane. As they reached autumn, Rachel returned to the region and joined the class. Patti and Rachel co-taught early on weekday mornings, before heading to their own college campus. Amina's stilted vocabulary developed steadily, and soon she spoke in fluid sentences. She was proud and grateful. She routinely complimented us for being "good teachers." When Rachel announced that she would soon leave to visit her parents in Texas, Amina led the class in a letter writing exercise. The letter was drafted to Rachel's parents and expressed gratitude for Rachel's help, kindness, and politeness.

Amina extended her appreciation to all aspects of her schooling. Upon passing through the heavy wooden doors of the cinder block building, she wiped her feet meticulously at the doormat. In the classroom, she turned the worn pages of the workbooks with extreme care. At the coffee stand, she was careful to wipe down stray granules of sugar or powered milk.

Amina's dedication served her well. She soon progressed beyond our entry level course and moved on to a higher level class. Her new teacher reported that Amina spoke glowingly of our efforts. We were able to return the compliment. Amina had spoken equally charitably about her new teacher.

Amina kept moving up through the classes, eventually acquiring proficiency and leaving MAEC. She and her husband found work at a local large scale retailer. Occasionally, we would run into her at community events or on the street. The gap in her teeth was now filled by two gleaming white dentures. Her affect was proud and happy. She introduced us as her "good teachers," and we always returned the compliment. Amina was a "good student," we would tell whomever accompanied her that day. She would beam.

Amina had lived the majority of her adult life as one of several wives in a highly sex-segregated culture. Her entrance into U.S. society had shifted key parameters of her life. In the United States, she attended school along with her husband. She learned to speak English and to read and write. She began to work outside of the home and was the only legally recognized wife of her husband's. Yet, her previous life was not washed away, nor did she enter the U.S. without constraints. Even as she (and her husband) found tentative ways to maintain traditional practices, such as establishing minimum degrees of separation within the confines of a small classroom, she also crafted new ways of being through enrollment in school. As a student she emphasized gratitude and perseverance, and was rewarded with returned affection and a degree of social mobility.

Like Amina, many women enrolled at MAEC respond with effusive gratitude for the resources made available to them in the United States. In doing so, they position themselves to mirror the more favorable of two prominent characterizations of newcomers. Much like the immigrant of the liberal imagination, female Somali students at MAEC talk about the ways in which life in the U.S. opens up formerly restricted avenues of opportunity and personal growth. Nasra notes that, as a woman, resettlement enables newfound access to education. In Somalia, as the oldest girl in a family with many children, Nasra was not able to attend school. While all of her siblings became educated, she was required to remain at home, cook, clean, and do laundry for her family. "In America, finally, I am … going to school, reading, reading, reading, like everyone else."

Indeed, upon entrance into the United States, many Somali women enroll in school for the first time. However, schooling is not the only public service for which female students express gratitude. Women also applaud the high quality healthcare and clean, spacious public housing projects. Women are apt to compare health care and housing to that provided in the refugee camps. To a person, they laud Milltown's quiet and safe environment and universal K-12 public schooling system. Repeatedly, they inform us that children could not attend secondary school in Kenya or Somalia without paying prohibitively expensive school fees. Women attend school with the oft-stated aim to improve their employability. In the face of the pervasive xenophobia, Somalis make every effort to enter the paid workforce. The women with whom we worked remain on constant lookout for positions of almost any type. Those who find employment use it as a source of personal pride with which to push back against anti-immigrant sentiment. Salwa, a woman in her late 70s, frequently refers to her experience as a housekeeper at a local motel. Though her English skills lag behind many of her younger counterparts' and her job demands exhausting physical labor, Salwa symbolizes successful economic integration. In class, she acts out her many responsibilities—slowly making imaginary beds and vacuuming carpeted floors—until she is able to describe her work in English. Many women with stronger language skills expressed envy that Salwa has found steady employment and regularly sends money back to relatives in Africa. For her part, Salwa echoes a common local refrain against Somalis who rely upon Temporary Aid For Needy Families (TANF) "They are lazy," she states matter of factly. "They say no work. I am old woman. I have job since I came." Able to avoid the Milltown welfare system entirely, Salwa proudly embodies the successful immigrant of liberal imagination.

One morning, Sue entered our classroom unannounced and was accompanied by three representatives from a local employment service. After introducing the White man, White woman, and Somali man to us, Sue asked if they could make an announcement to the group. The man began by asking in English if anyone was interested in employment. While 70-year-old Aman waited for a translation, Nasra blurted out, "Yes!" and Samira nodded enthusiastically. With translation provided by his Somali counterpart, the man briefly quizzed the women on their past work experience before asking if they would be interested in full-time or part-time positions. "Full-time, part-time—everything!" Nasra exclaimed in English. The man looked at his translator as if granting him permission. The woman nodded her silent assent. Speaking in Somali, the translator described jobs that were available at a local seafood processing plant. Aman and Nasra interrupted him with frequent questions. Finally, he turned toward his coworkers and announced: "They want the job and can find a way to carpool."

The three visitors formed a small impromptu circle from which they planned a course of action. Excited whispers bubbled around the table of women. After a few minutes, the speakers broke from their huddle and recommenced. The man explained that, while the job would be year-round, the seafood to be processed would rotate seasonally between crab, shrimp, and lobster. The Somali man translated in turn. If hired, the White man continued, the women would be responsible for cracking the shellfish and feeding meat into a processor. The female recruiter interjected: "It's very cold; it's like working in a refrigerator." Nasra said "Oooh" and feigned shivering, though her smile and enthusiasm did not wane.

According to the man, the women would not have to speak a lot of English, but they would need to comprehend verbal instruction. Nasra, who had for the past few moments been whispering excitedly in Somali, switched promptly to English to demonstrate her proficiency. Further, they would need to arrange their own transportation for the 45-minute commute from Milltown. Before leaving, the three passed around a legal pad for students to record their names and numbers. Once they had exited the room, Nasra looked at Rachel and said, "No more coming to school—working! Money!" with a big smile on her face. Samira, who was putting on her coat, said cheerfully, "Yeah, money, money!"

For many of the women who enroll at MAEC, school is above all an avenue to employability. They seek to learn English in order to increase the number of jobs for which they might be eligible, and they use school hours to update each other on local job opportunities. The women in our study dream of the day they will no longer rely upon TANF and can attain financial independence. The women's eagerness to find work is readily apparent even to classmates. One day, two Thai students in the class asked Felis, an advanced English student who sometimes attend class in order to assist her peers, to advertise an opening for kitchen staff to the assembled group. Before sharing the news, however, Felis accepted the position herself.

When seasonal employment opportunities come in the local retail industry, MAEC enrollment numbers dwindle. The rare few who find secure positions leave permanently, or attend MAEC on a part-time basis. In this sense, schooling serves a purely functional role for Somali women, a view that complements educational leaders' own prescribed vision of ELL programming. Many educators and students alike view the primary purpose of schooling as leading to economic self-sufficiency.

In addition to making themselves employable, women in our study often explain that they wanted to learn English in order to attend parent/teacher conferences, communicate with landlords independent of social service providers, form meaningful connections with non-Somali members of the Milltown community, and respond to racist taunts to "Speak English!" or "Go Back to Africa!" The promise of English fluency, attained through dedicated study, at once ensures greater success in the pursuit of jobs and enables women to make strategic inroads into mainstream Milltown institutions as a whole. In short, through participation in schooling, Somali women in our study worked to embody the "good immigrant" of liberal imagination.

Critique

While many women clearly utilize schooling as a space and process through which to give expression to an imagined ideal immigrant, their actions do not suggest a singular alignment with liberal ideology. Just as appropriating the language of enlightenment provides young women in Dadaab with the moral capital to make demands upon more resourced aid workers and visiting Westerners, women enrolled at MAEC do not uncritically absorb the liberal discourse of immigration. Having established themselves as dedicated students, they venture to speak with authority about areas of cultural incongruence between Somali and American ways of being. Through these acts of analysis, comparison, and critique, they formulate new senses of self as Somali women in the United States.

Rukio had lived in the United States for over two decades when we met her. She was one of the first Somalis to enroll in MAEC's first formal citizenship test preparation class. Rachel taught the course and quickly developed a close relationship with Rukio. One afternoon Patti and Rukio sat down for an interview. In the ensuing conversation, Rukio focused largely on her disillusionment about American culture and society. She explained that in the years preceding her migration, her husband, who had resettled in 1981, had written letters that outlined all of the "good things" about U.S. life but neglected to detail "the bad life." When Rukio finally made the long journey away from family and country, she had expected to enter a world in which everyone was rich and "life was like a movie." Instead, she observed, "The house was so small ... little T.V." She immediately regretted her choice and longed to return to Africa. Enduring political instability in Somalia and her husband's refusal to leave the U.S. precludes her return. Twenty years later, she remains unsatisfied.

Beyond the failure to meet with her material expectations, Rukio finds the United States a difficult place to build community. "Everyone work. In Somalia women don't work. They cook, clean, take care of the children, but they don't work. Here, everybody work." With so many women busy working, there is no one with whom she can spend her time. With domestic chores simplified by technological advancements, in the U.S. women do not gather together to wash clothes and dishes. Nor, do they prepare food in the way that Rukio had been accustomed in Somalia. "There is just no one there." While Rukio's husband is employed and in her estimation made "good money," given her loneliness and boredom, she has tried to enter the workforce herself. Taking pains to explain that she not need a job for "survival," that she does not "need the money," she nonetheless worked for a short time in a "packaging factory." She had not liked the work, though: her hands were cut badly on the job and she had to work the night shift. "It is a different way from the time you think till you see it [the United States]," she concluded. "I was surprised 24 hours somebody work. People don't sleep? When do they see the childrens?"

In her questions Rukio offers a poignant critique of America's obsession for work and material prosperity. Based on her own lived experience, for Rukio, realizing the American dream is a Pyrrhic victory in which Americans sacrifice intimate family and community relations in order to maintain a surprisingly low standard of living. Her own effort to give work an alternative purpose, to put employment to the service of community building, have also failed. According to her, colleagues are too tired to socialize and merely labor side-by-side in virtual silence. They do not have the time nor energy to invest in friendships. She has come to see Americans as alienated, unhappy, and overworked. By contrast, her own and other African peoples' lifestyles offer a more humane appreciation of leisure; family and community; and personal balance. For Rukio, the promise of schooling as an avenue to opportunity for newcomers is a vacuous one. As she explains, she did not participate in schooling in order to "become a doctor or lawyer." "I go to talk. To meet people. Not like Americans."

In addition to critiquing Americans' work ethic and materialism, women also find fault with the U.S.'s racialized social structure, and, again intimate that Somali culture is more advanced. One morning early in our study, Patti sat with Nasra as the latter read a story about Jackie Robinson's experiences with racism in the United States. In response to the story, Nasra announced that, unlike in the United States, in Somalia "there is no black and white. Somalia is international." According to Nasra, skin color only became apparent to her after coming to the United States because, "In Africa, it is all the same. We live together. We work together. We marry. There are Italians, French, and English all together."

Whether or not Nasra's perspective represents a "truth" about Somali national culture, which is itself colored by decades of European colonial occupation (as well as tenuous relations between ethnic Somalis and their Bantu counterparts), for her, racism and racial distinctions are a means through which she comes to understand the U.S. and her place, as a "Black" person, within the Milltown community. For Nasra, the strangeness of employing race as a category of social organization is linked to an Islamic sensibility. Appraising racism in the United States, she reasons, "Americans don't understand that everyone dies." In this phrase, Nasra invokes a common saying among the women at MAEC: "Everyone dies, everyone goes to *Allah*." For Nasra, Americans' myopia concerning the afterlife fosters chauvinistic attitudes: "[Americans say] 'This is the United States, I love my country. Everyone must speak English.' They [Americans] don't think we all die." In her words, Nasra vents frustration with a perceived insularity among Americans, whose lack of religiosity leads to a failure of imagination, an inability to see beyond the temporariness and superficiality of race, language, and national belonging. Certainly, according to Nasra, no amount of perceived racial superiority can thwart death—a fate shared by all.

Nasra expresses a belief that her experiences as a Black woman and English language learner in the U.S. are shaped (and limited) by Americans' approach to race and religion. She weaves an assessment of workplace discrimination through a larger narrative of racism in the United States. She believes that some employers will not hire her—a fluent English speaker and active community member—because of her Blackness. She recalls a previous experience at a blanket company where a White female coworker repeatedly failed to perform her assigned tasks. When Nasra went to complain to the management about the coworker, they accused her of lying and told her to go back to work. For Nasra, this incident is intimately tied to a larger problematic of race in the United States. She explained that the police are especially harsh to the Somalis because of their "Blackness," and she illustrated this by saying that if two [White] kids were to get in a fight at school, "it is nothing," but if the kids were

Somali, the police would be called upon and would respond harshly, often putting Somali youth in jail. She demonstrated this by physically mimicking police aggression, throwing an imaginary Somali youth to the ground. Nasra concluded our conversation by again reminiscing about how in Somalia, despite the presence of Italians, French, and English, "there is no black and white."

In her narrative, Nasra demonstrate a nuanced understanding of race politics in the United States. She identifies contradictions between espoused notions of meritocracy and liberal discourses of diversity and colorblindness and the realities of her lived experiences in which race affects hiring, firing, and access to economic success among Somalis and Black Americans as a whole. In doing so, she also reveals the ways in which Black women's voices and experiences are institutionally disregarded (see Collins, 2004).

As their resettlement experiences deepen with time, students like Rukio and Nasra particularized analytic lenses shaped by age, class, and education level to, assess the challenges and benefits of resettlement in the United States. life. Given a local dearth of employment opportunity, Rukio, Nasra and others have plenty of time and material for continued reflection.

One day Sumayah announced to the class that no jobs exist for herself or her peers because President Bush's economic policies favor the rich at the expense of the middle class and working poor. In response others began to interrogate Bush's tax cuts. Patti clarified that "to cut" meant "to lower" or "to decrease," before she wrote Sumayah's reference to the "rich" and "middle class" on the board. Patti had yet to complete the impromptu list of relevant words when Fardous, a beginning student, interjected "poor" and "lower class." As if to translate for her friend, Sadia pointed to herself and announced, "I working class.... Section 8—$375 a month." Despite the strangeness of such English words, students are intimately familiar with their symbolic position they occupy in the U.S. class hierarchy. It is not uncommon for students to at once critique the constraints of Milltown's economy and request that we devote time to learning vocabulary and skills that will increase their employability.

The women's discussion of the Bush tax-cuts, laced with critical commentary on the conundrum of being a newcomer in a globalized, postindustrial Milltown, transitioned quickly to more pragmatic concerns when one student requested that we spend the rest of class time practicing mock job interviews. Accordingly, for the remainder of class, we all took turns assuming the role of employer or potential employee and role-played sample questions and answers. When Hamda's turn came around, she decided to act as an employer seeking a housekeeper. Sadia, though engaged in the activity, laughed mockingly at Hamda's scenario and said, "You will be housekeeper because you can't speak English!" Sadia's response echoed the disgruntled complaints of many older women who resented their relegation to menial and/or physical labor.

Similarly, Hibo, a woman in her later 50s, lamented that "factory work is too hard and she is too old." For her part, Hamda compared employment experiences in Somalia, where she and her family ran a commercial farm, to those in Milltown. Like Hamda, many women fondly remember their day-to-day lives in Somalia working in small family businesses or on farms. Comparisons between quality of life across national contexts often turn to food; inevitably, they note that produce and meat in Somalia is fresh, unlike the frozen, packaged, and processed groceries to which budgets restrict the women in Milltown. According to Hamda, it is because of the poor quality food that she and her classmates are "getting fat."

Despite misgivings about the U.S. system, many students continue to take advantage of the newfound opportunity to attend school. Many became fixtures in classes at MAEC. Through the act of critique, women at MAEC work to craft unique ways of being Somali women in the United States.

Conclusion

As is the case in Dadaab, women in Milltown use schooling to make sense of themselves within a new political, economic, and cultural context. to align with a dominant ideology. While engaging the new, they simultaneously reach back to grasp hold of personal histories. With freshly reconstructed memories, learned strategies, and ingrained intuition in hand, they go about the work of making sense of the present and imagined future. The women with whom we worked developed senses of self in the U.S. that depend upon the activation of a functional memory of the past. For many, women's heretofore near complete illiteracy rate makes the novelty of schooling a luxurious pleasure.

In a surprisingly similar way, imagining an idealized Somali state highlights and provides a benchmark against which to measure racial dynamics of U.S. society. While Somalia has a highly racialized and racist history and has long suffered from high unemployment rates, the at least momentary revision of such history allows for a contrast to their current situation as a Black refugees in the United States. Their discursive slippage back and forth across imagined national borders reveals shifting contingencies of belonging and exclusion, and exemplifies how study participants come to utilize schooling as a space and process through which to make sense of themselves as Somali women in the United States.

CHAPTER 11

CRAFTING IDENTITY THROUGH COMMUNITY BUILDING

Somali refugee women in Milltown use schooling to actively negotiate shifting, multiple, and often contradictory expectations regarding gender ideals, norms, and practices. As study participants confront rearrangements of family, dislocating movement through various communities and nations, and finally, challenges of resettlement in Milltown, they encounter overlapping configurations of womanhood. They draw upon such multiplicity to build unique identities as Somali women in the United States. The distinctness of the women's developing identities lies in the particularity of their multinational experiences as well as their skill at weaving together networks of reciprocal giving within a new cultural context. Drawing upon past experience and frameworks of meaning, the women's community building represents a gendered expression of heritage work through which they invoke symbols of womanhood to establish connections across difference. For the women, the establishment of community reflects pragmatic acts of survival through which they are able to both re-establish networks of support among fellow Somalis and build relationships with other newcomers and longer term residents of the Milltown community. In this chapter, we explore both myriad gendered images at play in the lives of Somali refugee women at MAEC and the women's strategies of community building employed in relations in and around school.

Educated For Change?: Muslim Refugee Women in the West, pp. 255–279
Copyright © 2011 by Information Age Publishing
All rights of reproduction in any form reserved.

Gender Change Among Somalis in East Africa

Somali refugee women strategically position themselves in relation to an array of gendered images at play in their memories and everyday experiences in the United States. Given the multinational nature of their journeys and self-identifications, Somali women in the U.S. are aware of a variety of ways of being female, as well as the very real necessity to adapt to gendered change within the Somali community itself. As Werbner (1997, p. 6) indicates, "in a globalizing world, monological national languages cannot escape the sense of being surrounded by an 'ocean of heterglossia'" (Bakhtin, as cited in Werbner, 1997, p. 6). In *Somalia: The Untold Story*, Gardner and El Bushra (2004) vividly capture originating multiplicities of meaning within women and girls' gendered experiences of war and subsequent refugee journeys. Drawing upon empirical research and first hand accounts, the authors argue that the loss of men to war and drug abuse, as well as the rampant use of sexual violence as a weapon of war, have had a dramatically destructive effect upon families and the clan-based social organization of the Somali community. As marriages and clan-based protection systems are torn apart within Somalia and refugee camps, a two sided dynamic emerges: On the one hand, the dismantling of protections once afforded women through the clan structure has made women increasingly vulnerable to sexual violence and resulted in loss of status and power within their own families and clan. On the other hand, in response to the hardships of war, women have amplified their influence through increased involvement in trade, peace activism, and political representation. In the lattermost case, women have become integral to the functioning of the informal trade economy within Somalia and between Somalia, refugee camps, and surrounding East African countries. Taking advantage of dual clan identity that allows for greater movement across various territories as well as the understanding that women are not subject to revenge killings, women carry and trade money, rations, gold, and grain. According to Warsame (2004), women's ability to possess property and influence represents a significant cultural change.

> [Somali] society in general, and men in particular, have in the past had a negative attitude towards women owning property, even an *aqal* (nomadic home). There is a frequently quoted traditional expression: "Never allow a woman to own anything of value; if she brings a clay pot with her to the matrimonial home, break it." This attitude is gradually changing as more and more women earn and control their own cash. (p. 126)

Building upon their increasing economic power, women now play a lead role in "trying to save their families by whatever means available to them"

(Gardner & El Bushra, 2004, p. 189). In an effort to establish greater security, women try to institutionalize their increased influence in family and community through involvement in civil society organizations that work to provide immediate housing and food aid to families adversely affected by violence. Though men in positions of power consistently thwart their efforts, women continue to organize and make political demands that have resulted in small advances toward fuller representation. In 1993, an unprecedented 10 women were included as observers at The National Peace and Reconciliation Conference in Boroma, Somaliland. Over the intervening 10-15 years, women have held public demonstrations against fighting, set up committees to mediate talk between government and sub-clan elders, and pushed for a reinterpretation of debate over whether Islamic law allows for female participation in peace conferences and parliament. Despite strong resistance and slow progress toward greater political involvement, Somali women are intimately aware of their changing roles within Somali society. Along with a demonstrated need to unite and institutionalize their influence in the face of devastating vulnerability, a deep appreciation for women's leadership as peacekeepers also reverberates throughout the community. Somalia's postcollapse history and women's roles within it continue to evolve. Additionally, the women with whom we worked at MAEC may have been subject to rape, affected by the destruction of family, or personally involved in women's activism. Those who make their way to the U.S. bring with them a shared knowledge of Somali women's changing status and power that informs their developing self-perception as Somali women within the U.S. national community more broadly.

Gender in Global Perspective: Journeys of Resettlement

As described, once refugees are selected for resettlement, they often move through a variety of host countries before establishing permanent residency. Among the women at MAEC, some had lived in Yemen, Russia, Thailand, and/or France. During stays ranging from a few months to several years, Somali women become acquainted with a variety of ways of being female as they simultaneously reckon with the disruption of their traditional roles as daughters, wives, and sisters. Once in Milltown, the women continue to draw upon facets of their multinational experiences to situate themselves as Somali women in the United States.

One morning at MAEC, Patti worked with a class of six women as conversation turned to the prevalence of divorce in the resettled Somali community. One of the women in the class had lived in Russia and Thailand prior to settling with her husband and five children in the United States. As the only woman in the class with an intact marriage, Khadijo's assessment of the divorce rate seemed to bear special significance among fellow students who listened attentively to her interpretation. As she raised her normally quiet voice to speak, the boisterous and overlapping conversation of the others hushed. Khadijo explained that in her experience, Somali women post-civil war are the same as Russian and American women, in that they are "strong" and "are not quiet" in the face of men's demands. Given such unwillingness to back down, she continued to explain, Somali, Russian, and American women's marriages are characterized by conflict and subsequently often end in divorce. "Too much divorce because they [Somali women] say [to men]: 'Just go.' Russian, American, and Somali women the same. Strong." By contrast, Khadijo argued, Thai women are passive in their relations with men. As an example, she described Thai women who would "act like little girls" with U.S. soldiers stationed in Thailand and beg the men to marry them and bring them back to the United States. "They are very poor and hungry," Khadijo concluded. "They are not like us [American and Somali women]. Not independent, not take care of themselves. They depend on the man."

In this example, Khadijo draws upon her multinational experience to explain the phenomenon of marital dissolutionment among the Somali diasporic community. Claiming Thai women's propensity to obsequiously seek aid from U.S. men, she also offers a critique of dependency as a way of being female, championing instead strong willed women who do not accept men's efforts to dominate. Her observation/analysis is further nuanced by an implicit regret that such strength of character comes at a high price for Somali women. While Khadijo's assessments of Thai, Somali, and U.S. women are undoubtedly essentialized and not always favorable, what is immediately significant about her analytic framework is that she places Somali women's ways of being within an imagined international context. As a product of her ricochet-like journey through host countries, Khadijo and, consequently, other women at MAEC, draw upon a postmodern panorama of images of womanhood, a uniquely twenty-first century occurrence for a population of largely poor and rural women.

In addition to serving as a source of comparison, alignment, and distinction, women report that exposure to other ways of being female also inspire personal change. Asha, a single woman in her early 20s, was the only woman at MAEC to wear a full *burkha* and to cover all but her eyes when in public. For the most part, the way in which women dress at MAEC depends largely on the region of Somalia from which they originate. Some wear only simple scarves to cover their hair; for some, the color of the scarves is limited to grey and black. Most also wear *hijabs* that cover the neck, shoulders, and chest. Again, some of these are colorful while others are plain. That Asha chooses to more fully cover garnered her much attention from Rebecca, a White, middle aged teacher who runs a weekly women's group at MAEC. During one such meeting, Rebecca asked Asha why she wore the veil and whether she would lift it so that all in the room could see her face. When Asha obliged, Rebecca cooed and said, "Oh, that is so different! You have a face. Now, I feel like I can know who is hidden under there." Asha endured such attention with a patient bemusement and explained to all present that she first chose to wear the veil during her stay with family in Yemen. She observed that women there all wear veils and that, although she lives on her own in Milltown, she continue to dress the way her family in Yemen did as an expression of her religious beliefs and connection to community in Yemen. Interestingly, for Asha, the choice to cover does not reflect a stringent orthodoxy. Although it is traditional for Somali women to enter into arranged marriages as adolescents, Asha explained that she does not want to marry or have a man in her life. She maintains close friendships with other single women at MAEC, who by virtue of being in their 20s are also well beyond the average age of marriage. Rather than prepare for a future married life, Asha works to earn her GED so that she might go on to college. A steady presence at MAEC, Asha is one among only two women in our study who successfully passed from the ELL program into Adult Basic Education, signaling an acquired fluency in English. Asha's choices in regard to self-presentation and aspirations reflect her exposure to and adoption of various different ways of being female. She maintains the practice of veiling from her time in Yemen as a symbolic link to distant family and community. In Milltown, she carves out a lifestyle that is distinct from that lived by many Somali women, marking her continued ability to learn from and adapt to an array of opportunities and ways of being a young Somali woman in the United States.

Study participants are also exposed to different ways of being women by virtue of their enrolment at MAEC. The collapse of the Somali nation affected rural, urban, pastoral, agrarian, Bantu and ethnic Somalis of various class backgrounds. Consequently, day after day Somalis who might never have come in contact in their homeland find themselves gathered shoulder to shoulder around seminar style tables in overheated, small rooms. Alongside this diverse group of Somalis sits a handful of other African refugees, including Sudanese, Congolese, and Togolese women, as well as Latino/as, Chinese, and Thai men and women. Despite drastically different cultural and religious backgrounds, these students often share experiences of displacement, flight, and resettlement. Classroom discussion provides space for comparison and contrast between their stories, and sheds light on still more articulations of womanhood.

One morning, when Rachel was leading class, six women gathered around a small, square table. All of the women were Somali except Sarah, a Christian refugee from Southern Sudan. As a group, the women lamented the trouble caused by guns, noting their destructive impact upon both Somali and Sudanese social order as well as quality of life in inner city Atlanta, where many Somali refugees had originally resettled. Rachel asked whether or not the women thought it would be different if women were in positions of authority in each situation. Hamda replied, "Yes, the women don't fight. It was only men." Turning toward Sarah, Hamda casually asked if it was the same in Sudan, before waiting for her to agree. Sarah, however, promptly replied, "No, women, too." As shock registered on the women's faces, Zeynab looked up and incredulously asked if the women involved in the Sudanese civil war carry guns. When Sarah answered affirmatively, Zeynab was so taken aback she laughed out loud. That women in Sudan are active participants in the civil war and perpetrators of violence challenges Somali women's oft spoken belief that women are natural peacemakers.

In addition to complicating otherwise taken-for-granted understandings of gender, the women's immediate experiences at MAEC also provide Somali women with an opportunity to engage in dialogue with a diversity of U.S. women and interact with U.S. men. One morning, Patti sat among a group of women who were working individually in one of Jacqueline's tutoring rooms. William, a tall elderly White man well into his 70s, was also offering one-on-one tutoring in the room, and his presence elicited a humorous interaction. Hawalul, in a laughing tone, called out to him, "Mr. William, I should be your wife!" Hawalul had originally lived in Djibouti and has a casual style of dress. Unlike most every other woman at MAEC, she frequently wears jeans and shirts that reveal her collarbone. Her headscarves are colorful and cover her head loosely, allowing glimpses of her hairline. In a flirtatious tone she continued, "You like younger women? You marry me Mr. William. I cook, clean. No American woman [will do that]. I give you children. Brown children, Mr. William, but I give many children, Mr. William."

"You wish," William muttered ineffectually and looked at Patti.

In her flirtatious banter, Hawalul gently prods at symbols of cultural difference in gendered power relations, and offers a ribbing about their respective places within an implicit hierarchy of color. Hawalul's words ironically, if disingenuously, suggest her willingness to serve and produce offspring for William in ways that iconic modern American women would not, and that such treatment might persuade him to overlook the presumed unattractiveness of having "brown" children.

As Hawalul's interaction with William reveals, daily life at MAEC brings Somali men and women in contact with American men and women, thereby introducing complex and shifting configurations of social positioning informed by race, class, and gender differences. As a service-learning component of several of her courses, Patti has college students tutor at MAEC. In their fieldwork, young White men often work in close physical proximity with Somali women, and American women with Somali men. Hands and shoulders touch and eye contact is common. Young women direct older men—elders in the Somali community—to read particular lines, answer questions, and enunciate English words. Somali women often ask questions that speak of a desire to delve into culturally informed difference. Young American women are constantly asked whether they are married or have children. Despite Patti's hesitancy to reveal her sexuality, after a few years spent at MAEC and the development of close friendships with a couple of Somali women, rumors that she is gay spread among the community. Similarly, women ask Robin, a full time teacher in her late 30s, about her long-term, live-in boyfriend and whether they have plans to marry in the immediate future. Conversation at the weekly women's group features frequent discussion of the supposed liberal codes of sexual activity among young American women. The group also discusses the facilitator's long term partnership with a man. At the same time, the women encounter Sue, the ELL program director, who is both married with children and grandchildren and actively pursues a challenging career. In short, just as they have diverse trajectories leading to Milltown, Somali women encounter and are called upon to craft meaning out of myriad ways of being women, expressing sexuality, and relating to men at MAEC; as Berns McGown (1999) notes, through exposure, they "reinterpret" who they are as Muslim women in the West.

During the course of our study, many women devoted time at MAEC to such reinterpretation, working through dialogue with each other and the assorted people with whom they come in daily contact to make sense out of a multiplicity of images at play. Out of this dialectic and subjective negotiation process, the women help to forge a local Somali community that is both heterogeneous in background and in its articulations of gendered identity.

While there is no single way of being a Somali woman in the United States, many overlapping features mark the sense-making process as women tactically draw upon: self identifications as Africans and Muslim women; memories of common citizenship in a Somali state; histories shaped by civil unrest and traumatic violence; multinational refugee journeys; resettlement experiences; financial struggle; new educational opportunity; and finally, a need to establish what it means to be a Somali woman in a predominately White, Christian community. Women used community building both with one another and other women at MAEC as a strategy to dialogically make meaning out of shared experiences and frameworks of understanding. Accordingly, the nature of their community building is fluid, as its parameters of belonging and exclusion shift in relation to identified areas of commonality and distinction between various women at MAEC. The various methods of community building that emerge among Somali women at MAEC highlight the evolving multi-nationality of Somali women's identity work in the United States.

Building Networks of Support: MAEC as a Social Space

On the most basic level, MAEC serves as a central location for many Somali women, who often spend their evenings and weekends at home raising children, cleaning, and otherwise caring for family members, to congregate and socialize. Because a large percentage of the women do not drive and are therefore restricted in movement, the hours between 8 A.M. and 12 P.M. become a designated time when, in addition to meeting specific educational goals, women can simply chat, share stories, and build and strengthen friendships. When asked about their favorite or most memorable aspect of school, many refer to the opportunity to socialize, which enrollment at MAEC provides. Fatima is an upper level ELL student at MAEC who attends school regularly even after Rebecca, MAEC's ELL 4 teacher, left, and advanced ELL programming temporarily dissolved. With her husband living in Atlanta, Fatima cares for three children on her own while pregnant. Despite tremendous domestic responsibilities, she came to school throughout her pregnancy. After a brief stint in Adult Basic Education classes, Fatima decided to assist in our ELL 1 class every morning until just before her due date. As most of our class material was easy for her, Fatima helped other students by translating difficult concepts and vocabulary. In a conversation with Rachel, she described what she liked best about school. "I like everything about school. What they doin'—talking. Always first when I go I talking with my friends, everybody I see—what happened, what they did."

In January of 2004, Rebecca, an ELL teacher in whose class Patti had been observing, started what became known as "The Women's Workshop" in order to provide information for immigrant and refugee women on a variety of topics, including: birth control, nutrition, abuse protection, and local community resources. In the first meeting 10 women, including 1 from Morocco, 2 from Togo, 4 from Somalia, Rebecca, and the 2 of us, gathered around a table in a small back room of MAEC. Rebecca had asked each woman to introduce herself, describe when she had moved to Milltown, and tell the group what the experience of living in Milltown had been like so far. When her turn came, Yasmin released a floodgate of emotion. She explained that she was 20 and had moved to Milltown a year before with only her two young daughters. "I know nothing. The buses. The shopping. The job. Nothing." She explained that for the better part of that first year she stayed home alone with her two daughters and went out only occasionally by taxi to shop. Gradually, she came to know the system better, enrolled her daughters in Head Start, and attended school. "It was so nice. To see people. To talk to people. To see the people, they smile." The women surrounding her in a circle nodded their heads vigorously as she spoke and cried.

Yasmin went on to explain that her husband was still in Africa, and when Rebecca asked if she wanted him to join her here, she replied, "Yes, why not?" In a latter conversation with Patti, however, she revealed that in fact her husband had taken another woman into their home when she still lived in Kenya, that she believed the two of them had an affair, and that he had subsequently "disappeared." She tried to locate him, but his family members refuse to tell her where he had gone, and she feels helpless to support her two children. Desperate, she asked her own family members to help her apply for refugee status. When she arrived in the U.S. her parents, who had already settled in Virginia, turned her away, saying that she would have to support herself. While at first Yasmin felt stranded with her two children, once she was able to enroll at MAEC she was finally able to join and help sustain a community.

Ayaan, the minivan carpool driver who has been in the United States for 19 years, echoes Fatima and Yasmin's characterization of school as a social space. Answering a question we had posed about what she will remember about school when she is an old woman, Ayaan states:

> Sometimes just like fun fun we have [as a] group of friends. It just like that. Some people go for a reason, like to be doctor. Me, I never go that way. I never think school is [more] important [than being a] housewife.

While Ayaan is in a rare and privileged position in that she, because of family support, does not need a job, her emphasis on school as a social space and site for the gathering of friendship groups is shared among many. Basra, who attended school for the first time in Milltown, explains that she developed her community of friends at MAEC. On Valentine's Day, when class was discussing people's intended plans (or lack thereof), Basra replied, "No, my husband is away and I don't have any friends." After some protest, she added, extending her arms to gesture to the women on her left and right, "Well, my friends are here."

MAEC provides women an opportunity to share stories and stay informed about one another's lives. Every day, the first 5 to 15 minutes of our class were spent in lively conversation. Class members inquired about friends and relatives known to be sick or absent from school, and updated each other on mutual contacts. The first portion of a typical class might have begun with Hibo asking Sumayah about her pregnancy, followed by an evolving conversation in which Sumayah inquired about Alima's children, who were in a car accident. Ardo might have discussed her recent pilgrimage to Mecca for Eid, while others searched for an update on the status of Rashid, a Somali teacher at MAEC who had unexpectedly suffered from a stroke. Topics from these overlapping conversations often shape the thematic base of the day's lesson as we would guide students to collectively craft related stories. Such extended conversation once prompted William to refer to our class as "a coffee klatch." After class ended, the women often carried their conversations into a smaller tutoring room or an unused area under the stairs. In fact, Sue, who wanted to discourage the use of school as a "community center," had removed a comfortable couch and set of chairs from underneath the stairs so that women would stop gathering there. Nevertheless, women continue to occupy the modest space, chatting and sharing snacks. On any given day, Ardo might have pulled cookies wrapped in napkins out of her purse while someone else would have offered slices of homemade pound cake or *halwa*, a sugary dessert.

In addition to using MAEC as a social space, Somali women employ schooling as a process through which they lend one another support. Somali women, who are often far from family, assist one another in learning and the everyday challenges of Milltown life. Even getting to and from school necessitates coordinated effort and reveals informal systems of support created by women at MAEC. At the time of our study, no modes of public transportation existed to connect MAEC with the residential neighborhoods in the outskirts of the city, where most Somalis live. As a result, while many of the women who reside in MAEC's surrounding streets walk to school, those who live farther away set up carpool systems to ensure their friends and neighbors' ability to attend. For a brief period of time, MAEC was able to pay one of these women, Ayaan, to drive students in her minivan to and from school. While funding for the carpooling initiative dried up, Ayaan continues to transport the group in exchange for a small fee from each of the women. Ridesharing efforts extend beyond transportation to and from school, as women often leave early from class in pairs or small groups in order to get one another to doctor's appointments or meetings at the local General Assistance office.

Just as women pool transportation resources, informal conversations in and around school reveal efforts to assist each other in the negotiation of social and public institutions in Milltown. Women routinely share stories and advice on the local medical system, public schools, or career services program. The women also support each other in their learning ventures at MAEC. While the majority of women speak multiple languages, including Somali, Arabic, Kiswahili, Italian, or French, many are attending classes and learning English for the first time. Particularly for the older women who, given less frequent membership in the workforce, have mini- mal contact with long term American residents, learning English is an especially challenging endeavor. As these women struggle day to day to slowly pick up the ability to read, write, and speak English, younger, more advanced learners wait patiently, offering encouragement and assistance while never complaining that their own progress is delayed in the process. Nevertheless, older women sometimes become exasperated, sigh loudly and declare, "English. I hate English!" One morning in class, students asked about the distinction between the words "beach" and "bitch." As Patti tried to explain, Ebyan let out a frustrated groan, complaining, "Words sound same. How do you know?" Picking up on her irritation Kedma tried to calm her friend. "Okay. Okay. It is like this. Now we are like children learn to walk again. The English one step at a time."

On another morning we asked the women to work with a set of ques- tion posing vocabulary, such as "who," "what," "when," "where," and "why." One student would develop a question and pose it to another, who would try to respond appropriately. When we came to Salwa and Kedma, the two oldest women in the room who are both well into their seventies, Salwa looked at Kedma and asked, "Why you coming to America?" After Kedma successfully replied, "I came to America civil war," the class clapped enthusiastically. Each subsequent pair's efforts were similarly applauded.

While the classroom atmosphere is not always so cheerful, and women are not unfailingly patient, daily classroom interaction is governed by an overriding sense of collaborative effort, which women rely upon to soothe potential conflict. On those occasions when women's constant habit of correcting one another's grammar or pronunciation and openly hushing each other seem to irritate a member of the class, others would quickly jump in to mockingly berate or otherwise elevate the mood with humor. Periodically, women's tendency to speak Somali during class would annoy certain class members. Once a complaint is registered, emphatic debate often ensues. One morning Ebyan, an older woman with strong English skills and a slightly caustic demeanor, expressed her frustration both at our habit of translating into various languages and students' side chatter in Somali. Almost yelling, she insisted, "No Somali—English! English only!" Ikran, a newer and much shyer student whose English was less flu- ent than Ebyan's, responded with surprising fervor: "Somali, Somali!" At this point, Patti explained that we were incorporating Somali and other languages in order to be sure everyone understood the meaning of the words used. Apparently reassured, Ebyan nodded her assent. Both Ebyan and Ikran's willingness to declare what form they would like their school- ing to take was made possible by the larger sense of community the women had established within the classroom and throughout MAEC. In fact, members of our class often asked us to revise the lessons or assignments we used with them. In these cases, the ability to define the classroom as a collaborative space, and schooling as a participatory process, reflected their commitment to community building and active participation in community.

Strategic Use of Westernness

While social networks and systems of support set up at MAEC emerge most visibly among groups of Somalis, women also make an effort to build community with White, long-term residents of the United States. During our time at MAEC, this dynamic became especially poignant in women's relations with us. Among other strategies of relationship building, the women in our classes pragmatically employed our ability to negotiate U.S. public and social institutions to address their immediate needs. While a simple desire for friendship, general good will, and the strategic benefit of establishing connections with us are in fact inextricably interwoven in our relations with Somali women, for analytic purposes here we pay particular attention to the lattermost element.

Women at MAEC routinely asked us for advice or help with filling out job, rent, and social security applications. Often, they brought tax forms, letters from landlords, or information from local service agencies so that we might help them to understand their intent, and respond appropriately. We were also asked to make calls to doctors' offices, explain symptoms, and translate prescription labels. In short, the women tapped our English proficiency, cultural and social capital, and experience negotiating U.S. bureaucracy to help meet the challenge of surviving in the United States. Over the course of our time at MAEC, we routinely served as resources and points of leverage as women adapted to life in Milltown (Warriner, 2004).

Though significantly less common, a few of our closest friends also requested our assistance in accessing material resources. After the birth of her fourth child, one student planned and held an impressive celebration at her house. She invited us to attend, asking Patti to bring a video camera borrowed from the college to record the event. We agreed and arrived several hours before the party's official start to help prepare. Eager to host an elaborate event, the woman had already transformed her normally unfurnished basement into a rich and colorful space. Decorative fabrics hung along the walls and from the ceiling, as low lying, velvety couches lined the walls. Two tables had been pushed together and covered with food, including a mix of Somali dishes, meats, and rice with a large iceberg salad and heavy tray of lasagna. At least 20 women of varying ages were already in attendance, filling the room in bright and ornate silk dresses. As still more arrived, Somali music blared from the boom box and women gathered in clusters to dance around the mother and her new baby. Patti circled the room, video camera in tow, recording the celebration. Groups formed around Patti as the hostess instructed her to capture particular images. Women posed for the camera, displaying their dresses, dancing with one another, and smiling. Such homemade and professional video recordings often circulate among family and friends in various international locations. Just as we have watched tapes of weddings in Los Angeles and Minneapolis at women's homes in Milltown, this video, too, would traverse the globe, a digital announcement of the mother's joy and success in producing a male offspring.

After a few hours of eating, dancing, and visiting, Patti announced that she would need to leave soon so that she might begin her hour-long commute home. Distressed, women begged her to stay and continue videotaping. In the face of Patti's resolve, someone suggested that Patti leave the camera with a woman who had experience operating similar equipment, a suggestion that was met with widespread approval and enthusiasm. Unwilling to do so, Patti insisted that she needed to leave with the camera and steadily disengaged herself from a sea of disappointed and frustrated faces. While Somali friends and neighbors had been called upon to help cook, dance, and celebrate, Patti's contribution lay in her ability to provide a material resource.

On another occasion, when a participant's young daughter wanted to join a local youth group on a trip to England, Patti was asked to help her arrange for a fund-raising event at the college where Patti was on the faculty. Such occasions signify women's understanding that, as a professional woman, Patti has greater access to material resources. In general, however, there are in fact relatively few instances of Somali women's efforts to access material resources through connection with us; rather, most of the strategic community building with us and other long term U.S. residents centers on accessing crucial knowledge and skills. In addition to asking for help negotiating public institutions, women occasionally solicit advice and information regarding other unfamiliar situations. In these moments, individual women seek allies outside of the Somali community and use access to "Westernness" to traverse potentially new and controversial terrain.

In one instance, Zeynab, a woman in her forties who had sporadically attended both our ELL and citizenship classes, approached us after class. Though generally lighthearted, Zeynab had in the past demonstrated frustration with her inability to focus full-time on schooling as she raises 12 children, cares for her husband, and runs her household. While her husband, Mohammed, completed the citizenship class with ease and passed the exam soon thereafter, Zeynab has yet to take the exam. Zeynab also faces a variety of health concerns, often coming to school with a sore back or aching legs, and had been recently diagnosed with chronic high blood pressure. On this morning, Zeynab's face was particularly grim. Immediately, she relayed the news that she was pregnant again, explaining that, although she had consistently expressed to Mohammed her desire to stop having children, he had refused to use contraception or to "leave her alone." Having already been informed by a doctor that her situation placed both Zeynab and her baby at high risk, Zeynab told Patti flatly that she wanted to end the pregnancy. In response to Zeynab's request, Patti asked if Zeynab wanted her set up an appointment at the hospital. Zeynab nodded emphatically. When we parted ways that day, Patti agreed to make an appointment as soon as she could. A few days later, Zeynab called Patti in the midst of a crisis and was rushed to the hospital, where she miscarried.

For Zeynab, Patti serves as a cultural broker who can comfortably negotiate the Milltown medical system and advocate for her in a scary and unfamiliar situation. In reaching out to Patti, Zeynab demonstrates that her entrance into the U.S. national community brings with it expanded options for managing her reproductive role in the family. Despite the very real danger of ostracism within the Somali community, Zeynab elected to try to take advantage of her membership in a new national context and, in the process, added a heightened degree of complexity and nuance to her identity as a Somali woman.

A similar situation occurred when another student enrolled in our class became pregnant for the sixth time. Having had a previous emergency Cesarean section, the woman's doctor informed her that a c-section would be the safest birthing method. Her husband, however, strictly prohibited her from pursuing this option, arguing that the performance of c-sections tampered with *Allah's* will. When the woman insisted that her health would be in jeopardy if she chose to give birth vaginally, her husband told her that he would divorce her if she disobeyed his command. The woman faced a difficult decision. On the one hand, she now enjoyed access to high quality health care that could potentially save her life. One the other, taking advantage of such care potentially contradicted deeply held community dicta regarding women's relationships to reproduction and their husbands. For several weeks, the woman silently struggled with her decision before asking Patti to accompany her on a doctor's visit. During this visit, the doctor, a White, middle aged woman, and Patti listened carefully to the woman's concerns. In turn, Patti and the woman listened attentively as the doctor explained that the woman risked her own death and the death of her baby if she did not opt to have a c-section. Thinking strategically, Patti asked the woman whether her husband had considered that, even if she were to survive the birth, she would never be able to bear more children should her uterus burst. Holding Patti's gaze, Fatima nodded silently in recognition, "Let me call him." Returning to the room after speaking on the phone with Omar for only a few minutes, Fatima announced with certainty, "He said to go ahead with the c-section."

Both of the women who sought Patti's assistance are called upon to adroitly balance between newly available ways of managing their roles as wives and mothers in the United States. While not all Somali women embrace expanded reproductive options, the women's stories illustrate how Somali women in the U.S. act from a particular, often conflicted, positionality. Reaching out to Western women, who operate from an equivalently unique gender, race, and class salient standpoint, represents one aspect of Somali women's pragmatic strategy for managing everyday life. Patti's presence at such significant moments in participants' lives stems from the women's purposeful efforts to establish relationships across difference. In each of the described instances, the women draw upon Patti and Rachel as sources of social, cultural, and or material capital, allowing them to better position themselves in relation to the demands of Milltown life. Such usage constitutes a deliberate and poignant form of community building, and reflects one aspect of the women's ever evolving multinational consciousness. Knowing that we operate out of a very different set of values and expectation than the local Somali community, in developing relations with us, Somali women etch out a link between former, traditional ways of being Somali women and emergent identities as Somali women in the United States.

Invoking Western Idioms to Build Community

In addition to building and drawing upon relationships with U.S. citizens in order to better navigate the new terrain of life in Milltown, study participants often invoke "Western" idioms to build community at MAEC. These invocations take shape as expressions of tolerance for ways of being that they frequently refer to as "American women." In these crucial moments of acceptance, the women condone others' forms of dress or expressions of sexuality that are clearly not acceptable for them as Somali, Muslim women. On one occasion, a woman who held very traditional notions of marriage and family for Somali women, brought Rachel a generous gift of two tight, cropped halter tops to thank her for helping prepare the citizenship class. The woman would never have worn the blouses herself. Nor, would she have been likely to permit her daughters to wear them. In fact, the shirts were much flashier and more revealing than Rachel's own style. Yet, for the woman they are representative of Western ways of being a young woman.

The woman's desire to give the shirts to Rachel is itself symbolic of her work to recognize and accept Rachel on her own, culturally distinct terms.

Somali women's acceptance of Rachel's perceived lifestyle is also expressed by study participants during a classroom conversation in which it was revealed that Rachel had moved far from family in order to attend college. Women repeatedly assured Rachel that her independence is "good." Hers was not an unequivocal acceptance, however, as such encouragement was followed by observations that Rachel was in a prime position to marry and begin having children. Women asked her how many children she wants and cajoled her about the importance of having a family. Still, although Rachel was older than many of the women had been when they were married, the women nodded in approval when Rachel replied to their queries with an assertion that she had no intention of marrying soon. Nodding with approval, the women assured her, again, that she was "still young," that being educated was "very good," and that she still had time to marry in the future.

Although less explicit, several women also took steps to demonstrate an acceptance of Patti after determining that she was gay. Homosexuality is deeply disapproved of within the Somali community, so much so that the International Organization for Migration chooses to warn Somalis coming to the U.S. that they will have to live and work peacefully alongside people with a range of gender and sexual expressions. Indeed, homosexuality is so marginalized within East African countries as a whole that one Kenyan woman with whom we worked during our research in Nairobi responded to the news that the U.K. had legalized same-sex marriage by saying that homosexuality is a "Western thing" and that "Africans are not gay."

On two occasions, Patti came out to study participants with whom she spent the most time and had established especially close relations. Both women responded to Patti's admission with initial surprise followed by a brief period of withdrawal. Both soon recovered though and declared their loyalty as friends. Both stated in their own way that such things are different in the U.S. and that, because Patti is a good friend, they would continue to accept her. In each case, Patti maintains close friendships with the women, spending as much time at their homes and with the women's other friends and children as before her admission.

Despite her deliberate decision to hide her sexuality out of fear that most participants would not be willing to work with her if they knew she is gay, after working at MAEC for several years, rumor began to openly circulate. One woman, who was present in the first class Patti ever taught at MAEC and who routinely expressed an appreciation for Patti as a teacher, heard the rumor and went to another teacher to determine its veracity. Regardless of her interest in Patti's sexual orientation, the student's warmth toward Patti never changed. She continued to share hugs upon meeting, smiled throughout classroom interactions, and invited Patti and college students with whom Patti worked to her home. The woman's willingness to maintain close ties with Patti reflects her overall readiness to cross social category boundaries to build family and community and, accordingly, a pragmatic acceptance of what the women perceive as Western idioms of womanhood. While it is difficult to gauge whether relations with other, perhaps more traditional women might have been affected by the knowledge of Patti's sexuality, none of the main participants in the study showed any indication that they wanted to stop working or socializing with Patti based on this information. The fact that study participants were therefore willing to continue to work closely with Patti after she was identified as gay reveals a willingness to accept what they perceived as Western ways of being. Such tolerance for "Western" dress and sexuality reflects a positionality that characterizes the women's sense of self as Somali women in the United States.

Invoking Africanness

As discussed, a key part of establishing unique identities as Somali women in the U.S. includes building relationships both within the Somali community as well as with those outside of its margins. Again, this dynamic is well illustrated both in relations between various Somali women at MAEC and with the two of us: women often bring food or other culturally relevant goods into the school to share, and they also relay stories that highlight their "Africanness," offering unique experiences and cultural artifacts in the symbolic exchange for friendship and support.

Somali women often come to school with *hennaed* hands, which we tended to notice and remark on, complimenting the intricate designs. Seemingly pleased with our interest in the decorative practice, women explained that *henna* is traditional within Somali culture—a mark of beauty used like makeup for special occasions. We were taught that it is applied freshly in especially ornate designs for weddings, births, and other ceremonies, but never during menstruation. Decorative *hennaing* is a distinctly female practice; while men *henna* their hair and beards a ruddy tone, designs on hands, arms, and feet as well as darkened finger tips are worn solely by women. During one class morning, Rachel noticed that Yasmin had brought in a selection of temporary *henna* tattoos, and was passing them around to the class. As everyone perused the selection, Yasmin explained that she was selling them for five dollars apiece, and that Rachel should look through the book and pick out her favorite. Considering buying one from her like everyone else, Rachel admired her collection, interested that they were temporary tattoos versus the traditional *henna* done painstakingly by hand. After Rachel pointed to her favorite, Yasmin immediately left the room and returned with a cup of water and paper towels, intending to apply the tattoo to Rachel during the class. Yasmin explained that it was a gift, and refused to accept payment for it. As Yasmin pressed the tattoos on Rachel's hands, the rest of the class members gathered around to admire. After class ended and we all returned downstairs, other women who had not been in the class complimented Rachel's hands as Yasmin held them up proudly. For the rest of the time that the *henna* remained, many women took notice, both interested and pleased that Rachel had taken on a symbol of African or Arab female beauty.

The sharing of traditional Somali and other African foods is also a common vehicle for building community at MAEC. Sue reports that when Somali women first started attending MAEC, they frequently brought tea and other foods in to share with one another and with teachers. While Sue enjoyed the sentiment that propelled the sharing, after a while she and Jacqueline decided that they needed to implement a "no food" rule so that the women would concentrate more on school work than socializing. Nevertheless, women in our class often secreted in danishes, cookies, and juices to share during class time. After a brief discussion of the type of tea that Patti brought in a thermos to school each day, Alima came to class with a carafe of homemade chai for Patti to try. On a different day, during a discussion of the types of goods offered at the local *halal* market, Fawziya offered to bring in camel meat, a staple in Somalia now sold in Milltown, so that Rachel could taste it. On another occasion, after Patti had explained that she would have to miss several classes in a row because she was going to visit her parents out of state, Hawalul asked when Patti would be leaving for the trip and if Patti would be willing to stop by MAEC before she left. When Patti visited school on her way out of town, Hawalul presented her with a dish of baked chicken and rice, made decorative with food coloring and spices. She gave these dishes with a warm hug and greetings to Patti's mother and father, whom she had never met. Similarly, during the winter holidays a few months later, Rachel announced her intent to visit her family out of state. After Rachel explained why she would miss several upcoming classes, Alima proposed to the other women present that the class write a letter to Rachel's family in which they introduced themselves and expressed gratitude for Rachel's work at MAEC. Before class ended that day, Alima gathered all of the class members together around one end of a long table to compose the letter. Fatima, whose writing was the strongest, translated everyone's sentiments onto a handwritten letter that everyone signed. Alima proudly presented the letter to Rachel with a request that she deliver it to her mother and father. In the letter, the women described how they knew Rachel and thanked Rachel's parents for their daughter's efforts in Maine.

The women's practice of giving food, gifts, and letters of appreciation to us and our families invokes the centrality of family within Somali culture, as well as the women's efforts to incorporate us into networks of reciprocal giving. The women deepened their connection with us by showing respect for our elders, a practice that echoes traditional Somali and, arguably, African patterns of social organization, in which an individual's actions are seen to be both reflective and constitutive of status, family, and community. The women's efforts to acknowledge their gratitude for our work at MAEC necessarily found expression through communication with elder members of our family, to whom the women attribute our perceived goodness.

In addition to sharing or invoking physical and symbolic tenets of Somali culture to embed us within their local community, women at MAEC often tried to educate us about East Africa and, not surprisingly, appreciated what familiarity we do have with the particulars of their African lives. Against a contextual backdrop where Somali women are often told blatantly to "go back to Africa," grouped together as one homogenous entity, or viewed as exotic strangers from a distant part of the world, any culturally specific knowledge that we showed about Somalia, Kenya, or Africa more generally was received enthusiastically. Those moments in which we shared knowledge about or personal experience in Kenya or Somalia sparked extensive discussion. Before her move to Milltown, Rachel had studied in Kenya, where she learned some Kiswahili. Although she had stayed in a different region of Kenya than most Somalis who had lived there, she was often able to identify and recognize the names of towns and cities along the coast and carry out basic conversations with the women who had also learned Kiswahili while in Kenya. As a result, Kiswahili conversations and greetings often dotted classroom interactions. At the same time, Patti worked to learn basic Somali, a project students enthusiastically encouraged by providing new words and expressions for her to practice. Furthermore, over the course of our time at MAEC, we each received research grants to travel to Kenya which, in addition to facilitating the improvement of our language skills, enriched our ability to discuss specific places and dynamics of the women's Kenyan lives. We had visited the region of Nairobi where Somali nationals and undocumented Somali refugees live, and we had also attended the cultural orientation sessions students had sat through as part of their resettlement process. These research opportunities allowed us to share stories with the women, who were always delighted to recall details of the places we now shared in common.

On one of these trips, Rachel was able to visit Maryam's mother. Given a hefty package of pictures, videos, and gifts to deliver, Rachel traveled four hours from where she was staying in Kenya to the community in which Maryam's mother lived. By phone from the United States, Maryam had arranged for her cousin to pick Rachel up and transport her by car to her mother's home. When she arrived, Rachel found that Maryam's mother had prepared a beautiful lunch and tea—both of which were strikingly similar to those served by Maryam in Milltown. After tearfully receiving the package Rachel delivered, Maryam's mother walked Rachel through the small town and glowingly introduced her to Maryam's relatives and childhood friends. Upon return to Milltown, Rachel gave to Maryam pictures she had taken of her mother, other family members, and childhood friends. She also relayed specific greetings to her from a variety of friends and relatives. Maryam and her two children, who had been unable to travel to Kenya given Maryam's tentative status in the United States, sat shoulder to shoulder beside Rachel as she described all the people she had seen and what they had said during her brief visit. Alternating between tears and laughter, Maryam used the pictures to compare life in Africa with her and her children's current life in the US. Pulling out a picture of a much thinner version of her son from their days in Kenya, Maryam joked, "Here, he is African." Laughingly pinching his now plump belly, she added, "Now, he is American. Now they want to eat American food only." Continuing, she complained that her children wanted to dress "American," drive flashy cars, and were getting fat. Meanwhile, her constant work to support them financially meant she spent less time with them or friends. "It is different than Africa," she concluded, her voice no longer cheerful.

During such visits to their homes, women at MAEC often similarly combined evocations of African heritage with contemporary ways of life in the United States. We often went to Fatima's house together, both to provide some company while she was pregnant and to help out after the baby was born. On each of these occasions, Fatima would offer pound cake or cookies accompanied by tea. Each was served formally on trays carried into the living room, where we sat together on the low, velvety couches sold at the local African store. During our times at her house, Fatima would always bring out things to show us—stacks of pictures from Atlanta, her children's latest report cards and drawings, her well read copy of the *Quran*, and prayer beads. One afternoon, we asked about the meaning of the ornate hangings adorning her wall. The tapestries, which depict Mecca or contain Arabic characters in gold across dark, intricate backgrounds, are common at the houses of Somali women we have visited. After explaining and translating the message of each, Fatima brought out her *Quran* to show us, explained that her children attend *Quranic* school, and demonstrated how to use wooden prayer beads. Patti admired the beads and Fatima proposed that Patti keep them as a symbol of their friendship.

On another afternoon Nasra, after asking for a ride home from school, invited Patti into her apartment for tea. After showing Patti around the apartment, she pulled out a stylized electric teapot and explained that she had bought it at "the African store" in Milltown and that it was like those that they had used in Somalia. Though Patti had at this point been introduced to the distinction between American style and Somali (chai) tea on numerous occasions, she listened again as Nasra explained the use of various spices, sugar, and milk. And Patti tasted the tea as if for the first time, complimenting Nasra on how much more flavorful it was than the tea she normally drank. Nasra beamed proudly and waved for Patti to come into her bedroom where Nasra pulled several items out of a trunk. Each was wrapped in cloth: the first item revealed was a bottle of perfume in a container modeled after a *hooka*. Nasra demonstrated that each of the hoses coming from the main bottle sprayed a bit of perfume, and explained that "it is like the thing for smoking" as she looked at Patti for signals of recognition. Patti nodded in understanding and asked whether they smoked from similar devices in Somalia. Nasra shook her head no. "No smoking, just for show." Next, Nasra unwrapped a set of smaller bottles of perfume with Arabic script written on them and proceeded to uncap each, asking Patti to smell. She then revealed a tray with a matching set of ornate tea cups and dishes. Having unwrapped and set each item on the bed, Nasra leaned back on one elbow and asked Patti which of the perfumes she liked the best. Patti noted that she liked them all and then chose one bottle, saying that she liked the gentle scent of that one. Nasra declared in a tone that did not allow for question, "That one is yours. From my home to yours. Thank you to my friend."

On these occasions, when the women draw upon African idioms to connect with us, they entwine us within patterns of reciprocal giving that characterize their relations with one another. During our time at MAEC, we observed a constant exchange of goods, favors, and sentiments of good will. A woman who might frequently share homemade snacks with fellow students could be confident that when she brought in beauty products explicitly marketed toward African women, those same classmates would purchase her merchandise and supplement her meager income. Nasra, a high level English language learner who often offer her ability to translate between teachers and entry level learners, could rely on both teachers and fellow students to provide rides to the local career center, doctor's office, or grocery store. Similarly, the women bought us coffee and offered food in exchange for our services as volunteer teachers. And, when invited to women's homes for dinner, we knew to bring "American" dishes to share. In this way, the women skillfully draw upon African idioms to

weave us into social webs of reciprocal support that are themselves repro-
ductions of Somali patterns of social organization. The act of enmeshing
us into such patterns, which both draw upon practices understood as
Somali or African and include women who practice different ways of
being and represent distinct values, manifest their unique ways of being
Somali women in the United States.

Global Politics

As our illustration of community building has sought to show, women
at MAEC use schooling to build allegiances and connections. In addition
to socializing and providing support, using and accepting aspects of
"Westerness," and invoking and sharing African idioms, experiences, and
knowledge, the women employ class conversations to discursively position
themselves in relation to various macrolevel geopolitical issues. For example, while it is well established that language use has direct connection to
nationalism and long histories of territorial power struggle, the women
elect not to assert their potential dominance at MAEC, despite their
numerical majority in the classroom, as part of a larger effort to smooth
over areas of potential conflict and strife. The women respond with light-
hearted acquiescence to those occasional moments of potential conflict
over language use that arises between Somali language speakers and non-
Somali students. On a couple of such occasions, students whose first languages were in the minority became tired of the Somali women's common
use of Somali to communicate during class time and would insist—sometimes irritably, sometimes gently—that their classmates "speak English."
Over the course of the study, at least a half dozen of these requests were
vocalized, and each time the Somali women responded with equanimity
as they nodded their heads in assent, apologized, and laughingly vowed
to try harder to only use English in the classroom.

More poignantly, women use the classroom as a space to purposefully
extend offerings of peace across markers of historical and cultural difference. In moments when Rachel described her Jewish upbringing, women
enthusiastically identified the many historical and customary overlaps
between Judaism and Islam. One woman once detailed the shared biblical
roots of the two religions, noting that followers of each descend from
brothers. Women also shared that, in their initial cities of resettlement in
the United States, they used to buy *kosher* foods before *halal* meats became
available, because the preparation of the two were so similar. Another
time, after Rachel asked what type of meat was available at the local *halal*
markets, the women began listing: "chicken, fish, beef, goat, camel—not
pork!!" When Rachel added that she did not eat pork either, the women

around the table nodded understandingly and with apparent pride in the shared custom. Fawziya offered on behalf of the group, "We would eat in your home!" Finally, on another occasion, discussion of the two religions evolved into explicit conversation on the conflict in the Middle East. During that conversation, in which Rachel sat with six Somali women, it became immediately apparent that everyone shared very similar positions—each deeply regretting the violence, each eager for a resolution in which both an Israeli and a Palestinian state would emerge peacefully.

Discussion of Rachel and the women's position of shared regret in regard to war and violence parallels a common theme in women's conversations about various wars in Africa. One morning, Rachel asked Sarah, who was the only non-Somali learner in class that day, to explain the situation in Sudan to the group. Sarah stood tentatively at the board and began to draw a circle in chalk, dividing it into four quadrants, which she labeled North, South, East, and West. In a subdued tone, she began to explain that, while each region of the U.S. was currently unified, in Sudan the north and south were fighting against one another. After gesturing with frustration that she could not capture the situation's complexity in English, Sarah continued to explain that, due to prolonged warfare, the south enjoyed few amenities: "No schools, no hospitals, no streets." Her Somali classmates shook their heads in recognition as Sarah continued to elaborate that while Muslims lived in the north, west, and east of Sudan, the south was composed of Christians, like herself. Elaborating, she explained that since 1959 there had been many guns and a lot of fighting, with only a brief peaceful interlude. She finished by noting that, when she left Sudan, she traveled to the refugee camps where "the children had no shoes, no clothes, and there were no houses." Interspersing her English words with vivid hand gestures, she acted out how at night (she placed her hands under her face like she was sleeping), you could hear gunfire (she made machine gun noises). By this point in Sarah's narrative, Somali women in the class sat quietly with rapt attention to her words and gestures. When Sarah's voice finally fell silent, the women began to contribute their own accounts of war and shared experiences of life in Kenyan refugee camps. Hibo, her voice strong with urgency, exclaimed, "All Africa—Rwanda, Uganda, Sudan, Somalia, Mali, Sierra Leone." As she generated the list of African states with histories of civil strife, other women began to interject. "Not all Africa!" Ebyan countered. "All Muslim countries!" Hamda said with a regretful tone. Hibo meanwhile continued to compile her list, "Kenya." "No! No war in Kenya" several women protested. After Hibo agreed to remove Kenya from the list, Hamda tried to demonstrate that there were some peaceful African states, listing, "Egypt, Kenya, Libya."

As the women identified warring and peaceful African countries, Rachel asked why they thought African countries experienced such a propensity for civil strife. Hamda answered, "Different groups, in Somalia it was different groups even though 100 [percent] Muslim." Other women said "Christians and Muslims." Even as the women identified those social divisions that had led to war, they took pains to express a general antiwar sentiment. One morning we asked the class whether they would have declared war on Iraq if they were president of the United States. With only one exception, each of the roughly 10 women in the class that morning stated that they would not have gone to war because it killed many women and children who "have nothing to do with Saddam or terrorism." The one woman who did support the war stated that, if she were president of the United States, she would have gone to war with Iraq in order to secure oil so that Americans could have gas for their cars to drive to work. Other women laughed incredulously at her statement and one woman joked, "Ah, she is American now! But, she likes Bush. She voted Bush. She is confused. She does not know." Others chimed in with agreement. "Yes, she is poor but she thinks she is rich and that Bush is for her! She does not understand." Kedma, who had voted for Bush in a mock class election, laughed along and, looking down, shook her head from side to side, as if silently admonishing her friends for the rebuke.

While there was no resolution to such politically loaded conversations, nor agreement upon exact reasons for the widespread violence within African states and across the globe, the women are careful to approach these discussions in ways that highlight shared experiences and allegiances and minimize sources of difference or dispute. The women work deliberately to enact a discursive space in which they can commiserate over the violence that has torn apart and reshaped each of their lives.

Conclusion

The social organization of family and community among Somalis has undergone considerable change since the onset of war in Somalia. For the women in our study, transformation is at once a shared experience, as Somalis draw upon a common national heritage to make sense of multinational refugee journeys, and a fracturing force among a nation of people who have become increasingly scattered across the globe and subjected to vastly different demands and opportunities. During the course of our study, members of the Somali community in Milltown pull from established ways of being and memories of self, community, and nation to respond to local pressures and possibilities. In this creative process of remembrance and adaptation, newcomers give shape to a unique expression of Somali identity in the United States. As part of their negotiation of multinational identities and experiences, as well as the myriad gendered images at play in their journeys across the diaspora, the Somali refugee women in our study use schooling as a space and process through which to build community. The methods employed to build community include the development of social support networks, making use of Western women as sources of cultural knowledge, invoking Western and African idioms, and crafting a shared positionality in relation to global politics. Through use of these community building methods, women traverse multiple lines of difference, including ethnicity, gender, national origin, race, class, and religion, as they share ideas, company, food, goods, stories of past and present lives, and practical information about life in Milltown.

CHAPTER 12

"YOU BETTER SAY YOUR PRAYERS BEFORE PRAYERS ARE SAID FOR YOU"

Negotiating and Regulating Gender Change

In the previous chapter, we illustrate some of the ways that Somali women at MAEC use schooling as a space and process in which to build community. While Somali women's community building efforts occur across the various markers of social identity and difference present at MAEC, a good deal of the women's energies also go toward building and maintaining relations among Somali women more exclusively. In this chapter, we extend our analysis to consider the ways in which women use community to regulate gender change amongst one another. As is the case in associations across social markers of difference, the women employ a variety of methods for constructing a Somali women's community. In contrast to trans-national, race, and ethnic community building work, efforts to influence one another's ways of adapting to life in the U.S. is a primary means through which to establish and mark the boundaries of belonging among Somali women. Again, as we have noted, Somali women encounter myriad images of womanhood through multinational journeys and daily life in the small Milltown community. In what follows, we demonstrate that individual Somali women's choices in regard to a constellation of gender options are made within intricate webs of symbolic meaning in which the

Educated For Change?: Muslim Refugee Women in the West, pp. 281–303
Copyright © 2012 by Information Age Publishing

reiteration of ideal Somali womanhood is a commanding prerogative. Recognizing the inherent danger in essentializing a richly diverse and dynamic cultural and social history, and being careful to note that the particulars of women's roles in Somali society vary across time and region and according to class and age, we point to the centrality of marriage and child rearing in notions of ideal womanhood prevailing in Somali society because women in our study repeatedly evoke such ideals in the everyday exchanges through which they construct and regulated community.

As noted in Chapter 2, marriage in Somalia tends to follow distinct patterns and comprises the major avenue through which women can contribute to family, clan, and society. The war and international migration, however, have given rise to a community of women with vastly different marital arrangements and family structures. MAEC's population includes unmarried women well into their twenties; members of polygamous family arrangements who are now officially "divorced" as per U.S. law; and grandmotherly matriarchs of large transnational families. There are also women who, despite the constant teasing of others, have chosen not to marry. The two-parent, nuclear family normalized in the U.S. rarely reflects the family structure of those women in our study. Most are single heads of households and, when applicable, the primary (or single) caregivers for their children. It is within the context of fractured (from prevalent, prewar patterns of social organization in Somalia) family life that women in our study go about the work of reestablishing the preeminence of marriage and mothering in Milltown. In the midst of heterogeneity in marital practices, and regardless of the prevalence of negative feelings toward men, women's commitment to marriage and childrearing is seen as crucial to the conservation of core Somali and Muslim values and practices. According to Ibrahim (2004), child-bearing and child-rearing are women's paramount roles in the Somali family. She explains, "As mothers, [women] bear Somali culture, and foster among their children the distinctive role-playing which determines future male and female patterns of behavior" (p. 28).

Somali women reiterate an ideal of Somali womanhood in which marriage and child rearing remain central prerogatives within a markedly different national context. In the first part of the chapter we relay the stories of two women who do not express their commitment to family as wives and mothers in ways fellow Somali women found acceptable and, consequently, faced significant disapprobation. While extreme in nature, the women's experiences of exclusion and shaming speak to women's power and determination to monitor one another's gendered orientation to life in the United States. While few Somali women in Milltown make similar choices or become subject to such dramatic forms of reprisal, the marginalized women's experiences bring to light the normalizing function of community constantly at play in the lives of Somali refugee women more broadly. In the second half of the chapter, we turn from the extremes of gender regulation to the broader middle ground, in which multigenerational women collaboratively negotiate terms of acceptable gender change.

(Re-)Establishing Norms Through Exclusion

Bad Things Will Happen To You: Hell, If You Don't Do Ramadan

-Fatima's Story

We first met Fatima when she was enrolled in Rebecca's upper level ELL class in which Patti observed several days a week. We also came to know her through our joint participation in a weekly women's group meeting held at MAEC. At the time of our initial meeting, Fatima was divorced and had two children. The ELL class was composed of six women whom Rebecca frequently prompted to share personal stories. Out of Fatima's narratives, we learned that her divorce had been complicated and bitter. When she first came to the United States, Fatima enthusiastically embraced the styles of dress worn by many American women. She stopped wearing a head scarf, exposing her hair publicly, and began to dress in low cut blouses and jeans. Though her husband, friends and family severely disapproved of her choice, she refused to relent. After her husband insisted that she dress "like other Somali women," she ended the marriage. Fatima left her husband and children and went to stay with family in another state while she continued to dress, in her words, "like an American." According to Fatima, her husband kept custody of the children—his customary right within the patrilineal Somali clan structure—as leverage against her so that she would return to the marriage.

After leaving her marriage, Fatima took a job through which she met an African American man. The two formed a friendship, and the man expressed an interest in marrying. Fatima would later describe him as "a good man" who treated her well and worked hard. While Fatima enjoyed the man's company and appreciated that he treated her with respect, she soon ended the relationship because, as she reported, she knew that her family and the larger Somali community would ostracize her if she were to marry a Christian. Indeed, Fatima never told her family about the "American man," and soon after ending the relationship she began to date Omar, a Somali man. Her former husband soon got word that she was dating Omar and responded by sending their two children to her in order to hamper the new couple's freedom. Her family also tried to thwart the relationship. Omar, they complained, had been in the U.S. for 10 years without buying a car, marrying, or having children. For them, the inability to establish himself in the U.S. signified a failure to live up to gendered expectations that Somali men produce and provide for large families. Displeased with Fatima's choice of dress and decision to divorce, and deeply disapproving of Omar, her family threatened to cut all ties with her unless she agreed to make a fresh start in Milltown, a much quieter community, where an older, more conservative aunt lived with her husband and children. Reluctantly, Fatima conceded.

During her first year in Milltown, Fatima attended classes, took care of her children, and moved into her own apartment. Again responding to familial and community pressure, Fatima began to wear a head scarf. Her resignation to family and community was incomplete, however. Unlike the vast majority of Somali women in Milltown, she continued to wear jeans rather than full length dresses or skirts. Though she always wore a scarf, she wore it loosely, so that glimpses of hair would occasionally show. She decorated her living room walls with "glam shots" of herself unveiled and in tank tops. Her mother, who heard about the pictures through Fatima's sister repeatedly pressured her to remove them, arguing that little difference existed between being uncovered in public and immodestly portrayed for visitors to her home.

At school, classmates openly offered similar assessments of Fatima's behavior. When she wore her jeans and other "American clothes," Fatima was told by both Somali men and women that she shouldn't come to school dressed inappropriately because, as Fatima paraphrased to Rachel, "I'm becoming American and that if I continue like that, in 10 years I'll be Christian." Fatima would offer indignant replies to such comments and invite people into her home so that they could observe that she and her children read and studied the *Qu'ran*. Her critics were not deterred by her demonstrations of piety, however, and continued to voice the opinion that her choice of dress was a louder expression of her religious beliefs and practices than her private study of the *Qu'ran*. One morning Fatima came to school wearing a dress with wide knit sleeves that revealed the skin on her arms. While she was waiting in the parking lot at the end of the morning, people in the school began describing to Yasmin, Fatima's closest friend at the time, how improper it was for Fatima to wear that particular outfit, and how they thought she should cover more. Yasmin admitted that she agreed with them. They continued to explain to Yasmin that since she was Fatima's friend, she should tell Fatima not to wear clothes like that to school again. Yasmin explained that she had in the past, but that Fatima had not complied. Yasmin then went outside to relay the message. Fatima got angry, demanding to know who had said it. At this point a man standing outside spoke up and said that he had both heard it and agreed with the assessment. Fatima replied, "That is your opinion and I have my own and I don't care what any of you think."

Fatima's refusal to completely submit to the wishes of her family and the local Somali community also extended to her relationship with Omar, whom she continued to date even after moving to Milltown. Omar made occasional visits to Milltown, and the two discussed plans to wed. In Rebecca's class one morning, Fatima told classmates that Omar wanted to get married, but that she was concerned because he was frequently jealous and possessive of her, wanting to know where she was at all times of the day and night, and insisting that she cover her body more completely "like other Somali women." Rebecca groaned out a warning, "Oh, god! That is not a good sign. Wait! Don't do anything for a *long time*." Privately, Fatima explained that, while she had the same misgivings about marrying Omar because of his jealousy, she didn't feel that she could break up with him either "because I love him. I'm just in love with him." Soon after declaring her love for Omar to us, Fatima returned from a visit with him and announced to the class that she and Omar had married. In another month, she notified the class that she was pregnant and that Omar would soon be moving to Milltown. Fatima's family and members of the Milltown Somali community complained that she went forward with the marriage without her parents' or community's approval, and had been married by an *imam* out of state who had himself disregarded the communal custom for parents to arrange and sanction their children's marriages.

Fatima's attitude toward the critical standard bearers within the local community exacerbated tensions. During her pregnancy, she stopped wearing pants and began to dress more like the other women in skirts, long shirts, and headscarves. One day a group of women at MAEC accusingly asserted that the only reason she was wearing "Somali clothes" was because she was pregnant and wanted to cover her stomach. Fatima agreed with them and told the group that they disapproved of her out of jealousy because they "do not have a body like hers." She finished by declaring that if they were young and had her body, they would dress in the same way.

In another instance, during the approach of *Ramadan*, the Muslim holy month when observers fast during daylight hours, Rachel asked our class what plans they had for the holiday. Fatima replied quickly and defiantly, pointing to her pregnant belly, "I'm not going to do it."

"Oh, so in Islam when you're pregnant you're exempt [from fasting]?" Rachel asked. Fatima responded, "Well no, I supposed to, but...." and again pointed to her stomach. Hibo, a woman in her mid-50s, looked up from her notebook to glare at Fatima and began to speak passionately in Somali while making forceful scissor motions with her hands. Fatima, with an expression of bemused indifference, translated for our benefit what Hibo had said: "You know paradise? Hell? Bad things will happen to you: hell, if you don't do *Ramadan.*"

Fatima's defiance came at a high personal cost. One morning, Sue asked Fatima to teach a group of entry level ELLs a civics lesson based on material she had learned in her upper level ELL class. While Fatima agreed to do this, when Sue led her into the room where the women waited, the class rose in revolt, refusing to be taught by such an immoral woman. The women, after relaying their disdain for Fatima, stood and exited the room in unison. Fatima left MAEC in tears and did not return for over a week.

As the months of her pregnancy progressed, Fatima felt increasingly iso-lated from the Somali community at MAEC as well as from her family. Her father refused to communicate with her, forbade talk of her within the fam-ily, and disallowed her mother from speaking with Fatima by phone. Though they both attended MAEC and lived within a few miles of one another, Fatima rarely spoke to her aunt. We spent significant time with her at her home during this period, both in preparation for the baby and because she expressed loneliness and frustration with Omar, who had yet to move to Milltown as promised. Around this time, Rachel asked Fatima if she had confided in or sought advice from friends at school. She replied, "No, I don't trust these people. If I tell them, everybody knows." Though she did report receiving calls from Somali women at MAEC to check on her during her pregnancy, Fatima routinely complained of isolation and aban-donment during the days and weeks leading up to the delivery.

On an early January evening, Fatima gave birth to Qassim. A week later we went to visit the baby and Fatima at home. After introducing Rachel to Qassim and chatting for a while, Fatima led us out of the living room and opened up the small closet next to her kitchen to reveal a large tin of fresh cookies, as well as numerous uneaten pound cakes. Fatima explained that during her last week of pregnancy, when she was home from school, she had spent hours baking to prepare for all of the visitors that she had expected to receive after her delivery. Deeply disappointed by the lack of people who had stopped by, Fatima revealed her expecta-tion that the birth of her son would rally community support and help to dissolve community members' resentments.

Within a few months of the incident, Fatima began to bring her new-born on frequent visits to MAEC. While many women at MAEC normally ignored Fatima, on these occasions she assertively directed conversation toward her newborn and announced that she would soon be hosting a party to celebrate his birth. Over the course of several visits, she invited and re-invited many dozens of women to her home. Privately, she told Patti that, given the circumstances of her marriage, she had not been able to celebrate her wedding and so the party was meant not only to mark Qassim's birth, but her marriage as well. She also explained that "many are unhappy with her but they not be unhappy with baby. They come and say 'congratulations, you are a good mother.' Then," she continued sweeping her hands around her home, "they see, I have good home, good children, I not a bad woman, they think." Indeed, in many ways Fatima's party seemed to be successful. Nearly 50 women of all ages, including her older sister and many students at MAEC, attended and danced joyfully around Fatima. In the weeks and months after the party, Fatima continued to make visits with Qassim to MAEC. On these occasions, she wore loose fitting pants and blouses that fully covered her arms and sat high along the neckline. She was greeted with reserved welcome and brief, polite conversation about the baby. Over time, the frequency of her visits diminished, and in a resolved tone she confided to Patti, "This is all now. I am home mother, wife. Nothing more. No more student. Just home." Over time, members of the Somali community, including fellow women, wore away Fatima's rebellious streak and she returned to customary clothing and a traditional domestic lifestyle.

In another case, a woman broke with community norms regarding domestic abuse. Felis, who, like Fatima, had alienated peers by marrying against her family's wishes and supporting her daughter's participation in a growing trend among Somali girls to play sports publicly, became subject to physical abuse at the hands of her husband. After one terrible fight, Felis announced to our class that she had decided to end her relationship, and demanded that her husband leave the house and family. In response, several women in the class reminded her, in grave tones, that it was not her prerogative to end the marriage before following prescribed routes of action. Felis, head bowed, listened intently. After a prolonged silence following the women's admonishing words, we moved on to cover the day's lesson. Later, Felis raised the topic with Patti. She explained that she had already told her husband to leave but he had refused, reminding her that her choice was to call the police or learn to obey his will. Crying, Felis explained in distressed and exhausted tones that, because she had entered the marriage against her family's will, her father would not help to protect her against his physical abuse, nor would he support her decision to end the marriage. Nevertheless, "you must follow your community. Like (the women) today say. Or, it will be worse for you." Rather than call the police, Felis followed the unwritten procedures for handling spousal abuse within the Somali community, to which her fellow students had referred.

It is been customary within the Somali community to deal with domestic abuse in ways that reflect the patrilineal and clan structure of Somali society. According to Affi (2004):

> In Somalia ... domestic conflicts that might lead to divorce are often solved by one's in-laws and extended family, thereby saving the marriage. (This is particularly the case in clan-exogamous marriages where there is more at stake than the relationship between two people). (p. 113)

Domestic violence is often kept in check through clan based systems of respectability and retribution, as mistreatment of a wife is viewed as an insult to the clan from which she came (Ahmed, 2004). When a wife feels as if she has been subject to abuse, there are established channels through which she is to pass in order to redress the situation. A wife is first expected to seek counsel from elders within her husband's family or clan. If the elders agree that she had grounds for complaint, they reprimand the husband. *Imams* within the husband's clan can also be approached and can elect to speak with members of the husband's and wife's families in order to gather the points of view of each party. If it is determined that the wife has fulfilled her duties to the husband and has not invited physical punishment, the *imam* will reproach the husband and demand that he change his behavior. If these measures fail to improve the husband's behavior, the wife can then turn to males in her own family who can ask that greater pressure be placed upon the husband from within his clan. If all efforts to redress the situation fail, the woman's remaining option is to leave her husband and children in order to return to her father's home. While the outlined course of action represents a shared understanding of the appropriate procedures for grappling with severe cases of physical abuse, in practice every case is treated individually and depends upon the reputation and status of the husband as well as the relationship between the two spouses' clans.

Following traditional practices, Felis first contacted her husband's elder male relatives. While one of her husband's uncles who lived in Milltown conceded that his nephew was "no good," and agreed to speak with him about treating Felis better, he told Felis not to expect her husband to honor his advice and encouraged her to contact a local *imam* about the situation. The *imam* came to Felis' house, spoke with her husband and Felis separately, and then with members of each of their families. Based on all of their perspectives, the *imam* cautioned the husband not to hit his wife again and told Felis to heed her husband's will. Importantly, he concluded that, based on all he had heard about the husband, Felis had his permission to call the police should her husband become violent again. Rather than end the marriage as she had hoped, Felis followed the *imam*'s advice. In subsequent conversations with Patti, Felis explained that she no longer loved her husband and in fact had come to hate him, but felt that she had to remain in the marriage because "people told me he was bad and now they say, 'We told you; now you must stay with what you decided.'"

When we spoke with Felis 2 years after the initial incident of physical abuse, she continued to live with her husband, who spent his nights "chewing *khat*" with friends as Felis attended to their six children. He also retained seasonal employment, which the *Imam* had helped him to locate around the time of Felis' original complaint. Felis explained that, while her husband remains emotionally abusive and frequently threatens to leave her if she does not bear another child, he is careful not to give her reason to call either the police or the *imam* again. Rather, he insists that she stop attending school and remain home to care for him and their children.

Fatima's and Felis' stories reveal a variety of gendered regulatory dynamics at play throughout the Somali community, as well as the allure of other ways of being a woman encountered through multinational journeys and everyday life in the United States. The women's experiences make plain schooling's function as a space and process through which Somali women mark the contours of (dis)respectability within a new cultural landscape. Through choice of dress, attitude toward those who offer critique, or willingness to disobey family and community wishes in regard to divorce, marriage, and abuse, can women demonstrate a desire to resist traditional to ideals of Somali womanhood upheld within the Milltown Somali community. Over time, however, both of the women in our study who initially rejected conformity began to respond to community pressure and progressively conceded to family and community wishes. Initially willing to break with expectations, the corresponding backlash from within the community made the women increasingly cautious. While she had once been willing to risk disapprobation by marrying against her family's will, Felis' peers' warnings with regard to the proper etiquette for addressing domestic abuse had not fallen on deaf ears. Accordingly, Felis followed culturally prescribed guidelines for handling domestic abuse, even though the outcome was years of unhappy marriage rather than divorce, as she had hoped. Similarly, while Fatima had divorced her first husband and married her second against her parents' wishes, she rejected an opportunity to pursue a relationship with a Christian man who treated her well because she perceived that family and community would not approve; in Milltown, she adopted increasingly modest styles of dress; and finally, having experienced an instance of dramatic public rejection as well as more implicit, routine acts of exclusion from members of the Somali women's community at MAEC, Fatima elected to take on a more traditional Somali wife's lifestyle, spending the vast majority of her time at home caring for her children and fulfilling marital duties. Despite her efforts to reconcile with her peers, Fatima continues to experience social rejection. Perhaps as a signal to other women, Somali women are unwilling to accept Fatima's gestures of compliance and continue to marginalize her from the women's community. Such persistent exclusion, while rare, is not limited to Fatima; we know of other instances in which Somali women are excluded because they are perceived to have broken with fundamental ideals of Somali womanhood.

Halima joined Patti's ELL class. Married with several children, Halima comes regularly to MAEC, attending 2 consecutive 2 hour classes every weekday morning. After living for several years in Milltown, she has established a network of female friends at MAEC with whom she carpools, shares information and gossip, and struggles to learn English. Late one summer, Halima stopped attending school, and word spread that she had left her husband after local elders' efforts to smooth over tension in her marriage had failed to stop frequent instances of physical abuse. Halima's decision to leave her husband was widely disapproved of within the women's community at MAEC. She was blamed for breaking up her family and failing to respect both the authority of her husband and the wishes of community elders. After Halima contacted the police and gained a protection order preventing her husband from nearing their home, one member of our class and former friend of Halima's took the husband into her home. Another class member stated matter-of-factly, "Yes, is bad her hurt, but is the way. She is wife and children. Listen to husband is the way for woman." For her part, Halima acted with resolve, spreading word among her former friends that "Africans are backwards" and need to change how they think about domestic abuse and women's roles within the United States. Angered by her previous friends' willingness to shun her, Halima declared that from that point forward she would have nothing to do with other Africans and would only interact and establish friendships with Americans, even to the point of cutting off relations with the woman who had originally taken her in after incidents of physical abuse. Reportedly, Halima, who stopped attending classes, goes about her daily life without contact with other members of the Somali or larger refugee community in Milltown. Instead, she largely stays within her home, cares for children and refuses to discuss the possibility of reconciliation with her husband, family, or larger community. By leaving her husband, Halima aborted the course of action deemed appropriate for handling domestic abuse. As a result, she is viewed as having abandoned her responsibility to husband, family, and community, as well as to the reproduction of appropriate and traditional Somali gender roles. Just as in Fatima's story, Halima's actions are thought to invite exclusion and chastisement from other Somali women. In both cases, the punitive treatment of transgressive acts send a cautionary message to women in the larger community.

Defining Acceptable Gender Change

While MAEC serves as a space in which women actively etch out parameters of belonging and exclusion, work at the boundary of community isn't always as straightforward as in Fatima, Felis, and Halima's situations. While the polarities of acceptability and transgression are marked on the one hand by women who adhere to their place within the traditional patriarchal Somali social structure and on the other by those few women who dare to break markedly from established ways of being, most of the women at MAEC exist within the vast middle ground between these extremes. Each of the women in our study works to balance necessary adaptive concessions against culturally relevant standards of conduct. Rather than individual acts of meaning making, these negotiations occur dialogically as the women engage one another in the process of thinking through and responding to change. In these exchanges, both Islamic law and Somali tradition are evoked and referenced as guidelines marking proper ways of being women. Not surprisingly, however, such directives are themselves often contradictory and subject to interpretation, thereby opening up instances of ambiguity, disagreement, and transformation. While in some cases, such as the covering of one's hair in public, the women seem to have reached a shared level of understanding, establishing boundaries of acceptability is often a contentious process in which the women collaboratively—though not always harmoniously—draw upon heteroglossic notions of what proper Somali womanhood should look like given women's journeys and experiences in a new time and context. The specific terms of acceptability are forged with particular regard to finding new ways of expressing a customary commitment to marriage and childrearing.

Somali Women and Dress

During the course of our research, every Somali woman at MAEC—regardless of class or regional roots—covered her head with a tight scarf, loose shawl, *hijab*, or *burkha*. While considerable diversity exists among choices of head coverings or levels of skin exposure around the hairline and neck, the majority of Somali women in Milltown wear *hijabs*, and little debate exists around this practice. Berns McGown (1999) identifies the increased prevalence of the *hijab* among Somali women as a reinscription and revitalization of Islamic religious devotion in particular. She describes Somalis resettled in Toronto and London:

> Most of the adults ... have a heightened awareness of their religion, regardless of how positive or negative they feel about their existence as refugees

and immigrants.... Prior to their emigration, their religious and cultural identity was something that they could take for granted and not pay much attention to. After emigration, it has become a focal point in their lives. Far from contemplating "assimilation," they tend to take steps to make religion—as opposed to Somali nationalism or even clan loyalty—the primary material of their identities.... Many women newly wear the hjiab, and women frequently spoke of community pressure to dress in a 'Muslim' fashion, which they had not felt in Somalia. (p. 96)

While we can neither confirm nor disprove Berns McGown's assertion of increasing religiosity in the diaspora, for their part, Somalis in Milltown tend, with few exceptions, to regard the *hijab* as a religious marker and source of pride. During one section of our ELL class, we read the beginning of Satrapi's (2003) illustrated novel *Persepolis: The Story of a Childhood*, which features Persepolis, a young girl living in Iran during the Islamic Revolution. On one of the first pages of Chapter 1, Persepolis describes (and cartoon pictures depict) girls' reactions to the mandate that they veil at school. The girls in the story play various games with their *hijabs*, mockingly pretending to be ghosts. As we discussed the chapter during class that morning, women reacted to Perspepolis' acquisition of the veiling practice by nodding in affirmation and offering terse appraisals, "good" and "very good." As the story drew to a close, the women elaborated upon their reaction, explaining that children (like Persepolis) often do not like veils. Several noted that their own daughters resist wearing veils, especially to school. However, they contended, "they don't know." For women and Muslims, they stated conclusively, "*Hijabs* are very good."

For the women, though little question exists around the merits of covering in general, variation does emerge in response to other specifications of dress. As we illustrate in Chapter 7, employment opportunities for Somalis in Milltown, particularly those with minimal formal schooling, remain limited, and almost any job is viewed as an opportunity. Certain jobs, however, demand that women remove the *hijab* and/or wear pants. Despite the efforts of Catholic Charities, local career services, and refugee service coordinators at City Hall to distribute information to local employers about women's dress as an expression of Muslim religiosity, certain employers, out of safety concerns or for more openly xenophobic reasons, refuse to hire women who resolve to wear the *hijab* in the workplace. Accordingly, women are often required to determine which concessions in dress they feel comfortable or willing to make in order to help support their families. One day in class, women began to compare whether or not in their experience employers allowed workers to veil. One woman informed the others that she remained in her *hijab* when on the job at a local outdoor outfitter and clothing store. Fawziya is a single woman and advanced ELL student who raises young children, cares for a handicapped sister, works, and attends school. Always dressed in colorful and stylish fabrics, Fawziya explained that she was allowed to dress "as she wanted" while at work. Indeed, H. J. Perkins, the company for whom she worked, has a good reputation within the Somali community and a large base of Somali employees. The company hires seasonally from the fall through the holidays, and during this time many women at MAEC take extended leaves of absence from school in order to work for the manufacturer. Familiar with the company's policies, women in the room nodded in appreciation of the privilege Fawziya enjoyed there.

After Fawziya described her situation, Shukri noted that, while she covered her hair with a tight, simple scarf (the kind most women wore underneath their *hijabs*), she was not permitted to wear a *hijab* at work because, as her boss maintained, it would pose a health and safety hazard. Shukri, who wore *hijabs* to school, works in the cafeteria of a local nursing home, where she serves food and washes dishes. Shaking her head, Fawziya declared that she would not have taken the job under such circumstances. Hamda agreed, saying she would refuse any work in which she could not wear skirts and veil, "because of the religion." Everyone in the room subsequently echoed the sentiment, hinting that Shukri was compromising her religious values as a result. Looking at the table, Shukri remained silent. Though Shukri continues to work without a *hijab*, it was clear from the conversation that her friends do not condone her choice.

In addition to discussion about the *hijab*, women engage in contentious conversations about whether wearing pants is an acceptable. Throughout the cold New England winter, almost every woman at MAEC remains in skirts—layering underneath with long underwear, pants, thick wool socks, and winter boots. While this practice is widely sanctioned, wearing pants alone is more controversial. A few women at MAEC, however, do forego skirts and dresses in favor of slacks and jeans. One morning, Rhoda pointed out to Patti that it was Somali women from Djibouti or northern regions of Somalia who wear colorful fabrics and are often willing to wear pants alone. "You can tell where people are from by the ways they dress. Djibouti is less strict than in Mogadishu." While such women are in the minority at MAEC, their dress habits are deemed acceptable and they continue to be included in the social networking and community building practices of the larger Somali female community. Nevertheless, more traditional women indicate that they would not engage in similar dress practices. "It is okay for them. That is their way," Rhoda explained, "but not for, most will not do that (wear pants). That is for men; for women, it is skirts."

While some women's preferences for pants are attributed to regional background and are largely condoned, women are expected to conform to the dress of the region from which they come. If a woman from a region in which pants are not worn by women began to wear pants while in the United States, she would face criticism. Ruqia, who had enrolled in classes at MAEC in order to get certified as a dental assistant, faced such censure around her choice in dress. Fluent in English prior to enrollment at MAEC, Ruqia quickly met the nursing program's requisites and began to work at one of Milltown's two major hospitals with an otherwise all White department staff. Though she always covers her hair in public, Ruqia dresses more "like an American" in pants and short sleeve shirts. She also offers her daughter the choice of wearing pants to school.

In part because of her choice of dress, Ruqia is constantly told that she is "becoming American" by those within and outside the Somali community. While many of her White friends and coworkers enthusiastically claim her as American and emphasize distinctions between her and the larger Somali community in Milltown, her Somali contacts often perceive markers of Americanization negatively. Though she finds commentary from both sources amusing and mildly irritating, Ruqia does acknowledge that years of living in the U.S. have fostered changes in her ways of being.

> It's so different, really.... Staying here is changing some people. Let me tell you the truth, it change.... Staying here longer...and learning different cultures, American culture, it just, you know, change you. Really, you just change automatically. Day by day by day by day.... I can see the changes in myself.

At the same time that she recognizes personal transformation, Ruqia laughs off notions that her choice of dress reflects her cultural, religious, or national self-identification. Rather, she refers to fashion, comfort, and pragmatism as factors shaping her preferences. During one conversation, Patti asked Ruqia what she considered to be the biggest personal change since her arrival in the United States. Ruqia answered quickly, "wearing jeans," and continued to explain how she had only worn dresses once or twice throughout the Milltown winter. After Patti asked what that change represented to her, Ruqia responded that it was simply a choice shaped by climate, which was too cold most of the year for dresses. Although she maintained that she liked her Somali dresses very much, and intended to don them in spring and summer, she described their incompatibility with U.S. life in northern locations. She explained:

> I like [dresses], yes. But, the dresses need open shoes—to look cute, you know?... Because they're dresses made for summer. I don't think the one who was building [the dresses] thought of America. There was no America in their vocabulary. It was just Arab country with hot, and Somalia, Sahara Deserts—that's all. They had not thought these American people need to

wear this type of clothes. So, I cannot wear those clothes—It's just like people going out ... in like a nightgown—It's still cold.

With such practical views underpinning her choice of dress, Ruqia lightly critiques those who read her decision to wear pants as negative or as indicative of Americanization. After being asked what it felt like to be out in public wearing jeans, Ruqia replied,

I don't really, really ... I don't see any difference. It's just another, a cloth—you know? But still, I could get from Americans looking at me—they say, "Wow, you're becoming American!" I say, "With what?" They're saying, "Jeans." I say, "Oh really? To wear jeans is being American?"

Rather than viewing dress as a concrete, symbolic identifier of belonging and exclusion, Ruqia understands indicates her decision to wear pants as indicative of climate as well as her hybrid cultural weaving, and further justifies her choice of dress as a reasonable response to local economic pressures. She notes:

I pick a little from you, little from here, little from there ... you know and *[clap]* mix it together. And do it. Either it'll backfire, or—it'll work out! You know, or it'll be good! But, I'm not just saying because I was born like this and raised like this. I have a friend, she got a job and they told her to wear pants. She say "From her dead body!" She will never ever wear pants. So I said, "Oh really, but the day you'll miss food stamps, you'll work".... And that's true! Because, [until you miss food stamps], you don't care. "I don't want this job,"—You don't have a choice!

According to Ruqia, her friend's rejection of pants occurs "because of religion" and, more specifically, because pants are seen as an invitation for inappropriate sexual thoughts from men. While Ruqia agrees that her friend's concerns are valid, she views unsolicited sexual musings as indicative of problems with men who lack better things to do or think about, rather than with women who wear pants to keep a job. According to Ruqia, men are too idle and women, in response, should wear longer shirts over pants and just "do their own thing." Regardless of her reasoning, Ruqia's friend still refused the job, a choice Ruqia interpreted as a privilege afforded her as a result of her husband's support and her access to general assistance. Ruqia, on the other hand, had supported her three children entirely on her own since coming to the United States. Ruqia tried to explain her logical approach toward dress to her friend, saying "Yeah, [but if] you're one day to be a single woman. Kids at home will be waiting for food. What's that will be there? [You'll] wear pants." In describing her friend's reaction, Ruqia concluded:

> She thinks that I'm just crazy; she says "No" I say "Only if you have an option, me I don't have an option in life." I don't have, I don't have me, I don't have an option. My option, you know what is my option? My kids to go to school. The day the kids will come out of school educated—that's all my option is.

In her conversations with friends and with us, Ruqia alternately frames her decision to wear pants as a matter of cultural change and practical necessity.

In relation to dress practices, women like Ruqia dialogically work to etch out parameters of acceptability and transgression. Thusfar, little consensus is reached about what comprises appropriate modifications in dress. While, in general, extremes—such as uncovering one's head entirely—are deemed unacceptable, a large middle ground of negotiation exists around appropriate practices of veiling and the decision to wear pants. Women continue to critique and monitor one another's behavior and practices against an ambiguous, shifting, and contentious code of suitability. Other areas of potential transformation within the Somali community, particularly with reference to a commitment to family, reflect this dynamic.

Marriage and Childrearing

Negotiation over what comprises acceptable forms of commitment to family is incomparably central to women's efforts to establish boundaries of acceptability and belonging within the Somali community. Despite its significance, however, given the diversity of women's experiences and the new circumstances within which they live, there is little collective agreement about what commitment to marriage and childrearing should look like. Like Fatima's husband, Omar, men are often described as burdensome to families as they "chew *khat*," fail to help with housekeeping or childrearing, and are often subject to long periods of unemployment. Conversations about the troubles of living with men occur frequently at MAEC, and often form a basis for solidarity building among women. One morning, Patti was working with a group of women in Jacqueline's tutoring room and Hawalul asked Patti whether or not she was married, had children, or had a boyfriend. Patti replied that she was not married and was not looking for a boyfriend. Hawalul agreed, nodded and stated that "men are trouble" and that she didn't want a man. She did, however, want to have another daughter, and had heard about in-vitro fertilization. Hibo, who was sitting next to Patti and had until that point been busily working on math problems, looked up to report that she had been married for 18 years but now she did not want another man. Nasra, the only woman in the conversation in an intact marriage, replied, "Men aren't good, but children are good."

On another occasion Yasmin, Fatima's close friend who lives in Milltown with her two infant daughters, shared her impressions of men. After Fatima had announced her marriage to Omar and his plans to move to Milltown, Yasmin described the fear and regret she felt for her friend, "Sometimes men just go. They take off and leave you with the baby." After thinking about Fatima for a few seconds, she continued to add, "I don't want a man.... Some are good. But most think that they are smarter than you. They are a nuisance." Alima, a learner in her 50s who raised eight children in Milltown and regularly attended our class, repeatedly refers to her husband as simply "no good." While she proudly describes raising eight children and often tells stories of her family, she does not hesitate to clarify that she and her husband are permanently separated and that she runs her family on her own. Such conversations in which women divulge negative feelings toward husbands occur quite frequently, especially among the older women whose marriages predate migration.

Despite expressed displeasure with men and the increased prevalence of divorce in the Somali diaspora (Affi, 2004), women often reaffirm the importance of marriage and mothering within the larger context of change. Countless conversations highlight the sanctity of marriage and motherhood, while single women are teased for not having a husband. One morning Amal noted, "In America, a woman doesn't have to have a man." Amal, whose husband had recently migrated from Africa to join her after she had raised their infant daughter and lived alone in California for 4 years, was complaining in class about her husband's return. Despite her lack of English proficiency and admission that in California she had rarely left her home, Amal felt she had managed better without a man. Fatima, who had negative experiences with both of her husbands and also raises her children on her own, countered patiently, "Everyone needs a man."

Another day after class, Nasra explained that Patti needed to get married because it would help to make her happy. Nasra, who had remarked on an earlier day that men were bad but children were good, was, at the time, married without children. To support her point that Patti would benefit from male companionship, Nasra asked Patti if she had a good job. When Patti responded that she did, Nasra noted with a hint of challenge, "money isn't all you need. If I come home from work upset, I have a husband to talk with, but if you come home and sleep alone, that upset just stays." Assuring Patti that she was "happy and laughing with her husband" and that "you need the company," Nasra concluded with a grim warning that when Patti got older she would need kids to take care of her.

Although she made a steady income, money would only stay in the bank and wouldn't attend to her. "In a year from now I want you to be married!" she said with finality.

On another occasion in class, Patti asked students to use question-posing phrases. When it was her turn, Hibo turned to Patti and asked whether she was married and wanted children. Hibo, who was separated from her husband of 14 years and raised 12 children on her own, announced that it was "no good single" and advised Patti to have her own baby rather than to adopt. Alima, supporting Hibo's point, told Patti that she should marry if she found a "good man." Even as the women acknowledge the presence of "bad" men, their comments nevertheless persistently idealize the institution of marriage. Interestingly, out of the members of class that day, which included Kedma, Salwa, Qamar, Alima, Hibo, and Fatima, only Kedma and Qamar actually remain in intact marriages.

Motherhood, too, emerges as a crucial aspect of women's work. One day, in order to illustrate the meaning of the word "move," Rachel asked if Sumayah, who was 22 and pregnant, if she could feel her baby moving. After Sumayah affirmed that the baby had been kicking a lot, other women began to describe their memories and feelings about pregnancy. When we got to Jalila, a slightly eccentric younger woman, she said simply, "No, I don't like children." At this point, both Alima and Sumayah looked at Rachel and incredulously repeated Jalila's words. Everyone began teasing Jalila, laughing and smiling. Kedma added, "but she wants a husband!" and started playfully patting her, suggesting sexual desire, and asked provocatively, "Why?" Jalila, shrugging, did not answer. As other women at the table continued to joke about Jalila's desire for a husband, Kedma touched Jalila's lips playfully. At this point, Alima started laughing very emphatically out loud and began speaking Somali. Alima eventually translated that, in direct opposition to Jalila, she did not want a husband but did want children. Declaring that her husband "is no good," she explained that she now takes care of her children on her own. As if to offer an alternative perspective, Sumayah interrupted Alima to say that she loved her husband, who was her cousin, and that, rather than enter into an arranged marriage, she had personally decided to marry him. Alima agreed that Sumayah's husband was very good but that, again, hers "was not good." As Alima and Sumayah compared experiences, other women in the class listened attentively and smiled with genuine pleasure as Sumayah described her considerate and loving husband. Kedma, the oldest in the class, and whose English was probably the most basic, nodded repeatedly and stated of Sumayah's example, "It is good!"

In this vivid example, Sumayah, who was pregnant and happily married to a "good man," is positioned as an ideal example of Somali womanhood in the United States. Though her marriage is nontraditional in the sense that it is monogamous, unarranged, and features a companionate dynamic, it successfully reasserts the significance of men's role within the family, as well as women's commitment to childrearing and close relationship with men. Jalila, on the other hand, represents an undesirable outlier. Despite urging from others, she remains unmarried and expresses a most unpopular disinterest in children. For her part, Alima represents a significant portion of the population of Somali women in the United States. Older than Sumayah, Alima fled Somalia at the height of violence, migrated to Kenya, and has started a new life in the United States. While Alima is separated from her husband and therefore fails to personally exemplify a form of ideal Somali womanhood, she deeply values her role as a mother and continues to support and encourage marriage among her fellow classmates. Indeed, out of all of the women at the table that day, Alima was most vocal in her valorization of Sumayah's situation. In her own way, then, Alima reestablishes notions of marriage and childrearing as integral to proper femininity and female responsibility.

On another day, Rachel had the class read an article on Ellen Johnson Sirleaf, the current Liberian president who recently visited the United States. The article reports that Johnson Sirleaf has solicited assistance from Liberians in exile in order to bring prosperity and peace to the struggling country. Most of the women in class had heard of Johnson Sirleaf and knew that she is the first woman to be president of an African country. As we went through the associated vocabulary words from the article, which included "exile," "survive," and "prosper," the women made comparisons between Liberia and Somalia. They noted that both had long histories of violent civil strife that had scattered citizens across the globe in search of safety. Nodding in response to Johnson Sirleaf's promises, Khadra announced that she believed women would make better presidents in general, because "they are the responsible ones" who "raise children" and do not "carry guns." Reflecting her own war experience, Khadra referred to the ways in which women in Somalia have worked to safeguard their children and bring about peace rather than instigate or participate in violent struggles for power. The class nodded in agreement that indeed women would be more responsible world leaders. As class drew to a close, however, Alima, who had initially agreed with Khadra, asserted that most women could not be president, though, "unless they decided to be like men" and prioritize work over family. Fawziya confirmed Alima's insight, stating that women in the class would not ever be president because of their commitment to family, and that one would have "to be like Hillary Clinton" in order to be a political leader. Despite the fact that both Hillary Clinton and Johnson Sirleaf have children and families, for Alima and Fawziya, a woman's emphasis upon career precludes a strong commitment to marriage and children.

While marriage and childrearing are stridently defended as ideals, in practice considerable flexibility exists around proper ways of doing both. Just as many women accept Rachel's independence, in the United States, where possibilities for women are expanded, younger Somali women are allowed, even encouraged, to take time before marriage to pursue higher education or other goals. As long as marriage remains young women's ultimate goal, their now-single mothers most often support their aspirations. Saba, for instance, is respected among the Somali community as a fluent English speaker and self-sufficient young woman, even though she has yet to marry. A cheerful and vivacious woman in her mid-20s, Saba was raised in Djibouti rather than Somalia. As a child during most of the war, Saba came to the United States with her mother and sisters. After some time in Ohio, however, she decided to move on her own to New England—a practice common in the United States, yet almost unheard of in Somalia. While her mother struggled to understand why she needed to leave, Saba explained that she was 21 and wanted to live and work on her own. In Milltown, Saba lives with friends, occasionally travels with other Somali women to parties in nearby cities, describes having career goals, and proudly asserted, "I am independent." She consistently wears her scarf loosely around her head, often revealing a woven hairstyle. Unlike Jalila or other unconventional women at MAEC, however, Saba is not chastised by other women. Frequently and proudly stating that she aspired to marry and have children but that she wants to be independent first, she is able to assure classmates of her primary commitment to family. Despite the fact that Saba deliberately crafts the period of her early 20s as one focused on education and independence, while most of the other women her age at MAEC were already married and bearing children, she successfully established herself as a strong supporter of family and marriage and, in doing so, reinscribes the norm.

Women's ability to negotiate the terms of their compliance to community norms also exists in reference to the generational shift from polygamy to monogamy. Again, in conversation, women lay out various structural options of marriage, and weigh each against desirable aspects of traditional Somaliness and the realities of post war social and contextual change. In their deliberations, women explore their own locality in relation to the intersections of various cultural idioms, including the traditional Somali commitment to large family networks, Western notions of romantic love, and perceptions of jealousy or camaraderie among co-wives. On one day in particular, discussion emerged that highlighted the various positionalities women occupy in regard to changing configurations of marriage and family. In class, we were working with adjectives that described emotions. When we began to explore the meaning of the word "jealous," some women immediately began to demonstrate their understandings of jealousy in relation to polygamy. The women explained to us that in Somalia it was common for a man to have two or more wives. Kedma illustrated this by holding up three, then two, fingers saying, "three women" or "two women." As typical of most of our class-room interactions, the ensuing conversation featured women's overlapping voices, as each built upon one another's examples and explanations of what polygamous marriage meant to them. At one point Kalifa, a kind, older woman with an endearing smile, who usually remains quiet but for an occasional outburst in Somali, stated in English that she used to be the first of three wives. Laughing at what she knew to be a tantalizing possibility in the United States, she explained that now it was "only her" because one wife had "got divorced" while the other, whose name is Alima, was still in Africa. Hearing the third wife's name, the student sitting beside the Alima in class nudged her friend and started to laugh heartily at the innuendo. Looking at Kalifa with clear bemusement, Saba shifted sassily in her seat and noted that Kalifa was now the only wife and therefore her husband's only sexual partner. Still facing Kalifa, Saba asked whether the older woman had ever gotten jealous of the other wives. Kalifa, who had been smiling up until this moment, immediately frowned and emphatically answered, "No!" Turning to her right, she hugged Jalila and then Saba on her left to demonstrate friendship and solidarity between herself and her co-wives. Fleshing out her sentiment in English, women around the table began to explain to us that indeed multiple wives could be family. Then, translating for their friend who had begun to speak in rapid Somali, women explained that Kalifa and her co-wife Alima had given birth to sons at the same time, which had been "very nice." Co-wives are able to help one another cook, clean, and care for children. Another woman in the class earnestly explained that multiple wives allow for the distribution of a man's attention. Placing her hand inches before her face she said, "So he no right here always." Sumayah, who had up until this point remained quiet, but held a grimaced expression, inserted that she was "jealous just listening" to this scenario. Kedma repeated that having more than one wife was "very good." Sumayah said several times more that the situation was something she would not want to participate in and that even listening and thinking about polygamy made her jealous.

For the women in our study, schooling provides a space and process through which to share and negotiate positionality in relation to highly contrasted beliefs about, and experiences of, the value of polygamous relationships. While Sumayah could not comfortably imagine sharing her husband with other women, Kalifa, who raised multiple children and ran a household in Somalia, appreciated the companionship and cooperation her co-wives provided her. In their conversation, the women reinscribe the importance of marriage and childrearing, even as they use classtime to explore shifting configurations of ideal family life. In doing so, study participants work dialogically to adapt ideals of Somali womanhood to shifting realities of time and place. While the majority of women at MAEC do not face cultural regulation to the same extent as Fatima and Halima, through teasing, lecturing, and displays of disdain, the women more implicitly manage one another's decision making and behavior.

Conclusion

The Somali women in our study mark the boundaries of community belonging through dialogic differentiation between terms of acceptable and objectionable gender change. Through communication (sometimes verbal, but often just as poignantly through silence and exclusion), women trace the contours of a remembered ideal womanhood within new formulations of family and community evolving in the United States. In their efforts to build and regulate community, Somali women at MAEC license those gendered ways of being that are seen to foreground a primary commitment to serve the family as wives and mothers, if within new materializations, and simultaneously mark choices deemed intolerable. The everyday conversation, body language, and patterns of interaction through which women engage in processes of negotiation between terms of acceptable and objectionable gender change are most often light-hearted and punctuated with laughter. Nevertheless, the women's interchanges possess an implicit power to regulate one another's ways of being women in the United States. In rare instances when subtle efforts fail to suppress gender practices and ideals deemed transgressive, communications become more punitive and exacting in nature. Those who actively resist gender regulation and cling defiantly to their own patterns of cultural weaving or heritage work, lose full access to social support structures and are relegated to the fringes of community. Through lively—sometimes friendly, sometimes embittered—interchange, women use schooling to assess, normalize, and prescribe what it might mean to be good Somali women in the United States. Amidst far-reaching change in the social organization of Somali family and community as a whole, women at MAEC work together to integrate understandings and opportunities brought about through multinational journeys and identities, with invocations of Islam and Somali tradition. In doing so, they produce unique and hybrid Somali-specific expressions of religiosity, respectability, and commitment to family. Because both Islam and Somali tradition are subject to interpretation, the women's reference to them necessarily invokes a moving target. With so many potential expressions of womanhood, a significant grey zone exists between the polarities of ideal and transgressive ways of being Somali women. Accordingly, many potentially controversial issues pertinent to Somali women's everyday lives remain unsettled, works-in-progress.

CHAPTER 13

EDUCATED FOR CHANGE?

Some Concluding Thoughts

We began our examination of Somali refugee women's lives by asking what role newfound access to schooling plays in shaping cultural change at the confluence point of the West and Islamic East. We note that transformation is not only about location: the move across national borders into foreign lands. Nor, is it encapsulated as personal, social, cultural, political, and economic in nature. Significantly, understanding the nature of change concerning forced migrant Somali women entails an appreciation of the variant, often contradictory, perspectives of multiple stakeholders. Humanitarian aid policymakers and practitioners, Kenyan nationals, American liberals and nativists, Somali traditionalists, moderate members of the refugee community, Western researchers, social theorists, and multiethnic refugee peers have all developed orientations to Somali girls and women's schooling that reflect particular standpoints, self interests, and imagined futures. Some herald the education of Somali girls and women as pure progress; others perceive it as an unforgivable rape of Somali culture. Most importantly, a variety of nuanced views populate the territory between such extremes. It is in the middle ground that we find the most promise for the improvement of relations between the Islamic East and the West.

Educated For Change?: Muslim Refugee Women in the West, pp. 305–322
Copyright © 2012 by Information Age Publishing

Contexts: Traditionalism Versus Westernism in Dadaab and Milltown

Somalis' political, religious, and cultural identities are dynamic and have long been shaped by the push and pull of multiple spheres of influence, struggle and adjustment. In Chapter 2, we note that traditionalism is a fluid concept that has evolved throughout Somali history. Somalis' diverse and shifting notions and utilization of clan, *xeer*, and interpretations of Islam speak to the ways in which the strength and quality of familial, political, and religious authority morphs across Somali history. By extension we note that, while treated as static and essential within the contexts of Dadaab and Milltown, in fact, Somali traditionalism is nothing of the sort.

Whether a Somali refugee finds herself living out her life in a Dadaab camp or is granted a coveted resettlement slot in the United States, she faces an ever-evolving administration of Somali traditionalism. In the former case, she also confronts a similarly emergent understanding of female empowerment as promulgated by the UNHCR. In the latter scenario, a particularized brand of Somali traditionalism plays against a contentious meeting of American liberalism and nativism. In Chapters 3, 4, 8, and 9, we establish that, as spaces of cultural encounter between the Islamic East and the West, the Dadaab and Milltown landscapes are fraught with tensions, barriers, and moments of possibility. Seen through the lens of school practice, we note that life in Dadaab and Milltown catalyzes myriad forms of change and gives shape to unique transformations in cultural identity among Somali women.

In the refugee camps of Dadaab, Somalis encounter the UNHCR as a pseudo-state whose local authority is near absolute. Policies enacted by the UNCHR and its implementing agencies control most aspects of refugee life—from provision of their food and water to their sanitation, education, medical care, access to shelter, land, and firewood, and so forth. The UNCHR, coupled with Kenyan police on the ground in Dadaab, also enforce a restriction of refugee movement. Of course, for all of the ways in which the UNHCR limits the autonomy of Somalis granted asylum on Kenya soil, it also provides the assistance that sometimes separates life from death (and perseveres despite increasingly frequent declines in funding and relatedly, donor government interest). Agency agendas extend beyond simple life-saving measures. Paternalistic efforts to affect cultural change, for instance, emerge in campaigns against female circumcision, "wife-beating," or gender inequity; and, some might say, the inclusion of girls in schooling.

These efforts, often transmitted via a language of enlightenment, are met with an emergent traditionalist ideology, self-consciously enacted by members of the Somali community concerned about shifts in existent ways of being. Emergent traditionalism represents a strong counter pull to enlightenment discourse and, when brought together, the two countervailing forces result in a polarized sociopolitical terrain. Just as the UNHCR provides much of the limited economic opportunity available in Dadaab, traditionalist leaders among the Somali community exert tremendous social control through regulation of belonging and exclusion, honor and stigma. We see in Chapter 4 that traditionalists look upon UNHCR governance as a form of imperialism shrouding a Christian proselytizing mission. Dadaab's landscape is characterized by a social and political bipolarity, that refugees must respond to with insight, care, and creativity.

Youth are well aware of the schism that divides Dadaab and react to it with a wide range of orientations. Some share traditionalist perspectives; a few espouse a completely Western outlook. Most navigate a middle ground in which they lament the lack of political autonomy and substandard living conditions Somali refugees must endure in Dadaab, even as they express appreciation for humanitarian aid and access to schooling.

Thousands of miles across the diaspora, Milltown provides a stark contrast to the refugee camps of Dadaab. In Chapter 9, we note that on U.S. soil, a tripolarity structures the landscape. In Milltown, Somali Muslims are no longer in the majority, but rather have come to embody cultural and religious difference in a once largely homogenous, White, Christian community. Ironically, in the United States, the dominant conservative discourse finds expression in a strongly anti-immigrant, anti Muslim, and anti-Somali (nativist) perspective. Of course, emergent Somali traditionalism is also present. In Dadaab, enlightenment voices articulate a universalized human rights discourse. By contrast, in the United States, enlightenment ideals come to the fore via a liberal ideological framework in which newcomers are viewed sympathetically as victims of political violence and potential future economic and cultural assets to the U.S. nation. In Milltown, liberalism shapes the schooling to which refugees have access. At the level of adult basic education, pedagogy and curriculum are anachronistically focused on the acquisition of industrial-era work skills and employee/employer relations, that scarcely exist in the twenty first century United States. The effect is to undermine the democratic potential of schooling to produce informed citizens ready to fully participate in the cultural, civic, and economic life of their new community.

Women in Schools

Responding to Enlightenment and Liberalism

Girls and women in Dadaab are offered novel opportunities even as they face considerable challenge. They are encouraged to apply themselves academically in constant competition for tremendously limited scholarships and poorly remunerated incentive work. Female students face resistance that occasionally escalates to physical violence at the hands of Somali traditionalists, some of whom include male classmates. In Chapter 5, we identify some of the ways young women make use of schooling as a space and process through which to make sense of their new positionality. With access to formal education, young refugee women distinguish themselves as leaders of an imagined future Somali (diasporic and physical) nation; carefully adopt tenets of enlightenment discourse; and, appropriate rights-based discourse to critique aid agencies and the limitations a protracted refugee scenario imposes.

Similarly, in Chapter 10, we demonstrate that schooling in Milltown also offers a space and process for women to negotiate a local terrain marked by countervailing sociocultural worldviews. Refugee students in Milltown work to enact a form of Somali womanhood that both values education and pointedly critiques perceived faults in American society. In Chapters 6 and 11, we note that women in both Dadaab and Milltown claim membership in a global citizenry through interest in and interaction with different ways of being to which they are exposed as transnational migrants.

In Chapter 7 and 12, we find that through intragroup dialogue, Somali female students actively develop new ways of being Somali women that prove compatible with moderate interpretations of Islam, *xeer*, and access to Western-style education. They do so by discursively distinguishing culture and religion, staking out moderate positionalities on the continuum between cultural continuity and change, and identifying extremes in identity change that, in their assessment, stray too far from the more moderate space of compromise. Overall, they flexibly negotiate between the defining polarities of the particular locales in which they find themselves.

As a Whole

Whether in Dadaab or Milltown Somali women co-opt some aspects of Westernization including shifting from clan to class as a dominant marker of social status and belonging/exclusion, exploring new options for marriage and childbirth, showing a willingness to enter a Western based economy and society, and identifying as global citizens. They also maintain aspects of traditional Somali culture, such as dedication to family and community over individual gain; dress as a symbol of allegiance to Islam and their families and community; and alignment with moderate, though long standing, forms of Somali culture. Women also weave together elements of Western and Somali culture using traditional gender idioms to rationalize choices that might otherwise be viewed as Western. They justify delayed marriage and continued school participation with promises to care for family. They advocate a less drastic form of circumcision in to sustain a symbolic ritual, but eradicate pain, danger, and domination. They go to college to learn about community development and politics in order to lead Somalis toward a prosperous future. For Somali women in the diaspora, flexible citizenship takes shape in the movement between traditional and Western gender options, a movement through which they create a fresh set of options. Exercising flexible citizenship stretches markers of Somali belonging to include new ways of being Muslim women. In doing so, refugee women work at amending relations of power within the Somali community and between the Somali community as well as their Western host communities. While female students recognize their position at the forefront of cultural change, they do not want to abandon Somali culture wholesale. Nor, do they want to choose between Western and Somali ways of being. Instead, they try to weave the two in an elaborate, improvisational pattern.

(Flexible) Citizenship in the West

As we have seen, Somali women's work in school represents a form of flexible citizenship practice in which participants draw selectively upon proffered aspects of Somali and Western cultures. In her choice of nomenclature, Ong (1999) deliberately codes *flexible citizenship work* to the political realm. By alluding to the contract between the governed and the governing implied by the concept of citizenship, even as she offers a critique of such westphalian genealogy, Ong directs attention to the quality and nature of the relationship between governing bodies and newcomers as significant to the process of constructing a sense of belonging among newcomers. However, for Ong, the spheres in which such contractual actions take place are not simply civic. Rather, she construes such citizenship work rather broadly to include performance in cultural, economic, and civic spheres. Accordingly, she opens up new possibilities for theorizing governing authority. If, for example, active citizenship necessitates not only political representation and economic opportunity but also the expression of culturally derived mores, power brokers in the cultural realm additionally enjoy a contractual relationship with fellow citizens. And, of course, each realm of community/national life affects the other and each has an internal complexity, meaning that the governing bodies with which an individual or group might enter into a contract are numerous.

For women in the Somali diaspora, it is appropriate to conceive of participation in schooling as embroiling them in cultural, economic, and civic realms of production in which the localized set of institutionalized constraints and possibilities are shaped by various, often conflicting governing bodies. Study participants from Dadaab and Milltown have been forced from their homeland by violence and material deprivation. In crossing the national border of Somalia in response to political violence, they have automatically become a subject of international human rights law. Falling under the protection of the UNHCR opens up new opportunities, even as it complicates the long standing organization of their community according to implicit cultural principles—the heart of which concern gender norms and expectations.

While legally under the authority of either the UNHCR or the U.S. government and imbricated within Westernized sociocultural structures and practices, for the women, Dadaab and Milltown landscapes are in fact defined by the dominating bipolarity of Western enlightenment *and* emergent Somali traditionalist ideologies. As we have seen, traditionalists engender a worldview equally as encompassing as Western enlightment ideology and rife with its own ranked dualisms. Rooted in what feminist scholar Leila Ahmed (1992) refers to as a "technical, legalistic legacy of establishment Islam" (p. 242) traditionalists maintain that: men are superior to women; men occupy the public sphere while propriety circumscribes women to the private, domestic sphere; the East offers an elevated religious sensibility to the West's fixation with commerce and sexual depravity; and *Sharia* law is the optimal structuring social principle over individual choice and self expression.

Accordingly, when women in Dadaab and Milltown participate in schooling, they necessarily engage multiple master narratives, each of which is coded to particular imagined nation states. The nature of the citizenship practices called for from them in such imagined national communities varies dramatically. The nation of Somalia exists on multiple planes. There is the remembered peaceful Somali nation of the past in which women's prescriptions for citizenship contrasts the contemporary disordered Somali nation rife with gendered violence. There is an imagined future Somalia in which newly educated women envision playing key leadership roles. And, there is the diasporic Somali nation in which its citizens are bonded by a shared history and contemporary efforts to navigate new national environments in which they find themselves in the religious, racial, and ethnic minority. Beyond the multiple imagined Somali nations and corresponding forms of belonging, in Milltown there are the physical, legalistic, and imagined borders of the United States in which strands of liberalism and nativism compete to define and (re)define what it means to be belong or face exclusion. In Dadaab, the particular nation in question is a UNHCR-run territory that draws upon key tenets of Western nation building such as constitutionalism—for example, the 1951 Convention for the Status of Refugees—while selectively ignoring others, such as representative democracy. As a process then, Somali women's participation in schooling demonstrates a form of citizenship work that is inclusive of cultural, civic, and economic acts of belonging. Women's schooling is at once tied to nation and flexibly transcends of singular forms of national belonging.

While we can see that study participants actively attempt to engage all three forms of citizenship in their work in schools, their capacity to realize full rights in either Milltown or Dadaab is severely restricted. Take for example, women's use of schooling to realize a sort of flexible economic citizenship that makes use of the permeability of Western institutions in order to enact a new form of economic belonging in the diasporic Somali nation. In Dadaab to a person, Somali women who are able to secure employment within Western NGOs report using their pay to provide for their parents, siblings, and, oftentimes extended family. In doing so, they innovatively retain a family and community orientation, as well as responsibility for the domestic sphere that extends beyond the contribution of unpaid labor. We witness a rejection of the West's focus on the application of school knowledge for purposes of individualized social mobility. In the process, students lithely traverse two distinct sociocultural realms. In this example, we see participants exert agency as they actively negotiate a form of economic citizenship in two distinct spheres. Yet, their capacity to act as fully empowered economic citizens within the Western realm is severely restricted.

In Dadaab, while schooling often leads to incentive work for the highest academic performers, such positions are few and far between and increasingly available to only those rare few able to complete secondary school. Accordingly, the vast majority of young women who attend school in Dadaab likely face decades, even potential life times, of unemployment. Those who are fortunate enough to work for NGOs face the positions which pay very low wages, often in return for high skill labor. Despite bearing responsibility for high skill tasks, including highly translation, research, and report writing, teaching, and case management, workers have little decision-making power within the NGOs and have no leverage over working conditions or remuneration.

Those in Milltown face an equally bleak employment frontier. A post-industrial town with high rates of unemployment, poverty, and welfare dependency, Milltown offers few low skilled positions for newcomers. And, of course, as a whole the U.S. has an increasingly frail social safety net for those unable to secure employment, a weakening with particularly virulent consequences for women. Burbules and Torres (2000) write:

in an era of globalization, the consequences of the feminization of survival involve the increasing incorporation of migrants and women from the South, as the global world's newest proletariat, into the global capitalist activities of the North, all under severely diminished citizenship regimes. (p. 3)

Limited Economic Citizenship

For scholars, the performance of economic citizenship is based on the right of laborers to organize and bargain. However, such a right is only meaningful if local employers retain some autonomy. Such leverage is lost with the growth of multinational corporations which, rather than respond to demands made by of U.S. labor interests, increasingly turn to low skill labor sources in free trade zones outside the United States, where they are not accountable to local labor laws. Refugee camps are rarely, if ever, considered in theorization of economic citizenship, but it is easy to see that encamped refugees offer a pool of unemployed who will eagerly vie for excessively underpaid employment opportunity with employers with whom they have limited ability to bargain. As Woodiwiss (2002) adds:

> if the exercise of such a liberty [such as union labor demands] interrupts production, the corporation at the head of the commodity chain can readily reduce its orders or seek new suppliers and in this way render labour's local liberties and therefore the idea of economic citizenship largely meaningless. (p. 64)

From a labor standpoint, a form of global economic citizenship might offer redress to the opportunistic ease in which multinationals and, in this case, supranational organizations operate. Burbules and Torres (2000) argue that in weakening labor's influence over multinationals and [and, again, we add supranational organizations], grassroots democracy is enfeebled. For Burbules and Torres, while multinationals act in their own self-interest, the state is negligent in its reluctance to intervene. The state "withdrew from its role as an arbiter between labor and capital, allying itself with capital and pushing labor into a defensive position" (p. 5).

We note that in the case of refugee policy, the UNHCR, as a quasi-state, not only fails to act as arbiter, but in fact acts in the very same capacity as a multinational corporation with regard to refugee employment in camp settings. The product of that labor is the smooth operation of the very humanitarian aid regime, a regime that at once provides basic needs and denies freedom of movement and the ability to work for a fair wage.

A similar dynamic of limited economic rights holds true on U.S. soil where, taken together, the withdrawal of the state from labor interests and loss of autonomy among local employers has effectively undermined the ability of U.S. labor to bargain collectively. The detrimental impact of the dominance of neoliberalism at the federal level upon access to economic citizenship for those in the bottom half of a two-tier economy has significant consequences for the schooling of low-income newcomers from the global South.

Further, neoliberal faith in the market and disapproval of expenditure in the public sphere situates education as an economic drain that threatens international competitiveness. "Public institutions, like schools, are seen as 'black holes' into which money is poured-and then seemingly disappears—but which do not provide anywhere near adequate results" (Apple, 2000, p. 59). As we know, in the big picture of school policy in the United States, the state is exploring various privatization options including vouchers and choice plans, both of which promise the application of free market forces to education. In a similar vein, schools respond to funding pressures created by decreasing federal expenditure in the public realm by turning to the private sector for financial assistance. Channel One's contract with a number of school systems witnesses the penetration of commercial forces into the classrooms. As a result, students, for whom the state mandates school attendance, are subject to paid advertisements by various corporations (Apple, 2000). Alternatively, the neoconservative arm of the neoliberal umbrella aggressively seeks to further shift regulatory power to the federal level (Apple, 2000).

Together, these policies give shape to public school systems with minimal autonomy at the local level, increasing dependence upon local tax schemes that are dramatically unequal, and a mandate to serve a global capitalist order characterized in the U.S. by a bifurcated workforce and diminishing middle class. The effect is the creation of a tiered education system that mirrors patterns of socioeconomic and racial residential segregation (Kantor & Brenzel, 1993). Schools, which are keenly aware of the mandate to "reconsider their mission in light of changing job markets in a post-Fordist work environment" (Burbules & Torres, 2000, p. 20), shape their pedagogy in relation to the demographic profile of student body, offering rote and vocationally oriented education for the lower classes and stressing the acquisition of critical analytic and leadership skills among the future managerial, intellectual, and capitalist upper class (Anyon, 1980).

Within both the advantaged and disadvantaged tiers, students are seen as human capital worthy of educational expenditure only at levels that produce profitable rates of return. Apple (2000) writes, "The ideological effects of this are momentous. Rather than democracy being a *political* concept, it is transformed into a wholly *economic* concept" (p. 60). We see these dynamics enacted in the lives of Somali newcomers who attend underfunded schools operated without an appreciation for the students' desire and ability to have a voice in their education. Instead, schools favor a myopic focus on preparation for jobs that no longer exist.

In all then, whether in Dadaab or via resettlement in the West, the current international refugee policy limits economic citizenship of refugee girls and women and (re)situates resettled refugees at bottom of global neoliberal economies.

Limited Cultural Citizenship

A similarly restricted capacity to fully realize rights of cultural citizenship characterizes Somali women's work in schools. The practice of cultural citizenship includes ability to express culturally derived mores, traditions, ideologies, and ways of being without compromising economic or political forms of belonging or otherwise experiencing a loss of social status and efficacy. Discussion of cultural citizenship in the West first took shape as debate over identity politics and recognition in the post civil rights era.

One side of the dispute over identity politics argues that marginalized groups' efforts to end discrimination and freely express themselves culturally "have provoked widespread fear that assertions of group identity threaten national unity" (Minow, 2003, p. 67). Given such demands for recognition of the right to exist in various different and equal ways, those who idealize a common national culture worry that multiculturalism creates an environment in which newcomers will never assimilate to established ways of performing national identity. In this view, rather than absorbing newcomers, multiculturalism encourages immigrants to force their culture upon a so-called preexisting national identity. Racism raises the level of anxiety about immigration as a greater percentage of newcomers arrive from regions of the global South. Further, the steady flow of immigration forecasted into the future contrasts with historically sporadic waves of immigration. Comparing contemporary Jewish, Italian, Greek, Polish, and Slavic migrants of the twentieth century, Water (2003) writes, "These immigrants achieved their progress in an era ... [of] rising income equality and sustained economic growth" (p. 119). The opposite is currently true. Without a means of economic participation, cultural preservationists worry that new immigrants, denied similar opportunity and no longer subject to domination by majority cultural practices and ideals, will create an isolated criminal underclass.

The fears of antimulticulturalists are exhibited in Dadaab and Milltown. In Dadaab. Kenyan officials keep refugees circumscribed in order to avoid their entrance into Kenyan national culture. Under UNHCR jurisdiction, they are exposed to Western institutions as well as systems of reward and punishment that discipline behavior, and arguably, ideas. Indeed, refugee women have little or no control over their recognition within the quasi nation of the camps.

In Milltown, widespread fear of the expression of Somali culture is found not only in nativist reaction to newcomers, but also more implicitly in liberal efforts to acculturate newcomers into Western ways of being and within Western dominated institutional parameters that do not cede authority or give authentic decision-making power to newcomers.

Alternatively, proponents of multiculturalism argue that identity politics allow for the redress of oppressive marginalizations and therefore reflect and strengthen equality as a core national value. "Efforts to resist mistreatment on the basis of a shared trait naturally evolve into celebrating of the trait and seeking recognition and redress on its basis" (Minow, 2003, p. 69). Building this celebratory sentiment upon a postmodern understanding that any given individual enjoys multiplicities of "traits" or identifications means that there are multiple ways in which citizens can relate to one another. Identity politics in this vision become a unifying force that brings to light ways in which seemingly disparate individuals share characteristics and egalitarian ideals. Rosaldo (2003, p. 3) refers to demands made by "subordinated subjects" against the state on the basis of identity as cultural citizenship rights. Proponents of multiculturalism contend that cultural citizenship allows for a theory of belonging that does not rest upon the loss of cultural identity or core (quasi) national values (such as civil rights).

Whether in Dadaab or Milltown, schools serve as primary sites for cultural incorporation, as flows of new immigrants and refugees enter Western (quasi) national territory. We see study participants trying to enact forms of cultural citizenship as they engage in dialogue about gender salient practices such as dress, marriage, circumcision, political leadership, and the pursuit of education itself. Again, however, their capacity to realize full cultural citizenship is limited by context specific factors. In Dadaab, the realization of cultural citizenship is limited by the fact that Somali culture is treated as monolithically traditionalist even as the UNHCR takes it upon itself to eradicate traditionalist practices such as domestic abuse, circumcision, and early marriage. Because Somali culture is viewed monolithically, the UNHCR is reluctant to let go of any of its power into the hands of Somalis. Instead, it uses its leverage (through the provision of incentive work, scholarships, and resettlement opportunities) to divide the community and asks youth to join in the effort to undermine traditionalism. In a contradictory move, the UNHCR and its implementing agencies hold community meetings in which elder—frequently traditionalist—males are the only ones given voice thereby reinforcing the notion the traditionalism defines Somaliness and effectively silencing the very voices of change the agency has worked to foster. In the end, youth are treated as pawns in the UNHCR's efforts to affect cultural transformation without being given an authentic voice in the development of a narrative of contemporary Somali culture.

For its part, Milltown ends up the locale in which enculturation into an ironically anachronistic economic system takes place. As adult immigrants who, with emergent literacy and English language skills, are unlikely to enter into the paid labor force, participants could have used school time to offer democratic decision-making about their schooling, engage in community education about Somali culture in order to increase local awareness of the complexity of Somalia and its history, and participate in collective action to learn about and improve aspects of Milltown's community. Unfortunately, at MAEC, democratic cultural mores that would arguably emphasize voice and plurality of decision-making and potential contestation over what values and practices are to be institutionalized are overshadowed by the primacy of what are falsely perceived as pragmatic economic concerns.

Limited Political Citizenship

The restriction of economic and cultural citizenship in both Dadaab and Milltown results in part from a similar circumscription of political citizenship rights. The practice of political citizenship includes engagement with legal institutions that make laws and the exercise of political power through voting and the ability to run for office. Alongside the erosion of economic rights principally affecting those in the bottom of the two-tiered economy, (and therefore disproportionately first generation immigrants of color), political rights traditionally granted newcomers are increasingly under assault. Efforts to limit external membership, which Janoski and Gran (2002, p. 13) describe as "how aliens obtain entry and then become accepted or naturalized as citizens" reflect this anxiety and subsequent hostility. In Kenya, political leaders have responded to the groundswell of anti-immigrant sentiment by restricting Somalis' entrance into the country in ways that repeatedly break international human law and delaying the passage of a national refugee rights law that expanded migrants' ability to move and work. Within the camps, the UNHCR teaches about, but hardly grants, citizenship rights.

In the U.S. increasing immigration from the global South is met with a wave of restrictive legislation. Barreto and Munoz (2003) write, "to an extent barely recognized in public debate, a series of recent laws and policies has radically challenged the old immigration regime. American society has been quietly reconfiguring the boundaries of national community and sacred notions of citizenship" (p. 132). Delineation of boundaries takes shape through curbs in the provisions of welfare as well as within the federal immigration bills of 1996 and 1998. The 1996 immigration law added an intent clause that states that a victim of discrimination must prove employer intent. Barreto and Munoz write of this clause that "in essence" it "legally sanctions stereotyping and bigotry" (p. 137). The 1996 law also erodes civil and citizenship rights through elimination of judicial review of USCIS's (United States Citizenship and Immigration Services, formerly known as INS) decisions. Noncitizens can now be arbitrarily deported from the U.S. if they cannot establish residence and likewise, political asylum seekers can be turned away at the airport. The USCIS can also adjust an individual's status without a court hearing. Additionally, while the 1996 law allows employers to access the USCIS database, which reportedly contains such errors in 28% of the cases, and there is no protection for workers who are victims of errors (p. 39). Finally, in 2002 the justice department ruled that local police can enforce violations of immigration law. To lend an appreciation of the new vulnerability of immigrants, it is a reportable offense not to declare an address change in 10 days.

Barreto and Munoz (2003) hold that, as a consequence of these recent laws and policies, tiers of civic citizenship have been created.

> Over the past decade, immigration policy, rather than helping to forge a national community, has threatened to create separate societies, subject to vastly different standards when it comes to fundamental rights-the right to work, to receive services, even to walk down the street without having one's status as an American questioned.

Such restrictions upon membership signify a redefining of U.S. democracy. "Tragically" Barreto and Munoz contend, "the United States has taken several steps down the path, perhaps more precisely a slippery slope, of weakening core democratic principles" (p. 142)

In his *Educational Regimes and Anglo-American Democracy,* Manzer (2003) explores the assertion that the marginalization of civil society by global capitalism minimizes the role schools play in the production of civically engaged citizens. While the traditional goal of public education for democratic citizenship continues to be endorsed by governing agencies, Manzer maintains that responses to the dynamics of technological change and globalization, "give higher priority to the economic role of individual learners as future workers rather than to their political role as future citizens" (p. 301).

Even as educators and policymakers turn away from curricular and pedagogical prioritization of civic education, the increasing reliance upon the free market fosters a culture of individuality that inhibits coalition building. Stromquist (2002) articulates this point, noting that the justification for moving factory work abroad is couched as an unassailable capitalist prerogative regardless of the impact it has on American workers, the economy, or the civic sphere. She writes, "the assumption therefore is that the common good is unproblematically the sum of the individual preferences rather than a hard-won compromise on many issues" (p. 37). Burbules and Torres echo that neoliberal values, "promote less state intervention and greater reliance on the free market, and more appeal to individual self interest than to collective rights" (Burbules & Torres. 2000, p. 9). Apple (2000) argues more specifically that school choice detracts from the potential for radical collective action dealing with social inequalities in spheres outside of education. Indeed, the very language of educational social justice has been co-opted within the neoliberal paradigm. As Stromquist (2002) writes:

> In the United States, equity is invoked in assertions about "ending the injustice of social promotion," "holding all students to the same high standards," and creating "world class schools." Unfortunately, the translation of this principle into the specific mechanisms of school and student accountability ends up placing blame for failure on students, parents, teachers, and schools, while the real causation is more complex (depending on interactions among sociological, cultural, economic, and pedagogical factors). (p. 41)

The alignment of the education system to the global capitalist economy and the reduction of genuine attention given to social inequity concerns in school have particular impact upon the ways in which schools address pluralism and the nature of cultural citizenship accentuated in an era of global mobility.

In all, Somali women enjoy severely limited political decision-making power and have minimal-to-nonexistent access to quality education over which they exert influence. Perhaps reflecting a knee jerk reaction against the loss of power felt in domains previously controlled at the state level, in the global North, national education policy increasingly centralizes the governance of educational systems and processes. Burbules and Torres (2000) argue that the overall impact of neoliberal versions of globalization is, "reflected in an education agenda that privileges, if not directly imposes, particular policies for evaluation, financing, assessment, standards, teacher training, curriculum, instruction, and testing" (p. 15). In the U.S. and other postindustrial nations of the global North, the centralization of authority, reduction of public expenditure, increasing regulation and punitive accountability systems, commercialization and privatization, and alignment with economic versus civic or social justice concerns, produce two-tiered school systems that do not equally serve the needs of female newcomers from the global South. Underresourced urban school systems that serve majority minority communities feed the unskilled female labor force at the bottom half of the economy. "Education is complicit in the production of the 'docile and unskilled worker in foreign controlled enterprises' " (Blackmore, 2000, p. 136). Further, the centralization of educational authority means that Western feminists, who might have worked in partnership with immigrant and refugee communities, can no longer influence education policy, for, as local actors, they have been cut off from the power source.

In Milltown, neoliberalism has resulted in adult education that denies women political voice. Abysmally under resourced, MAEC offers citizenship classes that feature static versions of American history and government acquired through rote memorization. Refugees have no say over the determination of curriculum or pedagogy and interactional dynamics between faculty and students reinforce social status inequities between White middle class teachers and refugees.

In the global South, education policy is similarly subject to the hegemony of neoliberalism. Western anxiety over shifting global geographies of power (Sassen, 1996) has manifested in foreign aid policies which feature conditionalities that tie aid to enactment of neoliberal economic policy (Koeberle, Bedoya, Silarsky, & Verheyen, 2005). As a result, governments in the global South have not had the latitude to invest in public education to the extent that they might have preferred. Ironically, development policy has recently emphasized the importance of attaining universal basic education in the global South and made significant financial commitments to accomplishing an ambitious goal of attaining universal basic education by 2015 as laid out in the Dakar Framework of 2000 (UNESCO, 2000). The twinning of conditionality and the Education For All (EFA) agenda produces a neo-colonial arrangement of power in which Western supranational coalitions, such as the UNHCR, maintain significant control over the development of educational systems throughout the global South. While EFA and the Dakar frameworks increase girls and women's access to education, they are part of a larger geopolitical ecology that limits local control (just as NCLB does in the United States); thus, they circumscribe women's access to power even as they support a bifurcated system that produces a glut of female labor at the bottom of the economic food chain.

What we see overall, then, is a restriction of economic, cultural, and political citizenship rights for those Somali refugee women who have made their way into the structured synopticon of the West. By implication, what this means for Islamic East/West relations is that those who speak from a Western standpoint might forestall impugning traditionalist elements of Muslim communities in order to reflect upon the West's ability to successfully foster democratic processes and structures. Rather than focus on the extreme elements of Muslim communities, Westerners could honor democracy's promise to listen to multiple voices and share decision-making power. Once the most marginalized members of our (quasi) national communities have real power, Westerners can engage in discussion about Islamic East/West relations from an ethical position.

What Somali Girls and Women Have to Say

While we, the authors, offer a critical analysis of the West's orientation to the Somali refugee community in general and efforts to educate girls and women in particular, it should be recognized that study participants have strongly positive opinions about schooling. Access to education gives them a language of hope and self improvement; in school, they enjoy a diversity of ideas, a sense of personal accomplishment, expanded parameters, and belonging to a larger, global community of the educated. With Somali girls' women's perspectives in mind, we posit that the implication of our findings that Somali women realize only a circumscribed form of citizenship in the West is not to stop increasing access to schooling. Rather, we argue through recognition and representation (Fraser, 2010) female Muslims can help make institutions, such as schools, more polyvocal and democratic. In doing so, women's voices can be heard more clearly in conversations about relations between the Islamic East and the West.

Unterhalter offers a useful way to think about the changes that need to be made in school policy affecting girl' and women from the global South. In her 2005 text *Gender, Schooling, and Global Social Justice,* Unterhalter argues that global social justice employs a complex understanding of gender as a process of connection and change and articulates a moral basis of legal rights. In this form global social justice is characterized as dynamic and responsive to the demands of equality, difference, and diversity. The method through which justice is achieved is through dialogue between various constituents and institutions tasked to deliver goods, services, and protect rights. The object for Unterhalter is to develop what Sen (1999) and Nussbaum (2003) refer to as "capabilities."

The capabilities approach is distinct from both the human capital and rights approaches. Whereas the human capital orientation aims at economic and social development or education for the sake of society and the rights approach rests on abstract principles of freedom, for Sen (1999), capability is about having options between various potential "functioning combinations" (p. 75). Ulterhalter (2005) characterizes functioning combinations as "what a person is able to do or be" as distinguished from preference satisfaction in human capital theory that may be based on rate of return (to family) without thinking about what else might be valuable to the individual in question. The nature of obligation in this framework is a willingness to enter into dialogue with multiple other groups and/or institutions in order to cooperatively develop a suitable ends. Obligation also takes shape as an evaluative prerogative to gauge how a girl's opportunity to achieve the education she values is constrained by social arrangements concerning teachers' pay and work, lack of resources to support learning, norms concerning the sexual division of labor in families, and the appropriate education for women combined with decision-making processes that exclude girls from voicing concerns relating to their education (p. 76).

Ulterhalter's (2005) form of global social justice shares much in common with transnational feminist perspectives in its articulation of justice as a process, rather than "on the basis of principles and procedures" (p. 32). According to Ulterhalter, transnational theorist Nira Yuval Davis, "engages a process of dialogue which entails rooting and shifting. Rooting encompasses recognizing one's own historical and national specificity. Shifting requires an alertness to the needs and histories of others, an appreciation of different perspectives" (p. 32). Here, obligations, as well as the bodies in which such responsibility lies, remain elastic and subject to change across time and space.

The problem with such flexibility lies in its lack of specificity. As Fraser (2005) notes, what is missing is attention to who is able to make justice claims and to whom/what body. If the stage is filled with multiple actors of various political formations, who is able to voice claims and who is responsible for hearing and responding to them?

In the theorization of justice as it applies to girls' and women's schooling in the global South, there is indeed a lack of consideration of the particular value girls and women place on education and how they come to do so within the context of various constraining/enabling social arrangements. By turning to Somali refugee women in order to assess what education means in their lives, we give ourselves material from which to ponder whether, as a global society, we have achieved the purposes to which we set out to educate refugees, as well as whether those purposes are appropriately prioritized. We are able to look at their participation in schooling and ask, is this bringing about the kind of change desired? Which, if any, form of justice is realized in the experiences, perspectives, and actions of the study participants? Do the women's perspectives, experiences, and actions call for amendments to various theoretical notions of global social justice?

Drawing on Unterhalter's notion of global social justice, we reach the following conclusions about the direction the West could to take in its approach to Somali girls and women's schooling that we propose would improve the West's relations with the Islamic East. We know improvements need to be made to schooling in order to enter girls' and women's voices into the conversation about relations between the Islamic East and the West. We know that the change that has to happen is to make schools reflect a greater polyvocality in its structures, curricula, pedagogy, and systems of reward and punishment. Somali girls and women demonstrate a desire to create such change, but structural forces limit their capacity, and thus, the realization of global social justice. This needs to change. We find that while women are able to claim global citizenship, they are prevented from realizing global social justice by various barriers. As we have seen, cultural barriers from within the Somali community are most often identified in UNHCR rhetoric, but, in reality, the women face socioeconomic, representational, and political barriers that are much more potent. The UNHCR and countries of resettlement need to provide services in a way in which power is shared with the refugee community, in a way that is careful not to merely listen to emergent traditionalists but to authentically take into account the range of perspectives that exist within the Somali community.

Unterhalter's (2005) dialogic approach to the realization of global social justice assumes a set of transcendent principles that adhere regardless of setting, even as the enactment of which necessarily looks different depending on context. For example, education policy in Dadaab could, in the end, work with multiple models. Dadaab could feature Somali speaking schools, schools with other than Kenyan curriculum, and coed as well as all female schools. In Milltown, the MAEC could hire more Somali teachers and aides as well as integrate a site-based board with significant Somali representation.

Clearly, while newfound access to schooling for Somali refugee women has led to profound transformation within the Somali community, it has not yet led to the realization of global social justice. However, as we have seen, Somali girls and women are ready to claim full citizenship rights. Their demonstrated acumen at flexibly negotiating between the various aspects of Somali and Western culture indicate that, once girls and women realize the capability to act as full citizens, relations between the Islamic East and the West will change accordingly.

AFTERWORD

Final Reflections On Our Project

Research does not occur in a vacuum; instead, the demand for reflexivity in all feminist inquiry means that feminists (we) must acknowledge that we work within a deeply inequitable global system. The best-intentioned efforts to decolonize the research process, particularly between researchers from the global North and participants from the South, are contextualized within exploitative patterns of extraction and exchange. Feminists have asked aloud whether such structural imbalances, at scales far greater than that of the research interaction, nullify efforts to make ethnography a meaningful exercise (Naples, 2003). This is an especially poignant question in the context of a refugee camp, and one that we have struggled with throughout the course of researching and writing this book.

We have sought guidance from feminist, postmodern, and poststructural scholars who have long examined the concepts of representation and voicing (see Dominguez, 2000; Gorelick, 1991; Harding, 1987; Hesse-Biber & Leckenby, 2004; hooks, 1984; Maguire, 2001; Mohanty, Russo, & Torres, 1991; Said, 1978; Smith, 1992; Spivak, 1988); the epistemological significance of lived experience (see Bar On, 1993; Collins, 1990, 2000; Harding, 1987, 2004; Mohanty, 1992; Naples, 2003; Scott, 1992) and relatedly, the role of identity politics in ethnographic research (see Dominguez, 2000; Hesse-Biber & Leckenby, 2004; Spivak, 1988). For each question probed, another complication arises. Perhaps the uncertainty—this constant need for nuance and the resulting dialogue that emerges in critical scholarship—represents the best of feminist endeavors.

Educated For Change?: Muslim Refugee Women in the West, pp. 323–327
Copyright © 2012 by Information Age Publishing
All rights of reproduction in any form reserved.

In our case, we recognize the complexity that each of our distinct identities presents in research settings characterized by profound inequity (such as that of Dadaab). Our ability to come and go from the camps—both nationally, at a time when refugee movement is restricted by the Kenyan government, and internationally, with U.S. citizenship—symbolizes the dramatic privilege we have in comparison with the many forced by circumstance to be refugees. Further, with the explicitly political goal of expanding socioeconomic opportunities for Somali girls and women and an agenda that is linked by default to what are at times more problematic consequences of Western, NGO-sponsored schooling on refugee communities, our project is not uncomplicated. It is these deeply troubling inequities and ethical complexities that we believe demand a critical and self-reflexive feminist epistemological stance.

We agree with Mohanty and other postcolonial feminist scholars who recommend that cross-cultural feminist scholarship include theorization of difference and historicization of research in "careful, politically focused, local analyses" (Mohanty, as cited in Naples 2003, p. 25). Accordingly, we have worked to critically position ourselves in Sassen's (1996, p. 5) "global geography of power." We have also chosen to view "voicing" as a politicized transaction—one that includes both the women speaking and the researchers (who) first mediate, and later edit, their speech (Gray, 2007; Hesse-Biber & Yaiser, 2004). We have worked to heed Harding's (2004) call to avoid erasure of a researcher's voice and theoretical inclinations from the text.

In both Dadaab and Milltown, our identities indelibly shaped our research, just as they uniquely position us to impact policy and pedagogy. Patti was hired as educational consultant for CARE Kenya and, in that capacity, co-authored a report with Rachel that describes the barriers facing girls and women's enrollment and retention in schooling for use by CARE's educational sector and the UNHCR. In Milltown, as teachers and tutors, we were each empowered to design and implement curriculum units at MAEC. As we acknowledge our identity-based sociopolitical locations, we aim to heed Dominguez's (2000) call to identify another element in our project—a "politics of love." For we also believe that transparency about love/affection in scholarly work is a crucial component of self-reflexivity.

For Dominguez (2000), one way to foster a production of knowledge both just and nuanced in nature is to shift from solely valuing identity and identity politics to acknowledging "love" as a relevant, and indeed, appreciated factor in research. She calls for "a different criterion of value—namely, genuine love, respect, and affection, not categorically 'identity'" (p. 365) to be applied to projects which seek to bring marginalized voices to the fore. She highlights the difference between a "love-based" criterion and "the salvage paradigm," and remains wary of liberal condescension endemic to much feminist research. Dominguez explains:

> Loving does not mean (a) presenting only positive characteristics of people in our writing; (b) eliding conflict, violence, or debate; or (c) feeling so guilty about our own geopolitically defined position that we treat those we consult with kid gloves, both in "the field" (i.e., when we are spending time with them) and in our published writings. (p. 366)

In all, we have spent years getting to know and sharing our lives with women in our study. We have sat together over countless meals and weathered the ups and downs of life over an extended period of time. We have appreciated the women's desire to access education and heeded the requests of young women in Dadaab that we shift from exclusively scholarly roles to become advocates, working to actively expand opportunities for tertiary education for refugee students by seeking resources and fellowships in the United States. As such, our scholarship has become ever more entwined with activism through our incorporation and expansion of the nonprofit organization Matawi 501(c)(3) (see below). It is undeniable that, in our work with women in Milltown and Dadaab, love/care for participants is as salient an area to note as identity, even if love, like identity itself, is not uncomplicated. We hope that this has come across in this book.

In some ways we could not be more different than our study participants: We hold different views on, for instance, sexuality and enactments of gender, than most Somali women in Dadaab and Milltown, and, as a gay woman and a Jew, bear different (at least stated) identity politics than all of them. These distinctions have admittedly been hard to grapple with at times, especially in the camp setting where gender norms differ markedly from those in the States and where homophobia and anti-Semitism were both expressed, though certainly not by all participants. That Patti felt comfortable disclosing her sexuality with only two women with whom we worked in all eight years of this book's conception and Rachel shared her religious identification in Milltown but not Dadaab certainly shaped our experience of the research process. Whether or not such choices were most appropriate is something to consider moving forward, especially after disclosure in this text. Nonetheless, it is the very grappling with identity and difference—the process of making sense of these choices, of when to reveal or omit information (the same process that, no doubt, study participants faced in interaction with us), in a context of love and mutual respect that we believe enacts the very politics that Dominguez calls for. It is these everyday moments of negotiation and dialogue which both define our process/project and that make conducting scholarship of this type most valuable to us.

However, our story continues. During the process of researching and writing this book, we decided to pursue a parallel, more activist agenda. We did so knowing that it complicates the scholarly project in certain ways. The years of 2007-2009 were largely devoted to the conception and incorporation of Matawi 501(c)(3) (www.matawi.org), as noted in the acknowledgments.

Matawi, which means "branches" in Kiswahili, supports education, civic engagement, and leadership development in the global refugee community. Through a range of programs and initiatives, Matawi seeks to responsively identify and nurture strengths, skills, and potential for growth across the diaspora. With an awareness that refugee needs and contexts are in constant flux, we currently emphasize facilitation of access to higher education for young women as well as the gathering and dissemination of refugee life-stories.

Regarding the first "branch" of Matawi programming, we created the Dadaab Young Women's Scholarship Initiative. As part of the Initiative, we seek to expand access to higher education for young women graduates from Dadaab by liaising with U.S. colleges and universities interested in helping intrepid scholars, like those featured in *Educated for Change?*, achieve their dreams of a college education. We conduct essay-writing workshops with young women in the camps who plan to submit applications. We hold meetings with admissions teams from U.S. schools, where we work to contextualize the applications submitted by young women in Dadaab. Through a range of strategies, we work to explain how a C+ or B− grade on the KCSE exam in the context of a radically underresourced refugee camp represents far more than a letter on a page. And, if an institution of higher learning in the U.S. is interested in funding a young women's education, we aim to cover secondary expenses such as plane tickets, clothes, and books required to get her prepared for an academic life in the United States. We also work to create local support committees, composed of students, faculty, staff, and communities members interested in being available for the young women scholars as they transition to lives as students in the United States. Finally, as part of the Scholarship Initiative, we fundraise to provide scholarships for young women to attend degree-granting programs across East Africa as well as supplementary KCSE study material for young women in the camps. For more information, please see www.matawi.org/scholarship.php .

In all, creation and implementation of the Dadaab Young Women's Scholarship Initiative has been a learning process, and we are grateful for the guidance we have received from partner organization Windle Trust Kenya, as well as from deeply committed international admissions representatives who have been generous in their advice to us as how to best present refugee applications.

Related closely to the Scholarship Initiative is our other "branch" of programming, in which we work to make refugee life stories and challenges more accessible to audiences in communities of resettlement. To date, we have primarily accomplished this through publication of *"They Were Very Beautiful. Such Things Are": Memoirs from Lewiston, Maine and Dadaab, Kenya.* In 2007 and 2008, we compiled the life stories of refugees in Dadaab and in Maine, as well as longer-term Maine residents, organized them thematically, and co-edited *They Were Very Beautiful* as an anthology of memoirs. 100% of proceeds from the sale of *They Were Very Beautiful* benefit the Dadaab Young Women's Scholarship Initiative. We plan to continue projects of this sort with ever-expanding populations in the future. For more information on this project, please see www.memoirsforchange.org .

Like research itself, the path of our work with Matawi is not linear, but shifts and realigns as we learn better how to navigate the terrains of both the nonprofit and higher education communities. In the next few years, we hope to expand the number of scholarships we are able to provide, and in doing so, bring more awareness to the plight of warehoused refugees in Dadaab as well as create another incentive for families to send their young daughters to primary school in the camps. There are many ways for readers to get involved and we would be honored by any form of your support. If you are part of an academic community and would like to help us strategize an approach to your own admissions committee, or for any other inquiries, please contact us as info@matawi.org. Please see our website (www.matawi.org) for any additional information.

We would like to close here with an excerpt from *"They Were Very Beautiful. Such Things Are"* that we believe well illustrates what it may look like in the future when refugee young women are able to control to what ends—and for what change—they are educated. The words below were spoken by one secondary school graduate in Dadaab:

> I hope that Somalia will get peace one day. It may be that the [future] president is now in the camp [among] those that are educated in the camp. They are the only people who can do something for Somalia, because in Somalia, their things have been demolished.... Those that have been educated in the camp can at least do something there. I hope that one day I will be the president of Somalia, simply because I have the experience of being a refugee and being in a foreign country. And I know the importance of being a patriot and being in one's country. Though I can't remember anything about Somalia, I was four, but at least I can feel [what it is like] being in a foreign country. That's my hope. (Buck & Silver, 2008, p. 393)

REFERENCES

Abdi, A. A. (1998). Education in Somalia: history, destruction and calls for reconstruction. *Comparative Education, 34*(3), 327-340.

Affi, L. (2004). Domestic conflict in the Diaspora—Somali women asylum seekers and refugees in Canada. In J. Gardner & J. El Bushra (Eds.), *Somalia—The untold story: The war through the eyes of Somali women* (pp. 107-115) London: CIIR and Pluto Press.

Afrax, M. D. (1994). The mirror of culture: Somali dissolution seen through oral expression. In A. I. Samatar & J. M. Ghalib (Eds.), *The Somali challenge: From catastrophe to renewal?* (pp. 233-252). Boulder, CO: Lynne Rienner.

Ahmed, L. (1992). *Women and gender in Islam.* New Haven, CT: Yale University Press.

Ahmed, S. M. (2004). Traditions of marriage and the household. In J. Gardner & J. El Bushra (Eds.), *Somalia—The untold story: The war through the eyes of Somali women* (pp. 51-68). London: CIIR and Pluto Press.

Aihwa, O. (1999). *Flexible citizenship: The cultural logics of transnationality.* Durham: Duke University Press.

Aikman, S. (1999). *Intercultural education and literacy: An ethnographic study of indigenous knowledge and learning in the Peruvian Amazon.* Philadelphia, PA: John Benjamins North America.

Anderson-Levitt, K.M. (2003). Local meanings of global schooling: Anthropology and world culture theory. In K. M. Anderson-Levitt (Ed.), *Local meanings of global schooling: Anthropology and world culture theory.* Palgrave/St. Martins Press.

Anderson-Levitt, K. M., & Diallo, B. B. (2003). Teaching by the book in Guinea. In K. M. Anderson-Levitt (Ed.), *Local meanings of global schooling: Anthropology and world culture theory.* Palgrave/St. Martins Press.

Anyon, J. (1980). Social class and the hidden curriculum of work. *Journal of Education, 162*, 167-192.

Appadurai, A. (1990). Disjuncture and difference in the global cultural economy. *Theory, Culture, and Society, 7*(2), 295-310.

Appadurai, A. (1996). *Modernity at large: Cultural dimensions of globalization.* Minneapolis, MN: University of Minnesota Press.

Apple, M. (2000). Can critical pedagogies interrupt rightist politics? *Educational Theory, 50*(2), 229-254.

Ashworth, G. J., & Graham, B. (Eds.) (2005). *Senses of place: Senses of time.* Burlington, VT: Ashgate.

Badran, M. (2007). *Feminism beyond East and West: New gender talk and practice in global Islam.* West Sussex, England: Global Media Publications.

Baines, E. (2004). *Vulnerable bodies: Gender, the UN and the global refugee Crisis.* Hants, England and Burlington, VT: Ashgate.

Bar On, B.A. (1993). Marginality and epistemic privilege. In L. Alcoff & E. Potter, (Eds.), *Feminist Epistemologies: Thinking gender* (pp. 83-97). New York, NY: Routledge.

Barber, B. (1997). Feeding refugees, or war? The dilemmas of humanitarian aid. *Foreign Affairs, July/August,* 8-14.

Barlas, A. (2002). *"Believing Women" in Islam: Unreading patriarchal interpretations of the Qu'ran.* Austin, TX: University of Texas Press.

Barnes, V. L., & Boddy, J. (1994). *Aman: The story of a Somali girl.* New York, NY: Random House.

Bakhtin, M. M. (1981). *The dialogic imagination* (C. Emerson & M. Hosquist, Trans). Austin, TX: The University of Texas Press.

Barreto, M., & J. Munoz. (2003). Reexamining the politics of in-between: political participation among Mexican immigrants in the United States. *Hispanic Journal of Behavioral Sciences, 25*(November), 427-447.

Bartlett, L. (2003). World culture or transnational project? Competing educational projects in Brazil. In K. M. Anderson-Levitt (Ed.), *Local meanings of global schooling: Anthropology and world culture theory.* Palgrave/St. Martins Press.

Berns McGown, R. (1999). *Muslims in the Diaspora: The Somali communities of London and Toronto.* Toronto: University of Toronto Press.

Besteman, C. (1996). Representing violence and "othering" Somalia. *Cultural Anthropology,* 120-133.

Besteman, C. (1998). Primordialist blinders: A reply to I. M. Lewis. *Cultural Anthropology, 13*(1), 109-120.

Besteman, C. (1999). *Unraveling Somalia: race, violence, and the legacy of slavery.* Philadelphia, PA: University of Pennsylvania Press.

Blackmore, J. (2000). Globalization: a useful concept for feminists rethinking theory and strategies in education? In N. C. Burbeles & C. A. Torres (Eds.), *Globalization and education: Critical perspectives* (pp. 133-155). New York, NY: Routledge.

Borjas, G. J. (1990). *Friends or strangers: The impact of immigrants on the U.S. economy.* New York, NY: Basic Books.

Bouchard, K. (2002). Lewiston's Somali surge. *Portland Press Herald.* Retrieved from Retrieved from http://pressherald.mainetoday.com/news/immigration/020428lewiston.shtml

Bourdieu, P., & J.P. Passeron (1990). *Reproduction in education, society and culture*, London: SAGE.

Bowles, S., & Gintis, H. (1976). *Schooling in capitalist America: Education reform and the contradictions of economic life*. New York, NY: Basic Books.

Boyle, E. H. (2002). *Female genital cutting: Cultural conflict in the global community*. Baltimore, MD: Johns Hopkins University Press.

Buck, P., & R. Silver, (Eds.). (2008). *"They were very beautiful. Such things are": Memoirs from Lewiston, Maine and Dadaab, Kenya*. Bangor, MA: Booklocker.

Burboles & Torres. (2000). Globalization and education: Critical perspectives. New York, NY: Routledge.

Burke, B. M. (1995). *Trends and compositional changes in fertility: California circa 1970-1990*. Paper presented at the annual meetings of the Population Association of America, San Francisco, CA.

Burton, R. F. (1966). *First footsteps in East Africa*. (G. Waterfield, Ed.). New York, NY: Routledge & K. Paul.

CARE Kenya. (2007). Appendix A. Monthly Data for February 2007. Dadaab: CARE.

Cassanelli, L. V., & Abdikadir, F. S. (2007). Somalia: Education in transition. *Bildhaan: An International Journal of Somali Studies, 7*, 91-125.

Cassanelli, L. V. (1982). *The shaping of Somali society: Reconstructing the history of pastoral people, 1600-1900*. Pennsylvania, PA: University of Pennsylvania Press.

Chavez, L. R. (2001). *Covering immigration: Popular images and the politics of the nation*. Berkeley, CA: University of California Press.

Collins, J. (2011). Language, globalization, and the state: Issues for the new policy studies. In T. McCarty (Ed.), *Ethnography and language policy*. New York, NY: Routledge/Taylor and Francis.

Collins, P. H. (1990). *Black feminist thought: Knowledge, consciousness, and the Politics of Empowerment*. New York, NY: Routledge.

Collins, P. H. (2000). *Black feminist thought: Knowledge, consciousness, and the Politics of Empowerment* (2nd ed.). New York, NY: Routledge.

Collins, P .H. (2004). *Black sexual politics: African Americans, gender, and the new racism*. New York, NY: Routledge.

Dale, R. (2000). Globalization and education: Demonstrating a "common world educational culture" or locating a "globally structured educational agenda?" *Educational Theory, 50*(4), 427-448.

Daniel, E. V., & Knudsen, J. C. (1995). *Mistrusting refugee*. Berkeley, CA: University of California Press.

Dawson, G. G. (1964). Education in Somalia. *Comparative Education Review*. 199-214.

deHaan, A. (2009) *How the aid industry works*. Sterling, VA: Kumarian Press

Democracy Now. (2003). *4,500 people rally in support the Somali community of Lewiston, Maine against Neo-Nazi rally*. Retrieved from http://www.democracynow.org/2003/1/13/4_500_people_rally_in_support

Dominguez, V. R. (2000). For a politics of love and rescue. *Cultural Anthropology, 15*(3), 361-393.

Fairness & Accuracy in Reporting (FAIR). (2006). *CNN's immigration problem: Is Dobbs the exception—or the rule?* Retrieved from http://www.fair.org/index.php?page=2867

Farkas, S., Dufer, A., Johnson, J., Moye, L., & Vine, J. (2003). Now that I'm here: What America's immigrants have to say about life in the U.S. today. *American Educator, 27,* 28-36.

Fattah, M. (2006). *Democratic values in the Muslim world.* Colorado: Lynn Rienner Publisher or Cairo: AUC Press.

FAWE. (2001). Girls' Education in Africa: The FAWE Response to EFA Highlights for the Year 2000.

Federation for American Immigration Reform (FAIR). (2004). Refugees and the Refugee Act of 1980. Retrieved from http://209.25.133.193/html/03202603.htm

Finnegan, W. (2006, December 11). New in town: The Somalis of Lewiston. *The New Yorker,* 46-58.

Fitzgerald, N. (2002). *Somalia: Issues, history, and bibliography.* Huntington, NY: Nova Science.

Fox, D. J., & Hasci, N. (Eds.) (1999). *Women's rights as human rights: Activism and social change in Africa.* Lewiston, NY: Edwin Mellen Press.

Francis, S. (2003, January 9). South Africans vs. Somalis: Some immigrants are more welcome than others. *VDARE.* Retrieved from http://www.vdare.com/francis/more_welcome.htm

Fraser, N. (2005). Reframing justice in a globalizing world. *New Left Review, 36,* 1-19.

Fraser, N. (2008). Scales of justice: Reimagining Political Space in a Globalizing World. New York, NY: Columbia University Press.

Fukuyama, F. (2006). Identity, immigration, and liberal democracy. *Journal of Democracy, 17*(2), 28-36.

Gardner, J. (2004). Section 1: Changing roles and responsibilities in the family. In J. Gardner & J. El Bushra (Eds.), *Somalia—The untold story: The war through the eyes of Somali women* (pp. 99-106). London: CIIR and Pluto Press.

Gardner, J., & El Bushra, J. (Eds.). (2004). *Somalia—The untold story: The war through the eyes of Somali women.* London: CIIR and Pluto Press.

Ginther, M. (2006, June 28). Minnesota group to visit Somali education system. *Minnesota Daily.* Retrieved from www.pbs.org/weta/washingtonweek/voices/200606/0628world0.html

Global Security. (2010). *Global security.* Retrieved from www.globalsecurity.org

Gordon, A. A. (2001). Women and development. In A. A. Gordon & D. L. Gordon (Eds.), *Understanding contemporary Africa* (3rd ed.) Boulder, CO: Lynne Rienner

Gorelick, S. (1991). Contradictions of a feminist methodology. *Gender and Society* 5(4), 459-477.

Gray, J. (2007). (Re)considering voice. *Qualitative Social Work 6,* 411-430.

Gruenbaum, E. (2001). *The female circumcision controversy: An anthropological perspective.* Philadelphia, PA: University of Pennsylvania Press.

Hall, K. (2002). *Lives in translation: Sikh youth as British citizens.* Pennsylvania, PA: University of Pennsylvania Press.

Hall Jamieson, K. (2007). *Comments.* Retrieved from http://communities
.annenbergclassroom.org/blogs/050206jamieson/archive/2007/10/03/
ask-the-expert-05-02-06-dr-kathleen-hall-jamieson.aspx

Hanley, G. (1971). *Warriors and strangers.* London: Hamish Hamilton.

Harding, S. (2004). How standpoint methodology informs philosophy of social
science." In S. N. Hesse-Biber & P. Leavy, (Eds.), *Approaches to qualitative
research: A reader on theory and Practice* (pp. 62-80). New York, NY: Oxford University Press.

Harding, S. (Ed). (1987). *Feminism and methodology: Social science issues.* Bloomington, IN: Indiana University Press.

Hardt, M., & Negri, A. (2000). *Empire.* Cambridge, MA: Harvard University Press.

Harrison, F. V. (2008). *Outsider within: Reworking anthropology in the Global Age.*
Champaign, IL: University of Illinois Press.

Hatch, T., & Honig, M. I. (2003). Getting beyond the "one best system"? Developing alternative approaches to instruction in the United States. In K. Anderson-Levitt (Ed.), *Local meanings, global cultures: Anthropology and world culture
theory* (pp. 99-120). New York, NY: Palgrave.

Haynes, J. (2005). Islamic militancy in East Africa. *Third World Quarterly, 26*(8),
1321-1339.

Heavy Handed Politics. (2006, October 22). Will Muslim immigration destroy
Western democracy? *Heavy Handed Politics Blog.* Retrieved from
www.drivethrupolitics.blogspot.com/2006/10/will-muslim-immigration-destroy.html

Herpa, H. (Ed). (2009). Proceedings of the 2008 Oromo Studies Association
Annual Conference held at The University of Minnesota Coffman Memorial
Union Great Hall on August 2-3, 2008. Minneapolis, Minnesota.

Herzi, S. H.-D. (1999). Against the pleasure principle. In M. Agosin (Ed.), *A map of
hope: Women's writing on human rights—An international literary anthology*
(pp. 244-249). New Brunswick, NJ: Rutgers University Press.

Hesse-Biber, S. N., & P. Leavy (Eds.). (2004). *Approaches to qualitative research: A
reader on theory and practice.* New York, NY: Oxford University Press.

Hesse-Biber, S. N., & D. Leckenby. (2004). How feminists practice social research.
In S. N. Hesse-Biber & M. Yaiser (Eds.), *Feminist perspectives on social research.*
(pp. 209-225). New York, NY: Oxford University Press.

Hesse-Biber, S. N., & M. Yaiser. (2004). *Feminist perspectives on social research.* New
York, NY: Oxford University Press.

Higham, J. (1955). *Strangers in the land: Patterns of American nativism, 1860-1925.*
Rutgers, NJ: Rutgers, The State University.

Hill, M., & Docekal, S. (2006, October). Somali immigrants fight government
raids: In Seattle, women lead protest to free their husbands and brothers.
Freedom Socialist Voice of Revolutionary Feminism, 27(5). Retrieved from http://
www.socialism.com/drupal-6.8/?q=node/618

Hirsi Ali, A. (2007). *Infidel.* New York, NY: Free Press.

hooks, b. (1984). *Feminist theory: from the margin to MAEC.* Boston, MA: South End
Press.

Horst, C. (2006). *Transnational nomads: How Somalis cope with refugee life in the
Dadaab camps.* Oxford, England: Berghahn Books.

Hussein, I. (1997). *Teenage refugees from Somalia speak out*. New York, NY: Rosen

Ibrahim, R. M. (2004). Women's role in the pastoral economy. In J. Gardner & J. El Bushra (Eds.), *Somalia—The untold story: The war through the eyes of Somali women* (pp. 24-50). London: CIIR and Pluto Press.

International Covenant on Economic, Social and Cultural Rights. (1966). Retrieved from http://www2.ohchr.org/english/law/cescr.htm#art13

International Organization for Migration (IOM). (2005). *CO Africa Quarterly Report: 4th Quarter FY 2005*. Nairobi: Cultural Orientation, International Organization for Migration.

IRIN Humanitarian News and Analysis. (2002). *Kenya: UNHCR head accepts Nairobi corruption report*. Retrieved from http://www.irinnews.org/report.aspx?reportid=29962

Issa-Salwe, A. M. (2000). *Cold War fallout: Boundary politics and conflict in the Horn of Africa*. London: HAAN.

ITVS. (2004). The immigration myths & realities quiz. *Independent Lens*. Retrieved from http://www.pbs.org/independentlens/newamericans/quiz.html

Jamal, A. (2008). A realistic, segmented and reinvigorated UNHCR approach to resolving protracted refugee situations. In G. Loescher, J. Milner, E. Newman, & G. Troeller (Eds.), *Protracted refugee situations: Political, human rights, and security implication* (pp. 141-161). Tokyo: United Nations University Press.

Janoski, T., & Gran, B. (2002). Political citizenship: foundations of rights. In E. Isin, & B. Turner (Eds). *Handbook of Citizenship Studies* (pp. 13-52). Thousand Oaks, CA: SAGE.

Jungck, S. (with B. Kajornsin). (2003). Thai wisdom' and glocalization: Negotiating the global and the local in Thailand's national education reform. In K. M. Anderson-Levitt (Ed.), *Local meanings of global schooling: Anthropology and world culture theory*. Palgrave/St. Martins Press.

Kagwanja, P., & Juma, M. (2008). Somali refugees: Protracted exile and shifting security frontiers. In G. Loescher, J. Milner, E. Newman, & G. Troeller (Eds.), *Protracted refugee situations: Political, human rights, and security implication* (pp. 214-247). Tokyo: United Nations University Press.

Kantor, H., & Brenzel, B. (1993). Urban education and the truly disadvantaged, 1945-1990. In M. Katz (Ed.), *The "underclass" debate: Views from history* (pp. 366-403). Princeton, NJ: Princeton University Press.

Kapteijns, L. (1994). Women and the crisis of communal identity: The Cultural Construction of Gender in Somali History. In A. I. Samatar (Ed.), *The Somali challenge: From Catastrophe to renewal?* (pp. 211-232). Boulder, CO: Lynne Rienner.

Kapteijns, L. (1995). Gender relations and the transformation of the Northern Somali pastoral tradition. *International Journal of African Historical Studies, 28*(2), 241-259.

Kapteijns, L. (2001). The disintegration of Somalia: A historiographical essay. *Bildhaan: International Journal of Somali Studies, 1*, 11-52.

Katerberg, W. H. (1995). The irony of identity: An essay on nativism, liberal democracy, and parochial identities in Canada and the United States. *American Quarterly, 47*, 493-524.

Kemnitz, A. (2006). Immigration as a commitment device. *Journal of Population Economics, 19*(2), 299-313.

Kenya National Exams Council (KNEC). (2007). Summary of top 100 positions With respect to gender and category of schools. Retrieved from http://www.examscouncil.or.ke/UserFiles/File/kcpe/Summary%20Statistics%20top%20100%20positions.pdf

Khazim, Y. (2001, December 15). Islamic movements in Somalia: Their origin, configuration, and role in the Civil War. *Al-Hayat Newspaper.* Retrieved from http://www.somaliawatch.org/archivedec01/011231601.htm

Killian, C. (2003). The other side of the veil: North African women in France respond to the headscarf affair. *Gender & Society, 17,* 567.

Koeberle, S., Bedoya, H., Silarsky, P., & Verheyen, G. (Eds.). (2005). *Conditionality revisited: Concepts, experiences, and lessons.* The World Bank.

Laitin, D. D., & Samatar, S. S. (1987). *Somalia: Nation in search of a state.* Boulder, CO: Westview Press.

Lane, S., & Rubinstein, R. (1996). Judging the other. *Hastings Center Report, 26(3),* 31-41.

Levinson, B. A. U., & Sutton, M. (2001). Introduction: Policy as/in practice—A sociocultural approach to the study of educational policy. In M. Sutton & B. A. U. Levinson (Eds.), *Policy as practice: Toward a comparative sociocultural analysis of educational policy* (pp. 3-22). Westport, CT: Ablex.

Lewis, I. M. (1962). Lineage continuity and modem commerce in Northern Somaliland. In P. Bohannan & G. Dalton (Eds.), *Markets in Africa.* Evanston, IL: Northwestern University Press.

Lewis, I. M. (1965). *The modern history of Somaliland: From nation to state.* New York, NY: F. A. Praeger.

Lewis, I. M. (1988). *A modern history of Somalia: Nation and state in the Horn of Africa.* Boulder, CO and London: Longman.

Lewis, I. M. (1992, August 30). In the land of the living dead. *The Sunday Times, London,* 8-9.

Lewis, I. M. (1993). Literacy and cultural identity in the Horn of Africa: The Somali case. In B. Street (Ed.), *Cross cultural approaches to literacy* (pp. 143-155). Cambridge: Cambridge University Press.

Lewis, I. M. (2002). *A Modern history of the Somali: Nation and state in the Horn of Africa, Fourth Edition.* Oxford, England: James Currey.

Lightfoot-Klein, H. (1989). *Prisoners of rituals: An odyssey into Female Genital Circumcision in Africa.* New York and London: Haworth.

Lischer, S. K. (2005). *Dangerous sanctuaries: Refugee camps, Civil War, and the dilemmas of humanitarian aid.* Ithaca, NY: Cornell University Press.

Loescher, G. (2001). *The UNHCR and world politics: a perilous path.* Oxford, England: Oxford University Press.

Loescher, G., & Milner, J. (2008). Understanding the problems of protracted refugee situations. In G. Loescher, J. Milner, E. Newman, & G. Troeller (Eds.), *Protracted refugee situations: Political, human rights, and security implication* (pp. 20-42). Tokyo: United Nations University Press.

Loescher, G., Milner, J., Newman, E., & Troeller, G. (Eds.). (2008b). *Protracted refugee situations: Political, human rights, and security implications*. Tokyo: United Nations University Press.

Lytle, K. (2003). Constructing the criminal alien: A historical framework for analyzing border vigilantes at the turn of the 21st Century. *MAEC for Comparative Immigration Studies*. Retrieved from http://www.ccis-ucsd.org/PUBLICATIONS/wrkg83.pdf

Luykx, A. (1996). From Indios to profesionales: Stereotypes and student resistance in Bolivian teacher training. In B. Levinson, D. Foley, & D. Holland (Eds.), *The cultural production of the educated person: Critical ethnographies of schooling and local practices* (pp. 239-272). New York, NY: State University of New York Press.

Macgoye, M. O. (Ed.) (1986). *Coming to birth*. London: Heinmann.

Maguire, P. (2001). Uneven ground: Feminisms and action research. In P. Reason & H. Bradbury (Eds.), *Handbook of action research: Participative inquiry and practice* (pp. 59-70). London: SAGE.

Mahfouz, N. (1991). *Half a day. In the time and the place and other stories*. New York, NY: Doubleday.

Maine State Planning Office. (2005). Frequently requested Maine Data. Retrieved from http://www.maine.gov/spo/economics/census/frequent.php

Malkki, L. H. (1995). *Purity and exile: Violence, memory, and national cosmology among Hutu refugees in Tanzania*. Chicago, IL: The University of Chicago Press.

Mamdani, M. (1996). *Citizen and subject: Contemporary Africa and the legacy of late Colonialism*. Princeton, NJ: Princeton University Press.

Mansur, A. O. (1995a). Contrary to a nation: The cancer of the Somali state. In A. J. Ahmed (Ed.), *The invention of Somalia* (pp. 107-116). Lawrenceville, NY: The Red Sea Press, Inc.

Mansur, A. O. (1995b). The nature of the Somali clan system. In A. J. Ahmed (Ed.), *The invention of Somalia* (pp. 117-134). Lawrenceville, NY: The Red Sea Press.

Manzer, R. A. (2003). *Educational regimes and Anglo-American democracy*. Toronto, Canada: University of Toronto Press.

Markakis, J. (1987). *National and class conflict in the Horn of Africa*. Cambridge: Cambridge University Press.

Martin, D.C. (2009). Annual flow report: Refugees and asylees. Office of Immigration Statistics, U.S. Department of Homeland Security. Retrieved http://www.dhs.gov/files/statistics/publications/yearbook.shtm

Mazrui, A. A. (1997). Crisis In Somalia: From tyranny to anarchy. In H. M. Adam & R. Ford (Eds.), *Mending rips in the sky: Options for Somali communities in the 21st century* (pp. 5-11). Lawrenceville, NJ: The Red Sea Press.

McCarty, T. L., & Warhol, L. (2011. The anthropology of language planning and policy. In *A Companion to the Anthropology of Education* (1st ed.). Malden, MA: Blackwell.

McCarty, T. L., Colins, J., & Hopson, R. (2011). Dell Hymes and the New [Language] Policy Studies: Update from an underdeveloped country. *Anthropology & Education Quarterly*.

Milner, J. (2008). *Refugees, the state and the politics of asylum in Africa*. Basingstoke: Palgrave Macmillan.

Minh-ha, T. T. (2011). *Elsewhere, within here: Immigration, refugeeism and the boundary event*. New York, NY: Routledge.

Minow, M. (2003). *Breaking the cycles of hatred: memory, law, and repair*. Princeton, NJ: Princeton University Press.

Mohamed, H. S. (1997). The Somali refugee women's experience in Kenyan refugee camps and their plight in Canada. In H. M. Adam & R. Ford (Eds.), *Mending rips in the sky: Options for Somali communities in the 21st century* (pp. 431-440). Lawrenceville, NJ: The Red Sea Press.

Mohanty, C. (1991). Under Western eyes: Feminist scholarship and colonial discourses. In C. Mohanty, A. Russo, & L. Torres, (Eds.), *Third world women and the politics of feminism* (pp. 51-80). Bloomington, IN: Indiana University Press.

Mohanty, C. (1992). Feminist encounters: Locating the politics of experience. In M. Barrett & A.Phillips (Eds.), *Destabilizing theory: Contemporary feminist debates*. Cambridge: Polity Press.

Mohanty, C., Russo, A., & L. Torres, (Eds.). (1991). *Third world women and the politics of feminism*. Bloomington, IN: Indiana University Press.

Morris, E., & S. J. Stedman. (2008). Protracted refugee situations, conflict and security: The need for better diagnosis and prescription." In G. Loescher, J. Milner, E. Newman, & G. Troeller (Eds.), *Protracted refugee situations: Political, human rights, and security implication* (pp. 69-84). Tokyo: United Nations University Press.

Nadeau, P. (2007). City of Lewiston Report to Maine's Congressional Delegation: Federal Funding Deficiencies for Refugee and Secondary Migrant Services and Programming. Retrieved from http://www.ci.lewiston.me.us/news/2007/2007files/10-17-07CongressionalLewPortImmigrantBrief.pdf

Nadeau, P. (2003). The Somalis of Lewiston: Community impacts of rapid immigrant movement into a small, homogeneous Maine city. *Brown University Center for the Study of Race and Ethnicity Draft Paper*, 1-60. Retrieved from http://www.brown.edu/Departments/Sociology/faculty/silver/immigneng/papers.html

Napier, B. D., & Napier, J. D. (2003). Transformations in South African education: Policies and practices from ministry to classroom. In K. M. Anderson-Levitt (Ed.), *Local meanings of global schooling: Anthropology and world culture theory*. Palgrave/St. Martins Press.

Naples, N. (2003). *Feminism and method: Ethnography, discourse analysis, and activist research*. New York, NY: Routledge.

New York Times. (2007). New York Times Topics: Immigration and refugees. *New York Times*. Retrieved from www.topics.nytimes.com/top/reference/timestopics/subjects/i/immigration_and_refugees/index.html

Nnaemeka, O. (Ed.). (2005). *Female circumcision and the politics of knowledge: African women in imperialist discourses*. Westport, CT: Praeger.

Nussbaum, M. C. (1997) *Cultivating humanity: A classical defense of reform in liberal education*.Cambridge, MA: Harvard University Press,

Nussbaum, M. (2003). Capabilities As fundamental entitlements: Sen and social justice. *Feminist Economics, 9*(2-3), 33-59.

Office of Immigration Statistics. (2006). 2004 Yearbook of Immigration Statistics. *Office of Immigration Statistics, U.S. Department of Homeland Security*. Retrieved from http://www.dhs.gov/xlibrary/assets/statistics/yearbook/ 2004/Yearbook2004.pdf

Olden, A. (2008). Somali opposition to government education: R. E. Ellison and the Berbera School Affair, 1938-1940. *History of Education, 37*(1), 71-90.

Ong, A. (2003). *Buddha is hiding: Refugees, citizenship, the new America*. Berkeley, CA: University of California Press

Ong, A. (1999). *Flexible citizenship: The cultural logics of transnationality*. Durham, NC: Duke University Press.

Otoo-Oyortey, N., & Pobi, S. (2003). Early marriage and poverty: exploring links and key policy issues. In C. Sweetman (Ed.), *Gender, development and marriage* (pp. 42- 51). Oxford, England: Oxfam GB.

Ousman, A. (2004). The potential of Islamist terrorism in Sub-Saharan Africa. *International Journal of Politics, Culture, and Society, 18*(1/2), 65-105

Ouyang, H. (2003). Resistance to the communicative method of language instruction within a progressive Chinese University. In K. Anderson-Levitt (Ed.), *Local meanings, global schooling: Anthropology and world culture theory* (pp. 121-140). New York, NY: Palgrave MacMillan.

Parker, M. (1995). Rethinking female circumcision. *Africa 65*(4), 504-521.

Peace Through Interamerican Community Action (PICA). (2007). Trade-Related manufacturing job Losses in Maine, January 1993 to June 2005. Retrieved from http://www.pica.ws/fairtrade/images/TRAproportion.pdf

Perea, J. F. (1997). *Immigrants out! The new nativism and the anti-immigrant impulse in the United States*. New York, NY: New York University Press.

Pipes, D. (1999, July 22). It matters what kind of Islam prevails: Culture: Muslims can bring their strong values into U.S. life of try to dominate it. *Los Angeles Times*. Retrieved from http://www.cdn-friends-icej.ca/isreport/septoct99/ islam.html

Portland Press Herald. (2002). Mayor Raymond's letter to the Somali community. Retrieved from http://pressherald.mainetoday.com/news/immigration/ 021005raymondletter.shtml

Pratt, M. L. (1986). Fieldwork in common places. In J. Clifford & G. E. Marcus (Eds.). *Writing culture: The poetics and politics of ethnography*. Berkeley, CA: University of California Press.

Raissiguier, C. (1994) *Becoming Women, becoming workers: Identity Formation in a French vocational school* Albany, NY: Suny Press.

Randle, K., & Brady, N. (1997). Further education and the new managerialism. *Journal of Further and Higher Education, 21*(2), 229-239.

Rawson, D. (1994). Dealing with disintegration: U.S. assistance and the Somali state. In A. I. Samatar (Ed.), *The Somali challenge: From catastrophe to renewal?* (pp. 147-188). Boulder, CO: Lynne Rienner.

Reed-Danahay, D. (2003). Europeanization and French primary education: Local implications of supranational policies. In K. M. Anderson-Levitt (Ed.), *Local meanings of global schooling: Anthropology and world culture theory*. Houndmills, Basingstoke, Hampshire, England: Palgrave/St. Martins Press.

Rival, L. (1996). Formal schooling and the production of modern citizens in the Ecuadorian Amazon. In B. Levinson, D. Foley, & D. Holland (Eds.), *The cul-*

tural production of the educated person: Critical ethnographies of schooling and local practices. New York, NY: State University of New York Press.

Robson, B. (2001, November 21). Blaming the Somalis: Are local immigrants unwittingly funding Al Qaida? The numbers just don't add up. *City Pages.* Retrieved from http://tcb.citypages.com/2001-11-21/books/blaming-the-somalis/

Rosaldo, R. (2003). *The anthropology of globalization.* New York, NY: Routledge.

Rosen, L. (2003). The politics of identity and the marketization of schools: Negotiating the "common good" in a debate on parental choice in education. In K. M. Anderson-Levitt (Ed.), *Local meanings of global schooling: Anthropology and world culture theory.* Houndmills, Basingstoke, Hampshire, England: Palgrave/ St. Martins Press.

Rytina, N. F. (2005). Annual flow report: Refugee applicants and admissions to the United States: 2004. *Office of Immigration Statistics of the US Department of Homeland Security.* Retrieved from http://www.uscis.gov/graphics/shared/ statistics/publications/refugeeflowreport2004.pdf

Said, E. (1978). *Orientalism.* New York, NY: Vintage Books.

Salmon, M. H. (1997). Ethical considerations in Anthropology and Archaeology, or relativism and justice for all. *Journal of Anthropological Research, 53*, 47-63.

Samatar, A. (1992). Destruction of state and society in Somalia: Beyond the tribal convention. *The Journal of Modern African Studies, 30*(4), 625-641.

Samatar, A. (1994). Empty bowl: Agrarian political economy in transition and the crises of accumulation. In A. I. Samatar & J. M. Ghalib (Eds.), *The Somali challenge: From catastrophe to renewal?* (pp. 65-94). Boulder, CO: Lynne Rienner.

Samatar, A. I. (1994a). Introduction and overview. In A. Samatar & J. M. Ghalib (Eds.), *The Somali challenge: From catastrophe to renewal?* (pp. 3-20). Boulder, CO: Lynne Rienner.

Samatar, A. I. (1994b). The curse of Allah: Civic disembowelment and the collapse of the state in Somalia. In A. Samatar & J. M. Ghalib (Eds.), *The Somali challenge: From catastrophe to renewal?* Boulder, CO: Lynne Rienner.

Samatar, A. I., & Ghalib, J. M. (Eds.). (1994). *The Somali challenge: From catastrophe to renewal?* Boulder, CO: Lynne Rienner.

Sarkosy, N. (2010). Retrieved http://blogs.reuters.com/faithwork/2010/05/19

Sarroub, L. K. (2005). *All American Yemeni Girls.* Philadelphia, PA: University of Pennsylvania Press.

Sassen, S. (1996). *Losing control?: Sovereignty in an age of globalization.* New York, NY: Columbia University Press.

Satrapi, M. (2003). *Persepolis: The story of a childhood.* New York, NY: Pantheon Books.

Save the Children. (2008). *Education for a bright future.* Retrieved from http:// www.savethechildren.org/education-for-a-bright-future.html

Save the Children. (2008). *Mission and strategy.* Retrieved from http:// www.savethechildren.org/about/mission/

Scott, J. (1992). Experience. In J. Butler & J. Scott (Eds.), *Feminists theorize the political.* New York, NY: Routledge.

Segal-Levit, K. (2003). Transforming the culture of scientific education in Israel. In K. M. Anderson-Levitt (Ed.), *Local meanings of global schooling: Anthropology and world culture theory*. Houndmills, Basingstoke, Hampshire, England: Palgrave/St. Martins Press.

Sen, A. (1999). *Development as freedom*. New York, NY: Random House.

Shakespeare, W. (1600). *The merchant of venice*. New York, NY: Simon & Schuster.

Slaughter, A., & Crisp, J. (2008). A surrogate state? The role of UNHCR in protracted refugee situations. In G. Loescher, J. Milner, E. Newman, & G. G. Troeller (Eds.), *Protracted refugee situations: Political, human rights, and security implications* (pp. 123-140). New York, NY: United Nations University Press.

Smith, D. (1992). Sociology from women's experience: A reaffirmation. *Sociological Theory 10*(1), 88-98.

Smothers, R. (1997, February 6). Somali immigrant had won asylum before detetion. *The New York Times*. Retrieved from http://www.nytimes.com/1997/02/06/nyregion/somali-immigrant-had-won-asylum-before-detention.html?ref=ronald_smothers

Southern Poverty Law Center (SPLC). (2003). *Maine town's diversity rally outdraws hate-group gathering*. Retrieved from http://www.splcenter.org/center/splcreport/article.jsp?aid=28

Spivak, G. (1988). Can the subaltern speak?" In C. Nelson & L. Grossberg (Eds.), *Marxism and the interpretation of culture* (pp. 271-313). Urbana, IL: the University of Illinois Press.

Stabile, C., & D. Kumar (2005). Unveiling Imperialism: Media, Gender & the War on Afghanistan. *Media, Culture & Society, 27*(5), 765-782.

Stambach, A. (2003). World-cultural and anthropological interpretations of "choice programming" in Tanzanian education. In K. M. Anderson-Levitt (Ed.), *Local meanings of global schooling: Anthropology and world culture theory*. Houndmills, Basingstoke, Hampshire, England: Palgrave/St. Martins Press.

Stromquist, N. (2002). *Education in a globalized world: the connectivity of economic power, technology, and knowledge*. Lanham, MD: Rowman & Littlefield.

Swift, J. (1977). Pastoral development in Somalia: Herding cooperatives as a strategy against desertification and famine. In M. Glantz (Ed.), *Desertification: Environmental degradation in and around arid lands* (pp. 175-305). Boulder, CO: Westview Press.

Swift, J. (1979). The Development of livestock trading in a pastoral economy: The Somali case. In D. R. Aronson (Ed.), *Pastoral production and society: Proceedings of the International Meeting on Nomadic Pastoralism* (pp. 447-465). Cambridge: Cambridge University Press.

Taylor, S. (2002, May 15). Roomful, earful. *Lewiston (Maine) Sun Journal, C1*, A8.

Ten stories the world should hear more about. (2008). Retrieved from http://www.un.org/events/tenstories

Terry, F. (2002). *Condemned to repeat?: The paradox of humanitarian action*. New York, NY: Cornell University Press.

Thomas, O. K. (1987). *The circumcision of women: A strategy for eradication*. London: Zed.

Thomas, R., & Murr, A. (1993). The economic cost of immigration. *Newsweek, 122*(6), 18-20.

Timmons, D. (2004). *The sixth clan—women organize for peace in Somalia: A review of published literature*. Geneva: University for Peace.

Toh, S-.H., & Virginia Floresca-Cawagas. (1997). Toward a people-centered education: Possibility and struggle in the Phillipines. *Review of Education, 43*(5/6) 527-545.

Tripodi, P. (1999). Back to the Horn: Italian administration and Somalia's troubled independence. *International Journal of African Historical Studies, 32*(2/3), 359-381.

Troeller, G. (2008). Asylum trends in industrialized countries and their impact on protracted refugee situations. In G. Loescher, J. Milner, E. Newman, & G. Troeller (Eds.), *Protracted refugee situations: Political, human rights, and security implication* (pp. 43-68). Tokyo: United Nations University Press.

United Nations Development Programme (UNDP). (1998). The lost generations: Focus on education. *In Human Development Report Somalia* (pp. 68-84). New York, NY: UNDP.

United Nations Educational Scientific and Cultural Organization [UNESCO]. (2000). *Dakar framework for action, education for all: Meeting our collective commitments.* World Education Forum.

United Nations High Commissioner for Refugees (UNHCR). (2001). How to guide: Reproductive health in refugee situations, Kakuma & Dadaab, Kenya. UNHCR. Retrieved from http://www.unhcr.org/protect/PROTECTION/4039cfc54.pdf

United Nations High Commissioner for Refugees (UNHCR). (2005). Statistical yearbook: Kenya. Retrieved from http://www.unhcr.org/statistics/STATISTICS/4641be610.pdf

United Nations High Commissioner for Refugees (UNHCR). (2007). Convention and protocol relating to the status of refugees. *United Nations Refugee Agency.* Retrieved from http://www.unhcr.org/protect/PROTECTION/3b66c2aa10.pdf

United Nations High Commission for Refugees (UNHCR). (2008). Global Report.

United Nations High Commissioner for Refugees. (2010). History of UNHCR. Retrieved from http://www.unhcr.org/pages/49c3646cbc.html

Unterhalter, E. (2005). *Gender, schooling, and global social justice.* New York, NY: Routledge.

U.S. Census Bureau. (1999). Historical Census Statistics on the Foreign-born Population of the United States: 1850-1990. C. J. Gibson and E. Lennon. Retrieved from http://www.census.gov/population/www/documentation/twps0029/twps0029.html

U.S. Citizenship and Immigration Services (USCIS). (2003). Refugees. In *Yearbook of Immigration Statistics.* Retrieved from http://uscis.gov/graphics/shared/aboutus/statistics/Refugees/htm

U.S. Citizenship and Immigration Services (USCIS). (2006). The worldwide priority system. Retrieved from http://www.uscis.gov/graphics/howdoi/priority.htm/

U.S. Department of State. (2010). *Diplomacy in action: Associate community services officer—Dadaab, Kenya.* Retrieved from http://www.state.gov/g/prm/142294.htm

Vavrus, F. (2005). Adjusting inequality: Education and structural adjustment programs in Tanzania. *Harvard Educational Review, 75*(2), 174-201.

Vavrus, F. (2006). Girls' schooling in Tanzania: The key to HIV/AIDS prevention? *AIDS Care, 18*(8), 863-871.

Vecoli, R. J. (1996). The significance of immigration in the formation of an American identity. *History Teacher, 30*, 9-27.

Verdirame, G. (1999). Human rights and refugees: The case of Kenya. *Journal of Refugee Studies, 12*(1), 54-77.

Verdirame G., & Harrell-Bond, B. (2005). *Rights in exile: Janus-Faced humanitarianism.* New York, NY: Berghahn Books.

Wa Thiong'o, N. (1986). Decolonising the mind: The politics of language in African literature. London: J. Currey.

Walker, B. (2007). Taliban USA? Moslems target American democracy. Retrieved from http://www.limitstogrowth.org/WEB-text/taliban-usa.html

Warriner, D. (2004). 'The days now is very hard for my family': The negotiation and construction of gendered work identities among newly arrived women refugees. *Journal of Language, Identity and Education, 3*, 279-295.

Warsame, A. M. (2004). Crisis or opportunity? Somali women traders and the war. In J. Gardner & J. El Bushra (Eds.), *Somalia—The untold story: The war through the eyes of Somali women* (pp. 116-126). London: CIIR and Pluto Press.

Waters, J. (2003, September). Flexible citizens? Transnationalism and citizenship amongst economic immigrants in Vancouver. *Canadian Geographer, 47*(3), 219-234.

Washuk, B. (2006). Learning to thrive. *Lewiston Sun Journal.* Retrieved from http://www.sunjournal.com/index.php?storyid=175935

Washuk, B. (2007). Most Lewiston schools fall short. *Lewiston Sun Journal.* Retrieved from www.sunjournal.com/story/237093-3/LewistonAuburn/Most_Lewiston_schools_fall_short

Weedon, C. (1987). *Feminist practice and poststructuralist theory.* Blackwell.

Werbner, P. (1997). Introduction: The dialectics of cultural hybridity. In P. Werbner & T. Modood (Eds.), *Debating cultural hybridity: Multi-cultural identities and the politics of anti-racism* (pp. 1-26) London: Zed Books.

Willis, P. (1976). *Learning to labor: How working class kids get working class jobs.* New York, NY: Columbia University Press.

Windschuttle, K. (1999, January). Edward Said's "Orientalism" revisited. *The New Criterion.* Retrieved from www.newcriterion.com/articles.fm/Edward-Said-s-ldquo-Orientalism-rdquo-revisited-2937

Women's Commission for Refugee Women and Children. (2002). UNHCR Policy on refugee women and guidelines for their protection: An assessment of ten years of implementation [Electronic Document]. http://www.unhcr.org/3de78c9c2.html

Woodiwiss, A. (2002). *Postmodernity USA: The crisis of social modernism in postwar America.* Thousand Oaks, CA: SAGE.

Young, C. (1994). *The African colonial state in comparative perspective.* New Haven, CT: Yale University Press.

Zabus, C. (2004). Between rites and rights: Excision on trial in African women's texts and human contexts. In P. H. Marsden & G. V. Davis (Eds.), *Towards a transcultural future: Literature and Human Rights in a "Post"-Colonial World* (pp. 109-134). Amsterdam: Rodopi.

Zabus, C. (2007). *Between rites and rights: Excision in women's experiential texts and human contexts.* Stanford, CA: Stanford University Press.

ABOUT THE AUTHORS

Patricia Buck is Associate Professor Of Educational Anthropology at Bates College. Her work focuses on gender, forced migration, and schooling. Patricia has served Programming Consultant for CARE Canada and is cofounder of Matawi, a nonprofit organization that works to increase educational opportunities for girls and women from Dadaab.

Rachel Silver received a master's degree in African Studies from Yale University, focusing on gender and forced migration in East Africa and the Horn. She co-founded Matawi and serves as the director of its Dadaab Young Women's Scholarship Initiative. Rachel will pursue a PhD in Educational Policy Studies at the University of Wisconsin-Madison beginning in the Fall of 2011.

CPSIA information can be obtained at www.ICGtesting.com
Printed in the USA
BVOW030148310812

299281BV00002B/3/P